CHARLES HODGE REVISITED

CHARLES HODGE REVISITED

A Critical Appraisal of His Life and Work

Edited by

John W. Stewart & James H. Moorhead

WILLIAM B. EERDMANS PUBLISHING COMPANY
GRAND RAPIDS, MICHIGAN / CAMBRIDGE, U.K.

© 2002 Wm. B. Eerdmans Publishing Co.

All rights reserved

Wm. B. Eerdmans Publishing Co.
255 Jefferson Ave. S.E., Grand Rapids, Michigan 49503 /
P.O. Box 163, Cambridge CB3 9PU U.K.

Printed in the United States of America

06 05 04 03 02   7 6 5 4 3 2 1

Library of Congress Cataloging-in-Publication Data

Charles Hodge revisited: a critical appraisal of his life and work /
edited by John W. Stewart & James H. Moorhead.
p.   cm.
Based on a conference held Oct. 22-24, 1997
at Princeton University and Princeton Theological Seminary.
Includes bibliographical references (p.   ) and index.
ISBN 0-8028-4750-1 (pbk.: alk. paper)
1. Hodge, Charles, 1797-1878.
I. Stewart, John W.   II. Moorhead, James H.

B921.H63 C48   2002
230'.51'092 — dc21

2002029677

www.eerdmans.com

Contents

CONTENTS

Preface

Once, amid the thrusts and parries of a lively luncheon discussion, the editors of this volume tried to recount what American scholars did and did not know about Charles Hodge. We were, of course, well aware that most assessments of Charles Hodge paint him as either comic or tragic: comic because of his intentionally provocative statement that "there never was a new idea" at Princeton Seminary; tragic because, in the minds of many, he failed to appropriate the main currents of modern thought in the nineteenth century. We were also aware that contemporary scholars of nineteenth-century religious movements differ widely in their estimates of Hodge. On the one hand, standardized histories of nineteenth century American religion and culture usually acknowledge the depth and range of Hodge's influence. He mentored 3,000 students over five decades at Princeton Theological Seminary, and he edited a first-rate journal with an agenda of surprisingly wide reach. More recent scholarship, furthermore, has revealed Hodge's contributions as a political commentator, a social critic, a keen observer of American science, and a pivotal contributor to transatlantic discourse. On the other hand, specialists in American religion have chastised him for his construing Reformed and evangelical convictions on rationalistic, biblicist, and narrowly confessionalist assumptions.

We agreed that Charles Hodge needed a fresh look. The tired, standardized appraisals were too myopic and self-serving, and they lacked a future. What was needed was an informed inquiry that would weigh the abundant but largely unconsulted historical sources and, at the same time, interpret Hodge within his own cultural milieu and on his own terms.

Eventually, we found enough support and encouragement to sponsor a symposium to be held on campuses of Princeton University and Princeton Theological Seminary in the fall of 1997, the bicentennial year of Hodge's birth. As we laid plans and sought nominees for the lectures, we soon realized that others shared our enthusiasm for such a conference. From the outset, we determined that only first-rank, well-established historians and theologians would be invited and its sole agenda would be to revisit and reappraise the life, thought, and influence of Hodge.

The essays in this book are derived from the lectures given originally at that conference, October 22-24, 1997. With support from the Center for the Study of Religion at Princeton University, and especially a very generous bequest from Princeton Theological Seminary, a cadre of well-known scholars of American cultural and religious history gathered for three days to examine Hodge's thought and writings. We hope that these essays will help shape a much-needed reassessment of Hodge. As will become apparent, these essays reveal a diversity of opinion, and several point to unresolved questions about Hodge's assumptions and perspectives. Yet, each essay accomplished what we editors dreamt of: a first-rank examination of why and how Hodge participated in such a wide range of cultural, political, scientific, and religious discourse.

One final note about these essays: many critical responses were offered by other scholars during and after the conference, and most essayists in this volume acknowledge their critics' and respondents' contributions. Obviously, the editors are deeply grateful for the contributions of the essayists and for their consent to publish their studies. Their names, titles, and universities are listed below.

JOHN W. STEWART
JAMES H. MOORHEAD

Contributors

RICHARD J. CARWARDINE
Professor of History
University of Sheffield
Sheffield, England

B. A. GERRISH
John Nuveen Professor Emeritus
The Divinity School, University of Chicago
Chicago, Illinois

ALLEN C. GUELZO
Grace Kea Professor of History
Eastern College
St. Davids, Pennsylvania

E. BROOKS HOLIFIELD
Charles H. Candler Professor of American Church History
Candler School of Theology, Emory University
Atlanta, Georgia

DAVID H. KELSEY
Luther A. Weigle Professor of Theology
The Divinity School, Yale University
New Haven, Connecticut

BRUCE KUKLICK
Nichols Professor of American History
University of Pennsylvania
Philadelphia, Pennsylvania

JAMES H. MOORHEAD
Mary McIntosh Bridge Professor of American Church History
Princeton Theological Seminary
Princeton, New Jersey

MARK A. NOLL
Professor, McManis Chair of Christian Thought
Wheaton College
Wheaton, Illinois

RONALD L. NUMBERS
Professor of the History of Medicine and the History of Science
University of Wisconsin
Madison, Wisconsin

LOUISE L. STEVENSON
Professor of History and American Studies
Franklin and Marshall College
Lancaster, Pennsylvania

JOHN W. STEWART
Ashenfelter Associate Professor of Ministry and Evangelism
Princeton Theological Seminary
Princeton, New Jersey

JAMES TURNER
The Rev. John J. Cavanaugh Professor of Humanities
University of Notre Dame
South Bend, Indiana

Introducing Charles Hodge to Postmoderns

JOHN W. STEWART

S ome time ago the English scholar, Marcus Cunliffe, offered a sage comment about the writing of American religious history: "The record is confusing: partly because we have tended to stress the vigour of innovators and to forget the vigour of the religious orthodox; and partly because what happened is genuinely complex."[1] The first of these generalizations may appropriately apply to much of the scholarly opinion about Charles Hodge of Princeton Theological Seminary. Standard histories of nineteenth-century America usually emphasize and retail the origins and continuities of Protestantism's "modern impulse." Less attractive are hosts of conservative thinkers who give voice to the aspirations and convictions of many ordinary members of "mainstream" religious communities. Equally uncongenial to postmodern mentalities are Hodge's philosophical assumptions and worldview, which feel increasingly remote from the more pluralistic and relativistic affinities of contemporary discourse.

Cunliffe's second generalization, however, is equally suggestive. By any measure, Charles Hodge's intellectual energies and discourse were both vigorous and complex. To begin with, his early training as a biblical scholar and theologian was unusually thorough for a nineteenth-century American scholar. A sojourn of nearly two years in German universities of Halle and Berlin (October 1826 to September 1828) provided Hodge with an enviable foundation in historical theology and Semitic languages, as

1. Marcus Cunliffe, "American Religious History," *Journal of American Studies* 1 (1967): 126.

well as a first-hand encounter with the philosophical trends and energies on the Continent. Few American theologians in the first third of the nineteenth century were as aware and conversant with German biblical and theological discourse as Hodge. For nearly forty years he edited a lively and well-circulated journal, contributing by himself nearly two hundred articles. The range of topics and the vigor of argument are not inconsequential. While serving on dozens of ecclesial, voluntary, and educational boards, Hodge's influence was propagated through three thousand seminary students who spread out to three continents. His longer-range influence is less clear, and there is little consensus among American historians as to how to interpret Hodge.[2] Several historians of religion have contended that Hodge's worldview and particular biblical hermeneutic have provided the intellectual framework for twentieth-century Protestant fundamentalism.[3] Yet, more recent scholarship has revealed Hodge's contributions as a political commentator, a social critic, a keen observer of antebellum science, and a pivotal contributor to transatlantic discourse.[4] Perry Miller grudgingly acknowledged that Hodge's (and his colleagues') critique of America's Transcendentalists was "masterful."[5] To date, however, there exists no comprehensive treatment of Hodge that fully interprets this Old School Presbyterian as a theologian, biblical scholar, editor, and ecclesial leader.[6] Compared to other prominent theologians of Amer-

2. For a fuller explanation of how both historians of American culture and historians of nineteenth-century religion have treated Hodge, see John W. Stewart, *Mediating the Center: Charles Hodge on American Science, Language, Literature and Politics* (Princeton: Princeton Theological Seminary, 1995).

3. For an early treatment, see Ernest Sandeen, *The Roots of Fundamentalism* (Chicago: University of Chicago Press, 1970). For a more balanced account, see George Marsden, *Fundamentalism and American Culture* (New York: Oxford University Press, 1980); and Marsden, *Understanding Fundamentalism and Evangelicalism* (Grand Rapids: William B. Eerdmans Publishing Company, 1991).

4. See especially the essay in this volume by Richard J. Carwardine, as well as his *Evangelicals and Politics in Antebellum America* (New Haven: Yale University Press, 1993).

5. Perry Miller, *The Transcendentalists* (Cambridge: Harvard University Press, 1966), p. 232. See Stewart, *Mediating the Center,* pp. 1-5.

6. This is not to say that newer appraisals are not emerging. The late dean of historians of American religion, Sydney Ahlstrom, once wrote about Hodge, "Probably nobody in the country was so generously well-versed in all the sciences of theology." Bruce Kuklick has contended that Hodge was one of a triumvirate who "ruled Calvinistic theology" from the 1830s to the 1870s, and also that Hodge was one of the prime reasons for the demise of a robust American Calvinism. The historian of American culture James Turner sees Hodge as a pivotal force in nineteenth-century discourse, albeit not an overly constructive one. Richard Carwardine has given Hodge's political and social thought a significant role in antebellum

ica's antebellum period, such as Horace Bushnell, Ralph W. Emerson, or Charles G. Finney, Hodge has received little critical attention. And it is especially unfortunate that there exists no modern, critical biography that locates Hodge in his own social, ecclesial, and political environments.[7] One notable exception to this neglect or ambiguity is the scholarly work of historian Mark Noll; his several critical essays on Hodge remain the most informed and balanced assessments.[8]

This essay takes a different, but complementary, tack from Noll's work. I seek to locate Hodge in his own socio-cultural milieu and to explain why Hodge is so problematic to contemporary, postmodern readers. Hodge was a *certain kind* of *American* theologian and he labored to insure that his theological discourses were relevant to the American political, social, and ecclesial landscapes.[9] No other nineteenth-century American Reformed theologian commented on as many issues or analyzed them quite the way Hodge did.

politics. David Hollinger included a section from Hodge's *Systematic Theology* in a widely used textbook on American intellectual tradition. More recently, Paul K. Conkin, while tracing the "uneasy center" of American Reformed Christianity, placed Hodge at the center of a "golden age" when American Reformed theology matured and foundered. Unlike theologians, American historians continue to acknowledge that Hodge was a significant voice and personality in American religious thought.

Sources for the above comments are as follows: Sydney Ahlstrom, *The Shaping of American Religion* (Princeton: Princeton University Press, 1961), pp. 263-64; Bruce Kuklick, *Churchmen and Philosophers: From Jonathan Edwards to John Dewey* (New Haven: Yale University Press, 1985), pp. 66-80, 203-15; James Turner, *Without God, Without Creed* (Baltimore: Johns Hopkins University Press, 1985), pp. 185-96; Richard J. Carwardine, *Evangelicals and Politics in Antebellum America* (New Haven: Yale University Press, 1993); and David Hollinger and Charles Capper, eds., *The American Intellectual Tradition,* 2d ed. (New York: Oxford University Press, 1993), pp. 5-12; Paul K. Conkin, *The Uneasy Center: Reformed Christianity in Antebellum America* (Chapel Hill: The University of North Carolina Press, 1995).

7. The only full-scale biography written about Charles Hodge was written by his son. See A. A. Hodge, *Life of Charles Hodge* (New York: Charles Scribner's Sons, 1880), hereafter cited as Hodge, *LCH.* I have tried to relate Hodge's upbringing and its role in his theologizing in Stewart, *Mediating the Center,* pp. 1-14.

8. In addition to the essay "Charles Hodge as an Expositor of the Spiritual Life," see Mark Noll, ed., *The Princeton Theology, 1812-1921* (Grand Rapids: Baker Book House, 1983, 2001), pp. 11-48; and Noll, "Introduction" to Charles Hodge, *The Way of Life* (New York: Paulist Press, 1987).

9. Stewart, *Mediating the Center,* chapter 5.

1. The Life and Faith Formation
of Charles Hodge (1797-1878)

Charles Hodge was born December 28, 1797, in the throes of the "first new nation." He was the son of a Scotch-Irish Philadelphia physician, who died during a smallpox epidemic when Charles was only seven months old. Hodge often referred to the father he never knew in mythic terms. Along with his older brother, Hugh Lenox Hodge, Charles was raised by their widowed mother within the Presbyterian communities and cultural milieu of Philadelphia. Probably at the prompting of her former pastor, Ashbel Green (elected President in 1812 of the College of New Jersey, later Princeton College), an impoverished Mrs. Hodge moved to Princeton in 1812 and took in boarders and laundry in order to garner funds to enroll her two sons at the college.[10] Hugh L. Hodge later became a distinguished professor of women's medicine at the College (later University) of Pennsylvania, where he was a pioneer in the new fields of gynecology and obstetrics. He was also Charles's lifelong confidant and occasional financier. After graduating from Princeton College and for unexplained reasons, Charles forsook an expected career in medicine and entered Princeton Seminary in 1816, graduating in 1819. There is every indication that the young and impressionable Charles was affectionately mentored at the seminary by Archibald Alexander, the new institution's first professor. Not to be underestimated was Hodge's tutelage under the urbane Samuel Miller, whose encyclopedic, two-volume *A Brief Retrospect of the Eighteenth Century* (1803) ought to be counted among the basic documents of the old Princeton theology.[11] Though ordained to the Presbyterian ministry, Hodge did not consider himself a very good preacher and shied away from

10. Hodge never forgot his impoverished upbringing. He often chided Presbyterian congregations about their abandonment of America's poor. As late as 1871 he wrote, "It is with great reluctance that we are constrained to acknowledge that the Presbyterian Church in this country is not the church of the poor." See Charles Hodge, "Preaching to the Poor," *Biblical Repertory and Princeton Review* 43 (1871): 86.

11. See L. Loetscher, *Facing the Enlightenment and Pietism: Archibald Alexander* (Wesport, Conn.: The Greenwood Press, 1983). Samuel Miller (1769-1850) may well have been the most gifted of all the seminary's early professors. His *A Brief Retrospect of the Eighteenth Century* (New York, 1803) was first delivered as lectures in New York City and is a treasure trove of the history of American ideas. Miller wrote over 200 books, articles, and reviews. Unfortunately, the life and ideas of Miller have yet to receive serious examination by modern historians. For a brief survey of Miller's breadth of interests, see Anita Schorch, "Samuel Miller, Renaissance Man: His Legacy of 'True Taste,'" *American Presbyterians: Journal of Presbyterian History* 66 (Summer 1988): 71-87.

parish assignments. Instead, at the urging of Alexander, Charles pursued the study of Hebrew with a rabbi in Philadelphia and, later, in New England with the biblical scholar, Moses Stuart, of Andover Seminary. In 1822, Hodge cemented his ties with the scientific and socially prominent communities in Philadelphia when he married Sarah Bache, a great-granddaughter of Benjamin Franklin.[12] Together, Charles and Sarah raised eight children. Two became professors at the seminary, the theologian Archibald Alexander Hodge (1823-1886) and Caspar Wistar Hodge (1830-1881), a New Testament scholar. Sarah Bache Hodge, a woman of considerable talent and learning, died in 1849, leaving Hodge broken-hearted. In 1852 he married Mary Stockton, a widow belonging to an influential and wealthy Princeton family. After more than fifty years of teaching and writing, he retired in 1877 and died in June of 1878 in his eightieth year.

Building on a solid and classical education in Princeton's two institutions, Hodge's training as a scholar took on a significant elevation in 1826 when, at the age of 29, he was among the very first American scholars to travel to the Continent (rather than to English or Scottish universities) for advanced studies in Bible and theology. He expanded his earlier interests in Semitic languages with DeSacy in Paris and with H. F. W. Gesenius, the famed lexicographer of Hebrew at the University of Halle. At Halle Hodge was taken under the wing of August Tholuck, the well-known theologian of the *Vermittlungstheologie,* or mediating school of theology.[13] Letters home related how Tholuck and Hodge became close friends, detailing Tholuck's warm piety and immense learning. Tholuck was the best example, Hodge explained, of how not all German theology led to infidelity. In 1828 he traveled on to the University of Berlin where he listened to famed theologian Friedrich D. E. Schleiermacher, studied the Bible with influential Prussian scholar Ernst Henstenberg, read in the history of theology with Otto von Gerlach and A. Neander, and attended regularly the Royal Academy of Science where Humboldt, among other scientists, lec-

---

12. I know of no evidence that Charles Hodge belonged to the famed American Philosophical Society, headquartered in Philadelphia and the center of the new nation's most advanced scientific and philosophical discourse. However, his father, brother, and many of his friends at the College of New Jersey (Princeton College) were lifelong members.

13. For a brief introduction to these theologians who sought to bridge Lutheran confessionalism with more modern ways, see Walter H. Conser, *God and the Natural World* (Columbia: University of South Carolina Press, 1993), pp. 48-54. Several Americans, including H. B. Smith, Edward Robinson, and George Prentiss, studied with Tholuck, as did the German-American Philip Schaff.

tured.[14] Though the documentation is sparse, it was probably during these years that Hodge realized how inimical German romanticism was to his confessional upbringing.

He wrote home often, detailing his many social encounters, the emergence of newly acquired friends, and his extensive travels. He reported to "Doctor" Alexander that he learned to drink beer in German pubs, sang the melodies of a newly discovered German composer (J. S. Bach), and visited regularly art museums and historical collections. Of course, he argued (endlessly it seems) for his understanding of the Reformed theology heritage and "common sense."[15] His letters, many written in French, also reveal a lonely husband and father. "I have seen the Alps!" he wrote to Sarah. "If now I never see anything great or beautiful in nature, I am content . . . [I] beg you to forgive my beholding such a spectacle without you, my love."[16] By the end of his sojourn, few American theologians could rival Hodge's excellence in scholarly preparation and credentials.

Sporting considerable facility in both French and German languages, Hodge returned to Princeton in September 1828 to take up the tasks assigned to him by the seminary and the denomination's General Assembly, namely, to teach biblical languages and literature. Over the next five decades of teaching, Hodge rarely neglected this original calling. In January 1829 Hodge recast his journal in order to alert American audiences to the most current German biblical and theological scholarship. He renamed his journal *The Biblical Repertory and Princeton Review* (hereafter, *BRPR*), which is now available online.[17] This journal is unquestionably the best source for contemporary scholars to measure the depth and range of Hodge's thought and influence. Between 1830 and 1840, he produced three New Testament commentaries, including a popular commentary on the epistle to the Romans in 1835. Hodge defended his "Old School" as-

14. See Hodge's comments about these German scholars in portions of Hodge's journal excerpted in Hodge, *LCH,* pp. 163-88.

15. See Hodge, *LCH,* pp. 152ff.

16. Hodge, *LCH,* p. 197.

17. It is to be noted with pleasure and appreciation that the University of Michigan has placed all the issues of the *Biblical Repertory and Princeton Review* online in their "Makers of America" series. The journal from 1831-1882 may be retrieved electronically at http://moa.umdl.umich.edu/moa_browse.html. A search engine is also available. Hereafter, Hodge's journal will be cited as *BRPR.* Hodge himself wrote a history of this journal; see *Biblical Repertory and Princeton Review: Index Volume, 1825-1868* (Philadelphia: Peter Walker, 1871), pp. 1-39. There are also two recent studies of this journal: Leslie W. Sloat, "American Calvinism Speaks," *Westminster Theological Journal* 7 (1944-45): 1-22, 112-35; and Mark Noll, "The Princeton Review," *Westminster Theological Journal* 50 (1988): 283-304.

sumptions in his *The Constitutional History of the Presbyterian Church in the Unites States of America,* which came on the heels of the denominational split in 1837. With the publication of this scholarly volume, Hodge earned a respected voice in American Presbyterian circles. In 1841, a year after he was appointed to succeed the aging Archibald Alexander as Professor of Exegetical and Didactic Theology, Hodge published *The Way of Life* (1841) for the American Sunday School Union. It was immensely popular and was translated into several languages. It also stands as a convenient starting place for any analysis of Hodge's theological assumptions and commitments.[18]

By the 1840s, Hodge was a formidable figure in America's antebellum theological and ecclesial circles. Through his articles in *BRPR*, Hodge's reputation in England, Scotland, Ireland, and France grew. Hodge's biographer tells of the warm and lengthy correspondence Hodge maintained with William Cunningham, Principal of New College in Edinburgh, and with his former teacher in Halle, August Tholuck. His lengthy critiques of nineteenth-century figures — David F. Strauss, Horace Bushnell, Ralph Waldo Emerson, Edwards A. Parks, to name only a few — rarely displaced his responsibilities to theologize about the mission of the Presbyterian churches in America and abroad. In the mid-1840s, Hodge was elected moderator of the 1846 General Assembly (Old School), served frequently as chairman of various denominational boards, and was a lifelong trustee of Princeton College. In the late 1840s Hodge initiated a twenty-year-long controversy over the nature of and membership in the Christian church with the South's foremost Presbyterian theologian, James H. Thornwell of South Carolina.[19] Reading between the lines of their correspondence, one can see that Hodge and Thornwell never got along very well. Their edgy relationship was strained and then severed in 1861 over the twin issues of slavery and the Civil War. When Thornwell argued that the church had no responsibility to comment or intrude on public issues, Hodge

---

18. Hodge, *The Way of Life*. The "New School" theologian Henry B. Smith of Union Theological Seminary in New York City, a friend of Hodge, greatly preferred this book to Hodge's later *Systematic Theology*.

19. In light of the considerable attention given to Thornwell by historians of the South, see James O. Farmer, *The Metaphysical Confederacy: James Henley Thornwell and the Synthesis of Southern Values* (Macon, Ga.: Mercer University Press, 1986) and recent writings of Eugene Genovese, especially his "James Thornwell and Southern Religion," *Southern Partisan* 7 (Summer 1987): 17-21. Hodge's controversies with Thornwell are summarized in *BRPR* 37 (1865): 645ff. See also H. Sheldon Smith, "The Church and the Social Order in the Old South as Interpreted by James H. Thornwell," *Church History* 7 (1938): 115ff.

summarily dismissed Thornwell's so-called doctrine of the spirituality of the church as "mischievous."

While many of Hodge's intellectual and ecclesial energies were consumed by the coming of the Civil War, his 1860 article "What Is Christianity?" was another key document in the emergence of his theological framework:

> Christianity objectively considered, is the testimony of God concerning his Son, it is the whole revelation of truth contained in the Scriptures, concerning the redemption of man through Jesus Christ our Lord. Subjectively considered, it is the life of Christ in the soul, or, that form of spiritual life which has its origins in Christ, is determined by the revelation concerning his person and work, and which is due to the indwelling of his Spirit. In one [the first] sense we may affirm that Christianity is a doctrine, and in another [second] sense we may with equal truth affirm that Christianity is a life.[20]

This article was something of a prolegomenon to Hodge's magnum opus, the three-volume *Systematic Theology* (1872-73).[21] In 1874 Hodge summarized his dissenting views of Darwinism in a famous salvo, *What Is Darwinism?* His answer — "Darwinism is atheism" — propelled the elderly Hodge into national and international arenas of controversy, a controversy that is still being examined.[22]

Two aspects of Charles Hodge's personality warrant comment. Hodge was nurtured in the Christian faith by a devout mother and by the pastors (including Ashbel Green) of his Philadelphia congregation. As readily as he acquired his mother's tongue, the young Hodge's language was steeped in biblical literature, especially the Psalms. Soon afterward, his theological vocabulary was honed by his memorizing the Westminster Catechisms in both English and Latin. That early training was supplemented under Archibald Alexander's tutoring. Along with a generous immersion in the works of Protestant theologians, the *Institutio Theologie Electicae* by Francis

---

20. Hodge, "What Is Christianity?" *BRPR* 32 (1860): 119.

21. Charles Hodge, *Systematic Theology*, 3 vols. (New York: Charles Scribner's Sons, 1872-73), hereafter cited as *ST*.

22. Charles Hodge, *What Is Darwinism?* (New York: Scribner, Armstrong, 1874), reprinted edition ed. Mark A. Noll and David Livingstone (Grand Rapids: Baker Books, 1994). The literature about Hodge and Darwinism is growing rapidly. See Stewart, *Mediating the Center*, pp. 36ff. It should also be mentioned that the notes of Hodge's many sermons preached at the Seminary's "Sabbath Afternoon Conferences" are reprinted in *Conference Papers* (New York: Charles Scribner's Sons, 1879).

Turretin served as the foundational textbook at the seminary.[23] Hodge boarded with the Alexander family and maintained lifelong ties with the Alexanders' many children, especially Joseph Addison Alexander and James Waddell Alexander.[24] Hodge rarely wrote anything without the sanction of "the Doctor." The elder Alexander responded in kind. He wrote to Hodge in Germany, "I feel anxious to hear from you, to know how you are and what progress you are making in the literature. You must come home loaded with riches. Much will be expected of you."[25] In light of this relationship, it is not surprising that Charles and Sarah would bypass their own family namesakes and name their first child Archibald Alexander Hodge.

While psycho-history is a precarious venture, it is tantalizing to ponder the implications of Hodge's fatherless upbringing and Alexander's role as surrogate father and watchful mentor.[26] Whatever else typified

23. See Timothy Ross Phillips, "Francis Turretin's Idea of Theology and Its Bearing Upon His Doctrine of Scripture" (Ph.D. dissertation, Vanderbilt University, 1986). See also Francis Turretin, *The Doctrine of Scripture: Locus 2 of Institutio Theologie Elencticae,* ed. and trans. by John W. Beardslee (Grand Rapids: Baker Book House, 1981).

24. The best biography of Archibald Alexander is Lefferts Loetscher, *Facing the Enlightenment and Pietism: Archibald Alexander and the Founding of Princeton Seminary* (Westport, Conn.: Greenwood Press, 1983). Very little has been published about Archibald Alexander's two sons, who were extraordinary scholars in their own rights. For J. A. Alexander (1809-1861), a well-known biblical scholar and master of twenty-seven languages, see Marion Ann Taylor, *The Old Testament in the Old Princeton School (1812-1929)* (Lewiston, NY: Mellen Research Press, 1992) and James H. Moorhead, "Joseph Addison Alexander: Common Sense, Romanticism and Biblical Criticism at Princeton," *Journal of Presbyterian History* 53 (1975): 51-66. For James W. Alexander (1804-1859), a theologian, seminary teacher, and New York City pastor, see Gregory M. Anderson, "The Religious Rhetoric of James W. Alexander: Texts and Contexts of an Antebellum Rhetorical Tradition" (Ph.D. dissertation, University of Minnesota, 1994). There is a gold mine of insights about the Princeton theologians' participation in American culture in J. W. Alexander's *Forty Years' Familiar Letters of James W. Alexander,* ed. John Hall, 2 vols. (New York: Charles Scribner, 1860).

25. Quoted in Hodge, *LCH,* p. 161.

26. There is a tender and revealing interchange between Alexander and Hodge mentioned in Hodge, *LCH.* In October 1851, Hodge was summoned across campus to the deathbed of Alexander. After telling Hodge that he could accomplish little more for the seminary or his family and affirming that his Christian faith was secure and comforting, Alexander said quietly to Hodge, "I want you to know that it has been my greatest privilege to have brought you forward." Deeply moved, Hodge kissed him and fell on his knees to pray as Alexander had requested. Immediately after leaving, Hodge wrote a verbatim to remember the poignant occasion. See "Memorandum to Myself, Princeton, October 21, 1851," in the archives at Luce Library, Princeton Theological Seminary. This memo appears, though in slightly different form, in Hodge, *LCH,* pp., 382-83.

Hodge's manner of thinking, he had a deep quest for structure and a distinct intolerance for ambiguity. His quarrels with Emerson's Transcendentalism and the Mercersburg theologians harbored a deep distrust of any mysticism in theological construction. Surely some of his theological need for bedrock certainty was related to his fatherless rearing. Secondly, there is abundant evidence that Hodge was a warm-hearted, gregarious, and much-liked person. He made friends easily and kept them for a lifetime. There are extant letters to nearly 800 different persons gathered in several archival collections. A sixty-year friendship that started in college with John Johns, an Episcopal bishop from Virginia and onetime President of William and Mary College, is just one example of Hodge's outgoing personality. "Hail Columbia," Hodge wrote to Johns in 1872, "tell me on what train you are coming in that I may meet you. I can't afford to lose one minute." In 1872, Princeton Seminary threw a festive party in Hodge's honor. The published speeches and documents of that occasion attest that it was an extraordinary celebration, with hundreds of distinguished persons in attendance. When Leonard Woosley, ex-president of Yale College, spoke of their long friendship that had started in 1828, Hodge, crippled and walking with a cane, walked across the stage to the podium and kissed him. His old friend, Bishop John Johns, asked Hodge how he was tolerating all the accolades. "Oh," said Hodge, "it is easy. I just pretend they are talking about someone else." Lutheran theologian Charles Krauth once said that "next to having Dr. Hodge on one's side, was the pleasure of having him for an antagonist." In 1873, in what was a very unusual move, the General Assembly of the Presbyterian Church meeting in Baltimore heard that Hodge was too ill to attend and was resting in Washington, D.C. When the Assembly adjourned to take a train to Washington, they first gathered at the Willard Hotel to sing to him and pray for his well-being before going on with their visitations and lobbying in the capital city.[27]

Hodge's vaunted conservatism needs to be understood, in part, in light of his close-knit academic community and upbringing. Tight com-

27. Here is how a member of that General Assembly described the occasion: "Dr. Hodge, very feeble, and showing signs of great emotion, took his seat at the head of the table. . . . This action of the Assembly touched him very deeply. When first told of the desire to thus honor him, he was almost overcome, and the cordial greetings he received on every side, he said, were among the most cherished recollections of his life" (quoted in Hodge, *LCH*, p. 546). The speeches and Hodge's response are recorded in *Proceedings Connected With the Semi-Centennial Commemoration of the Professorship of Rev. Charles Hodge, D.D., LL.D.* (New York: Anson Randolph Company, 1872).

munities can create a "horizontal hermeneutic," as one scholar has ob-served.[28] His gregarious personality merely exacerbated his commitment to his "community of interpreters" in Princeton. I doubt that one can ever separate a person from his or her theology. One clearly cannot do so with Hodge.

In the most elemental sense, Christian theology is a very human in-quiry that asks what a community believes about God, what it under-stands about being human, and what it means to act wisely. In the process of such a critical inquiry, "Every theology has to offer some account of the basis of its affirmations."[29] For a Christian theologian as prolific and pro-longed as Charles Hodge, such an accounting is not instantaneously grasped. Moreover, the paucity of sustained, scholarly analyses of Hodge's assumptions and contributions as an American systematic theologian handicaps contemporary scholars who seek to understand him within his own socio-cultural milieu. What follows in this introductory essay is a very preliminary discussion about Hodge's theological project: its philo-sophical underpinnings, its theological affirmations, and its heady dialog with the cultural norms, science, ecclesial practices, and social and politi-cal movements during two-thirds of the nineteenth century.

2. Hodge's Theological Vision and the "Princeton Paradigm"

By "Princeton paradigm" I mean Hodge's strenuous agenda to integrate (1) all reasoned inquiry (science, theology, politics, and ethics) with (2) all human behaviors and piety — and to do so *sub species aeternitatis* or, as New England Puritans put it, "under the holy watchful Eye" of the God revealed in the Bible. Hodge believed that all human thought and all pri-vate and social behaviors were to submit, *where appropriate,* to this divine revelation. To sustain this enterprise, Hodge drew simultaneously on four nourishing sources: (1) the Scottish-bred "common sense" way of ra-tionality and valuing; (2) the Bible as mediated through the Reformed Protestant tradition and especially nuanced by the Westminster Confes-sions; (3) American Presbyterian ecclesial communities; and (4) the socio-

28. Robert Corrington, *The Community of Interpreters: On Hermeneutics of Nature and the Bible in the American Philosophical Tradition* (Macon, Ga.: Mercer University Press, 1987). For a very helpful explanation of how Hodge fit into the life and politics of Princeton Seminary, see David D. Calhoun, *Princeton Seminary,* vol. 1 (Edinburgh: Banner of Truth, 1995).

29. Daniel Migliore, *Faith Seeking Understanding* (Grand Rapids: Eerdmans, 1991), p. 19.

political tradition of American Whiggery. These four constituents flowed congruently in Charles Hodge's mind. Such an attempted confluence is what makes Hodge's nineteenth-century theology distinctly Reformed, comprehensive, and American. It also makes him seem increasingly distant from the postmodern world.

A. Scottish Common Sense Realism

Charles Hodge once observed that "every theology is, in one sense, a form of philosophy. To understand any theological system we must understand the philosophy that underlies it and gives it peculiar form."[30] There is little doubt what philosophical system prevailed at Princeton Seminary for most of the nineteenth century. All who revisit Hodge's thought must explain the pivotal role of Scottish common sense realism, a philosophical tradition "bred in his bones" while a student (1812-15) at the College of New Jersey (Princeton College).[31] Samuel Miller, Hodge's seminary teacher, called it "the paramount tribunal for all appeals of philosophy." By the last quarter of the eighteenth century, Princeton College was the bastion of this influential, if not imperious, philosophical orthodoxy. Prominent teachers at the college were the Presbyterian Scotsman John Witherspoon and his successor, Samuel Stanhope Smith. They were thoroughly schooled in the works of the Scottish Enlightenment and Thomas Reid. Like many other Christians, these philosophers were all haunted by the epistemological skepticism of David Hume. Many have argued that this common sense realism became something of a philosophical "lingua franca," particularly in the middle colonies and the South, by the mid-nineteenth century.[32] To put Hodge's Princeton paradigm into perspec-

30. Hodge, "What Is Christianity?" p. 121. See especially John Hicks, *The Philosophy of Charles Hodge: A 19th Century Evangelical Approach to Reason, Knowledge and Truth* (Lewiston, N.Y.: The Edwin Mellen Press, 1997). See also J. W. Stewart, "The Tethered Theology: Biblical Criticism, Common Sense Philosophy, and the Princeton Theologians, 1812-1860" (Ph.D. dissertation, University of Michigan, 1990), chapter 7.

31. See Douglas Sloan, *The Scottish Enlightenment and the American College Ideal* (New York: Columbia University Press, 1971). See also Mark Noll, *Princeton and the Republic, 1768-1822: The Search for a Christian Enlightenment in the Era of Stanhope Smith* (Princeton: Princeton University Press, 1988).

32. The literature about Scottish common sense realism in American culture is expanding rapidly. For an excellent introduction, see Elizabeth Flower and Murray Murphey, *A History of Philosophy in America*, vol. 1 (New York: Capricorn Press, 1977); Theodore D. Bozeman, *Protestants in an Age of Science* (Chapel Hill: University of North Carolina Press,

tive, I need to outline briefly the salient features of this antebellum philosophical tradition at Princeton Seminary.

Scottish common sense realism has been appropriately labeled a "metaphysics of actuality." The author of that perceptive phrase, Terrence Martin, suggested that the common sense philosophers were driven "to concentrate on the actually existing object, the perceivable entity; it begot a tendency to narrow the limits of reality to [the] actually existing being."[33] They were committed to an uninhibited confidence in the world *outside* the human mind. Subject and object were thus sharply delineated. Such a claim implied that humans neither created the real world nor were they able to alter it. "The Scottish system," Perry Miller once wrote, "was a 'Realism,' meaning that man does perceive reality and need never to bother about what Whitman called 'the terrible doubt of appearance.'"[34] In short, neither "social location" nor human imagination could ultimately skew or distort the external realities that common sense consciousness illuminated. As Theodore Bozeman has so handsomely described, this "naive realism" also undergirded the Baconian inductive method for all sorts of intellectual activity.

From this unassailable epistemological realism the Scottish philosophers derived a "principle of universality." Reid had argued that his "first principles" were endorsed by "the universal consent of mankind, not of philosophers only, but of the rude and unlearned. . . . The practice of life is grounded upon [them]." A century later, James McCosh of Princeton College, whom Hodge helped to bring to America from Scotland, claimed that it was not too extravagant to claim that this Scottish realism "enunciated principles that were . . . SELF EVIDENT . . . [and] UNIVERSAL, be-

---

1977); and Mark Noll, "Common Sense Traditions and American Evangelical Thought," *American Quarterly* 37 (Summer 1985): 216-38. For an excellent introduction to Thomas Reid, see Keith Lehrer, *Thomas Reid* (London: Routledge, 1989). The scholarly literature about theology and Scottish sense realism is already vast and still growing. For an excellent treatment of the relationship of this Scottish philosophy and its theological constructions, see Richard B. Sher and Jeffery R. Smitten, eds., *Scotland and America in the Age of Enlightenment* (Princeton: Princeton University Press, 1990). With these efforts acknowledged, a thorough explanation of the relationship of Scottish realism and the Princeton theologians has yet to be written.

33. Terrence Martin, *The Instructed Vision: Scottish Common Sense Philosophy and the Origins of American Fiction* (Bloomington: Indiana University Press, 1961), p. 85. Martin's helpful phrase and judgment is further supported in Richard Olson, *Scottish Philosophy and British Physics, 1750-1880* (Princeton: Princeton University Press, 1975).

34. Perry Miller, *American Thought: Civil War to World War I* (New York: Holt, Rinehart and Winston, 1954), p. x.

ing entertained by all men."[35] Such an assumption was eminently congenial with the Christian belief in the divine creation of humans and the
"unity of mankind" doctrine. Thus Hodge could write in 1859,

> Whenever we meet a man, no matter of what name or nation, we find
> he has the same nature with ourselves. He has the same organs, the
> same senses, the same instincts, the same faculties, the same under-
> standing, will and conscience, the same capacity for religious cul-
> ture. He may be ignorant and degraded; he may be little above the id-
> iot brother who sits with us at our Father's table, but we cannot but
> recognize him as a fellow-man.[36]

Everywhere the telltale phrase "by the constitution of our nature" occurs
in these theologians' writings, one can be sure the assumptions of Scottish realism are operative or implied.

To these two pivotal assumptions a third needs to be added. Reid and
his successors paid considerable attention to the nature and function of
human language in human discourse.[37] They had read John Locke's writings about language and developed their own theory of "signs." "Language," Reid wrote, "is the express image and picture of human thought;
and from the picture, we may draw very certain conclusions in regard to
the original." On the basis of this presupposition they not only believed
that language possessed an inherent "power" to communicate the actual
world, but also that there was little obfuscation in the transmission. "To
conceive the meaning of a general word, and to conceive the truth of that
which it signifies, is the same as the thing itself. . . . The meaning is the
thing conceived." While they acknowledged that language lacked the precision of mathematical formulae, they contended that "all humans *think*
as well speak by means of words." Dugald Stewart insisted that words

---

35. James McCosh, "Scottish Philosophy, As Contrasted with the German," *The Princeton Review*, New Series, III (1882): 331.

36. Hodge, "The Unity of Mankind," *BRPR* 31 (1859): 148-49. In another article Hodge argued

> The Scriptures indeed recognize a common nation as belonging to all men; that is,
> that all men belong to one and the same class and species of the beings, have a
> common origin and same physical structure, same rational and moral faculties
> and they are in the same state of alienation from God.

See Hodge, "What Is Christianity?" p. 136.

37. See Hans Aarsleff, *The Study of Language in England, 1789-1860* (Princeton: Princeton
University Press, 1967).

were the sole instrument of human thought, since ideas were conveyed from person to person by means of words alone. Apparently, it was impossible for humans to have a wordless thought. In a lecture Hodge employed this Scottish philosophical heritage when he claimed,

> It will be remembered that in ordinary circumstances it is the object of every one using a language to be understood. . . . The only way in which the writer can be understood is to use words in the sense commonly attached to them by his readers. As this is perfectly obvious, it follows with equal clarity that . . . [one] must first ascertain however the words and expressions understood by the person to whom the writing was addressed. And in ascertaining that, *he may be sure* he has the meaning of the author. . . .

That lecture was given in 1823. Fifty years later Hodge argued similarly in his *Systematic Theology,* "Thoughts are in the words."[38]

As we shall see in the section below, this view of the nature of language was enormously important for these Princetonians' views of the Bible and their hermeneutic. From an early tract, "The Bible in Education" (1831), to the opening chapters of his popular *The Way of Life* (1841), to the first volume of his *Systematic Theology* (1872-73), Hodge insisted that any viable theory of divine inspiration of the Bible must extend to its words and wording, not just to its ideas, or much less, myths.[39] By implication, he believed that a passage possessed only *one* primary meaning, the so-called

---

38. For the sources of theses quotes from Thomas Reid's *Essays on the Intellectual Powers of Man* (1785) and other philosophers, see Stewart, "Tethered Theology," pp. 270-80. Scholars who follow this discourse about language in the antebellum era will know that Hodge fiercely combated Horace Bushnell's "A Preliminary Dissertation on Language," published in 1849. I have also outlined that Hodge-Bushnell exchange in the abovementioned dissertation.

39. Here is how Hodge put this conviction in 1857:

> We can understand how a man can regard the Bible as a mere human composition; we can understand he can regard inspiration as a mere elevation of religious consciousness; but how any one holds that the sacred writers were inspired [only] to their thoughts, but not to their language, is to us perfectly incomprehensible. . . . No man can have a wordless thought, any more than there can be a formless flower. By such a law of our present constitution [a favorite common sense formula], we think in words, and as far as our consciousness goes, it is as impossible to infuse thoughts into our minds without words, as it is to bring men into the world without bodies.

See "Inspiration," *BRPR* 29 (1857): 677.

authorial intention. With such a view, Hodge was left with the perplexing problem of discerning how one word or verse of the Bible was more or less important than any other.[40]

I contend that these Scottish philosophical assumptions contributed not only to the Princeton paradigm but also to Hodge's distinctive identity as a Reformed American theologian. They are clues as to why and how Hodge differed from his eighteenth-century American predecessors as well as contemporaries and twentieth-century successors.

Hodge often noted his discomfort with the earlier towering American figure in this Reformed Christian tradition, Jonathan Edwards. On several occasions Hodge dismissed "President" Edwards for basic philosophical reasons. "In America," Hodge once wrote, "the earliest school of metaphysics was founded by the followers of Locke; and with the clew of this great inquirer in his hand, Jonathan Edwards ventured into a labyrinth from which no English theologian had ever come out safe."[41]

Meanwhile, other mid-nineteenth-century Protestant theologians, particularly the "New Divinity" scholars in New England, were realigning themselves with the "modern impulses" of Kant, Hegel, and Schleiermacher. Hodge's paradigm, however, slowly sequestered him from his nineteenth-century counterparts. The reasons for this separation are complex. For one thing, Hodge rarely endorsed the *separation* of human reason, faith, feelings, and piety, a position be belabored in his elongated debates with Edwards A. Parks of Andover Seminary.[42] For another, the newer philosophical hegemony of Immanuel Kant was dislodging those of Reid and other Scottish realists.[43] All Kantian-based theologies with their unbridgeable delineation between the "phenomenal" (the realm of science) and the "noumenal" (the realm of religion) were toxic to Hodge. Reason, for Hodge, was to be *within* the bounds of religion, not vice versa, as Kant had

40. This is, essentially, the conclusion in one of the most sobering critiques ever penned of the early Princeton theology by the Scottish theologian Thomas N. Lindsay. See Lindsay, "The Doctrine of Scripture: the Reformers and the Princeton School," *The Expositor,* Fifth Series, vol. 1 (1895): 278-95. Hodge was not unaware of this dilemma. See Hodge, *ST,* vol. 1, p. 164.

41. Hodge, et al., "Transcendentalism," *BRPR* 11 (January 1839): 38. See also Lyman H. Atwater, "Jonathan Edwards and the Successive Forms of New Divinity," *BRPR* 30 (October 1858): 585-620.

42. See the introduction to this Hodge-Park controversy in Noll, *The Princeton Theology,* pp. 185-207.

43. For how Kant understood (and dismissed) Scottish common sense realism, see an important book by Manfred Kuehn, *Scottish Common Sense in Germany, 1768-1800* (Montreal: McGill-Queens University Press, 1987).

written. At the same time, Hodge rejected the theological inroads made by Hegel and his followers, usually dismissing their theologizing as implicitly pantheistic. The writings of F. E. D. Schleiermacher, however, were a separate issue for Hodge. In light of his earlier training in Germany, Hodge nursed a lifelong "love/hate" relationship with Schleiermacher. He wrote about that quandary often. Perhaps in ways later echoed by Karl Barth in the twentieth century, Hodge never reconciled the Princeton paradigm with the philosophical Romanticism implicit in Schleiermacher's way of doing Reformed theology. One American outcome of Hodge's misgivings about Schleiermacher's Romantic theology led to Hodge's bitter disputes with John Nevin, his former student and advocate of the "Mercersburg Theology." In like manner, his deep alienation from Horace Bushnell was grounded in this same philosophical impasse.[44]

Hodge had a hound's nose for sniffing out the philosophical assumptions of others, yet he was rarely critical of his own. He never seemed to fathom why his common sense realism was being jettisoned during the last half of the nineteenth century. I know of no reference to John S. Mill's famous critique of William Hamilton, which insisted that Scottish realism was too imprecise and insufficient for the needs of science. Neither can I discover whether Hodge ever read the earliest American pragmatists. Those more modern philosophers were plowing in altogether different philosophical fields.[45] At the same time, other countervailing issues were mounting as threats to the Princeton paradigm. The growing *empirical* evidence of the human family's physical and social diversity as evidenced in America's socio-cultural pluralism must have played havoc with Hodge's deepest assumptions about the uniformity of the human race and the universality in human ways of thinking. These formidable shifts to newer modes of thought seemed to render earlier common sense assumptions sluggish and flatfooted. Yet, even in the early 1870s, during the writing of

---

44. See especially Hodge, "Bushnell on Christian Nurture," *BRPR* 19 (1847): 536-39. "Schleiermacher, whose views are so zealously reproduced and between which and his own Dr. Bushnell seems often at a loss to choose, taught that Christ introduced a new life-principle into the world. . . . It is not with the historical, personal Christ that we have communion, any more than it is with Adam as an individual man with whom we have to do. Both are reduced to a mere power or principle. . . . In this way all the precious truths of the Bible are sublimated into unsubstantial philosophical vagaries, and every man pronounced a Rationalist . . . [or] a Puritan, who does not adopt them."

45. See especially John Diggins, *The Promise of Pragmatism: Modernism and the Crisis of Knowledge and Authority* (Chicago: University of Chicago Press, 1994); Cornel West, *The Evasion of Philosophy: The Genealogy of Pragmatism* (Madison: University of Wisconsin Press, 1989); and Louis Menand, *The Metaphysical Club* (New York: Farrar, Straus and Giroux, 2001).

his *Systematic Theology,* Hodge sought to stay the common sense course and defend his Princeton paradigm, with its particular views about the Bible. And to that aspect of the paradigm we now turn.

B. Hodge's Understanding and Use of the Bible

Benjamin B. Warfield, Hodge's onetime student and eventual successor, once recalled Hodge's manner when teaching seminarians about the Bible:

> After his always strikingly appropriate prayer had been offered, and we were settled back in our seats, he would open his well-thumbed Greek Testament — on which it was plain that there was not a single marginal note — look at the passage for a second, and then, throwing his head back and closing his eyes, begin his exposition. He scarcely again glanced at the Testament during the hour: the text was evidently before his mind, verbally, and the matter of his exposition was at his command. In an unbroken stream it flowed from subject to subject, simple, clear, cogent, and unfailingly reverent. Now and then he would pause a moment, to insert an illustrative anecdote — now and then lean forward suddenly with tearful, wide-open eyes to press home a quick-risen inference of the love of God for lost sinners.[46]

Modern scholars who grapple with Charles Hodge and his Princeton paradigm concede that the Bible was the gravitational center for all of his theologizing.[47] There is no historical justification to doubt Hodge when he wrote in 1842, "We have reason to assert and defend, the position that the Bible, the Bible alone, is the religion of Protestants; we want no other and we want no more."[48] For a lifetime, he held unswervingly to that core conviction. The Bible was not the object of his Christian faith, but rather the irreplaceable and normative medium through which he professed to encounter the triune God revealed in Jesus of Nazareth.[49] "All Protes-

46. For this quote, see Charles Hodge, *Princeton Sermons: Outlines of Discourse, Doctrinal and Practical* (London: Banner of Truth, 1958), p. xvi.
47. For Hodge's role as a biblical interpreter, see the essay in this volume by David H. Kelsey entitled "Charles Hodge as Interpreter of Scripture."
48. Charles Hodge, "Rule of Faith," *BRPR* 14 (1842): 629.
49. In a capital article, Hodge wrote,

To the believer, the Lord Jesus Christ, as the eternal Son of God, . . . is the supreme object of love and worship. All religious affections terminate in him. The believer lives in daily and hourly communion with him; relying on the merit of his righ-

tants," he wrote, "agree in the teaching that 'the word of God, as contained in the Scriptures of the Old and New Testaments, is the only infallible rule of faith and practice.'"[50] In retrospect, Hodge's core convictions about the Bible were unremarkable when compared to most other conventional Christians of his day, even if the word "infallible," lifted from the Westminster Confessions, would prove problematic and contentious for Hodge and his Presbyterian successors.[51]

Hodge's view of the Bible was, of course, grounded in the Reformed tradition. That tradition brought to bear at least two other claims for this Princeton theologian that give contemporary scholars pause. Sealed in Hodge's memory from childhood tutoring were the teachings of the Westminster Confessions, which maintained that the essential message of salvation for humans was plain and accessible to any person who could read the Bible:

> The Bible is a plain book. It is intelligible by the people. . . . It is not denied that the Scriptures contain many things hard to understand; that they require diligent study; that all men need the guidance of the Holy Spirit in order to [acquire] right knowledge and true faith.

---

teousness as something outside of himself. . . . He looks to him as his Shepherd. . . . He longs for his personal presence and to be perfectly devoted to his service.

See Hodge, "What Is Christianity?" p. 158.

50. Hodge, *ST,* vol. 1, p. 151.

51. Compared to English and German surveys of biblical scholarship, American historians have yet to provide a comprehensive survey of the Bible and its role in American theology and thought in the nineteenth century by which to assess Hodge's beliefs about the Bible. One earlier study that helps measure Hodge's views is Nathan O. Hatch and Mark A. Noll, eds., *The Bible in America: Essays in Cultural History* (New York: Oxford University Press, 1982). Another way to understand Hodge's biblical conviction is to place him within his own hermeneutical context by consulting the large literature about biblical interpretation in the nineteenth century. See for example Robert Morgan, *Biblical Interpretation* (New York: Oxford University Press, 1988); and R. J. Coggins and J. L. Houlden, eds. *A Dictionary of Biblical Interpretation* (London, SCM Press, 1990). See also Mark Ellsingsen, *A Common Sense Theology: The Bible, Faith and American Society* (Macon, Ga.: Mercer University Press, 1995). Jerry W. Brown's *The Rise of Biblical Criticism in America* (Middletown, Conn.: Wesleyan University Press, 1969) remains an excellent survey of biblical criticism in antebellum America.

With regard to Presbyterian-based controversies about the Bible, however, a small industry of literature has emerged. One excellent place to begin this investigation is Jack B. Rogers' two foundational works, *Scripture in the Westminster Confession: A Problem of Historical Interpretation for American Presbyterianism* (Grand Rapids: Eerdmans, 1967) and Jack B. Rogers and Donald K. McKim, *The Authority and Interpretation of the Bible* (San Francisco: Harper and Row, 1979). See also Stewart, "The Tethered Theology."

But it is maintained that in all things necessary for salvation they are sufficiently plain to be understood even by the unlearned.[52]

Hodge's commitment to common sense ways of thought made this claim of "perspicuity of the Scriptures" even more convincing.

Yet at the same time, Hodge insisted with his Reformed forebears that all *faithful* understanding of the Scriptures was integrated with the mysterious, electing intervention of Holy Spirit. For Hodge, the Spirit's active mediation in the original composition of the Bible's texts extended also to the believer's reading and appropriation of them. Without the participation of the Spirit — "the Spirit bearing witness with our spirits" (Romans 12) — the Word of God lacked convicting power and definitive guidance. "The ultimate ground of faith," Hodge repeatedly insisted, "is the witness of the Spirit." The pivotal and problematic word here is "witness."[53] Nevertheless, *without* the Spirit's persuasive powers, even an infallible Bible, though clear and unambiguous in its essential message, remained moot, ineffectual, and little more than a relic of ancient Near Eastern literature. *With* the Spirit's presence, however, it became the Word of God to humans.

Where, then, are contemporary historians to locate this Old School professor in the tradition of American Reformed thought? Current judgments among contemporary historians beg for a consensus. Most acknowledge that his training in biblical studies exceeded most of his contemporaries, and a notable historian of American religion has insisted that Hodge's views of the Bible differed little from other evangelical Protestants in antebellum America. Yet prominent scholars of American Presbyterianism has argued that the early Princeton theologians, including Hodge — pressed by modern skepticism, the rise of biblical criticism, and America's ecclesiastical diversity — skewed the Reformed tradition's understanding of the role and function of Scripture.[54] A contemporary Princeton theologian has maintained that Hodge's reliance on the Bible

52. Hodge, *ST,* vol. 1, pp. 183ff.

53. Hodge, *ST,* vol. 3, p. 60. Andrew Hoffecker's careful book about Hodge and religious experience is suggestive and important. He maintains that the place to begin in Hodge's theology is with Hodge's doctrine of the Holy Spirit. See Hoffecker, *Piety and the Princeton Theologians* (Grand Rapids: Baker Book House, 1981).

54. See the "Introduction" in Noll, *The Princeton Theology.* Rogers and McKim in their *Authority and Interpretation* are more critical. See also George Marsden, "Everyone One's Own Interpreter? The Bible, Science and Authority in Mid-Nineteenth-Century America," in Hatch and Noll, eds., *The Bible in America,* pp. 79-100.

inexcusably obscured the basis of true Christian confidence.[55] On the other hand, Mark Noll has observed that Hodge's biblical and propositional theology in the *Systematic Theology* belonged to the same era as the First Vatican Council (1869-70), when many Christian communities were addressing issues of religious certainty in a era of "enthusiasm, nascent rationalism and creeping modernization."[56]

Despite these widely differing appraisals, this much seems clear: (1) while Hodge was fully apprised of mid-nineteenth-century beginnings in biblical scholarship, his formative and lifelong convictions about the Bible *predate* his encounters with modern biblical criticism;[57] (2) his elaborate theory of divine inspiration of the biblical texts precedes his less explicit and underdeveloped hermeneutical norms and protocols;[58] (3) his confidence in the certainty of commonsense reasoning rendered a biblical reader's subjective energies and imagination dormant; (4) he capitalized on his role as editor of the *BRPR* to participate in a transatlantic conversation about the Bible, but he tended to translate and reprint *conservative* German scholarship for American audiences;[59] and (5) he believed that Protestant doctrine of *sola scriptura* implied that the Bible was authoritatively sufficient not only for Christian doctrinal formation, but also for the practice of Christian discipleship in both private and public realms of human existence.[60]

Most, if not all, of Hodge's convictions about the Bible ran counter to

---

55. Migliore, *Faith Seeking Understanding*, chapter 3.

56. Noll, *The Princeton Theology*, p. 34.

57. See Stewart, "Tethered Theology."

58. While Hodge wrote about this topic often, his most complete argument may be found in Hodge, "Inspiration," *BRPR* 29 (1857): 660-98. The section in the *ST* that addresses the inspiration of the Bible adds little. See *ST*, vol. 1, chapter 6.

59. While reflecting on the editorial policies of the *BRPR* in 1868, Hodge declared that

> The conductors of this *Review* have always endeavored to adhere faithfully to the principle that the Scriptures are the only infallible rule of faith and practice. Therefore, when any matter, either of doctrine or morals, came under discussion, the question with them was "What saith the Lord?" Nothing that the Bible pronounces true can be false; nothing false can be true; nothing obligatory on the conscience but what it enjoins; nothing can be sin, but what it condemns.

See Charles Hodge, "Retrospect of the History of the Princeton Review," in *The Biblical Repertory and Princeton Review: Index Volume*.

60. For the primary (though not only) sources of Hodge's views of the Bible, Hodge, *Way of Life*, chapter 1, entitled "The Scriptures Are the Word of God;" Hodge, "Inspiration," pp. 660-98; and Hodge, *ST*, vol. 1 (esp. chapters 1, 4, 6, and 12). Other essays in this volume, especially those of Brian Gerrish and David Kelsey, are especially important.

the "modern impulse" and the rising tide of nineteenth-century biblical scholarship. Hodge knew the declaration of Oxford scholar Benjamin Jowett, who declared in 1861 that modern scholars ought to interpret the Bible like any other document of antiquity. Hodge, along with many others, could hardly make a concession to such a desacralization. Yet there is something more in the substrata of Hodge's hermeneutical writings. Hodge nursed a profound aversion to any sort of historical development in the Bible or any dialectical process in human thought and doctrinal construction. I suspect this antipathy went deeper than his rejection of Kant and Hegel and was rooted in his unswerving and uncritical endorsement of a Newtonian worldview. His stout belief in the Bible as "the only infallible rule of faith and practice" was inextricably woven into his Scottish Enlightenment assumptions of stability, equilibrium, and order in the world of nature. Pivotal beliefs about the doctrinal unity of the Bible, its utter historical reliability *as written,* and the supernatural inspiration of its traditional authors ran counter to the "historicist drift" that came to dominate most liberal biblical studies in the nineteenth century. One historian has summarized this seismic nineteenth-century shift as the "biologizing of history and the historicizing of biology." We can trace Hodge's uneasiness and opposition from his earliest encounters in the 1820s with the biblical critics in Germany to his watershed article in 1857 (entitled "The Inspiration of the Bible") and on to his formulae in the *Systematic Theology.* This suspicion and chagrin was especially discernible in his caustic and dismissive reviews of several editions of *Das Leben Jesu* (1835-36) by the radical critic D. F. Strauss, who reduced the New Testament narratives to "creative legend" or second-century myths. And the same dissonance over evolutionary processes emerged again in Hodge's critique of Darwinism in 1874, where, incidentally, he referred to Strauss's radicalism again.[61] In this sense, Hodge was not only deeply at odds with the great intellectual drift in the nineteenth century but was also unable or unwilling to envision an alternative hermeneutic for his own day. James Turner has suggested that theologians like Hodge were unaware that the unitary language of science, philosophy, and ordinary discourse was breaking down under the specialization and expansion of knowledge in the nineteenth century, especially in the universities.[62] During Hodge's long life and career, Susan Handelman once observed, the "assumptions guiding the interpretation of the Bible — that it was totally

---

61. For an expansion of this view about Hodge and Darwinism, see Stewart, *Mediating the Center,* pp. 36-44.

62. Turner, *Without God, Without Creed,* pp. 159-63.

consistent, infallible, the source of its own interpretation — were transferred to the other Book, the Book of Nature."[63]

Postmodern scholars are preoccupied with the hermeneutical assumptions of biblical theologians. With one notable — and revealing — exception, Hodge never developed what later scholars would call a thoroughgoing hermeneutical theory.[64] That exception was Hodge's hermeneutical essay that opens his *Systematic Theology*. "The true method of theology," he began, "is, therefore, inductive, which assumes that the Bible contains all the facts or truths which form the content of theology, just as the facts of nature are the content of the natural sciences."[65] However wooden and arthritic this introduction now appears, for four decades Hodge had sought to anchor the Christian faith — and its mandates for a Christian way of life and a more just society — in an utterly reliable, "as written," Biblical record rather than in the muddy bottoms of Kantian rationality or Romanticism's many moods.[66]

63. Susan Handelman, *Slayers of Moses: The Emergence of Rabbinic Interpretation in Modern Literary Theory* (Albany: State University of New York Press, 1982), p. 125. She adds,

The interpretative method of science depended on the assumption of utterly consistent laws in nature, but the new and crucial idea was that the formulation of these laws was not only a *human attempt* at interpretation, an hypothesis; there was also no longer any direct divine pronouncement, only human formulations of divine meanings.

64. Strangely enough, while Hodge wrote a thirty-page critique of various heterodox theories of inspiration of the Bible, there are only *two* pages in his *Systematic Theology* on the "Rules for Interpretation" of the Bible. See Hodge, *ST*, vol. 1, pp. 187-88. He contended over and over again that the Bible's *essential* meaning and message was plain enough, and that commonsense readings of biblical texts were within the grasp of all persons with a "congeniality of mind." Such convictions carried wider implications:

If the Scriptures be a plain book, and the Spirit performs the functions of a teacher of all the children of God, it follows inevitably that they must agree in all essential matters in their interpretation of the Bible. And from that fact it follows that for an individual Christian to dissent from the faith of the universal Church (i.e., the body of true believers), is tantamount to dissenting from the Scriptures themselves.

See Hodge, *ST*, vol. 1, p. 184.
65. Hodge, *ST*, vol. 1, p. 17. For further exposition of this method of doing theology, see especially Noll, *The Princeton Theology*.
66. I suspect that Hodge would have sympathized with Flannery O'Conner's dig at American liberal Protestantism when she wrote in *Habits of Being*,

One of the effects of modern liberal Protestantism has been gradually to turn religion into poetry and therapy, to make truth vaguer and more and more relative, to

Usually Hodge was content to assess — and assail — the hermeneutical labors of others who were opening new frontiers in modern biblical scholarship.[67] Hodge was especially scornful of the hermeneutics in Horace Bushnell's *God Was in Christ* (1849). "He is only half out of his shell. And therefore his attempt to soar is premature."[68] "The Bible is not," Hodge charged, "a cunningly devised fable, — a work of fiction, addressed only to the imagination. . . . The revelations of God are addressed to the whole soul, to the reason, to the imagination, to the heart and to the conscience. But unless they are true to reason, they are as powerless as a phantasm."[69] He had equally unsympathetic estimates of Samuel Coleridge's *Aids to Reflection*, which was making swift inroads in New England academic circles.[70]

Hodge, the biblical theologian, wrote commentaries only on the Pauline Epistles.[71] If there was a "scholastic" streak in Hodge's hermeneutics, it was displayed in the selected portions the Bible that he chose to interpret. The Pauline Epistles appealed to his confessional instincts and way of theologizing. Meanwhile, except for his sermonizing, he bypassed other portions of the Scriptures, notably the Gospels and the Psalms, which would have required the engagement of human imagination and poetic insight.

One final aspect of Hodge's convictions about the Bible usually puzzles contemporary scholars. Hodge insisted that any hermeneutical method must include a behavioral component. That is, a faithful, Spirit-

---

banish intellectual distinctions, to depend upon feeling instead of thought, and gradually to come to believe that God has no power, that he cannot communicate with us, cannot reveal himself to us, indeed has not done so and that religion is our own sweet invention.

See Flannery O'Conner, *Habits of Being,* ed. by Sally Fitzgerald (New York: Farrar, Straus & Giroux, 1979), p. 462.

67. For further exploration of this large topic, see Stewart, "Tethered Theology."

68. Hodge, "Bushnell's Discourses," *BRPR* 21 (1849): 260.

69. Hodge, "Bushnell's Discourses," p. 269.

70. See the exchange of correspondence between Hodge and James Marsh, President of the University of Vermont and American promoter of Coleridge's works. The manuscripts detailing this dialog are available in Hodge's manuscripts collection at Princeton Theological Seminary.

71. Hodge, *A Commentary on the Epistle to the Romans* (Philadelphia: Grigg and Elliot, 1835); Hodge, *A Commentary on the Epistle to the Romans* (New York: R. Carter & Bros., 1857); Hodge, *An Exposition of the First Epistle to the Corinthians* (New York: R. Carter & Bros., 1857); Hodge, *An Exposition of the Second Epistle to the Corinthians* (New York: R. Carter & Bros., 1857). Hodge's commentary on Romans went through several revisions.

led interpretation had to be interwoven with a faithful Christian piety. As early as his inaugural address in 1822, Hodge argued that "No man can follow the common principles of exposition of the interpretation of the S.S. [Sacred Scriptures] who is destitute of a vital piety." Faithful biblical reading required a logic of obedience. "Beware," he warned his students," of a strong head and a cold heart."[72] There was nothing really new in this "hermeneutic of piety." Hodge knew, of course, that he was in synch with his parents in Reformed faith who always insisted that "Truth is in order to goodness." John Calvin had said the same thing when he offered his famous question at the beginning of the *Institutes of the Christian Religion* (I:2:2). Why do you want "to know about a God with whom you will have nothing to do?" Calvin asked. Hodge often contended that the radical critics linked their historical rejections to a repudiation of Christian discipleship. As others have said, for Hodge, "divine truth, both natural and revealed, was the seal of which piety was the impress."

C. Hodge and the Church

Hodge's theological vision required a church. He knew Calvin's famous endorsement of the early Church's dictum, that no one could know God as Father without having the Church as Mother. "God has imposed his duties upon his people," Hodge wrote in his *Systematic Theology,* "which render it necessary for them thus to associate in a visible organized body."[73] Postmoderns may opt for "spirituality" while dismissing the institutional church, but Hodge did not. He was a lifelong member of the First (now Nassau) Presbyterian Church in Princeton, a member of dozens of church and college boards, and moderator of the Presbyterian national General Assembly (Old School) in 1846. Between 1835-69, he labored annually to report on the Assembly's work in the *BRPR,* attending most of these conventions in person. Hodge always did his theologizing with an ear tilted toward the Church's theological tradition and an eye focused on Presbyterian well-being and responsibility. Yet a thorough exposition of Hodge's ecclesiology still awaits publication.[74] My goal here is not to reconstruct fully Hodge's ecclesiology, but to point the modern reader to

72. Hodge, *Princeton Sermons,* p. xvi.
73. Hodge, *ST,* vol. 3, p. 547.
74. A first step toward this end is John J. Deifell, Jr., "The Ecclesiology of Charles Hodge" (Ph.D. dissertation, University of Edinburgh, 1969).

some important aspects of Hodge's views about the nature, mission, and governance of the Christian church.

As is the case with most other aspects of Hodge's thought, his articles in the *BRPR* are the best places to start to understand his ecclesiology. Beginning in 1835, he wrote lengthy commentaries and critiques in the *BRPR* on the proceedings and decisions of the denomination's General Assembly (Old School). In addition, he wrote dozens of articles about the ecclesial issues that confronted antebellum Presbyterians, including sacraments, liturgies, the role of clergy, excommunication over slavery, revivalism, governance controversies, ecumenical cooperation, and the church's political involvement and allegiances when secession threatened the nation. Apparently, these opinions were widely read and often quoted in Protestant circles. In 1878 a former student gathered into one 600-page volume many of Hodge's comments about the church published earlier in the *BRPR*.[75]

Hodge's notorious 1836 article "Slavery" also carried revealing clues concerning his ecclesial reasoning. It was generated within the throes of Presbyterian debates over whether or not ecclesial authorities could excommunicate members for holding slaves or advocating slavery. That possibility had been proposed during the 1835 General Assembly and was scheduled for final resolution at the following Assembly in 1836. Apart from Hodge's controversial argument about slavery, he contended that Presbyterian judicatories had no such authority to excommunicate members over *this* issue because the Scriptures did not command such an excision. Of course Presbyterians could excommunicate wayward members, but not over this issue, Hodge argued. Apparently his view prevailed, at least for the moment.

Equally insightful were Hodge's caustic controversies with John W. Nevin, a former student and proponent of the Mercersburg theology. These articles were written in the 1840s, when he was the moderator of the General Assembly, and they help to explain Hodge's antipathy toward an episcopal or hierarchical understanding of bishops and clergy. They also plainly reveal his rejection of a Roman Catholic understanding of the Eucharist.[76]

In 1846 and 1860, Hodge penned three long articles on topics central to

75. William Durant, ed., *Discussions in Church Polity* (New York: Charles Scribner's Sons, 1878). It should be noted that this massive work, which contains an introductory essay by A. A. Hodge, concentrates on issues of governance and organizational structures in the Presbyterian and other Christian churches rather than ecclesiology.

76. See "The Mystical Presence: A Vindication of the Reformed or Calvinistic Doctrine of the Holy Eucharist," *BRPR* 20 (1848): 259-97.

ecclesiology: "Theories of the Church," "The Idea of the Church," and "Presbyterianism." Among the many arguments offered were harsh responses to the "spiritualized" ecclesiology of James H. Thornwell, a position that came to be identified in Protestant circles as the "passivity doctrine of the Church."[77] In contrast to Thornwell, Hodge had long argued that the church possessed not just a biblically based right but a moral obligation to encourage or critique a nation's political and societal agendas.

That stance was soon severely tested. Like his counterparts in other American denominations, Hodge was unable to persuade the 1860 General Assembly to keep his beloved Presbyterian church from splitting over *political* issues, not theological ones. Hodge's lament after the 1861 General Assembly remains in print:

> The country was engaged in a civil war. . . . Presbyterians were in arms against Presbyterians. . . . The General Assembly was called upon to take sides. . . . But alas! . . . our church was as divided as the country. It was the case of a mother who was called upon to take part for one child against another. It was in vain she urged that both were children. . . . This plea availed nothing. She was in the hands of the more powerful of the two. . . . The Assembly has had severe conflicts in her past history, but none were analogous to this. . . .[78]

In addition to these many articles in the *BRPR,* Hodge produced two books before 1850 that examined issues of ecclesiology. One was a large and erudite tome entitled *The Constitutional History of the Presbyterian Church* (1839). Published shortly after the 1837 "Old-School/New School" split in the Presbyterian denomination, Hodge sought to defend a presbyterian polity rather than an American-styled congregationalism, claiming the former was more biblical, Reformed, Scottish, and desirable. The other book was *The Way of Life: A Guide to Christian Belief and Experience* (1841), a popular volume written for the Sunday School Union. Some of

---

77. Hodge, "Slavery," *BRPR* 8 (1836): 268-305; Hodge, *Way of Life,* chapter 8; Hodge, "The Mystical Presence [Lord's Supper]," *BRPR* 20 (1848): 259-97; Hodge, "Theories of the Church," *BRPR* 18 (1846): 137-58; Hodge, "Is the Church of Rome a Part of the Visible Church?" *BRPR* 18 (1846): 320-44; Hodge, "Idea of the Church," *BRPR* 25 (1853): 339-89; Hodge, "Presbyterianism," *BRPR* 32 (1860): 547-67.

78. Hodge, "The General Assembly," *BRPR* 33 (July 1861): 542-43. Hodge noted with respect that it was right for the Southern Presbyterians to refuse to "sing the 'Star Spangled Banner' at the Lord's Table" when commanded by an "excited multitude." I have expanded Hodge's perspectives about Presbyterians and the Civil War in Stewart, *Mediating the Center,* pp. 87-110.

his earliest systematic thoughts about the church and its "means of grace" can be found here.

As is often noted, Hodge's *Systematic Theology* contained surprisingly little with regard to a systematic or constructive doctrine of the church. The answer to this curiosity seems to be satisfied by his son's comment that Hodge had intended to add a fourth volume to the *Systematic Theology*. It was to be a work "embracing the department of Ecclesiology," but it was never written, due to "infirmities of his advanced age."[79] Nevertheless, at least three ecclesial tenets surfaced often throughout the *Systematic Theology*. First, in a long exposition of the Fifth Commandment, in which honoring of parents was extended to the honoring of the church, Hodge reaffirmed an earlier and very generic definition the church. After describing the several ways in which the word "church" was used in the Scriptures, Hodge summarized his argument:

> In the present discussion, by the Church is meant what is called the visible Church; that is the whole body of those who profess the true religion, or any number of such professors united for the purpose of public worship of Christ, and for the exercise of mutual watch and care.[80]

Exegesis of this very broad and ecumenical definition can lead us to surmise what Hodge meant when he used the word "church." A church was a community of Christian disciples who affirmed established doctrinal convictions, worshipped God, disciplined each other, organized themselves "decently and in order," and were subject to communal oversight. Such a definition allowed Hodge considerable latitude and flexibility during his many ecumenical encounters.

A second ecclesiological touchstone in the *Systematic Theology* was a

79. This claim is made in the preface of Durant, ed., *Discussions in Church Polity*, p. iii.

80. Hodge, *ST,* vol. 3, p. 547. See also Hodge, *ST,* vol. 3, pp. 545ff. Earlier, in 1846, Hodge wrote in the same broad-church way: "By the word church . . . we mean an organized society, profession of true religion, united for the worship of God and the exercise of discipline under the same form of government and under some common tribunal." Charles Hodge, "Is the Church of Rome a Part of the Visible Church?" p. 328. As would be noted, this discussion of the church in the *ST* was precipitated by his defense of the baptism of infants and his insistence that children of faithful Christians were to be "numbered with the saints." "Whenever a father or mother seeks admission to the Christian Church, their heart prompts them to say, 'Here Lord am I and the children whom thou has given me.' And His gracious answer has always been, 'Suffer the little children to come unto me and forbid them not.'" Hodge, *ST,* vol. 3, p. 557.

long exposition (335 pages!) on the nature and efficacy of the sacraments of baptism and the Lord's Supper. Along with Bible reading and prayer, Hodge incorporated the two Protestant sacraments under the category of "the means of grace." He regularly employed this traditional Reformed term in his writings and defined it in the *Systematic Theology:* "The phrase is intended to indicate those institutions which God has ordained to be the ordinary channels of grace, i.e. the supernatural influences of the Holy Spirit, to the souls of men. . . . Means of grace are those means which God has ordained for the end of communicating the life-giving and sanctifying influences of the Spirit to the souls of men."[81] Hodge was perfectly consistent with the Reformed affirmations that sacraments, prayers, and worship services were instrumental to believers' deepening experience of divine grace rather than ends or virtues in themselves.

Third, Hodge's convictions about the Holy Spirit were not inconsequential for his ecclesiology. For all of his supposed rationalism and his congenital suspicion of mysticism, Hodge's ideas about the church were infused with a Trinitarian doctrine of the Holy Spirit. He knew of course that the Apostolic creeds placed the church *after* the statements about the Holy Spirit. Following that venerable confessional ordering, Hodge coupled theological convictions about the sovereignty, freedom, and divine election of God with the inscrutable workings of the Spirit. Rarely, if ever, was the Spirit's primacy and mystery underrated in the essential practices of the church. One quote from his *Systematic Theology* will have to suffice here:

> The efficacy of the sacraments is due solely to the blessing of Christ and the working of his Spirit. The Spirit, it is to be remembered, is a personal agent who works when and how He will. God has promised that his Spirit shall attend his Word; and He thus renders it [Spirit] an effectual means for the sanctification of his people. So He has promised, through the attending operation of his Spirit, to render the sacraments effectual to the same end.[82]

81. Hodge, *ST,* vol. 3, pp. 466, 547, 708.
82. Hodge, *ST,* vol. 3, p. 500. In Hodge's heated controversy with John Nevin in 1848, Hodge argued that establishing a solitary Reformed doctrine of the sacraments was difficult and complex. "This difficulty arises from many sources. The subject itself is mysterious. The Lord's supper is by all Christians regarded as exhibiting, and, in the case of believers, confirming their union with the Lord Jesus Christ. . . . It is agreed, further, that this union includes on our part a participation of the Spirit of Christ. It is the indwelling of the Holy Spirit . . . who dwells also in his people, so they become one body in Christ Jesus." Hodge, "The Doctrine of the Reformed Church on the Lord's Supper," *BRPR* 20 (1848): 227-28.

During most of Hodge's lifetime, Roman Catholic and Protestant relationships were usually nasty, shrill, and often combative. In an earlier article, he reacted severely to an 1845 General Assembly proposal to declare any baptism in the Roman Catholic Church as "null and void." Hodge countered by affirming that all Trinitarian baptisms in *any* Christian community, including Roman Catholic, were valid and permanent and were not to be repeated.[83] This irenic orientation came to the fore in 1868 on the occasion of Pope Pius IX's invitation to most American Protestant denominations to attend the upcoming Vatican Council. The 1868 General Assembly of the Northern Presbyterian denomination eventually voted to decline the invitation and, in a little-known decision, a committee assigned to Hodge the delicate task of responding to the pope. Hodge's hand-written letter to Pope Pius IX, extant in Princeton University's archives and fully reprinted in the official documents of the Council, was a memorable testimony to Hodge's conciliatory attitude toward Roman Catholicism. On behalf of Presbyterians in America, Hodge wrote that all persons were considered true Christians "who professed Jesus Christ as Savior and Lord, together with their children." That was not an insignificant declaration in an era when Protestants regularly labeled the pope the antichrist.[84]

One final comment remains about the sources of Hodge's ecclesiology. Throughout his career, Hodge displayed little sympathy for the preemptive religious individualism typified in Emerson's "Self Reliance" or implicit in the revivalism of Charles G. Finney. Neither did he endorse a church that was reducible to a "voluntary association," as Tocqueville had described.[85] Undoubtedly, some of his ecclesial convictions lay at the base of his opposition to "New School" Presbyterianism. Hodge was deeply annoyed at those tendencies in American Protestantism that led Christians to participate in religious communities on their

83. Hodge, "Is the Church of Rome a Part of the Visible Church?" pp. 320-44.

84. The manuscript of Hodge's letter is in the archives the Firestone Library, Princeton University in a file entitled, "Letter to Pope Pius IX." It was translated into French and published in *Act Et Decreta: Sacrorum Concliorum Recentiorum. Collectio Lacensis*, vol. 8, ed. S. J. E. Domo, et al. (Friburgi, Brisgovei: Herder, 1870-1890), pp. 10-12.

85. See Hodge's critique of voluntary "Boards and Agencies" in Protestant communities in his "Voluntary Societies and Ecclesiastical Organizations," *BRPR* 9 (1837): 101-20. It is not clear whether Hodge and other Presbyterians had read Tocqueville's *Democracy in America*, whose first volume was published in 1835 and a second in 1840. Hodge's dismissal of the church as a "voluntary association" suggests, however, some linkage with a term usually attributed to Tocqueville. For further insightful comments on Hodge's view of the church, see the essay by James Turner in this volume.

own terms. The contemporary "Sheilaisms" described by Robert Bellah would be utterly alien to Hodge.[86] For him, being Christian necessarily meant a participation in *some* Christian community.

D. Hodge and the American Social Order

Until recently, it was not generally recognized that Hodge was an astute observer and commentator on American social, cultural, and political life.[87] Hodge addressed a remarkable number of political topics and controversies in the *BPPR*. This willingness to engage the social and political issues of his day — whatever his particular opinions were — distinguishes Hodge from the later Princeton theologians such as A. A. Hodge and B. B. Warfield, who were more intramural and narrowly focused.

Generally, Hodge was aligned with the Whig tradition in American society and politics. With notable exceptions, the Whigs, as the Republicans after them, stood in the heritage of the old Federalists (Madison, Hamilton, and John Adams), with an emphasis on national economic development, urbanized cultural values, an assertive central government, and a network of cultural institutions that transmitted values and shaped opinion.[88] Surprisingly, Hodge voted for Free Soiler John C. Frémont in 1856 and campaigned for the newly established Republicans. He also became an admirer of Lincoln. Hodge often reiterated his intense patriotism by recalling that his physician father was imprisoned by the British during

86. Robert Bellah, *Habits of the Heart* (Berkeley: University of California Press, 1985), p. 221. For important insights about this topic, see Daniel Walker Howe, "Protestantism, Voluntarism and Personal Identity in Antebellum America," in *New Directions in American Religious History,* ed. Harry S. Stout and D. G. Hart (New York: Oxford University Press, 1997). Howe claims that "American religious diversity and freedom of religious choice were central to the massive effort at self-definition that helped usher in individualism and the pluralism of the modern world" (p. 226).

87. For a fuller exposition of Hodge's engagement with American culture, see Stewart, *Mediating the Center.*

88. An excellent treatment of American Whigs can be found in Daniel W. Howe, *Political Culture of the American Whigs* (Chicago: University of Chicago Press, 1979). For the weaving of Reformed theology, culture, and politics in the antebellum period, see Fred J. Hood, *Reformed America: The Middle and Southern Colonies* (Tuscaloosa: University of Alabama Press, 1980). See also David Murchie, "Charles Hodge and Jacksonian Economics," *Journal of Presbyterian History* 61 (Summer 1983): 248-56. To appreciate the political context of Princeton, New Jersey during Hodge's era, see William Gillette, *Jersey Blue: Civil War Politics in New Jersey, 1854-1865* (New Brunswick: Rutgers University Press, 1995).

the Revolutionary War and was released by the personal intervention of George Washington. The other "mainstream" political tradition, that of the Democrats (typified by Thomas Jefferson and Andrew Jackson), emphasized local government, a "rural" vision for America, and a strenuous commitment to individualism. The Democrats never appealed much to Hodge. He was as distrustful of "Jacksonian democracy" as he was disparaging of Charles G. Finney. It is not merely coincidental that Democrats were strong in the South, while the Whig-Republicans were prominent in the North.

Hodge rarely backed away from the political controversies of his day. He supported the establishment of a national bank, he affirmed Jackson's position in the "nullification controversy" in South Carolina, he called for government intervention to spur manufacturing by levying tariffs on foreign goods, he promoted the national postal system, and he was critical of America's entry into the war with Mexico, just to name a few of the issues he took on. Moreover, his many essays about the Civil War were outstanding editorials. On the other hand, his public views about women's roles in society were, by our current standards, irresponsible.[89] In an era that witnessed the flowering of the earliest American "women's rights movement," Hodge remained an defender of the then-fashionable "cult of domesticity." While acting as a caring husband and tender father to eight children, he was oblivious to his own hierarchical views about social structures that excluded women from public discourse and ecclesial offices. His opposition to women's suffrage was caustic and unyielding. Hodge published, and apparently endorsed, a review by Archibald Alexander of Catherine Beecher Stowe's *Letters on the Difficulties of Religion*. Alexander, with patriarchy in full force, concluded that women, "however gifted and learned [should be discouraged] from mixing in theological and ecclesiastical controversies."[90] Unlike his views about slavery in American society, Hodge never changed his ideas about women and their leadership roles in society and churches.

Hodge's views about American slavery have stirred, confused, and alienated many Presbyterians in his day and ours. Two perspectives are foundational for the reviewing of Hodge's convictions about slavery. First, for a limited period of time after his return from Germany in 1828, Hodge himself owned one or more slaves. How and why he acquired them while

89. See especially the essay in the volume by Louise Stevenson entitled "Charles Hodge, Women and Womanhood, and Manly Ministers."

90. Archibald Alexander, "*Letters* . . . by Catherine E. Beecher," *BRPR* 8 (1936): 544.

living in Princeton is not altogether clear and begs for further research. But Hodge, like Samuel Miller, did in fact own some slaves for some time in the 1830s. Secondly, at the closure of his editorial responsibilities for the *BRPR* in 1871, Hodge summarized the position of the many references to the slavery issue in the *BRPR*: "The conductors of this *Review*, from first to last, maintained that the doctrine that slaveholding is in itself a crime, is anti-scriptural and subversive of the Word of God." Immediately Hodge added, "The consequences of these [biblical] principles would be the speedy and peaceful abrogation of the slaves, and the gradual elevation of the slaves to the rights of free citizens."[91]

I have contended elsewhere that Hodge's views are more multifaceted and fluid than they first appear to modern readers.[92] Hodge rarely wrote about the slavery controversy without reference to the controversy's impact on the Presbyterian church. There were many moves and countermoves within Presbyterian judicatories to make the holding of slaves or the advocacy of slavery punishable by excommunication, a stance which Hodge opposed.[93] By the middle third of the century, Presbyterians were as deeply divided as the rest of the nation. James H. Thornwell's defense of slavery in the late 1840s led to a bitter exchange between the two theologians. Hodge called an 1861 sermon by Benjamin Palmer (the first moderator of the Southern Presbyterian Church) a "monstrous perversion" when Palmer claimed that the South's divine assignment was to perpetuate slavery.[94] That same year the editors of Augusta's prominent newspaper,

91. "Slavery," in *The Biblical Repertory and Princeton Review: The Index Volume from 1825-1868* (Philadelphia: Peter Walker, 1871), pp. 15ff.

92. For a preliminary discussion of this large issues of slavery and race in Hodge's writings, see Stewart, *Mediating the Center*, pp. 71-87. See especially David Torbett, "Theology and Slavery: Charles Hodge and Horace Bushnell on the Problem of African American Slavery in the United States" (Ph.D. dissertation, Union Theological Seminary and the Presbyterian School of Christian Education, 2002). In this volume Alan Guelzo argues, "That Hodge could move almost at once from marshalling together Christ and the apostles to defend slavery to a moment of apparently sober entertainment of black emancipation and civil rights presents a double somersault of dizzying proportions." Guelzo provides a wider context for Hodge's slavery comments in "Slavery and Original Intent," *Books and Culture* 8 (May-June, 2002): 36-37.

93. Charles Hodge, "*Slavery* by William E. Channing," *BRPR* 8 (April, 1836): 268-305. It should be noted that this essay appeared shortly before the meeting of the 1836 General Assembly of the Presbyterian church, where the excommunication of slaveholders was to be voted upon. For an insightful and contrary exposition of this article, see the essay by Allen C. Guelzo in this volume.

94. Charles Hodge, "Short Notices . . . [Palmer's] Thanksgiving Sermon," *BRPR* 33 (1861): 167.

the *Constitutionalist,* caustically called Hodge a traitor to the church and the Bible.[95]

It was not until the 1850s that Hodge fully appreciated the moral repugnancy of America's "peculiar institution." Still, he never acknowledged or comprehended the moral outrage of the abolitionists, even when those abolitionists were within the Presbyterian church. For the most part, Hodge dismissed "immediate" abolitionists as irresponsible and divisive. By the time of Lincoln's election, Hodge had written extensively about slavery. He offered a long defense of the controversial Emancipation Proclamation, though it could be argued that it was more political than moral in thrust and argument.

While Hodge's views on race and racial difference beg for more research, it can be argued that Hodge's assumptions about racial differences were liberal for his day.[96] One senses that Hodge's understanding of racial diversity in the human family was linked with his understanding of scientific beginnings of the examination of racial differences in the early research efforts of America's first cultural anthropologists. Hodge, remembering the writings of Stanhope Smith of Princeton College, wrote often about the "Unity of Mankind." His views of race ought to be seen within these scientific and historical contexts.[97]

Hodge was also a keen observer of the Civil War and Lincoln's leader-

95. In a review of Hodge's notable "State of the Country" essay in the *BRPR* (1861), the Southern editors wrote, "Many warm admirers of Dr. Hodge feel constrained . . . to exclaim, 'et tu Brute!' . . . The impression produced by the [Princeton] *Review* will be not less false that those by Mrs. Stowe's work of fiction." See *Constitutionalist,* March 22-24, 1861, p. 1.

96. Eugene Genovese put it this way: "Hodge and his compatriots looked like ultraconservatives in Princeton and the North but looked like liberal temporizers in Columbia, South Carolina and the South." Genovese, *The Southern Front: History and Politics in the Cultural War* (Columbia: University of Missouri, 1995), p. 87.

97. By 1860, Hodge discerned more clearly the relationship of "unity of mankind" beliefs and America's slavery practices and the attending racial denigration. In an article that followed the death of President Lincoln, Hodge wrote admiringly of Lincoln's handling of the slavery and emancipation issues: "Since all men are the children of Adam, made of one blood and possessing the same nation, therefore all are entitled to be regarded and treated as men. No symptom of permanent slavery can be justified, except on the assumption that the enslaved class are a different and inferior race. . . . From this it would follow, by parity of reason, that every man who has the intelligence and moral character for proper exercise of the elective franchise is entitled to enjoy it. . . . In other words, these rights and privileges cannot justly be made dependent on the colour of the skin or any other adventitious difference." Charles Hodge, "President Lincoln," *BRPR* 37 (1865): 456-57. An older treatment of Hodge's views is by Andrew E. Murray, *Presbyterians and the Negro — A History* (Philadelphia: Presbyterian Historical Society, 1966), pp. 106ff.

ship. His brother-in-law (by Hodge's second marriage) was the famed Union general David Hunter. Hunter, who rode Hodge's personal horse during the war, apparently arranged for Hodge to visit the Union's "war room" in Washington each May during the war years. Long and detailed letters to his physician brother in Philadelphia revealed Charles's careful following of the "second American revolution."[98] Hodge never viewed the war as anything but a profound tragedy. In contrast to many other intellectuals of his day, such as Emerson and Bushnell, who in the early 1860s celebrated the glories of the war and its promotion of American democracy, Hodge was not so sanguine. He was stunned by the outbreak of war: "And oh, what was it but a ghastly hallucination which could lead them [Southern politicians] to commit wholesale robbery, perjury, and treason, verily thinking they were doing God's service."[99]

E. Reflections on Hodge's Princeton Paradigm

Some of Hodge's seminarians, like Henry James, Sr., in the 1840s, found the Princeton paradigm too myopic and taut. Many others among Hodge's 3,000 students found the his teachings congenial and carried them into America's South, middle colonies, and the opening West. Some relayed Hodge's program abroad, especially in Scotland, England, France, India, and Korea. Hodge's *Systematic Theology* was used as a major text in several American seminaries as late as 1960 and remains in print. A knowledgeable friend told me recently that the it is still the primary textbook for theology in the one remaining Protestant seminary in North Korea.

Hodge's Princeton paradigm, however, was problematic from the beginning. The demise of Scottish common sense realism and the rise of American pragmatism, the *factual* evidence that Darwin supplied for his theory of evolution, the growing diversities in American life and culture, and the burgeoning of scholarship known as the historical criticism of the Bible — all of these factors leaned on Hodge's paradigm unmercifully. All four of these foundational changes point to a more modern worldview that was process-oriented rather than static, more evolving than established. If the "modern impulse" was headed toward the likes of Alfred N.

---

98. A sampling of these letters may be found in Hodge, *LCH,* pp. 451ff.

99. Quoted in "American Nationality," *BRPR* 33 (1861): 639. For how Hodge might be compared with other intellectuals, see George Fredrickson, *The Inner Civil War: Northern Intellectuals and the Crisis of the Union* (New York: Harper & Row, 1965).

Whitehead and John Dewey, Hodge's paradigm was too content with the ways of Isaac Newton and Thomas Reid. Moreover, there is suggestive evidence that Hodge realized that the Presbyterians' Civil War experience rendered suspect if not moot many of his assumptions about a universal morality and a common sense rationality. Particularly devastating was Hodge's realization that his beloved Presbyterian church's influence was rendered impotent when Presbyterians split along Union and Confederate lines in 1860-61 and ended up killing each other.

By the last third of the nineteenth century, Hodge's grand and gothic system teetered under the weight and burden of its own making. Viewed through postmodern perspectives, Hodge believed too much. His "meta-narrative" had too many *essential* subplots. He lived and wrote in an age when most theological energies were centrifugal rather than cohesive. With that said, no informed and critical reappraisal of Hodge is reliable without attending to this Princeton paradigm on its own terms and in its own Victorian-era context.

3. Hodge and the American Reformed Tradition

Sydney Ahlstrom of Yale University insisted that without Charles Hodge, American Calvinism would have taken an entirely different shape.[100] While not necessarily intending to include Hodge in his astute generalization, Bruce Kuklick has argued that American Reformed theology, especially in its New England form, "represents the most sustained intellectual tradition in the United States."[101] Within the boundaries of these two broad comments, Hodge was a distinctively American Reformed theologian.[102] By that I mean his Calvinistic orthodoxy was not only constructed with American styles and audiences in mind, but his theological enterprise encompassed prolonged encounters on major issues in American religion, culture, and socio-political movements. E. Brooks Holifield puts a similar judgment this way: Hodge "could draw on Edwards. He could even borrow an idea from Hopkins, and he could recognize his affinities with the Old Calvinists of eighteenth-century New England, but finally Hodge belonged in a different American tradition."[103]

---

100. Sydney Ahlstrom, *The Shaping of American Religion*, p. 263.
101. Bruce Kuklick, *Churchmen and Philosophers*, p. 43.
102. Stewart, *Mediating the Center*, pp. 111ff.
103. See the essay by E. Brooks Holifield in this volume.

Two conceptual frameworks help to explain why Hodge was a peculiarly *American* theologian. The first framework is methodological. Hodge was a "public theologian" in the sense that Martin Marty has defined.[104] Marty said that religious beliefs become public when believers seek to bridge public and private spheres in a reflective and analytical manner. The antithesis of "public theology" would be a theology that is privatized, interiorized, or even solipsistic in its faith expression. Hodge's theological methodological stance was clearly and habitually public. Further, his "public" discourse might be further nuanced by what George Lindbeck of Yale University has called an "intratextuality." In this sense, the task of the "public theologian" is to engage the Christian "text" with the other and prevailing "texts" of American culture. While Lindbeck applied this process to more recent theological discourse, his explanation could well apply to Hodge. Hodge's sustained project was to interpret the world around him through his biblical, Augustinian, Calvinist, Westminster Confessional lens. Illumined by these authoritative texts, Hodge strove to find meaning for his private and corporate lives and interpreted reality within those "textual" frameworks.[105] In a discourse that lasted a lifetime, Hodge employed these interpretive texts and processes, point and counterpoint, to engage multiple issues particular to American society and culture. And he did so in such a way that was neither myopic nor fundamentalist. To the contrary, he addressed such hefty and expansive issues as political agendas, modern philosophy and literature, Victorian science, American racism and slavery, and the tragic Civil War. His positions and postulates may now appear quaint, untenable, and unworkable, but they were neither trivial nor shallow-minded. Arguably, no other American Reformed theologian in the nineteenth century commented on as many and as diverse issues to the same extent as Hodge did.

A second framework flows from the first. Hodge needs to be located within the current debate among American cultural historians surrounding "American exceptionalism." Admittedly, the debate about America's uniqueness and particularity is unresolved. A worthy case has been made that America's foundational values and structures are clearly distinct from English, Continental, and African counterparts. The distinguished historian Jack P. Greene has maintained that the concept of "America" in-

104. See Martin Marty, *The Public Church: Mainline, Evangelical, Catholic* (New York: Crossroad Publishers, 1981).

105. George Lindbeck, *The Nature of Christian Doctrine* (Philadelphia: Westminster Press, 1984).

corporates not only a specific geographical place but also particular and specific cultural meanings and characterizations attached to that space. During the emergence of the new nation, Greene argued, Americans "defined more fully than ever before what made their societies different from those of the Old World and similar to each other. In the press of elaborating their American-ness, they quickly began to develop an infinitely more favorable sense of collective self." By the early part of the nineteenth century, Greene insists, American writers affirmed and intensified their positive identification of America as an exceptional place, people, and culture.[106]

Such a generalization is not inappropriate for Hodge, who often noted America's peculiarity. It was not inconsequential that Hodge was tutored early on by Samuel Miller, whose two-volume *Brief Retrospect of the Eighteenth Century* (1803) has been labeled "the first systematic study of intellectual history by an American."[107] As early as 1829, shortly after his return from Germany, Hodge wrote, "There is a personality in nations as well as in men, and as every individual has peculiar responsibilities arising out of his peculiar circumstances and character, so have nations." Thirty years later, in 1859, he reiterated the same idea: "Every nation has its peculiar character and usages, the product of and manifestation of its organic life. This country is no exception to this law."[108]

Every systematic theological enterprise, as Douglas John Hall has noted, is inevitably contextualized. Hall has maintained that theology, at its best, is a disciplined reflection and commentary upon the faith's engagement with "the everyday, complicated, beautiful, ugly and threatened world of our experience. It [theology] means, in short, our *context*."[109] Seen in this light, Hodge's Reformed theology was distinctively American. Hodge's philosophical underpinnings, his attempts to place faith claims in America's public arena, his ecclesial definitions and polemics, his designs for a substantial educational institution, and his linkage of piety and public faith expression are telltale signs of his deep roots in the soil of American culture and society. Interpreted though this lens, Hodge has

---

106. Jack P. Greene, *The Intellectual Construction of America* (Chapel Hill: University of North Carolina Press, 1993), p. 162.

107. John Higham, *Writing American History* (Bloomington: Indiana University Press, 1970), p. 44.

108. Charles Hodge "Anniversary Address," *The Home Missionary* 2 (July 1829): 17; Hodge, "Sunday Laws," BRPR 31 (1859): 758.

109. Douglas John Hall, *Thinking the Faith: Christian Theology in a North American Context* (Minneapolis: Fortress Press, 1989), p. 74.

more in common with Reinhold Niebuhr and H. Richard Niebuhr than with Benjamin B. Warfield or J. Gresham Machen.

4. Hodge in Retrospect

This essay began by revisiting Marcus Cunliffe's observation that the detailing of religious orthodox thinkers is both complex and full of vigor. Both of these generalizations can be tailored to fit Charles Hodge. Certainly he was no innovator in theology, if by that we mean that he transformed or redirected the foundational commitments of Protestant theology. To the contrary, he stood stalwartly in opposition to many of the nineteenth-century trends in modern theology, philosophy, biblical studies, and ethics. His unflinching commitment to Reformed theological orthodoxies, coupled with Whig-bound cultural proclivities, distanced Hodge from the liberalizing trajectories of nineteenth-century American theology. With that complex and vigorous conservatism acknowledged, it is most inappropriate to continue to dismiss Hodge as a squinty-eyed scholastic or a Presbyterian curmudgeon. E. Brooks Holifield invites a more balanced appraisal:

> Hodge the professional theologian, the theologian that tackled just about every big issue of nineteenth-century theology, was, in both history books and theological polemics, pushed into the tight boundaries of the Darwinian and infallibility debates. When viewed in the broader context . . . , however, Hodge exemplified the nascent ideal of the professional theologian as an incisive and broad-ranging thinker able to comment on any question of theology that might arise.[110]

In his illuminating essay in this volume, James Turner sums up Hodge's importance by writing that Hodge "stands as a synecdoche for the intellectual history of orthodox Christianity in the nineteenth century."

---

110. See the conclusion of Holifield's essay in this volume.

Charles Hodge in the Intellectual Weather of the Nineteenth Century

JAMES TURNER

To read Charles Hodge is to place oneself under the orders of a captain who pilots his vessel with rare assurance. The tone of voice is commanding. The range of knowledge is daunting. The hand on the tiller is rock steady.

This unwavering certitude belongs to the polemical style of the Victorian age, and few polemicists in Victorian America could trump Hodge. He never hesitated to put an opponent in debate firmly in his place. (Always *his* place; women could not properly take the field.) Reviewing a book by the Congregationalist biblical scholar Moses Stuart, for instance, Hodge declared that Stuart had "signally failed": "misapprehended the subject in debate; misconceived the meaning of the authors whom he quotes; contradicted himself; done violence to his own theoretical rules of interpretation, and gratuitously denounced" essential doctrines of Protestantism elsewhere professed by Stuart himself. How had Stuart fallen into this swamp of error? "Unconscious of the influence of certain works over his mind," the poor dolt had been led by the nose by German metaphysical theologians "and his own prejudices," a hapless victim of the "instabil-

---

BRPR signifies the *Biblical Repertory and Princeton Review*, which Hodge edited from 1825 to 1868 (under variant titles). Most *BRPR* articles, conventionally for reviews of the period, masqueraded as book reviews, rarely carrying formal titles; I have identified them by abbreviated running title. I am grateful to Raymond Cannata for supplying photocopies of many of Hodge's articles in the *BRPR*.

ity" of his "mental temperament."[1] On our thinner skins, words like these would rasp till we bled. This only shows what wimps we have become, or at least that we play the game by different rules.[2] Far from regarding Stuart as an enemy, Hodge paid him "unfeigned homage as the great American reformer of biblical study" and stood with him on terms of professional amity and private friendship.[3] And Stuart knew better than to take the formalized arrogance of debate personally.

Yet even by the polemical precepts of his day, Hodge behaved extraordinarily like Zeus, pronouncing his high judgments and hurling his thunderbolts accordingly on the inferior mortals below. In part this Olympian attitude may have mirrored the elevated status and didactic role of the Presbyterian minister along the northern seaboard in the early national period, which Hodge inherited; in larger part it justly derived from his own remarkable learning. Alone among American theologians and biblical scholars of his generation he had studied, and studied seriously, in Germany, the great fatherland of erudition; even in the next generation, probably only the Swiss-born and German-educated Philip Schaff could boast equivalent exposure.[4] And only Schaff among Hodge's immediate peers seems to have been more comfortable in the German language, the native tongue of the most influential theological and biblical scholarship. Hodge also handled Greek, Latin, Hebrew, and of course French competently and had studied Arabic and Persian, while his diverse writings reflect the staggering breadth of his reading in fields as seemingly remote from his professional concerns as craniometry. I, too, bow to his learning; and his more technical work in theology and biblical criticism — areas in

---

1. "Stuart on the Romans," *BRPR* 5 (July 1833): 382-85. This was for Hodge fairly mild stuff; see the savage ridicule heaped on the high church Episcopal bishop George W. Doane in "Bishop Doane and the Oxford Tracts," *BRPR* 13 (July 1841): 451-52.

2. The rules of engagement were well known. For example, regarding an article signed "A Friend to the A[merican]. E[ducation]. Society," known to those *au courant* with the controversy in question to have come from the pen of Moses Stuart, Hodge mentioned in replying to it that "we were not authorized to know the writer" until Stuart himself had publicly acknowledged his authorship. "Professor Stuart's Postscript," *BRPR* 2 (January 1830): 125.

3. "Stuart on the Romans," *BRPR* 5 (July 1833): 382.

4. Edward Everett and George Bancroft laid similar foundations but turned to other careers soon after returning from Germany. A high proportion of Americans who attended German universities in the first two-thirds of the nineteenth century only brushed up against German erudition, owing to deficiency of language or brevity of exposure; see, e.g., the records printed in P. G. Buchloh and W. T. Rix, *American Colony of Göttingen* (Arbeiten aus der Niedersächsischen Staats- und Universitätsbibliothek Göttingen, Bd. 15; Göttingen, 1976).

which I am utterly incompetent — I have not dared to assess. Indeed, even the judgments I do venture leave me feeling uncomfortably like a gnat hectoring an elephant. Hodge could speak with greater authority than most of his interlocutors for the very good reason that he *knew* more than they did.

But not always; and his habit of confident assertion sometimes outran his erudition. He could blandly declare that, during the colonial era of American history, "ninety-nine hundredths of our population came from Great Britain," a claim that even a novice in American history would have recognized as balderdash and that Hodge himself would probably have withdrawn had he bothered to think.[5] Pontification affected more substantial issues. Hodge not uncommonly — and, I think, increasingly as the years passed — delivered himself of asseverations such as that both Old and New Testaments *"everywhere"* distinguish "between the soul and the body as two subjects" and teach "the full conscious existence of the soul between death and the resurrection"; or, likewise, that the doctrine of a generic human existence shared by all individual persons (a belief held by Augustine) was novel in the nineteenth century; or, again, that "ninety-nine hundredths of all good men utterly repudiate" the "theory that all sin consists in acts." Such declarations were so at variance with reality, and so at odds with what Hodge himself must at some level have known, as to make the reader blink in astonishment.[6] Such propositions could not plausibly be argued; they could only be asserted.

Granted, much of what Hodge wrote for his journal, the *Biblical Repertory and Princeton Review,* he wrote at high speed with little chance for revision; and some of his more astounding overstatements probably owe their origin to this circumstance. But the trait was too deeply engrained to be so easily explained away. John W. Stewart has shrewdly suggested that Hodge's "intolerance for ambiguity" did not at all reflect a self-assured personality. Quite the reverse: Hodge's fatherless and impoverished childhood probably left a nagging insecurity at the core of his psyche.[7] The same psychology might account for his chronically hyper-certain rhetoric. Hodge, one might well believe, armored his vulnerability with that exter-

---

5. "England and America," *BRPR* 34 (January 1862): 147.

6. "What Is Christianity?" *BRPR* 32 (January 1860): 135; "Professor Park's Sermon," *BRPR* 22 (October 1850): 657. Emphasis mine.

7. John W. Stewart, *Mediating the Center: Charles Hodge on American Science, Language, Literature, and Politics* (Princeton: Princeton Theological Seminary, 1995), pp. 7-9. I am in general much indebted to Stewart for my understanding of Hodge, though I do not want to implicate him in my misunderstandings.

nal confidence, at times amounting almost to arrogance, so evident in his writings and so sharply in contrast with the tenderness and even emotional neediness apparent in his personal relations. I at least find Stewart's scenario highly plausible.

But I would add to this explanation of Hodge's compensatory overconfidence a different order of insecurity, one that helps us to place him not only in his individual psychological world but also in the mental world of the nineteenth century. The intellectual revolutions of that tumultuous century — revolutions to no small degree arising in the Germany that Hodge all his life admired and despised — did not treat him kindly. The winds of change blew with a deadly chill upon the fundamental axioms of his worldview. Perceptive as he was, he early realized that in such heavy weather any variance in course, still more any tacking to the storm, might well result in shipwreck. Hodge's confident assertions not only denied to himself the possibility that he might err in navigating through the treacherous waters of the nineteenth century; they served to mark clearly for his audience the course that he insisted must be followed to avoid going on the reefs.[8]

The most threatening risks were of three different orders, though often overlapping. The first was the growing individualism underlying phenomena apparently as unrelated as evangelical revivalism, utilitarian liberalism, and political democracy. The second was the subjectivism commonly linked with "Romanticism": the stress on inward feelings and intuitions as sources of human knowledge or insight and the related intimation that human beings mediate or even construct reality rather than directly perceiving it. The third, and perhaps the most toxic to Hodge, was the new sensitivity to history as a shaping force, evident in areas as diverse as biological evolution and Hodge's own special field of biblical criticism. These perils loomed all the greater because in no case did they offer utter novelty; rather, Hodge believed, these ominous new departures carried obvious truths to grotesque extremes. Out-and-out falsehood would have persuaded almost no one, but unbalanced half-truths had a treacherously seductive appeal. Hodge's responses to these dangers cast light not only on his own thinking but also on the dilemmas of his era.

---

8. In the case of most thinkers whose careers spanned as many decades as Hodge's, the historian would take care to respect the evolution of the subject's thought and distinguish accordingly between earlier writings and later. So far as I can tell, however, the lineaments of Hodge's worldview changed remarkably little over his lifetime: becoming only clearer and, as usual in middle and old age, more rigid. In this overview I have therefore drawn on his work without regard to dates of composition.

With a polymath like Hodge, the question is where to begin. A convenient entry into his thinking is his views of the church, since probably to no subject did Hodge devote more ink. A good Protestant, Hodge insisted on the priority of the individual's relationship with God over any ecclesiastical mediator and of the word of God in Scripture over any church tradition: principles that he believed to have been "taught by Christ and his apostles."[9] The true church comprised all true believers in Christ, the visible church all "professors of the true faith," spiritually united though institutionally divided by history and by doctrine inessential to salvation.[10] Even the Roman Catholic Church counted as part of the visible church, for it still professed the "essential doctrines of the gospel" despite adulterating them with a welter of false teaching and "idolatrous" practices; and Hodge liked to think that most of its members would be saved.[11] Otherwise, his contempt for the "Romanists," as he preferred to call them, could scarcely be measured. "Popery" was "by far the most dangerous form of delusion and error that has ever arisen in the Christian world"; it inured its members to "habitual commission of crime," posed a graver danger to America than German infidelity.[12] Hodge dreaded even the "romanizing" tendencies of the Oxford Movement and of, closer to home, the Mercersburg theology of Schaff and Nevin.[13]

Within these Protestant parameters, however, Hodge took so high a view of the church that other Americans may have suspected him of sympathy with Oxford. The American tendency to schism at the drop of a hat appalled him; in the cauldron of the Civil War he insisted that "the command of Christ" bound Northern and Southern Presbyterians "to hold together as a church" even while the nation disintegrated.[14] (They disobeyed.) He jealously guarded the prerogatives of the officially constituted governing bodies of the church against lay organizations, especially in matters of clerical recruitment and education. "The organization which Christ and his apostles have ordained" was not to be displaced by mere "societies of man's devising."[15] He felt uneasy about the American

9. "Bishop Doane," p. 456.

10. "Theories of the Church," *BRPR* 18 (January 1846): 145.

11. "Is the Church of Rome a Part of the Visible Church?" *BRPR* 18 (April 1846): 341, 343.

12. "Church of Rome," 344; "Theories of the Church," 157; "Schaf's [sic] Protestantism," *BRPR* 17 (October 1845): 630.

13. "Oxford Tracts," *BRPR* 10 (January 1838); "Bishop Doane"; "Dr. Schaff's Apostolic Church," *BRPR* 26 (January 1854).

14. "The Church and the Country," *BRPR* 33 (April 1861): 323, 375.

15. "Voluntary Societies and Ecclesiastical Organizations," *BRPR* 9 (January 1837): 106.

Protestant "error" — that is, routine practice — of a congregation supplying its pastor's salary: ministers being "ordained to the service of the whole church," the church as a whole ought to guarantee them adequate support.[16] He even dreamed of a parochial school "in connexion with every presbyterian church in our country."[17]

So powerful was Hodge's hankering for a stronger church that it led him briefly into an astonishing intellectual alliance with the proto-modernist American theologian Horace Bushnell, a man whom Hodge in later years could approach only with anathemas. In 1847 Bushnell published the first version of his *Christian Nurture,* repudiating revivalism and arguing in essence that, in the usual course of God's dispensation, parents brought their children to saving faith by a proper Christian upbringing within the bosom of the church. Hodge did caution that Bushnell tended to explain "Christian nurture" in almost naturalistic terms of organic law rather than "the covenant and promise of God." But his criticisms were almost swamped in his enthusiasm for Bushnell's leading point: the "great and obvious truth" of "organic, as distinguished from individual life." Despite the little book's doctrinal divagations, Hodge expected "immeasurably more good than evil from its publication."[18]

Like Bushnell, Hodge deprecated revivalism and the corollary image of the lone individual face-to-face with God. He insisted instead on the raising of children under the tutelage of the church (and, compared to Bushnell, Hodge stressed church more than parents) as "the natural, the normal and ordinary means" of grace. The revivalist regime "easily induced" believers to "become utterly remiss as to all social religious duties of an ordinary character." And here Hodge edged closer to what lay at the center of his own high view of the church. He seized on Bushnell like a dog on a bone not because he lay awake nights worrying about how parents were raising their youngsters, but because he was appalled by the modern philosophy "that every man has power to determine and to change at will his own character, or to make himself a new heart." This hyper-individualism, "as every one knows," had come to prevail in the United States. "It represents every man as standing by himself" — a denial of core Christian doctrine and an affront to Hodge's understanding of society and polity as well as salvation.[19]

16. "Preaching the Gospel to the Poor," BRPR 42 (January 1871): 87, 90; cf. "Stuart's Postscript," pp. 130-32.
17. "Claims of the Free Church of Scotland," BRPR 16 (April 1844): 258.
18. "Bushnell on Christian Nurture," BRPR 19 (October 1847): 535, 502, 504.
19. "Bushnell on Christian Nurture," pp. 510, 520-22. "They are called *American* revivals,"

For the nineteenth-century notion that every individual stood on his (or even worse, her) own feet Hodge perceived as a heresy deadly in secular as well as eternal affairs. He adhered to a distinctively American tradition of republican conservatism with a powerful communitarian ethos, a political outlook that flourished between the death of the older Federalist conservatism after the War of 1812 and the rise of laissez-faire economic conservatism after the Civil War. This important tradition of political thought still awaits its historian, but we can see its lineaments in Hodge.[20]

"Radical principles," Hodge reminded the readers of the *Princeton Review* at the end of the Civil War, "are alien to" the *Review's* "character and spirit" — and they certainly were to its editor's.[21] Like Burke, Hodge developed a strong sense of the salience of particular conditions in making political judgments; what might be "rational under one set of circumstances, is the height of infatuation under another."[22] He likewise had little patience with speculative talk of "inalienable rights"; he called it "a great fallacy to suppose that the abstract rights of men can be enforced at all times and under all circumstances."[23] Though he came to believe that slavery as actually practiced in the American South involved grave sin, he consistently refused to condemn slavery as sinful in principle: the question was how human beings in fact treated others and what sort of treatment a particular system fostered, not the theoretical relation of master to servant.[24]

As all of this suggests, Hodge understood government not in terms of any speculative theory, but as a historically conditioned institution. Although God intended human beings as social creatures to live under gov-

---

Hodge noted. "There is nothing American however in true religion. It is the same in its nature, and in its means of progress in all parts of the world" (p. 520).

20. Some, though by no means all, Whigs belonged in this tradition; and one gets some sense of its parameters in the essay on Rufus Choate in Daniel Walker Howe, *The Political Culture of the American Whigs* (Chicago: University of Chicago Press, 1979). A classic statement by a younger figure is Charles Eliot Norton, *Considerations on Some Recent Social Theories* (Boston, 1853), which is helpful in that it explicitly treats at a theoretical level contemporaneous European political ideas.

21. "The Princeton Review on the State of the Country and of the Church," *BRPR* 37 (October 1865): 628.

22. "Slavery," *BRPR* 8 (April 1836): 270.

23. "Slavery," p. 289; "Emancipation," *BRPR* 21 (October 1849): 597.

24. In his early writings on the subject, Hodge tended to minimize ill treatment by slaveowners and to accept the "wage-slavery" argument that English factory workers were worse off than American slaves ("Abolitionism," *BRPR* 16 [October 1844]: 576-77). His opinion changed during the crisis years following the Mexican War; the 1849 article "Emancipation" was a turning point.

ernment, the forms of it had varied through history. A child of the Scottish Enlightenment, Hodge tended to view such development through the lens of the Scottish notion of the progress of civilization.[25] An American Protestant, he breathed a sigh of relief that his own country's history had firmly shaped its institutions "before the floods of [Irish] ignorance and Romanism were opened upon us."[26] History left other peoples (including American slaves) in less happy circumstances; but Hodge felt entirely comfortable with the fact that "accident of birth" determined "the relative position of men in society."[27] Not even political despotism was wrong in itself.[28]

Given these historical realities, no individual bore the blame or credit for social or political conditions. Whatever guilt slavery entailed — and Hodge's impression of this did deepen over the decades — the culpability fell not primarily on the slaveholder but on the community as a whole, for slavery was not the creation of any individual. "The community is responsible for its existence," he insisted.[29] This strong communitarian sensibility may help to explain the vehemence with which Hodge rejected the individualistic utilitarian liberalism that increasingly captured the American intellectual imagination in the 1840s and 1850s.[30]

Although his sense of history reinforced Hodge's resistance to the rising tide of individualism, he in no way handed over the political realm to historical contingency. Although God had not ordained one type of government for all peoples, the principle remained that "all events depending on human agency are under his control." "The existence of any particular form of government is as much his work, as the rising of the sun or falling of the rain." More directly to the point, the Bible made clear that government was "not optional": "government, whatever its form, is of God. He has ordained it." It followed that government officials, although in one sense representing the people, "in a far higher sense" represented God. One's "civil duties" therefore had a "religious character"; and obedience to the law was required "on the authority of God." This did not imply that a citizen must *always* obey the government; the state could not, for instance,

25. See, for example, "Emancipation," p. 605, and "Slavery," p. 300.
26. "Emancipation," p. 599.
27. "Abolitionism," p. 562.
28. "The State of the Country" *BRPR* 33 (January 1861): 13.
29. "Emancipation," p. 593.
30. See, for example, "Civil Government," *BRPR* 23 (January 1851): 158. I say "help to explain"; Hodge had other clear objections to utilitarianism. His communitarianism was very obviously reinforced by his belief in "the participation of the life of Adam by the whole race, and of the life of Christ, by all believers" ("Christian Nurture," pp. 502-3).

legitimately order a citizen to sin. In such rare cases, the citizen had no "right to resist the execution of the law" but, rightly refusing to comply, had to submit to its penalty. Only the people collectively had a right of revolution — and even this Hodge derived from the divine command that human beings organize *some* form of government.[31]

Hodge took as high a view of government, then, as of the church. Indeed, just as he believed that the church was morally bound to support its clergy adequately — and, if necessary, pay for their education as a matter of right — so, by exact analogy, "a wise government" would do the same for its civil service.[32] And in both cases it was the welfare of the organic community, not of some impossible collectivity of unconnected individuals, that Hodge had in mind.

These complex commitments left Hodge of two minds regarding American democracy. He valued the republicanism of the United States, not because he believed people to possess any natural right to govern themselves, but because democracy had an "elevating effect upon the mass of the population"; for participation in politics raised the minds of ordinary people from the dulling grind of their "daily labor," requiring them "to think and act in reference to important and general objects."[33] As to the people's actual ability to "think and act," Hodge had pretty low expectations. Like other conservative republicans, he thought a fairly high level of "moral education" absolutely essential for popular government to work without disaster; and he worried that the public's "passions" might overwhelm their "mind" and "conscience."[34] Not surprisingly, then, he was no friend to any version of direct or participatory democracy. To the contrary, he took something like the old Puritan view that, while the people might elect their magistrate, they had no business telling him what to do once elected.[35]

---

31. "Civil Government," pp. 138, 133, 132, 134, 139, 143, 151, 152. More precisely, Hodge claimed that the right of revolution was "a necessary inference" from the fact that God willed "that government should exist" but "left the form to be determined" by "those to whom the general command is given," as well as from "the end which God designs government to answer"; viz., "the welfare of the people" ("Civil Government," pp. 152-53).

32. "Professor Stuart's Postscript," p. 132.

33. "Introductory Lecture," *BRPR* 1 (January 1829): 76-77. Curiously, Hodge did believe that, "as one of the necessary adjuncts of the right of private judgment," Christians should "have a voice" (though not necessarily more than a veto) in choosing their pastor. ("Church of Scotland," 241.) Given his strong version of the religious role of the state, his failure to extend this right to the choice of political rulers was probably a lapse in logic.

34. "Introductory Lecture," p. 87; "Slavery," p. 299.

35. "The Church and the Country," *BRPR* 33 (April 1861): 340.

JAMES TURNER

Yet this was not the whole story of democracy. Try as he might to restrain the power of the people and to deny the high claims for the individual conscience advanced by abolitionists, Transcendentalists, and other unsavory types, Hodge kept tripping over his own religious principles. The problem arose from the "vital principle of Protestantism" itself: "that God is now accessible to all men by Jesus Christ" without going "through the church, or through the mediation of other men as priests."[36] From this followed relentlessly the ultimacy of the individual conscience: "It is a primary principle that the right of private judgment extends over all questions of faith and morals. No human power can come between God and the conscience." So, as much as Hodge yearned to tell abolitionists (and later seceding slaveholders) that they could not take the law into their own hands, he had in the end to concede that they could. "Who is to determine whether a particular law is unconstitutional or immoral?" he asked in 1851, regarding the Fugitive Slave Law (which he himself endorsed). With a palpably heavy heart, he answered, "it cannot be denied, and ought not to be concealed, that the ultimate decision must be referred" to each individual's "own judgment."[37] The radical individualism inherent in Protestantism thus made Hodge more of a democrat than he wanted to be.

His Scottish Enlightenment philosophical principles reinforced the effect. The doctrines of common sense realism — at least as Hodge understood them — suggested that, in reasonably uncomplicated matters, the collective judgment of ordinary people provided a test of truth. This was especially true in moral questions, such as those that slavery raised, because of the "moral sense" that Scottish philosophers from Francis Hutcheson onward had ascribed to every properly functioning human being. "Every great moral truth has," as Hodge pointed out, "a self-evidencing light." This light may not be visible to "the ignorant or depraved," but it can be seen by "the great body of the intelligent and pious men of the country."[38] (Note that the qualification is *not* supernatural regeneration but natural human knowledge and morality.) It followed that ordinary citizens, if properly educated and well behaved, could be relied upon to participate politically as responsible and perceptive citizens. True, the question of education, particularly moral training, always remained a problematic one for Hodge; but he did not hesitate to invoke

36. "Schaf's Protestantism," p. 627.
37. "Civil Government," p. 145.
38. "Abolitionism," p. 551.

the consensus of ordinary American Protestants to refute his enemies.[39] It seemed hard for Hodge intellectually, as a Scotsman and a Protestant, not to be a democrat, however reluctantly.

In these tensions and even contradictions, we begin to see how radically out of step Hodge was with the leading intellectual trends of his century — as perhaps were most thoughtful Old School Presbyterians. The key issue was neither mistrust of democracy nor misgivings about individualism (doubts shared by many conservative Americans), but rather Hodge's philosophic refusal to accept history as a fundamental force shaping the human condition. This put him at odds with most other leading conservatives in the nineteenth-century transatlantic tradition: with Edmund Burke, Alexis de Tocqueville, and Benjamin Disraeli across the water, with John Randolph of Roanoke, Daniel Webster, and Charles Eliot Norton in the United States. Hodge did, of course, understand that particularities of human existence changed over time: forms of government, even the church's understanding of Christ's teaching. But for Hodge, despite all his communitarian instincts and almost against his wishes, the ultimate unit of human reality remained the individual, and the individual endured essentially unaltered by history.

It should be emphasized that this denial of the power of history did not follow logically from Hodge's Reformed presuppositions about the *potestas ordinata* of God. Just as human agency was compatible with divine determination (God ordinarily choosing to achieve his ends by human hands), so an orthodox Calvinist could accept God accomplishing his will through the less personalized form of human agency called history. Historicism, then, did not necessarily imply naturalism, as Hodge sometimes seemed to suggest.

But historicism did imply the shaping of the individual by his or her culture and the shaping of that culture by the history that had produced it; and this mediation between the individual and ultimate reality was what Hodge could not swallow.[40] He had grounds both philosophic and

39. "Abolitionism," p. 553.

40. "Historicism" is a notoriously slippery term, with perhaps as many shades of meaning as users. By it I mean no more than what I say above: the belief that individuals are shaped by their cultures and cultures by their unique histories. Any such claim certainly has relativistic implications, and some writers use "historicism" to denote the opinion that historical understanding dissolves all transcendental norms and any objective order of things. I use it in the more general and modest sense that allows Burke, for example, to be called a historicist thinker even though he combined his powerful sense of history with belief in objectively existing natural law.

religious. Philosophically, his Scottish common sense realism insisted that each individual perceives reality immediately, this perception conditioned by the unchanging structure of human consciousness but not by any historical particularity. The atemporal perceiving mind stood, as it were, outside of history, face-to-face with reality. Religiously, Hodge's "vital principle" of Protestantism likewise put the individual immediately before God, as revealed in Scripture. Neither the essential doctrines of the gospel nor the grasp of these by the regenerate were in any way conditioned by history; nor did any institution existing in history — that is, the church — need to mediate between the individual and the saving grace of God. The atemporal perceiving soul stood outside of history, face-to-face with eternity. And so, despite considerable cost to the plausibility of his communitarianism, of his otherwise Burkean understanding of political institutions, and of his high view of the clergy and the church, deeper commitments wedded Hodge to a radically atemporal individualism.

This ahistorical individualism meshed neatly with his sometimes vicious anti-Catholicism. Hodge came by his hostility to the Roman Catholic Church automatically, for anti-popery had provided a core element of Anglo-American political ideology since the seventeenth century. Many of his anti-Catholic outbursts, though they may make our more ecumenical skins crawl, need to be put in context as simply reflexes of this culture. However, his more reasoned critiques of Catholicism — and of the catholicizing Oxford Movement, which he feared and despised almost as much as Rome itself — serve to flesh out for us his repudiation of history.

The role and nature of historical development figured crucially in Hodge's polemics against "Romanism." In these attacks, Hodge probably most often assailed "the error of a mediating church or priesthood"; but he also declared that the "whole question between Protestants and Papists" boiled down to "whether there is any unwritten traditionary rule of faith or practice now binding on the church," a formulation that focused precisely on the relation of the church to history.[41] For Hodge, the only norm that could bind the church, and the only criterion by which it was to be judged, was the changeless "authority of scripture."[42] Though Christianity was a historical religion in the sense that Christ revealed its truths and founded the church *in illo tempore*, the faith once delivered to the saints was handed over entire and pure, once and for all, in the Scriptures. And it was imbecilic to believe that mere historical continuity testified to

41. "Schaf's Protestantism," p. 627; "Oxford Tracts," p. 113.
42. "Church of Rome," pp. 332-33.

verity. "A church may have been originally founded by the apostles, and possess an uninterrupted succession of pastors, and yet be now a synagogue of Satan."[43] The "road of history" *did* lead to Rome — proof that it led astray.[44]

Hodge was far too good a scholar to deny that development had occurred in the church's understanding of doctrine, but this did not imply that history had shaped doctrine itself. In "different ages," "one or more great truths of revelation" became "the subjects of perpetual conflict, until the mind of the Church was brought to a clear and comprehensive view of what was revealed concerning them" — as in the Christological controversies of the early church. But Hodge insisted that the Christian "system of doctrine" had been "recorded in the Bible" "distinctly," "fully," and "clearly." Of this system "there can be no *development*," only better grasp. Denying that any "doctrine can ever be unfolded or expanded" beyond its biblical statement, Hodge set himself explicitly against John Henry Newman's theory of doctrinal development, as well as against Philip Schaff's teaching of the "organic development" of the church from an embryonic beginning. For Hodge history mediated neither the church nor its beliefs. "The Church of the present does not derive its life by way of transmission from the Church of the past, but immediately from Christ by his word and Spirit, so that while inheriting the results and attainments of former ages to aid her in understanding the Scriptures, her faith always rests immediately on the word of God."[45]

This last phrase suggests the most powerful reason why Hodge was skittish about history. The idea of historical development threatened more than the Presbyterian church and its creeds; it threatened the Bible itself. And, in gauging Hodge's response to historicist biblical criticism, one must remember that his world pivoted on the Bible. "There can be no solid foundation for theological opinion," he always insisted, "but the original text of Scripture fairly interpreted."[46] His abhorrence of the Oxford Movement owed much to the Tractarians' acceptance of tradition as an authority parallel to Scripture: "When men begin to forsake the scriptures for tradition, and dote about fables, they seem to lose the ordinary power of discriminating truth."[47] Whatever was "the doctrine of the Bi-

43. "Theories of the Church," p. 147.
44. "Schaff's Apostolic Church," p. 152.
45. "Schaff's Apostolic Church," pp. 159, 157, 179, 165 (emphasis mine). Hodge was inconsistent in capitalizing "Scripture," and I have let his inconsistencies stand.
46. "Stuart on the Romans," p. 382.
47. "Oxford Tracts," pp. 102-3.

ble" on any subject, that was "also the doctrine of the church"; and Hodge believed all true Christian doctrines to be fully and unambiguously stated in Scripture.[48]

There was more here than the generic Protestant principle of *sola scriptura*. Hodge held firmly the Reformed view that the "universe is not a machine left to go of itself" but rather that God ordains every happening.[49] Therefore he regarded God's revelation of His will in the Bible as the handbook of ultimate authority for questions in politics or science as much as in theology. No matter how overwhelming the arguments supporting some political conclusion, for instance, "they would be driven to the wind by one clear declaration of scripture" to the contrary.[50] The Bible in its entirety had therefore to be shielded against every imputation of ambiguity or uncertainty. Yet ambiguity and uncertainty were precisely the result of nineteenth-century historical criticism of the Bible.

Hodge was far from contemptuous of the achievements of the German scholars who dominated the field. After all, he believed, the Scriptures had to be "historically interpreted" in a limited sense; "that is, we are bound to take them in the sense in which they were intended to be understood by the persons to whom they were addressed."[51] And the philological scholarship of "the modern German school of expositors" had immensely benefited "the careful student of the Scriptures, who is desirous of ascertaining with accuracy and certainty, the meaning of the word of God."[52]

But, not content with clarifying the meanings of the words of the biblical text, some of the most influential German scholars had gone on to challenge the received understanding of the nature of the Bible itself. Where Hodge and other traditionally minded Reformed Protestants maintained that the Bible shone with a "self-evidencing light" that proved its truths intuitively (like a mathematical axiom) to a regenerate reader of any time or clime, these Germans treated its books as historical products of particular ancient cultures, decisively shaped by those cultural contexts and only fully comprehensible within them.[53] Where Hodge believed the Bible to have an "obvious sense" that only "violent exegesis" could distort, the Germans argued that existing knowledge of historical context did not

48. "The Latest Form of Infidelity," *BRPR* 12 (January 1840): 35.
49. "Civil Government," p. 137.
50. "Abolitionism," p. 554.
51. "Bushnell on Vicarious Sacrifice," *BRPR* 38 (April 1866): 172.
52. "Stuart on the Romans," p. 382.
53. "Thornwell on the Apocrypha," *BRPR* 17 (April 1845): 270-72.

suffice for a good understanding of some books.[54] Where Hodge saw the work of authors led by the plenary inspiration of the Holy Spirit to pen words "as though spoken directly by the lips of God himself," the Germans perceived words written by limited men very much of a particular time and place. Where Hodge regarded the Old and New Testaments as "one book," the "product of one mind" (God's), presenting "one grand concatenated system of truth, gradually developed during fifteen hundred years," the Germans claimed that the Bible comprised a welter of distinct texts, with their own separate authors and outlooks, each to be understood in terms of its own history.[55]

The most extreme of the German historicist critics, most notoriously David Friedrich Strauss in *Das Leben Jesu,* completely "reject[ed] the gospel history as a history." They claimed that there existed no historical evidence to justify treating the gospels as narratives of actual events; they represented the New Testament as a very different kind of book, "a mere mythology" or "collection of fables, destitute in almost every case of any foundation in fact." To read the gospels as an actual record of Jesus Christ's life, teaching, death, and resurrection was simply to misunderstand the nature of the texts. Rather, their "truth must be sought" through "a mytho-symbolical interpretation" of the supposed history. The virus was spreading even in the United States; "even among the orthodox," people began to "talk of a mythology of the Hebrews," while some Unitarians abandoned "not only the miracles of the Old Testament, but those of the New."[56]

Hodge dug in his heels.[57] For, as *Das Leben Jesu* seemed to him to show, it was one short step from a Bible entangled in history to a Bible unmoored from any permanent meaning. Hodge understood with remarkable clarity what was at stake. His recognition of the fissile tendencies within American society and American Protestantism perhaps made him more sensitive to the hyper-individualist, anti-traditional threats to religious belief, and vice versa. (He lamented the advantage that their solidar-

---

54. "Slavery," p. 276.

55. "Inspiration," *BRPR* 29 (October 1857): 664, 663, 679.

56. "Latest Form of Infidelity," pp, 54, 68.

57. How little Hodge was affected by historical criticism is shown by his enthusiasm for one argument for the reliability of the biblical account of the creation and fall. Accepting literally the ages of Adam and the patriarchs recorded in the Old Testament, Hodge was much taken by the idea that Adam could have related the story directly to Methuselah, Methuselah to Noah's son Shem, and Shem to Jacob, in whose epoch "minute and particular history commences." "Neill's Lectures on Biblical History," *BRPR* 18 (July 1846): 456-61.

ity gave "Romanists" in the struggle for America's soul.)[58] Horace Bushnell certainly saw more lucidly than Hodge that no theological formula could escape having a culture-bound contingent character; even for a Victorian, Hodge was unusually blind to the salience of cultural diversity. But Hodge realized, as Bushnell did not, the crucial importance of stable orthodox definitions as guideposts and anchors for meaning, without which beliefs tended to dissolve into vapor.

And vapor was rising. The corrosion of "the objective form of truth as presented in the Scriptures" by historicist criticism made it easy to regard Christianity as merely "a feeling, or inward life," more or less "independent of a system of doctrines revealed by God and obligatory on men as objects of faith."[59] Thus the way was opened for the pantheistic philosophy rooted in Hegel and broadcast in more popular terms by Cousin, which Hodge regarded as the animating principle of German "infidelity": "that God is the only real existence of which the universe of mind and nature is the phenomenon."[60] In his earlier years Hodge did not worry that German aberrations would ever prevail in England or the United States, Anglo-Americans having too much "sanity of intellect" and being too deeply steeped in the Bible.[61] But he grew more alarmed after American Reformed theologians like Horace Bushnell and Edwards Amasa Park began to publish their German-influenced proto-modernist works around 1850, and he thereafter dedicated his pen to warning his fellow citizens against the dangerous currents flowing from German theology.[62] He certainly thought that Americans like Bushnell, Park, and John Nevin were spreading destruction, even if unaware of the true causticity of their still timid importations of German teaching.

"In all its forms" the "new philosophy" undermined the orthodox conception of Christianity as an unchanging and eternally true "system of doctrine." It rejected "the fundamental doctrine of a God who is the real Creator and Governor of the world, distinct from it, though everywhere

58. "Princeton Review on State of the Country," p. 652; see "The Education Question," *BRPR* 26 (July 1854): 526-27.

59. "Theology in Germany," *BRPR* 25 (July 1853): 449. This article summarizes well Hodge's view of the intellectual history of German theology and philosophy in the eighteenth and first half of the nineteenth century.

60. "Cousin's Philosophy," *BRPR* 28 (April 1856): 347. Hodge thought the doctrine relatively harmless to ordinary Christians in the impenetrable prose of Hegel, far more dangerous in the "popularized Germanism of Cousin" (which "we understand" was even "taught to girls"). "Cousin's Philosophy," p. 339.

61. "Latest Form of Infidelity," pp. 69-70.

62. See especially "Park's Sermon," "Bushnell on Sacrifice," and, for Nevin, "What Is Christianity?"

present in it, who is not bound to a process of development, and to act according to fixed laws, but may act how and when he pleases." Instead, "the world and history" became "a process, a development of God."[63] Hodge presciently identified such immanentism as the most salient religious consequence of historicism and as the bridge that would carry many Protestants away from traditional orthodox Christianity.

This radical theological historicism opened the way, Hodge judged, to an equally radical and destructive religious individualism. In the developmental theory religion was no longer a "form of knowledge" nor a "mode of action," but "a life, a peculiar state of feeling": Christianity specifically being a "form of the religious consciousness produced by Christ, or in some way due to him, and derived from him." The "intuitions of the religious consciousness" by their nature could have no fixed and permanent forms, but varied from time to time and from individual to individual.[64] And if "the facts and doctrines of the Bible are the mere forms of the spirit of Christianity," then the interpretation of both the Bible and the creeds became labile and individual, subject to "the opinion and prejudices of the reader" — everyman his own interpreter.[65] Language itself lost its limpidity. The "fixed rules of interpretation" fell into confusion; "Christian language" was twisted into unheard-of and "anti-christian" meanings.[66] The "divine character of Christ" might mean only that he was an extraordinarily good man. "Let philosophers and errorists," Hodge cried, "find words for themselves, and not profane the words of God by making them a vehicle for the denial of his truth."[67]

Hodge's rhetoric could grow overheated, formulations leaning to caricature; but in substance his complaints came tolerably close to what Horace Bushnell was writing, allowing for Bushnell's own animus against individualism. "Dr. Bushnell could sign any creed by help of that chemistry of thought which makes all creeds alike."[68] "Nothing can be more opposed to Scripture," Hodge believed, than such "depreciation of the importance of doctrine."[69] Bushnell, to be sure, did not think that he was depreciating doctrine, only appreciating it in a different way.

---

63. "Inspiration," p. 688.
64. "Inspiration," p. 689.
65. "Park's Sermon," pp. 642, 673.
66. "Park's Sermon," p. 658; "Latest Form of Infidelity," p. 38.
67. "Latest Form of Infidelity," p. 59.
68. "Park's Sermon," p. 646.
69. "Inspiration," p. 693. Hodge was not referring specifically to Bushnell in this passage, but in general to theologians who took a position like his.

For Bushnell had fallen under the spell of history, learned to admire her formative power, whereas Hodge had not succumbed to this new siren of the nineteenth century. Bushnell's epistemological watchword was *growth,* Hodge's was *fact.* Hodge believed of course that human knowledge *accumulated over time,* so that Victorians collectively knew more than ancient Romans; he accepted that the *expressions* of knowledge would reflect the idioms peculiar to a given society; but he did not consider knowledge itself in any fundamental way *conditioned* by historical context. A fact recognized by Plato would (assuming a normally functioning mind) be recognized in the same way by Charlemagne, Ignatius Loyola, and Charles Hodge.

This radically atemporal character of knowledge followed from Hodge's adherence to the common sense realism of the Scottish Enlightenment, especially as formulated by Thomas Reid. According to this approach, the human mind functions in the same way in all peoples, providing self-evident truths (or "facts of consciousness" or "laws of belief impressed upon our nature") that make knowledge possible and the truth of which one can neither prove nor deny without absurdity.[70] "A man undertakes a desperate task who attempts to argue against the intuitive judgments of the mind or conscience," wrote Hodge, self-evidently.[71] Equipped with "instinctive beliefs" such as causation and duration, we can make coherent the relations of the various objects that we perceive directly (as we also intuitively believe) through the senses.[72] And thus we produce facts, which we assemble into larger bodies of knowledge. The Bible is a special case, because only persons "under the influence of the Spirit of God" can reliably recognize its self-evidencing truths.[73] But not entirely special, since in the end we can only trust that the Creator has not "impressed upon our nature" false and misleading "laws of belief." "The ultimate ground of knowledge," Hodge made clear, "is confidence in the veracity of God."[74] Just as God did not change, just as human nature did not change, neither did facts change.

While imagination certainly had a place in human life, that place was nowhere near knowledge. Hodge distinguished sharply between "the logi-

---

70. Quoted phrases from "Can God be Known?" *BRPR* 36 (January 1864): 134, 143. For my account of common sense realism, I rely on Keith Lehrer, *Thomas Reid* (London and New York: Routledge, 1999), while attending to Hodge's own scattered statements.

71. "Bushnell on Sacrifice," p. 161.

72. Quoted phrase from "Can God be Known?" p. 148.

73. "Latest Form of Infidelity," pp. 33-34.

74. "Can God be Known?" p. 134.

cal understanding" and "the imagination"; and he regarded as respectable but unreliable "sentimental religionists, whose devotion must be kindled through the imagination." Bushnell, Hodge fumed, tried "to seduce us from cleaving to the letter of the scriptures" by appealing to the imagination; Hodge's own appeal in matters of doctrine was to "clear and decisive proof."[75] To his common sense realism Hodge added a robust "Baconian" distinction between "fact" and "theory," a suspicion of premature theorizing (at least by others), and an insistence on staying close to the facts.[76]

This "Baconianism" provided his self-described theological method. Hodge defined "Christian theology" as "nothing but the facts and truths of the Bible arranged in their natural order and exhibited in their mutual relations." Hodge did not try to answer the questions begged in "natural order" and "mutual relations." But he did expatiate on this definition in a passage worth quoting in its entirety:

> Such being the nature of theology, the duty of the theologian is first to ascertain and authenticate the facts of Scripture, that is, make it clear that they are indeed contained in the word of God. This induction of facts must, as far as possible, be exhaustive. All must be collected, and each must be allowed its due value. No one is to be ignored or modified. Then secondly, the theologian, having obtained his facts, is to present them in their natural order; that is, the order determined by their nature.
>
> The philosophy of the facts is in the facts; underlies, and arranges them, and determines their mutual relation. The theologian has no more right to explain the facts by his own philosophy, than he has to manufacture the facts for his philosophy. His business is simply to exhibit the contents of the Bible in a scientific form. His relation to the Scriptures is analogous to that of the man of science to nature.[77]

The same fact was always the same fact. The Bible belonged to the realm of immutable truth, not to that of history.

75. "Park's Sermon," p. 645; "Oxford Tracts," pp. 118, 102.

76. I use quotation marks to distinguish the nineteenth-century American (and to some extent British) understanding of Francis Bacon's views from how Bacon or others might have understood them. See especially Theodore Dwight Bozeman, *Protestants in an Age of Science: The Baconian Ideal and Antebellum American Religious Thought* (Chapel Hill: University of North Carolina Press, 1977). "The Unity of Mankind," *BRPR* 31 (January 1859), exemplifies Hodge's "Baconianism."

77. "Bushnell on Sacrifice," pp. 184-85.

And, as Hodge's last analogy suggested, it also belonged to the realm of science. Scientists and theologians tended to investigate different orders of questions and properly worked "independently yet harmoniously." However, as Hodge rightly pointed out, they often "overlap each other." Both, for instance, inquired into the "origin, nature, prerogatives, and powers" of human beings; and, the field being "common to both," neither had a right to warn the other off his ground. But Hodge went further. Facts being facts, the facts of the Bible, such as "sin and redemption" — "just as certain, and infinitely more important, than the truths of science" — ought to weigh in scientific theorizing with facts derived from other sources. "It is not only unwise but unphilosophical for the man of science to conduct his investigations on the assumption that nothing more than scientific facts can legitimately be taken into view." Hodge did not apply a simple-minded or one-sided criterion to the relation of science and the Bible. Biblical critics also needed to take scientific conclusions into account, and modern astronomical and geological theories had changed the church's understanding of some passages.[78] But facts, from whatever source, were true for all times and universally applicable across all domains of knowledge. No assertion could make clearer how the nineteenth century was distancing itself from Hodge.

An inevitable air of melancholy hangs about Hodge's career. Only a tiny handful of Americans of his day commanded the erudition he did; perhaps still fewer intellectuals of his generation exerted influence as broad. Yet in the end neither his learning nor his ascendance could protect his worldview from being swept under by the tide of historicism. At Princeton itself a remnant of loyalists did continue Hodge's work, but in the twentieth century even they were forced to abandon ship and ended marooned on the margins of American culture.

Hodge remains for us today a remarkable figure. He was among the last, and in many ways one of the most admirable and clear-sighted, of the thinkers who lived "before history" — that is, who lived in a world of stable laws and stable essences, before historicism and its offspring (such as the concept of cultures) had transformed the way in which we understand our world and how it came to be. One might even venture the claim that

---

78. "Unity of Mankind," pp. 104-6. I omit consideration of Hodge's famous encounter with Darwinism, because the key issue there seems to me to have been Darwin's naturalism rather than historicism, although Darwin's evolutionary hypothesis certainly had profoundly historicist implications for knowledge. Hodge's *What Is Darwinism?* has recently been reissued (together with related writings) with an illuminating introduction by Mark A. Noll and David N. Livingstone (Grand Rapids: Baker Books, 1994).

Charles Hodge was the last major American intellectual fully a citizen of the Enlightenment, immune to the ravages that the nineteenth century worked on the axioms of the eighteenth.

One might further argue that had Hodge not been so lovingly wedded to the atemporal common sense realism of the Scottish Enlightenment and the anti-theoretical conception of science that went with it, had he instead been willing to adapt to his own apologetic purposes the hermeneutic conception of knowledge that historicism fostered and even to weld historicism to his strong conviction of divine providence, he might have fared better, and so might the Christian worldview he defended. But to propose this is itself profoundly ahistorical. It is hard even now to imagine what an Old School historicism might have looked like in the nineteenth century. Certainly, the proto-modernist theologians like Bushnell who followed the historicist course found themselves in the end with a version of Christianity that would have appalled Hodge.

No, Hodge does not merit becoming one more victim of the enormous condescension of posterity. He deserves our respect. The Old School ship of traditional Presbyterianism could not have enlisted an abler captain in his time and place. It was not his fault that he found himself sailing on a strange new sea, with no adequate charts to guide him. Charles Hodge's career stands as a synecdoche for the intellectual history of orthodox Christianity in the nineteenth century.

The Place of Charles Hodge
in the History of Ideas in America

BRUCE KUKLICK

This essay has two parts. The first is historiographical and tries to explain how Hodge has illegitimately been read out of many narratives of the development of American thought. In the second part I take up, not to Hodge's advantage, more disputed questions concerning the value of systems of ideas.[1]

*   *   *

The constitution of the history of American philosophy is contested. Calling attention to problems of canonization and of presentism, many scholars have tried to revise our notions of who "the great American thinkers" are. These revisions have hardly analyzed if greatness is an appropriate category for historians to use, but have rather urged that different people need to be considered great. The surprising beneficiary of the revision has been, of all people, Ralph Waldo Emerson. According to the conventional wisdom Emerson is an American original, a sage or seer, owned by departments of literature, but he has not been regarded as a thinker of the first rank. Now revisionists tell us he is really a philosopher, and a good one at

---

1. For the intellectual background to my understanding of Hodge I have relied on my own work: *The Rise of American Philosophy: Cambridge, Massachusetts, 1860-1930* (New Haven: Yale University Press, 1976); and *Churchmen and Philosophers: From Jonathan Edwards to John Dewey* (New Haven: Yale University Press, 1985). The methodological notions that underpin my work are elaborated in a series of essays listed in my *Puritans in Babylon: The Ancient Near East and American Intellectual Life* (Princeton: Princeton University Press, 1996), p. 235.

that.[2] How does Hodge, a contemporary of Emerson's, fit in to these on-going reappraisals?

Talking about an American philosophical tradition makes good sense from the late nineteenth century on. That tradition is professional, academic, and coterminous with the rise of the new university system in the 1870s. It encompasses at its start Charles Peirce, William James, Josiah Royce, and John Dewey. Before that time the conception of American philosophy is dubious, and it is more accurate to speak of American speculative thought. This is a more inclusive notion whose extension encompasses several groups in the eighteenth and most of the nineteenth centuries. High on the list are parish ministers who wrote on high theology and participated in a dialogue that embraced a religious elite in England, Scotland, and Germany. Jonathan Edwards and Horace Bushnell are in this group, but so also is Emerson, who lived at a time when such men were escaping the parish and turning their efforts away from some of the ancient concerns of Reformed Protestant doctrine. Because they were unconnected to institutions, I have sometimes called them amateurs.

Another branch of American speculative thought was located in the divinity schools that grew up in the Northeast, the South, and the old Midwest throughout the nineteenth century. The divinity-school theologians had the preeminent institutional power base in the nineteenth century. They trained the ministers and controlled much learned publication. Their outlook tended to be more narrow and sectarian than those speculators who were not professors of divinity, but it is difficult to argue that they were not the intellectual equals of the men outside the divinity schools. Leonard Woods, Henry Ware, Nathaniel William Taylor, Henry Boynton Smith, and Edwards Amasa Park belong to this cadre.

It is possible to make a case that during the revolutionary and constitutional periods speculators who had a tenuous connection both to institutions and Christian orthodoxy — Benjamin Franklin, Tom Paine, Elihu Palmer, Joel Barlow — are worthy of consideration. But it is hard to include such people after 1800. They are few, isolated, and hardly engaged in

2. See David Van Leer, *Emerson's Epistemology: The Argument of the Essays* (Cambridge and New York: Cambridge University Press, 1986) and Stanley Cavell, *Philosophical Passages: Wittgenstein, Emerson, Austin, Derrida* (Oxford and New York: Oxford University Press, 1995). Stephen H. Daniel, *The Philosophy of Jonathan Edwards* (Bloomington: Indiana University Press, 1994) tries this revision for an earlier period of "American philosophy." In terms of power in the university, the revaluation reflects the strength of English departments and their modes of thinking over philosophy departments and their traditions.

a dialogue at all. The only one I would argue for even half-heartedly is Alexander Bryan Johnson, the positivist philosopher of language, who had a tiny revival some years ago.[3]

A final group, however, is crucial — the holders of chairs in mental, moral, or intellectual philosophy at the burgeoning American colleges in the nineteenth century. Their function, effectively, was to lend theoretical support to the more clearly theological concerns of the divinity school theologians and the most serious ministers on the hustings. The philosophers were inevitably ministers and committed Protestants, but in addition to showing that reason was congruent with faith they also elaborated on the grounds of the social order and politics, and commented on the affairs of the world. Frequently the presidents of their institutions, they had captive student audiences and easy access to publication. Although provincial, they conducted a transatlantic conversation and were on an intellectual par with the other people I have mentioned. Worthies here include Francis Bowen, James McCosh, and Noah Porter.

My American speculative tradition is thus formed from three intersecting dialogues of ministerial amateurs, divinity-school theologians, and college philosophers. It extends from the time of Edwards, at least, to the end of the nineteenth century. At that time the intellectual space religion occupied in American public life shrank in a revolutionary way; in the scholarly world divinity schools lost their primacy and, indeed, many closed their doors; and the Christian thought that dominated American intellectual life all but disappeared.

The later philosophical tradition was built on the ashes of the speculative tradition. One might argue that American philosophy is rooted in the ideas of the college philosophers.[4] But my parsing of the speculative and philosophical traditions into two is meant to be more than semantic: the latter is distinctive and includes the names of the pragmatists and their philosophical cousins whom contemporaries conjure with. This tradition provides the framework for the ideas of twentieth-century political theorists and reflective social scientists. More important, the pragmatists and their descendants were relatively unconnected to the standard tropes of American thought around them; the young pragmatists and their peers

---

3. The revival began with the publication of David Rynin's edition of Johnson's *A Treatise on Language* (Berkeley: University of California Press, 1947) and ended with Charles L. Todd and Robert Sonkin, *Alexander Bryan Johnson: Philosophical Banker* (Syracuse: Syracuse University Press, 1977).

4. To see how this argument must be complexly made for one person, John Dewey, see my *Churchmen and Philosophers.*

rejected many of the ideas of their elders, generated new ones, and grew up in universities and not colleges.

What should we make of the mélange of the older speculative tradition in the eighteenth and nineteenth centuries? It is hard to imagine that these men, as thinkers, will ever engage our sustained attention again, although that judgment certainly invites the view that they can serve as endless fodder for studies in social and cultural history. That is to say, there is something to the questions: Who are the great thinkers in American philosophy? Who are the great thinkers in American speculative thought? And it is not just a long fashion of scholars silently to argue that the great American thinkers are largely *not* in the eighteenth and nineteenth centuries; that Nathaniel Emmons is no Hume, Levi Hedge no Hegel. The revisionist interest in Emerson does attest to something.[5] But it is an unsurprising resurrection, one based not on rediscovery so much as re-appreciation; nobody has rescued Laurens Perseus Hickok, the most innovative of the college philosophers.

Overall, no compelling reason exists to study the vast majority of these thinkers in order to grasp their ideas: what they say has been said better by others. This does not mean they cannot have a sort of local interest, or that, as I have suggested, their work can not be read for other purposes.[6] It does mean that we are not dealing with a lot of junior Søren Kierkegaards or John Stuart Mills; and that a certain kind of American intellectual history of the eighteenth and nineteenth century should not be very important for historians or philosophers.

Was Hodge a part of this speculative tradition, my own reconceived canon? Yes, of course. Indeed, he was a critical part. The divinity-school theologians were at least first among equals in the loosely connected intellectual communities of nineteenth-century America, and Hodge was a formidable force among the theologians. Tireless in debate, long lived, and institutionally well situated, he was someone to contend with in every

---

5. The work here that is most relevant is that by Stanley Cavell noted above; and Russell Goodman, *American Philosophy and the Romantic Tradition* (Cambridge and New York: Cambridge University Press, 1990). For an exception see Robert Richardson's *Emerson: The Mind on Fire: A Biography* (Berkeley: University of California Press, 1995). Edwards is a different sort of case. His many defenders are almost all of a religious persuasion; they lament that he is overlooked in the philosophical tradition and want this tradition reconstituted to take him seriously. Edwards is, moreover, treated by everyone as exceptional. He *tests* my generalizations.

6. Such other purposes are outstandingly exemplified by Herbert Schneider's *A History of American Philosophy,* 2d ed. (New York: Columbia University Press, 1963).

important conversation from the Unitarian controversy to the struggle over Darwinism.

In general, those speculators outside the collegiate and seminary world were more creative and innovative in their use of ideas than those inside institutions. The new ideas that appeared in academia usually had more extreme ancestors expounded by men outside colleges or seminaries. But the non-institutionalists had less clout. And although it is now a cliché to say it, the sway of the amateurs lessened over the nineteenth century even among popular audiences. One can compare the careers and influence of revolutionary thinker Tom Paine in the eighteenth century; Emerson; and John Fiske or Francis Abbott, struggling independent philosophers at the end of the nineteenth. The flowering of the university that sent the amateurs to the wall, however, also had evil consequences for the theologians. As between college philosophers and divinity-school theologians, the latter probably had a greater authority and visibility in the culture. Although the power of the theologians waned into the nineteenth century, the philosophers were subordinate to them. Then, the revolution in higher education at the end of the nineteenth century diminished the importance of theologians and divinity schools to intellectual life. Neither the seminaries nor divinity itself recovered; they joined the amateurs on the fringes of intellectual life.

When historians began, some fifty years ago now, to look at the latter part of the nineteenth century, they saw clearly an American philosophical tradition that had gotten off the ground with pragmatism after the Civil War and extended this tradition backwards. Scholars found a small though still exaggerated role for the nineteenth-century college philosophers but also included Edwards and Emerson, for a variety of twentieth-century institutional, geographical, and political commitments that had little to do with speculative life in the nineteenth century. The big losers were the theologians of the schools that were inconsequential to secular twentieth-century intellectuals like the great historian of Puritanism and American ideas, Perry Miller.

I hope I have now deconstructed the history of American philosophy, in which Hodge does not appear. He deserves a large role in the speculative tradition I have delineated. The histories that fail to give him a significant place in the eighteenth- and nineteenth-century dialogue are, in that respect, a failure, their failure usually a product of a bias toward secular thinking.

*   *   *

For scholars interested in such matters, the composition of the American philosophical tradition is of some significance. This tradition has some present prestige and, it can be argued, is worth studying: the pragmatists who form its core said what they had to say better than anyone else. They are superior epigoni of Kant, and perhaps more. Even if this tradition, beginning after the Civil War, does not include Edwards and Emerson, it does justifiably embrace the fin de siècle philosophers of what is known as "the Golden Age" and latterly people like Thomas Kuhn and Richard Rorty.

The American philosophical tradition is the canon for historians of American ideas. It includes people whom it is profitable to study. That Hodge is not part of this tradition means, in the real world of the classroom, that Hodge will not be read, no matter what his place in the speculative tradition that is relevant only to a few experts. But this analysis speaks mainly to institutional and political issues in intellectual history and not directly to the vexed issue with which I have been indirectly grappling: Is Hodge a great thinker? Is he worth reading, whatever his place in the canon wars?

It is easy enough to locate Hodge in the American speculative tradition and then to argue that he will not be read because this tradition could not solve systematic problems, could not strategically locate itself in the university world of the twentieth century, and could not speak to the concerns of modernism. The emphasis on absolute Christian truths in this speculative tradition and its absence of a sense of history — of the limits that cultural situatedness places on thought — left it mortally vulnerable to the skepticism and historicism of the twentieth century.

Nonetheless, this explanation will not do. Most of the people in the speculative tradition have not found a contemporary audience but, for example, Jonathan Edwards has. He need not fear the condescension of posterity.[7] He was, like Hodge, an individualist without a recognizable historical sense, attached to absolutist religious doctrines rejected by modernists. Why do even secular thinkers want to read Edwards — want to read him enough to extend the American philosophical tradition unjustifiably backwards to include him? If Hodge were as prepossessing as Edwards, a way would be found to canonize him. Why do intellectual historians not want to read Hodge?

---

7. Another obvious choice here is Emerson, but Edwards is so much closer to Hodge that he makes for a better example. One could also point, perhaps less persuasively for some readers, to Horace Bushnell's ability to attract an audience, despite the fact that he has not been picked up in the American philosophical tradition.

To explore what Hodge's limitations were, I want to examine the implicit set of philosophical doctrines that guided him and their connection to the views of the triumphant pragmatists.

Hodge, like almost all members of the speculative tradition in the nineteenth century, can be labeled a Scottish realist. Scottish realism emerged in Scotland at the end of the eighteenth century as the first competent attempt to answer David Hume's anti-religious skepticism. In America the Scots Thomas Reid and Dugald Stuart were regarded as heroic defenders of common sense and true religion. Against Hume's skepticism, the two argued that the mind directly apprehends the natural world — hence the approving label "Scottish Realism" — and the basic truths of Christianity.

In the United States, Scottish ideas were taken up in different ways by different thinkers to serve different communal purposes in a variety of local and doctrinal cultures; the ideas themselves changed over a century. Yet the Scottish position standardly embraced three connected strands: an epistemology or theory of how the mind comes to know what it knows; a psychology — assertions about the nature of the mind and how it works; and a philosophy of science — an argument about how we accumulate systematic knowledge about the world.

Overall, the Scottish epistemology is static: the mind knows an externally existing universe. The mind itself is substantive — it is a sort of thing that has certain features or characteristics. The philosophy of science — commonly called Baconian — is based on recipe: to obtain scientific knowledge, the natural philosopher follows certain rules, more or less mechanistically.

To the extent that pragmatism has a progenitor in the speculative tradition it is in some extreme developments in Scottish Realism. In the course of the nineteenth century, realism underwent an evolution that pushed it, in various times and in various ways, to meet local intellectual crises. The pragmatists of the end of the century developed ideas that emerged from a matrix of Scottish problems but denied what the Scots espoused.

Whereas Scottish epistemology is static, that of the pragmatists is dynamic and interactive. Consciousness is not a *thing* for pragmatists; it is a *function*. Pragmatic psychology stresses not what the psyche is but what behavior defines the mental. The mind does not have being, but is a form of doing. In the theory of science rules are not emphasized, but the practice of scientists is; what is important is what the communities of scientists do.

If one wished to trace the origins of pragmatism to the waning speculative tradition, one would be well advised to look at the most extreme moves that varied Scottish thinkers had been forced to take. In pragmatism the most outré Scottish positions are stretched and extended; in effect, the pragmatists altered realism to meet the demands of their own time. They were sensitive to the psychological crises of the Gilded Age, the loss of some Protestant certainties, and changes in the life sciences and the understanding of the nature of the human past.

How did Hodge, in comparison, respond when he was called upon to defend his philosophical and theological ideas after the Civil War? How did he use the three components of Scottish realism that were his inheritance?

For David Hume at the basis of our knowledge of the world is sensation, the momentary contents of consciousness that individuals have before them at a given time. Observing the ordered changes in these sensations, we are able to construct a world and predict the alterations in it. But this knowledge is based on custom and habit, not reason; and we do not have what Hume termed "rational" grounds for our beliefs, grounds that have any indubitable basis. The basis is not logic and deduction but the uncertainty that accompanies the mere experimental evidence of the senses. From a theoretical point of view, Hume was a skeptic: he saw no argumentative foundation for beliefs, which were only the practical extrapolations from what was solipsistically given. Moreover, even this practical basis for activity was limited to empirical data; there was no room at all for commitment to super-sensual knowledge.

In America the Scottish epistemology denied the premise of Hume's skepticism, that we are directly aware only of the contents of consciousness; rather, we grasp things as they are in themselves and, therefore, as they really interact. Physical objects and also mind itself are "presented" to us. In consciousness we know each basic substance. Common sense teaches us that the five external senses and consciousness — the internal sense — give us a direct apprehension of the external world and of mind itself. To deny such common sense is not just a philosophers' trick but self-destructive; belief about the world and the self is necessary to any sort of reasoning.

Doubting such beliefs undercuts the very doubt itself. In assuming he could show the impossibility of knowledge, Hume presupposed the reasoning he ruled out. What did it mean for him to say we only know the phenomena that pass before our minds? He adopted a standpoint from which he could look at what was in his consciousness and claim it told him truly of the relation of objects to mind; but this presupposed what he wished to deny — that consciousness can adequately depict itself and the external world.[8]

This *reductio ad absurdum* clinched the case against Hume. The reasoning involved in demonstrating that skepticism presupposed a framework that could not be doubted was called "the principles of common sense." Individual truths of this importance were known as "intuitions." They were given, and could not be yielded without surrendering thought itself.

The intuitions of Scottish epistemology had a limited if crucial role for Reid and his followers. By the end of his career, however, Hodge had magnified the role of intuition. At Princeton intuition guaranteed the mind's grasp of all sorts of individual truths about the world.

Hodge chastised any beliefs he did not like by insisting that they tried to circumvent intuitions plainly necessary to thought itself. Thus, he defended many of his cultural prejudices that came under attack as prerequisites to the essence of thought itself. In a way for him, scientific atheism was impossible. A teleological universe was "almost . . . self evident." Scientists who believed in Charles Darwin arrayed themselves against "intuitive perceptions and irresistible convictions of all mankind — a barrier which no man has been able to surmount." To become a Darwinist was to try to escape the "constituion of our nature" or the "laws of [one's] own being," to become "derationalized or demoralized," to plunge into "the abyss of outer darkness."[9]

Hodge never asked how, as he admitted, a whole class of people could be gravitating to a constellation of beliefs that by his lights it was impossible to hold. *What Is Darwinism?*, from which I have been quoting, rightly urges that on a reasonable interpretation, Darwin leads to atheism. Hodge wants to go further, however, to contend that *therefore* no one can adhere to such a view.

How could so many people be operating with such ideas if they were indeed counter to the fundamentals of reasoning? The dialogue among social scientists posed a special problem for this line of thought: they began in earnest after Hodge's death to examine the factors that, over time,

8. For some American examples of Scottish reasoning, see John Witherspoon, *Works of John Witherspoon*, 9 vols. (Edinburgh: J. Ogle, 1815), vol. 7, pp. 21-23; and Francis Bowen, *Critical Essays on a Few Subjects Connected with the History and Present Condition of Speculative Philosophy* (Boston: H. B. Williams, 1842), pp. 6-30, 128-30, 302.

9. Hodge, *What Is Darwinism?* (1874); I have used the helpful edition edited and introduced by Mark A. Noll and David N. Livingstone (Grand Rapids: Baker Books, 1994), pp. 64, 66, 137, 153-54.

gave rise to differences in the world's cultures. These new men of science attempted to explore why different societies affirmed different beliefs. One does not have to be a cultural relativist to see why Hodge's argument to intuitions was unappealing even at the end of the nineteenth century.

American speculators from the late eighteenth century developed what we would today call psychological theories investigating the nature of the mind. This was a response to the work of Jonathan Edwards that had been required reading since the middle of the eighteenth century. The mind for Edwards was not so much an entity as a function, with two reciprocally related functions — cognition and volition. Edwards advanced his views mainly as a way of elaborating his deterministic position on the troubling question of human freedom for Calvinism. In the nineteenth century his solution provoked much opposition that found comfort in a different conception of mind and that divided the mental realm into a series of separate powers.

For the opposition to Edwards and for many Scottish realists, the mind had three functions, not two, and they were more clearly separated into ontological faculties. The understanding was not so much an activity as a substance that *did* the cognizing. So also the will, which was divided into a substance capable of *affection,* which might include sensation and emotion; and the will *proper,* which was the capacity for choice, or a substance that often clearly had what was known as a power to the contrary. Thus, in human behavior the reason (or understanding or cognition) set out goals; the affections provided the motives; but the will made action possible. Psychology in America in the nineteenth century was elaborated by college philosophers but most clearly served a theological purpose. For lack of a better designation I have called the enterprise philosophical psychology or mental science. It was an ancestor of present-day psychology, but lodged in a religious conversation and without an experimental component. The faculty psychology gave theologians a way to respond to Edwards on the will; it was a separable and freely acting entity. The Scots and their disciples in the United States shifted discussion away from the Edwardsean functionalist view of mind to a three-substance view.[10]

As psychology emerged as a separate empirical discipline in the new university system, the Edwardsean functional view again gained credibility, although now its activity was found to be self-generated and not a product of God's power. That is, by the end of the nineteenth century, as

---

10. See for example, Noah Porter, *Elements of Moral Science* (New York: C. Scribner's Sons, 1885).

Scottish realism declined, a different voluntaristic psychology arose. Its most famous proponents were William James and later John Dewey; and their functional voluntarism was structurally more similar to the writings of Jonathan Edwards on the mind than to McCosh's or Porter's writings on the faculties.

The faculty psychology was clumsy, and by the end of the nineteenth century had been rejected by practitioners of both philosophy and the new science of psychology. Hodge defended it because, in the ways I have noted above, it gave him the best hope of warding off Edwards and yielding a conception of the will useful for Princeton theology.[11] Throughout Hodge's writings on the will and on faculty psychology, disagreement with Edwards is the primary motivating force. Nonetheless, Hodge's ideas are complex and not unsubtle. The will is a separate faculty that acts freely; to be effective for Hodge, however, it must act in accord with the reason and the feelings. Just how the will's freedom is compatible with the certainty of God's decrees may be unclear for Hodge, as is appropriate for someone who believed in the limitations of our knowledge. But we are given the facts of freedom and of certainty, says Hodge, and their intellectual reconciliation is simply a risky enterprise.

I sympathize with Hodge's participation in the 150-year-old theological debate over the nature of the will. Edwardseanism, moreover, has enough problems for commentators to pay respectful attention to Hodge. Perhaps his only sin here was to have embroiled himself in a dialogue that involved psychological reasoning that was going permanently out of fashion. It is nonetheless true that unlike younger scholars — William James, for example — Hodge could not think his way around the faculty psychology. Nor could he develop a view of mind that was independent of theology and of the theological question of the freedom of the will. Perhaps this was only a failing because an independent discipline of psychology was coming into existence.

The theory of science Hodge defended was taxonomic or naturalist, following the position of the early naturalist-philosopher Francis Bacon. The "natural philosopher" observed the world around him systematically and from his observations induced generalizations (theories) about the world that gained the status of laws of nature, if they were sustained and acceptable. A lot here wants unpacking.

---

11. See Hodge, "Free Agency," *Biblical Repertory and Princeton Review* 29 (1857): 101-35, and Enoch Pond, "Dr. Hodge and the New England Theology," *Bibliotheca Sacra* 30 (1873): 377, 380.

First, it was premised that the American scientist was effectively a methodical observer, even a collector. The observations were presumed to be "objective," that is, they depended on the impartial character of the scientist's findings and his capacity to see what there actually was. Second, the naturalist did not engage in philosophy, that is metaphysics; empirical theories were different from hypotheses or speculations. The difference was just that theories had been "induced" from the facts collected. The precise nature of this kind of Baconian induction is mysterious. Ostensibly the scientist teased out of his information universal statements that were more than merely the sum of all the individual data; yet the universal statements or theories did not go beyond what was given in any unwarranted way. *That* would be metaphysics, speculative hypothesizing. Finally, it needs to be remembered that although the practice of science in America did not in all ways conform to this ideal, science *was* heavily naturalistic. The more strictly empirical Baconian philosophy of science *was* compatible with much of the science.

As science changed in the late nineteenth century, Hodge was unable to alter his preconceptions about it — his zealous, if peculiar, Baconianism. New scientific practices in the late nineteenth century were not limited to psychology. Innovation was key to biologists whose taxonomic undertaking became much more theoretical. To put it briefly, Darwin-like biology was more conceptual than what had come before. It gave greater emphasis to a hypothesizing mind than its hyper-empirical predecessor, which demanded little in the way of human creativity in science. Baconian philosophy of science could not much accommodate Darwin. While Hodge had good reason not simply to disregard the old philosophy of science, he made his Baconian philosophy of science (and his intuitions) the measure of science, rather than the reverse. His predisposition became more pronounced as other sciences followed Darwin away from taxonomic naturalism. Here is damaging evidence of Hodge's flaws. It was one thing to challenge Darwin; it was another to make one's theory of science the measure of what science was. Ironically, Hodge's devotion to the notion that science was only fact-driven put him in the position of disallowing many facts and, as matters turned out, all manner of science.

It is still worth quoting the extraordinary statements from his *Systematic Theology* on science and theology:

> It is a fundamental principle of all sciences, and of theology among the rest, that theory is to be determined by facts, and not facts by theory. . . . The true method of theology . . . assumes that the Bible

contains all the facts or truths which form the contents of theology, just as the facts of nature are the contents of the natural sciences. It is assumed that the relations of these Biblical facts to each other, the principles involved in them, the laws which determine them, are *in the facts themselves,* and are to be deduced from them, just as the laws of nature are deduced from the facts of nature. In neither case are the principles derived from the mind and imposed upon the facts, but equally in each department, the principles or laws are deduced from the facts and recognized by the mind.[12]

What is Hodge saying here? He has adopted what I would call Princeton Baconianism. He first assumes where there are realms of facts — in this case, in nature and in the Bible — and then wishes to us to apply induction on the facts. But why should we accept what is given in the Bible? Hodge has structured his inquiry so that he does not question the status of some writings that all of nineteenth-century scholarship — philological science, if you will — had urged the learned to worry about. His Baconian verbiage — that we should look at all the facts — covered up a set of assumptions that overlooked a lot of uncomfortable facts. More important, most other scholars were not overlooking these facts. The practice of inquiry — here in Bible studies itself — was getting increasingly away from Hodge's conception of it.

There have been some recent attempts made to show that Hodge was cognizant of and sympathetic toward the science of his day. On the contrary, he explained the tendency that he saw of scientists to be areligious by what he called an "addiction" to science. He hinted that the tendency was also a product of the fact that non-cultured scientists were rebelling against their class betters in divinity schools.[13] Hodge measured *all* science by his studies of the Bible and, more important, had no sense of how the activities of the scientific community defined that community itself and defined what science was.

The period after the Civil War was one in which the entire structure of knowledge was changing, in which the practices of men (and later women) of mind were altering. Rather than adapting his worldview to these practices, or even playing one off against the other, Hodge chose a different course. He made his ultimate beliefs about the cosmos the sole measure of what the men in the new universities could know. At the very

12. Hodge, *Systematic Theology* (New York: C. Scribner's Sons, 1872), vol. I, pp. 14-15, 17.
13. Hodge, *What Is Darwinism?* pp. 131, 134-35.

least this was not a prudent move; he now belongs to a world we have lost. More to the point, if one has any respect for practice as a measure of scientific achievement, we must conclude that Hodge failed to adapt to basic concerns that scholars and scientists came to have about the nature of the mind and of science itself.

* * *

Historians often like to evade questions that pertain to the quality of thought, but such questions are intrinsic to the history of philosophy and to some genres of intellectual history. The answers to implicit questions about the genius of thinkers, about their giftedness, guide the historical philosophical reading of late-twentieth-century intellectuals. What makes a Christian thinker worth reading in an age when many intellectuals have rejected Christianity? Why do commentators not need to conjure up historical sympathy to persuade people to appreciate someone like Edwards? A necessary condition is that the speculator must have the ability to juxtapose the sacred texts of his tradition with his own life experience and the knowledge of his culture. The thinker must give due regard to both to the texts *and* to the experience and knowledge. It is the synthesis that vivifies the writing. If that synthesis is absent, the writing remains dead, no matter what the technical brilliance of the author. In Edwards this synthesis exists. Indeed, some commentators might claim that he sacrifices sacred doctrine to the demands of his own experience and his culture's knowledge. In Hodge, there is no such synthesis. He subordinates his own experience and the knowledge of his culture to the inspired book over whose interpretation he presided. That is why Hodge has been called a Biblicist and a dogmatist.

Charles Hodge and the
Beauties and Deformities of Science

RONALD L. NUMBERS

Charles Hodge loved science. The son of a successful Philadelphia physician, who died within a year of his son's birth, Charles entered college hoping to follow in the footsteps of his father and older brother, Hugh Lenox Hodge, who was preparing for a career in medicine. Instead, after graduating from Princeton College (the College of New Jersey), he enrolled in Princeton Theological Seminary, where he studied with Archibald Alexander, a sometime science professor, and Samuel Miller, author of the first American history of science. After finishing seminary, Hodge spent a winter in Philadelphia improving himself and attending lectures on anatomy and physiology at the medical school of the University of Pennsylvania. In part because of a chronically painful right leg that often left him incapacitated, he maintained a lifelong interest in physiology and medicine and came to possess an "unusual knowledge" of medical matters for a layperson.[1]

1. Alexander A. Hodge, *The Life of Charles Hodge, D.D., LL.D.* (London: T. Nelson and Sons, 1881), pp. 46, 68, 98; John W. Stewart, *Mediating the Center: Charles Hodge on American Science, Language, Literature, and Politics* (Princeton: Princeton Theological Seminary, 1995), pp. 1-114, especially p. 7; Theodore Dwight Bozeman, *Protestants in an Age of Science: The Baconian Ideal and Antebellum American Religious Thought* (Chapel Hill: University of North Carolina Press, 1977), p. 40. Samuel Miller included scientific developments in his pioneering *A Brief Retrospect of the Eighteenth Century* (New York: T. & J. Swords, 1803).

I am indebted to Tomomi Kunakawa for her research assistance and to William O. Harris and Raymond D. Cannata of the office of Archives and Special Collections, Princeton Theological Seminary, for providing me with much-needed sources. I am especially grateful to Jon H. Roberts for his suggestions, criticisms, and encouragement.

In 1822 Hodge joined the new nation's first family of science when he married Sarah Bache, a great-granddaughter of Benjamin Franklin and a cousin of Alexander Dallas Bache, the most powerful man of science in the United States during the middle third of the nineteenth century. After four years of teaching biblical literature back at the seminary, Hodge left his wife and young children for a three-year study tour in Europe. Although he devoted most of his time there to biblical languages and theology, he eagerly sought opportunities to hobnob with distinguished European men of science and listen to their lectures. In Paris he made a point of going to a meeting of the Institut de France, where the great mathematician and astronomer Pierre-Simon Laplace presided over the city's literary and scientific intelligentsia. In Berlin he visited the Royal Academy of Sciences and faithfully attended the lectures of the world-famous naturalist Alexander von Humboldt, who had befriended him in Paris. In Goettingen he visited the museum of the anatomist and physical anthropologist J. F. Blumenbach, who showed his American guest his vast collection and human skulls and enlisted Hodge's help in obtaining additional New World specimens.[2]

Back home in Princeton after his years abroad, the frequently couchbound Hodge several times a week gathered his friends and colleagues in his study for spirited evening discussions. These occasions brought together not only distinguished religious thinkers but also some of the finest scientific minds in the country: the physicist Joseph Henry, the botanist John Torrey, the chemist John Maclean, and the mathematician Albert B. Dod, Hodge's cousin-in-law and one of his closest friends. Morning after morning, year after year, Hodge took the time to record vital meteorological data. As editor of the *Biblical Repertory and Princeton Review* (hereafter *Princeton Review*), the leading American theological quarterly of the day, he made a point of keeping subscribers abreast of recent developments in science. For a brief period he experimented with a section devoted to "Quarterly Scientific Intelligence." He routinely published short reviews of scientific books, ranging in topic from astronomy to zoology. In addition to numerous articles on the relations of science and religion, he printed a number of essays on general science, covering such subjects as agricultural chemistry, analytical geometry, western geography, and respiratory physiology. To help generate support for the U.S. Coast Survey, under the superintendency of Bache, he induced their mutual friend Henry to contribute an article on the institution's practical

2. Stewart, *Mediating the Center,* p. 17; Hodge, *Life of Charles Hodge,* pp. 112-14, 162, 170, 190-91.

and moral virtues. According to the calculations of John W. Stewart, roughly 20 percent of the articles published in the *Princeton Review* during the heyday of Hodge's editorship addressed scientific issues. Hodge viewed science, which disclosed the work of God, and religion, which interpreted the word of God, as "the twin daughters of heaven"; he venerated "men of science who, while remaining faithful to their higher nature, have enlarged our knowledge of the wonderful works of God."[3]

Hodge may have loved science, but he also feared and distrusted some of its practitioners, especially as he advanced in age and the pace of scientific progress quickened. Scientific theories were changing so fast — "almost as often as the phases of the moon" — that laypersons were experiencing difficulty keeping up. To explain the movement of the planets, Hodge complained, astronomers once "said that they were moved by spirits, then by vortexes, now by self-evolved forces. It is hard that we should be called upon to change our faith with every new moon." As editor of the *Princeton Review* during the 1840s and 1850s he published occasional warnings against the tendency of some scientific men to promote their speculative, often anti-Christian, opinions in the name of science. And by the late 1850s he was growing increasingly frustrated by the tendency of men of science to treat theologians who expressed themselves on scientific subjects as "trespassers" who should mind their own business. As a theological conservative who once boasted that "a new idea never originated in this Seminary," he decried the "recklessness" of men of science who gave no thought to the possible adverse impact of their views on Christianity

---

3. Hodge, *Life of Charles Hodge,* pp. 236-40, 364; Bozeman, *Protestants in an Age of Science,* p. 35; review of *The Annual of Scientific Discovery,* ed. David A. Wells, in *Biblical Repertory and Princeton Review* (hereafter cited as *BRPR*); [Samuel Tyler], "Agricultural Chemistry," *BRPR* 16 (1844): 508-17; [Albert Baldwin Dod], "Analytical Geometry," *BRPR* 13 (1841): 523-38; "Survey of the Valley of the Great Salt Lake of Utah," *BRPR* 24 (1852): 687-96; [John Stillwell Schank], "What's the Use of Breathing?" *BRPR* 37 (1865): 135-47; [Joseph Henry], "The British Scientific Association," *BRPR* 13 (1841): 132-49; [Joseph Henry], "Coast Survey," *BRPR* 17 (1845): 321-44; Hugh Richard Slotten, *Patronage, Practice, and the Culture of American Science: Alexander Dallas Bache and the U.S. Coast Survey* (Cambridge: Cambridge University Press, 1994), p. 83; Stewart, *Mediating the Center,* p. 25; Charles Hodge, *What Is Darwinism?* (New York: Scribner, Armstrong, 1874), p. 131. The sections on "Quarterly Scientific Intelligence" appeared in *BRPR* 24 (1852): 350-56, 526-31. On Hodge's meteorological activities, see also Joseph Henry to James Henry Coffin, September 9, 1842, in *The Papers of Joseph Henry,* ed. Nathan Reingold and Marc Rothenberg, 6 vols. to date (Washington: Smithsonian Institution Press, 1972), vol. 5, pp. 266-67. I have placed brackets around the names of authors writing in the *Biblical Repertory and Princeton Review* to signify that those names do not appear with the articles; in such cases, I have identified the authors by using *The Biblical Repertory and Princeton Review: Index Volume from 1825-1868* (Philadelphia: Peter Walker, 1871).

and who often ignored "all facts which do not fall within their own department," such as the historical facts revealed in the Bible. In the years following the American Civil War he expressed exasperation at the swiftly moving drift of modern science toward naturalism and materialism. He attributed the growing "alienation" between men of science and men of the cloth in part to the former's "assumption of superiority" and practice of stigmatizing their religious critics "as narrow-minded, bigots, old women, Bible worshippers, etc." He resented the lack of respect frequently shown to religious men, who were instructed by their scientific colleagues to quit meddling in science, while they themselves belittled religious beliefs and values. At times Hodge worried that science, devoid of religion, was becoming downright "satanic." He had no doubt that religion was in a "fight for its life against a large class of scientific men."[4]

In view of such conflicting sentiments, historians should probably be excused for disagreeing so strikingly about Hodge's understanding of and attitudes toward the science of his time. Some scholars have portrayed him as being "particularly paranoid about science," as demonstrating "an immature hostility to science," as lacking a proper understanding of science, and as serving as an intellectual "forerunner" to the fundamentalist creation scientists of the twentieth century. Others have described him as "one of the most astute writers on the theological implications of Darwin's work," as a "perceptive and even-tempered" analyst of Darwinism, and as a cultural mediator in troubled times.[5] There are grounds, however

4. Charles Hodge, *What Is Darwinism?* pp. 132, 134-35, 140-42; [Charles Hodge], "The Unity of Mankind," *BRPR* 31 (1859): 103-49, quotations on pp. 104-105; Hodge, *Life of Charles Hodge*, p. 521; Charles Hodge, "Address at the Inauguration of James McCosh," 1866, Hodge Papers, Princeton University Library, as quoted in Stewart, *Mediating the Center*, p. 25. Unfortunately, Hodge's correspondence in the Hodge Papers contains few references to science.

5. Herbert Hovenkamp, *Science and Religion in America, 1800-1860* (Philadelphia: University of Pennsylvania Press, 1978), p. 216; Joseph E. Illick III, "The Reception of Darwinism at the Theological Seminary and the College at Princeton, New Jersey," *Journal of Presbyterian History* 38 (1960): 152-65, 234-43, quotation on p. 157 (the phrase "immature hostility" is used to describe some articles in *BRPR*, some of which were written by Hodge); Hugh Foster, *The Modern Movement in American Theology: Sketches in the History of American Protestant Thought from the Civil War to the World War* (New York: Fleming H. Revell, 1939), p. 49; Walter J. Wilkins, *Science and Religious Thought: A Darwinism Case Study* (Ann Arbor, MI: U.M.I. Press, 1987), p. 37; Neal C. Gillespie, *Charles Darwin and the Problem of Creation* (Chicago: University of Chicago Press, 1979), p. 112; James R. Moore, *The Post-Darwinian Controversies: A Study of the Protestant Struggle to Come to Terms with Darwin in Great Britain and America, 1870-1900* (Cambridge: Cambridge University Press 1979), p. 204; Stewart, *Mediating the Center*. For an additional positive assessment, see Mark A. Noll and David N. Livingstone, Introduction to Charles Hodge, *What Is Darwinism?* (Grand Rapids: Baker Books, 1994), p. 22.

shaky in some instances, for most of these assertions, but not for the charge that he failed to understand science. As we shall see, Hodge's growing disillusionment with science stemmed not from his ignorance of the field but from his perceptive insights about its changing character.

In this essay I want to take a fresh look at Hodge's engagement with science. I am particularly interested in identifying any patterns to his scientific pronouncements and the motivations that prompted his public statements. Did he, for example, see himself primarily as a defender of the Holy Scriptures, of natural theology, or of a particular scientific method? What was at stake for him personally and for Christianity generally? Because I think it is important to see Hodge — and science — in the context of his times rather than ours, I have tried to situate his beliefs within the religio-scientific world in which he lived and worked. To do so, I have drawn extensively on essays and reviews that appeared in the *Princeton Review* during his long tenure as editor. These sources may not tell us exactly what Hodge thought about particular topics, but because of his disinclination to publish views that diverged from his own, they do reflect the direction of his thinking. On one of the few occasions when he did accept an essay at odds with his own beliefs, he attached an editorial note alerting readers that the accompanying article should not "be regarded as presenting the estimate of the *Princeton Review*." Except for pieces attributed to Hodge in the published index to his journal, we have no way of identifying what came from his own pen.[6] The portrait that emerges from my reading of the available sources reveals an unusually complex man, both rigid and flexible, dogmatic and open-minded, torn between his genuine love of natural knowledge and his loathing for what sometimes passed as science.

The Nature of Science and Religion

In 1863 the *Princeton Review* published an anonymous essay on "The Scepticism of Science," later attributed to a Pennsylvania cleric-businessman named Joseph Clark. Clark repeatedly warned of an impending attack on Christianity by modern science, which in recent years had "realized more than the wildest dream of poet, seer, or madman." "It has come to be generally conceded among discerning men, that the great battles of Christianity henceforth are to be fought with the various forms of unbelief gen-

6. [Julius H. Seelye], "Dr. Hickok's Philosophy," *BRPR* 34 (1862): 369-406, editorial note on p. 369; *The Biblical Repertory and Princeton Review: Index Volume from 1825-1868.*

erated by scientific inquiry," he wrote ominously. "And it has come to be boldly, and even boastfully declared, that the positive claims of Christianity, so far, at least, as they are founded upon the infallibility of Scripture, must now assuredly succumb under the last great assault, slowly but steadily, as with the tread of destiny, preparing against them." Rather than urging Christians to fight to the death against the menace of science, he recommended that the church "avoid ill-natured and unbecoming abuse of science and scientific men" and grant them "the largest liberty. . . . to carry on the pursuits and investigations of their respective sciences according to their legitimate mode." After all, he noted, the coming conflict would pit Christianity not against true science but false science, "against ignorant pretenders, sciolists, and vain boasters."[7]

An upset reader of Clark's article brought it to the attention of the editor of the staunchly conservative Presbyterian *Observer,* complaining that "the whole drift and tendency of it is to depreciate the Bible and exalt Science," to make "Science *lead* the way and the Bible *follow.*" The *Observer* editor agreed that the *Princeton Review* had gone too far toward elevating science above revelation. He especially disliked Clark's claim that "the discoveries of science rest upon a basis peculiarly their own — a basis of actual experiment and observation — and nothing can claim authority in a scientific view which does not so rest." To his way of thinking, this statement was a "distinct declaration that in *scientific* matters, faith in Moses and Paul must yield to Humboldt and Agassiz."[8]

This public charge of "abetting infidelity" provoked Hodge into writing a defense that spelled out his view of the relationship between science and Scripture, a message he reiterated in his monumental three-volume *Systematic Theology.* The *Princeton Review,* he insisted, had always "asserted the plenary inspiration of the Bible, in such sense that what the sacred writers say, the Holy Ghost said." This meant that the Bible could "teach no error, whether in reference to doctrines, morals, or facts; whether those facts be historical, geographical, geological, or astronomical." However, because God had revealed himself through nature as well as the Bible, the *Review* had simultaneously taught that "this infallible Bible must be interpreted by science." Thus when sixteenth- and seventeenth-century astronomers demonstrated that the Earth revolves around the sun, the church abandoned its longstanding commitment to geocentrism and re-

7. [Joseph Clark], "The Scepticism of Science," *BRPR* 35 (1863): 43-75, quotations on pp. 43, 47, 63, 65, 68. On Clark's identity, see Noll and Livingstone, Introduction, p. 51.
8. "Scripture and Science," *New York Observer,* March 12, 1863, p. 82.

interpreted the Scriptures to harmonize with science. As a believer in God's dual revelations, nature and the Bible, Hodge also held that true science could never contradict "the clear teachings of the Scripture." Although others sometimes found it difficult to distinguish between clear teachings and allegories, Hodge never doubted the perspicuity of Scripture, especially as it related to the plan of salvation.[9]

As a young man at Princeton and later in Europe Hodge had imbibed of the notion that theology was as much a science as geology or zoology, and as editor of the *Princeton Review* he had published a number of essays identifying induction as the distinctive method for doing science. In 1831 the *Review* called for "the full application of the inductive philosophy," commonly associated with the seventeenth-century English philosopher Francis Bacon and his eighteenth-century Scottish common sense disciples. Adopting the Baconian method meant stressing the primacy of facts, which served as a vivid "line of demarcation" between true science and pseudo-science and linked the science of theology with the sciences of nature. "The Bible is to the theologian what nature is to the man of science," wrote Hodge in his *Systematic Theology*. "It is his store-house of facts; and his method of ascertaining what the Bible teaches, is the same as that which the natural philosopher adopts to ascertain what nature teaches."[10] As we shall see, the passage of time soon undermined the common ground shared by science and religion, but in the meantime Hodge took satisfaction in their fundamental unity.

Pseudo-Science

The first signs of discomfort over scientific developments appeared in the *Princeton Review* in the 1830s, when phrenology, the science of the human mind developed by the German physicians Franz Joseph Gall and his student Johann Gaspar Spurzheim, reached America. According to phreno-

9. Charles Hodge, "The Bible in Science," *New York Observer,* March 26, 1863, pp. 98-99.

10. Walter H. Conser, Jr., *God and the Natural World: Religion and Science in Antebellum America* (Columbia: University of South Carolina Press, 1993), p. 69; "Advancement of Society," *BRPR* 3 (1831): 306-19, quotation on p. 315; "Rauch's Psychology," *BRPR* 12 (1840): 394-410, quotation regarding demarcation on p. 396. As Peter Hicks has perceptively noted, Hodge adopted the language of Baconianism and common sense philosophy "because they gave adequate expression to his theological and philosophical ideas, rather than because they controlled those ideas"; Hicks, *The Philosophy of Charles Hodge: A 19th Century Evangelical Approach to Reason, Knowledge and Truth* (Lewiston, Maine: Edwin Mellen Press, 1997), p. 79.

logical theory, the human brain comprised various "organs" — the exact number varied considerably — each corresponding to an exotically named mental "faculty," such as amativeness (love of sex), acquisitiveness (love of money), or philoprogenitiveness (love of children). Because the relative strength of any propensity could be determined by measuring the size of its matching organ, skillful phrenologists could readily "read" a person's character by carefully examining the skull. Although individuals could influence the strength of a particular organ by exercising it, the basic thrust of phrenology lay in the direction of psychological determinism, materialism, and infidelity. On occasion phrenology merged into another German import of the 1830s, Mesmerism, or animal magnetism, associated with an eighteenth-century Austrian physician, Franz Anton Mesmer. Late in the century Mesmer had announced the discovery of an invisible fluid, like electricity, that coursed through the human body. He reasoned that obstructions to the flow of this "animal magnetism" caused disease, which could be cured by the magnetic emanations from another person's hands or eyes. Treating patients in this manner often put them in a deep trance (later described as hypnotic), with unpredictable and sometimes entertaining results. Like phrenology, Mesmerism raised doubts about the doctrine of free will and aroused concern among Christians.[11]

Writers for the *Princeton Review* typically dealt with these potential threats to the harmony between science and religion by dismissing them as "quackery," "pseudo-science," or "a miserable abortion of folly," representative not of modern times but "the days when astrology and the theory of 'herbal signatures' were sciences." They described Mesmerism as simply "so absurd and incredible, that it cannot be true." Only persons "liable to be hoaxed" needed to be concerned. Though phrenology at first attracted some distinguished scientific supporters in America — Yale's revered Benjamin Silliman, the founding editor of the *American Journal of Science*, personally hosted Spurzheim in New Haven — after a while the best scientific and theological minds tended not to take it seriously. Thus Hodge risked little by publishing attacks on its scientific standing.[12]

11. On phrenology in America, see John D. Davies, *Phrenology, Fad and Science: A 19th-Century American Crusade* (New Haven: Yale University Press, 1955); on Mesmerism, see Robert C. Fuller, *Mesmerism and the American Cure of Souls* (Philadelphia: University of Pennsylvania Press, 1982).

12. "Phrenology," BRPR 10 (1838): 279-320, quotations on pp. 319-20; review of *Phrenology Examined*, by P. Flourens, BRPR 18 (1846): 354-58, quotation on p. 355; review of *Phrenology Examined, and Shown to Be Inconsistent with the Principles of Physiology, Mental and Moral Science, and the Doctrines of Christianity*, by N. L. Rice, BRPR 21 (1849): 298-300.

The sciences of the mind continued to attract critical attention in the 1840s, especially in connection with debates over the relationship between religion and insanity. Excessive religious enthusiasm had long been a topic of medical and theological interest, but the level of concern grew in the wake of the Finneyite revivals of the 1820s and 1830s, which sometimes reduced entire congregations to wailing and writhing, behaviors that could be interpreted as either pathological or spiritual. An epidemic of "religious insanity" reached its apex in the 1840s, when the excitement generated by William Miller's prediction of the imminent end of the world accounted for half of all religion-related admissions to some insane asylums in the Northeast. The prospect of widespread hereditary insanity resulting from such madness prompted the prominent asylum superintendent Amariah Brigham to rank Millerism above even yellow fever and cholera as a threat to the public's health. Brigham attributed the "outward signs" associated with revivals to overstimulation of the nervous system rather than to the *special outpouring of the Spirit of God.* His implication that clergymen could not distinguish between "the ravings of the insane or semi-insane and the operations of the Holy Spirit" did not go unchallenged. As Frederick A. Packard explained in the *Princeton Review,* "An enthusiast preaching wildly would at once pass among us for an insane man, and his influence would extend but little if at all beyond those who are predisposed to the same class of mental aberrations or already under their power." Packard granted that some Millerites among the thousands duped by "the false prophet" from upstate New York had become "crazed" by the excitement of preparing for the imminent Second Coming of Christ — or by the disappointment experienced when Christ failed to appear on the appointed date in 1844. However, Packard and other contributors to the *Princeton Review* emphatically denied that "true religion" played any role in the epidemic of insanity sweeping the Northeast, and they resented the impertinence of medical men who suggested otherwise. "The subject trenches so closely upon the domain of theology, and enters so far into that of experimental and spiritual religion," wrote one, "that it required more than mere medical knowledge to do it justice."[13]

13. Amariah Brigham, *Observations on the Influence of Religion upon the Health and Physical Welfare of Mankind* (Boston, 1835), pp. 260, 284-85, 291, 312; [Frederick A. Packard], "The Relations of Religion to What Are Called Diseases of the Mind," *BRPR* 22 (1850): 1-41; [Matthew Boyd Hope], "Religious Melancholy," *BRPR* 16 (1844): 352-79, quotation on p. 353. On Millerism and insanity, see Ronald L. Numbers and Janet S. Numbers, "Millerism and Madness: A Study of 'Religious Insanity' in Nineteenth-Century America," in *The Disappointed:*

As early as 1839 Hodge himself entered "the labyrinth of medico-metaphysical speculations about nervous diseases" and their relations to religion. As a cerebral Calvinist skeptical of highly emotional religious displays, he offered no defense of the "fainting, convulsions, jerking, etc.," commonly associated with rabble-rousing Methodists. Instead, he proposed a naturalistic explanation of their bizarre behavior and recommended medical treatment for the victims. "I am persuaded," he wrote to his physician brother, that such phenomena

> are nothing but one form of an infectious nervous disease, generated by strong impressions on the imagination and lively emotions. If so they have nothing to do, properly speaking, with religion, and instead of being encouraged or tolerated, as they almost always have been by good men to the great injury of religion, they ought by all means to be guarded against and suppressed as much as epilepsy or hysterics.

Clearly, scientific naturalism in the defense of religion was no vice.[14]

Despite this one medicalizing venture, Hodge and his circle kept a wary eye out for the encroachment of naturalistic psychology on the territory of moral philosophers. They strongly condemned the mid-century notion of "moral insanity," according to which outwardly normal persons changed with heinous crimes could be judged as insane. "We regard the notion of 'moral insanity,' lately promulgated, as a device for the protection of wicked and ungovernable men from the just punishment of their crimes," declared Packard. The concept of moral insanity reminded Lyman H. Atwater too much of phrenological theory, which explained sinful behavior anatomically rather than theologically, and he suspected that the advocates of moral insanity had "been influenced by the method of phrenology."[15]

By the late 1860s the *Princeton Review* was lashing out at the propagandists for physiological psychology, such as Herbert Spencer, Charles Darwin, and Thomas S. Huxley, who were attempting to create a scientific psychology devoid of spiritual elements — and doing so in a "loud, if not

Millerism and Millenarianism in the Nineteenth Century, ed. Ronald L. Numbers and Jonathan M. Butler (Bloomington: Indiana University Press, 1987), pp. 92-117.

14. Charles Hodge to Hugh Hodge, August 15, 1839, quoted in Hodge, *Life of Charles Hodge,* pp. 244-45.

15. [Packard], "The Relations of Religion to What Are Called Diseases of the Mind," p. 40; [Lyman H. Atwater], "Moral Insanity," BRPR 29 (1857): 345-75, quotation on p. 354.

blatant," manner. The materialist advocates of the new psychology, noted one author with alarm, "propose to reconstruct education, society, morals, and religion in accordance with it; to make physical science, pure and applied, the chief element in education; to banish from it the classics, psychology, metaphysics, ethics, Christianity, and to replace them with physiology, biology, and a semi-brutish sociology, founded on mere bestial gregariousness." With so much at stake, accommodation seemed out of the question.[16]

The desire of many mid-century physiologists to explain the workings of biological organisms, including the human body, in mechanical and chemical terms without invoking "vital forces" was also an occasion for alarm. One reviewer for Hodge's quarterly blamed comparative physiology for "converting the well-taught and religiously disposed youth, into the bold, careless, and sceptical physiologist or physician." Fearing that Christians did not fully appreciate the subversive influence of this science, he called on the "friends of religion . . . to baptize this new, brilliant, and fascinating science, into its legitimate discipleship to Christianity, to compel it . . . to bring its tribute of worship to the great Creator." Hodge consoled himself with the thought that a number of prominent men of science, including his trusted friend Joseph Henry, had not bowed to the feet of this materialistic science, which, in Henry's words, denied "the immediate presence of a direct, divine, and spiritual essence."[17]

Genesis, Geology, and Astronomy

Hodge and the authors whose works he published in the *Princeton Review* opposed the new psychology and physiology because they represented the cutting edge of naturalism, seemingly drove God out of the scientific enterprise, promoted infidelity, and undermined the biblical doctrines of the soul and free will. Their fears were well founded: mid-century men of science were indeed trying to erase the last traces of religion from the domain of science. In fact, methodological naturalism rather than Baconian

---

16. "Materialism — Physiological Psychology," *BRPR* 41 (1869): 615-25, quotations on pp. 623-24. See also [Hope], "Religious Melancholy," p. 377.

17. Review of *The Indictions of the Creator; or, The Natural Evidences of Final Cause,* by George Taylor, *BRPR* 24 (1852): 141-46, quotation on p. 145; Charles Hodge, *Systematic Theology,* 3 vols. (New York: Scribner, 1871-73), vol. 1, pp. 292-93. See also review of *Essays on Life, Sleep, Pain, &c.,* by Samuel Henry Dickson, *BRPR* 24 (1852): 507; and review of *A Treatise on the Forces Which Produce the Organization of Plants,* by John William Draper, *BRPR* 17 (1845): 345-47.

inductivism was rapidly emerging as the chief distinguishing characteristic of modern science. Under such circumstances, Hodge saw little room for compromise — except, surprisingly, in dealing with the disciplines of astronomy and geology that challenged the traditional reading of the Mosaic story of creation.[18]

Beginning in about the second decade of the nineteenth century, geologists on both sides of the Atlantic, most of them Christians and some of them clerics, abandoned the speculative theories of the Earth that had typified so much of eighteenth-century scholarship in favor of empirical investigations that took them out of their studies and into the mountains and valleys around them. Using the distinctive assemblages of fossils found in the different strata of the Earth's surface, they constructed the so-called geological column and reconstructed the history of life on Earth. In place of the Mosaic account of a recent creation in six twenty-four-hour days that was destroyed by a worldwide deluge at the time of Noah, they found compelling evidence of vast geological ages and no signs of a great flood that wiped out all but eight of the Earth's inhabitants. By the early 1840s no geologist of note, Christian or otherwise, could be found still defending a 6,000-year-old creation of the world or a geologically significant universal flood.[19]

As late as the middle of the century, an estimated "half of the Christian public" in America remained faithful to the traditional reading of the first chapter of Genesis, but the rest seem to have adopted harmonizing schemes that accommodated geologists' findings about the antiquity of the Earth and its inhabitants. Many followed the Scottish divine Thomas Chalmers, who proposed allowing an indefinite period of time between an initial creation "in the beginning" and the relatively recent Edenic creation, during which the planet had experienced a series of catastrophes and creations. As described by its foremost American advocate, the cleric-

18. On methodological naturalism, see Ronald L. Numbers, "Science without God: Natural Laws and Christian Beliefs," in *Science and the Christian Tradition: Twelve Case Histories,* ed. David C. Lindberg and Ronald L. Numbers (Chicago: University of Chicago Press, forthcoming).

19. See Martin J. S. Rudwick, "The Shape and Meaning of Earth History," in *God and Nature: Historical Essays on the Encounter between Christianity and Science,* ed. David C. Lindberg and Ronald L. Numbers (Berkeley and Los Angeles: University of California Press, 1986), pp. 296-321; James R. Moore, "Geologists and Interpreters of Genesis in the Nineteenth Century," in Lindberg and Numbers, *God and Nature,* pp. 322-50; Rodney L. Stiling, "The Diminishing Deluge: Noah's Flood in Nineteenth-Century American Geology and Theology," Ph.D. dissertation, University of Wisconsin-Madison, 1992.

geologist Edward Hitchcock, Chalmers's explanation "supposed that Moses merely states that God created the world in the beginning, without fixing the date of that beginning; and that passing in silence an unknown period of its history, during which the extinct animals and plants found in the rocks might have lived and died, he describes only the present creation, which took place in six literal days, less than 6000 years ago." An "extension of this interpretation," as Hitchcock phrased it, was advanced by the British theologian John Pye Smith in 1839. Like Chalmers, Smith believed that Moses had described two separate creations, but he argued that the latter had been a local event, restricted to *"the part of our world which God was adapting for the dwelling of man and the animals connected with him."*[20]

Another view, popularized in the early 1830s by Benjamin Silliman in the United States and later by Hugh Miller in Scotland, met the geological challenge to Genesis by interpreting the "days" of the first chapter as vast geological ages. Silliman divided the period of the Earth's development into six epochs, each corresponding to a day of the creation week. During the fourth epoch the previously made sun and moon had begun to measure time, and at the end of the sixth epoch — approximately 6,000 years ago — God had created humans. Interpreting Genesis in this manner did not imply, for Silliman at least, that the Bible was in error. Geology and the Mosaic record remained in full accordance, he assured his readers, "but more time is required for the necessary events of the creation than is consistent with the common understanding of the days. The history therefore is true, but it must be understood so as to be consistent with itself and with the facts."[21]

In the early 1850s Hodge's Princeton colleague Arnold Guyot, a physical geographer recently arrived from Switzerland, modified the day-age theory to incorporate Laplace's nebular hypothesis about the origin of the solar system into the scheme. The French mathematician and astronomer had explained the birth of the solar system in terms of physical laws acting on a gaseous nebula. As the nebula cooled and contracted, it abandoned a series of rings along its equator (much like the rings of Saturn), which then broke up to form the individual planets. In like manner, the planets spun off their respective satellites. Greatly taken with this idea, Guyot, instead of equating all of the creative days with *geological* epochs,

20. Ronald L. Numbers, *Creation by Natural Law: Laplace's Nebular Hypothesis in American Thought* (Seattle: University of Washington Press, 1977), pp. 89-90.

21. Numbers, *Creation by Natural Law*, pp. 90-91.

assigned the first days to *astronomical* developments. If the formless "waters" created by God in the beginning symbolized gaseous matter, then the light of the first day undoubtedly had been produced by the chemical action resulting from the concentration of this matter into nebulae. The dividing of the waters on the second day represented the breaking up of the nebulae into various planetary systems, of which ours was but one. During the third epoch the Earth had condensed to form a solid globe, and during the fourth, the nebulous vapors surrounding Earth had dispersed to allow the light of the sun to shine through. The fifth and sixth epochs had witnessed the population of the Earth with living creatures. "Such is the grand cosmogonic week described by Moses," declared Guyot. "To a sincere and unprejudiced mind it must be evident that these great outlines are the same as those which modern science enables us to trace, however imperfect and unsettled the data afforded by scientific researches may appear on many points." Although the Swiss naturalist, who suffered from a severe case of writer's block, proved to be a poor publicist for his views, his message reached the book-reading masses through the works of Silliman's son-in-law James Dwight Dana and John William Dawson, the principal of McGill College in Montreal.[22]

Of immense significance to Hodge and his Princeton colleagues in evaluating these radical departures from the common-sense reading of Genesis were the identities of their leading promoters. Virtually all of the men mentioned above were pious Christians in the Reformed tradition: Chalmers, a noted Presbyterian minister and writer on natural theology; Hitchcock, an evangelical Congregational minister and accomplished geologist; Silliman, a devout geologist of Congregational persuasion; Miller, a celebrated Presbyterian geologist and popular author; Guyot, a Presbyterian geographer and geologist who had once studied for the ministry; Dana, a widely respected Congregational geologist and contributor to theological journals; and Dawson, an internationally acclaimed geologist, known for both his Presbyterian piety and his scientific accomplishments. Even Smith, by far the most radical of the group, was a Bible-believing British theologian. With exegetes such as these, one could scarcely argue that the efforts to adjust the Mosaic narrative of creation to the findings of modern geology and astronomy represented the work of skeptics and infidels.

Besides, such views were being taught right in Princeton, both in the college and in the seminary. At least by the fall of 1841 Joseph Henry was

22. Numbers, *Creation by Natural Law,* pp. 91-100.

not only endorsing geologists' efforts to lengthen the history of life on Earth but also praising the nebular hypothesis as "one of the boldest and most sublime conceptions of the human mind." His brother-in-law Stephen Alexander, a former seminarian who taught mathematics and astronomy in the college from 1833 to 1877, devoted more energy to promoting the nebular hypothesis than any other American astronomer but one, the Presbyterian Daniel Kirkwood. By the late 1840s Alexander was describing the nebular hypothesis as God's method of creating the solar system. For years he devoted the last lecture of his popular astronomy course to the subject, drawing crowds of admiring auditors from both college and town. After joining the college faculty in 1854 as professor of physical geography and geology, Guyot too promoted the nebular hypothesis, and for several years he lectured at the seminary on the harmony of Genesis with modern science.[23]

In view of the above, we can see why biblical inerrantists such as Hodge and his colleagues at the *Princeton Review* generally supported the geologists and astronomers who were rewriting the story of creation. In fact, contributors to the *Review* repeatedly defended these men of science against conservative Christian critics, who worried that the Princeton harmonizers were giving precedence to science over the Bible, as indeed it seemed. From the earliest essay on geology, in 1841, *Review* authors generally defended both the facts of geology, though "totally incompatible with the belief, that the material of the earth was created only a few days before man and congenera," and the interpretation of those facts by Christian geologists. Invoking the authority of early church fathers who had deviated from the conventional reading of Genesis 1, as well as "eminent biblical scholars of our own age," one contributor concluded that there was not "much ground for apprehension." Another assured the faithful that there was "no need to be much concerned about the age of the globe on which our race resides. The chronology of Moses is that of the human race, and not of the material part of the earth." For the time being such writers defended a universal deluge at the time of Noah, because "the fact is asserted in scripture as positively and clearly as it possibly could be in words," while noting that "no practical geologist, of any school whatever, . . . refers the formation of the geological strata *solely* to the action of Noah's flood."[24]

23. Numbers, *Creation by Natural Law*, pp. 25-26, 60-63, 87.

24. [Matthew Boyd Hope], "Relation between Scripture and Geology," *BRPR* 13 (1841): 368-93, quotations on pp. 379, 389, 390; review of *The Principles of Geology Explained and Re-*

When some "zealous friends of revelation," such as the Lord brothers, Eleazar and David, attacked geologists for violating the Scriptures, the *Princeton Review* put them in their place. Joseph Henry, dismissing Eleazar Lord's archconservative *Epoch of Creation* as gratuitous and unscientific, pointed to the "remarkable fact, that every practical geologist known to us, whatever his religious belief, and whatever his prior convictions may have been, is brought to the conclusion, by a thorough and minute study of the facts, that there were races of organic beings on the earth living, and succeeding one another on definite and settled principles, before the existence of the human race." For him, that settled the matter. Perhaps because of the lingering association of the nebular hypothesis with the notoriously atheistic Laplace, some contributors to the *Princeton Review* urged greater caution in embracing it. However, one reminded readers that "very few scientific theories are essentially impious" and that, regardless of Laplace's own opinions, "any old-fashioned Christian, beginning with the nebular hypothesis and resolving the fire-mist into chaos, might, if need be, proceed to the creation of the world in six ordinary days."[25]

Although Hodge's early views on pre-Adamic history remain uncertain, his published opinions from the 1870s closely reflect those of his associates. Relegating the question of *how* the world was made to "minor importance," he nevertheless devoted space in his *Systematic Theology* to describing the nebular hypothesis. While conceding that the original Laplacian version of the cosmogony left little work for God to do, he deemed it common knowledge "that there is a form in which the nebular hypothesis is held by many Christian theists." Along with Guyot, he felt that the first verses of Genesis "clearly intimated that the universe, when first created, was in a state of chaos, and that by the life-giving, organizing power of the spirit of God, it was gradually moulded into the wonderful cosmos which we now behold." His studies over the years had convinced him that development from preexisting material fell "within the Scriptural idea of creating." He declined, however, to pick the correct interpretation of Genesis 1, preferring to leave that matter an "open question," to

---

viewed in Their Relations to Revealed and Natural Religion, by David King, *BRPR* 23 (1851): 164-65. For optimistic assessments about reconciling Genesis and geology, see also review of *Geognosy; or, The Facts and principles of Geology against Theories*, by David N. Lord, *BRPR* 28 (1856): 161-63; and "Primeval Period of Sacred History," *BRPR* 32 (1860): 90-100.

25. [Hope], "Relation between Scripture and Geology," p. 391; [Joseph Henry], review of *The Epoch of Creation*, by Eleazar Lord, *BRPR* 23 (1851): 696-98. Hodge invited Henry to review Lord's little work on geology in an undated latter, Box 12, Folder 21, Joseph Henry Collection, Record Unit 7001, Smithsonian Institution Archives.

be settled in the future by "duly authenticated" facts. Though open to using the latest astronomical and geological data in deciphering the meaning of the first chapter of Genesis, he drew the line at naturalistic explanations of the origin of present-day plants and animals. The introduction of life, he believed, necessitated the acceptance of "the Scriptural doctrine of an immediate creation ex nihilo by the power of God."[26]

When Hodge drafted his *Systematic Theology* in the early 1870s, he gave his imprimatur to Guyot's (and Dana's) hermeneutic scheme, which viewed the "days" of Genesis 1 as cosmic ages and fully incorporated both the nebular hypothesis and the findings of historical geology. "The best views we have met with on the harmony between science and the Bible," he quoted Dana as saying, "are those of Professor Arnold Guyot, a philosopher of enlarged comprehension of nature and a truly Christian spirit." Since the mid-1850s Hodge had come to know and trust Guyot as both a first-rank naturalist and a discerning Christian. "Friends of the Bible," wrote Hodge, owed the Princeton professor and his Yale publicist Dana "a debt of gratitude for the able vindication of the sacred record." Several years later, when Princeton was looking for someone to take over Guyot's duties in geology, Hodge eagerly sought the services of Dawson of Montreal, one of Guyot's leading exegetical disciples.[27]

The Unity of Races

The relative ease with which Hodge succeeded in dismissing phrenology, Mesmerism, and materialistic physiology as pseudo-sciences and in bringing once-suspect theories in astronomy and geology into harmony with the Bible gave him confidence that the same methods would work in the future. True, astronomy had once given cause for concern, but "no man now pretends that there is a word in the Bible, from Genesis to Revelation, inconsistent with the highest results of astronomy." Indeed, the agreement between the cosmogonies of Laplace and Moses was so great that men of science were now bowing "with wonder before the prescience of Moses." Geology,

26. Hodge, *Systematic Theology,* vol. 1, pp. 224-25, 550, 552, 556-58.

27. Hodge, *Systematic Theology,* vol. 1, p. 573. Much of this section on "The Mosaic Account of the Creation," though not the comments about Guyot and Dana, comes from a MS titled "Creation," ca. December 1846, Item 22, Box 1, Charles Hodge MS Collection, Princeton Theological Seminary Library. On Hodge and Dawson, see Charles F. O'Brien, *Sir William Dawson: A Life in Science and Religion* (Philadelphia: American Philosophical Society, 1971), pp. 19-22.

too, had raised some alarms, "but any one who has attended to the progress of this new science, must be blind indeed not to see that geology will soon be found side by side with astronomy in obsequiously bearing up the queenly train of God's majestic word." If scientific men could prove the antiquity of the Earth, "the Bible will be found not only to agree with it, but to have anticipated it." Despite such optimism in the late 1850s, Hodge fretted that one science, anthropology, would not so easily be brought into harmony with the clear teachings of the Bible. Indeed, as one of his book reviewers predicted, "the last of the long series of battles against the inspiration of the scriptures, pitched upon the ground of the natural sciences," would probably be fought on the field of anthropology.[28]

For decades Americans had been speculating about the origin of the various human races. Some attributed racial differences to supernatural intervention, such as God's curse on Noah's son Ham, which had allegedly produced the Negro race. Others, such as Princeton College President Samuel Stanhope Smith, suspected that natural factors, such as climate, had played a crucial role. In the late 1830s, in a book called *Crania Americana,* the Philadelphia naturalist-physician Samuel George Morton had drawn on his comparative study of human skulls to offer still another explanation: that God had created each racial group separately and, therefore, that all human beings had not descended from Adam and Eve. Morton soon enlisted two vocal supporters, George R. Gliddon, the United States consul at Cairo, who collected Egyptian skulls for him, and Josiah Clark Nott, a physician from Mobile, Alabama, both of whom possessed a zeal to free anthropology, like astronomy and geology before it, from the shackles of Scripture. Together in 1854 they brought out a 738-page treatise, *Types of Mankind,* dedicated to the late Dr. Morton and devoted to the propagation of the polygenetic origin of humans. Included in the volume was a contribution from Louis Agassiz, the leading naturalist in America, who had embraced polygenetic theory a few years after emigrating from Switzerland in the mid-1840s.[29]

28. [Charles Hodge], "The Inspiration of the Holy Scripture: Its Nature and Proof," *BRPR* 29 (1857): 660-98, quotation on p. 683; review of *The Races of Men,* by Robert Knox, *BRPR* 23 (1851): 168-71, quotation on p. 171. I am indebted to Jon Roberts for bringing the former article to my attention.

29. J. C. Nott and George R. Gliddon, *Types of Mankind* (Philadelphia: Lippincott, Grambo, 1854). For historical accounts of the American school of anthropology, see William Stanton, *The Leopard's Spots: Scientific Attitudes toward Race in America, 1815-59* (Chicago: University of Chicago Press, 1960); and Lester G. Stephens, *Science, Race, and Religion in the Nineteenth-Century American South: John Bachman and the Charleston Circle of Naturalists* (Chapel

Gliddon and Nott might easily be dismissed as "heretics" and "charlatans," but the same could hardly be said of Agassiz or even Morton, whose very presence in the polygenesist camp made it difficult to dismiss their anthropology as pseudo-science. Hodge clearly felt uncomfortable criticizing Agassiz, who, he said, belonged to "a different class" from that of his collaborators and who had simply lent his name to the polygenesist project "as a jewel to be worn as on a stage and for a night." Hodge hoped that readers would not accuse him "of the presumption of even sitting at the feet of Agassiz as a naturalist." His quarrel was with "the logic and metaphysics of [Agassiz's] speculations," not with his scientific facts. Hodge did however, find fault with Morton's sloppy techniques for determining the skull sizes of the different racial groups, such as ignoring the substantial differences in size between the skulls of men and women.[30]

In explaining the distinctive characteristics of the human races, Hodge followed his former teacher, Stanhope Smith, in attributing them to "the differences of climate, diet, and mode of life, and to the effect of propagation in case of acquired peculiarities." However, he insisted that natural causes alone had not produced the defining characteristics of race, because those causes had been "intelligently guided by God for the accomplishment of some wise purpose." By secondary means God had fashioned "the different races of men in their peculiarities to suit them to the regions which they inhabit." In response to the ethnologists' argument that distinctive racial features could be seen in primitive art dating to thousands of years before Christ, and that there was too little time between the creation and the appearance of these features for them to have developed naturally, Hodge cited the work of his seminary colleague William Henry Green, whose study of biblical chronology had led him in the early 1860s to argue for extending the post-Edenic time scale beyond 6,000 years.[31]

Hodge's refusal to compromise with the anthropologists, even in the face of Agassiz's formidable authority, resulted from his conviction that

---

Hill: University of North Carolina Press, 1999). On Smith's views, see Mark A. Noll, *Princeton and the Republic, 1768-1822: The Search for a Christian Enlightenment in the Era of Samuel Stanhope Smith* (Princeton, NJ: Princeton University Press, 1989), pp. 115-24.

30. [Charles Hodge], "The Unity of Mankind," *BRPR* 31 (1859): 103-49, quotations on pp. 112, 144; [Charles Hodge], "Examination of Some Reasonings against the Unity of Mankind," *BRPR* 34 (1862): 435-64, quotation on p. 446. Hodge recycled some of the material from "The Unity of Mankind" in his *Systematic Theology*, vol. 2, pp. 77-80. Stephen Jay Gould has criticized Morton for the same methodological shortcomings; see Gould, *The Mismeasure of Man* (New York: W. W. Norton, 1981), chapter 2.

31. Hodge, *Systematic Theology*, vol. 2, pp. 39-40, 86.

the pluralist doctrine threatened the foundations of both Christianity and the social order, the latter by providing a scientific justification for slavery. Unlike questions about the antiquity of the Earth and the structure of the solar system, he argued, the anthropologists' speculations about the origins of the human races contradicted "the explicit declarations of the Bible, as it subverts the great doctrines of the common apostasy and redemption of the race, and is opposed to the universal faith of the church." The developments in astronomy and geology had been assimilated "on the ground that the scriptures were not given to man for the purpose of teaching science," explained a contributor to the *Princeton Review*. But the same reasoning could not be applied to anthropology, because "the very object of the Bible was to clear up the history of the fall of man, to explain the condition in which he is found, and to reveal a plan for his recovery." Another essayist echoed these sentiments. "Whether the sun moves around the earth, or the earth round the sun; how many continents and what mountain ranges were above the surface of the ocean in Noah's day; are questions which seem to lie beyond the scope of those for the solution of which the aid of the spirit of God is promised to believers," he declared. "But questions which include the spiritual relations of the races of men to Adam or Christ, or which involve the connection between the sin of man and death, are of a very different nature."[32]

Complicating the issue for Hodge was his well-founded suspicion that some of the anthropologists were simply using their theory to undermine biblical authority. "It is indeed principally for the sake of disproving the Scriptural statement that all men are the children of Adam, and to break up the common brotherhood of man," he claimed, "that diversity of species is insisted upon." Hodge also resented the anthropologists' claim of exclusive rights to interpret early human history while warning "the theologian off of this ground as a trespasser." The "recklessness" displayed by some men of science in discussing the unity of mankind he found "not only lamentable but revolting." However, Hodge's "grand objection" to the hypothesis of multiple human races always remained its opposition "to the authority of the Bible, and to the facts of our mental, moral, and spiritual nature."[33]

32. [Hodge], "The Unity of Mankind," p. 107; [Matthew Boyd Hope], "Professor Bachman on the Unity of the Human Races," BRPR 22 (1850): 313-20, quotation on p. 315; "The Logical Relations of Religion and Natural Science," *BRPR* 32 (1860): 577-608, quotation on p. 605.

33. Hodge, *Systematic Theology*, vol. 2, p. 91; [Hodge], "Unity of Mankind," pp. 104-105, 148. For similar complaints about the arrogance of naturalists in this debate, see [Hope], "Professor Bachman on the Unity of the Human Races," p. 316.

Development

Even the despised anthropologists did not "advocate the same origin . . . for man and the monkey," Hodge noted in 1862. "This belongs to the opposite pole of sceptical speculation in natural history; of which the latest form appears in a remarkable book, from a very high authority," the English naturalist Charles Darwin. Since the appearance of the anonymous *Vestiges of the Natural History of Creation* in 1844, which chronicled the history of the world from nebula to humans by way of apes, Hodge and the *Princeton Review* had carefully monitored so-called theories of development (or what came to be called evolution). Fortunately for them, most men of science repudiated the thesis of *Vestiges* and continued to insist on the permanence of species. Even the Irish physicist John Tyndall, whom Hodge described as "one of the highest authorities in the scientific world," was reputed to have said that "if matter be what all the world believes it to be, materialism, spontaneous generation, and evolution, or development, are absurdities 'too monstrous to be entertained by a sane mind.'" But then in 1859 came Darwin's *Origin of Species,* aimed specifically at overthrowing "the dogma of separate creations" and establishing the theory of natural selection in its place.[34]

In his first extended discussion of the *Origin of Species* (and the subsequent *Descent of Man*) Hodge in his *Systematic Theology* credited Darwin with standing "in the first rank of naturalists . . . respected not only for his knowledge and his skill in observation and description, but for his frankness and fairness." Hodge also granted that Darwin himself was not an atheist and that it was possible to be a theistic evolutionist. Nevertheless, in opposition to the Harvard botanist Asa Gray, he insisted that Darwin's theory was essentially atheistic, because it removed God from the work of creation. It was also antibiblical, because it contradicted the statements in Genesis that "man was created in the image of God" and that "each species was specially created" — and unscientific, because instead of

---

34. [Charles Hodge], "Examination of some Reasonings against the Unity of Mankind," *BRPR* 34 (1862): 435-64, quotation on p. 461; Hodge, *Systematic Theology,* vol. 2, p. 10. For a sampling of opinion on the development hypothesis in the *Princeton Review* before 1859, see [Albert Baldwin Dod], review of *Vestiges of the Natural History of Creation, BRPR* 17 (1845): 505-57; review of *The Course of Creation,* by John Anderson, *BRPR* 24 (1852): 146-51, especially pp. 149-50; "Lectures at the University of Virginia," *BRPR* 24 (1852): 250-94, especially pp. 280-81. On Darwin's goals, see, for example, Ronald L. Numbers, *Darwinism Comes to America* (Cambridge: Harvard University Press, 1998).

dealing with the facts and laws of nature in Baconian fashion, it offered only unverifiable probabilities.[35]

Gray, a fellow Presbyterian who had been working on Darwin's behalf in America by giving his theory a theistic gloss, faulted Hodge for examining only the atheistic version of Darwinism and for pronouncing Darwin's "whole system 'thoroughly atheistic.'" Appealing to the previous experience with physics and geology, Gray argued that theologians had already conceded what evolutionists demanded, namely, "that there is a system of Nature with fixed laws." Hodge's complaint that Darwin was trying to account for developments that could only be known by revelation represented, in Gray's opinion, a fundamental misunderstanding of Darwin's goal. "For the very object of the evolutionists, and of Mr. Darwin in particular, is to remove these subjects from the category of origination, and to bring them under the domain of science by treating them as questions about how things go on, not how they began."[36]

On October 6, 1873, while attending the Sixth General Conference of the Evangelical Alliance being held in New York City, Hodge attended a session in which the president of Princeton College, James McCosh, presented a paper on "Religious Aspects of the Doctrine of Development." In the ensuing discussion Hodge pushed the participants to answer "the great question which divides theists from atheists — Christians from unbelievers . . . : Is development an intellectual process guided by God, or is it a blind process of unintelligible, unconscious force, which knows no end and adopts not means?" His own view, he explained, was that Darwinism teaches that "all the forms of vegetable and animal life, including man and all the organs of the human body, are the result of unintelligent, undesignating forces; and that the human eye was formed by mere unconscious action." If so, Darwinism clearly opposed both Scripture and reason.[37]

Hodge returned to Princeton the next day and almost immediately be-

---

35. Hodge, *Systematic Theology*, vol. 2, pp. 12, 16, 18-19, 26-27.

36. Asa Gray, "Evolution and Theology," *The Nation*, January 15, 1874, pp. 44-46, reprinted in Asa Gray, *Darwiniana: Essays and Reviews Pertaining to Darwinism* (New York: Appleton, 1876). For additional negative commentary on Hodge's discussion of development in his *Systematic Theology*, see "Lyell's Principles of Geology," *Bibliotheca Sacra* 31 (1874): 785-90. On Gray, see A. Hunter Dupree, *Asa Gray, 1810-1888* (Cambridge: Harvard University Press, 1959).

37. "Discussion on Darwinism and the Doctrine of Development," in *History, Essays, Orations, and Other Documents of the Sixth General Conference of the Evangelical Alliance, Held in New York, October 2-12, 1873*, ed. Philip Schaff and S. Irenaeus Prime (New York: Harper & Brothers, 1974), pp. 318, 320.

gan writing down his thoughts about the development hypothesis, which he published the next year under the title *What Is Darwinism?* In it he expanded on the themes he had raised at the meeting of the Evangelical Alliance. Once again he praised Darwin as "a careful and laborious observer; skillful in his descriptions, and singularly candid in dealing with the difficulties in the way of his peculiar doctrine." He correctly identified "the heart of Mr. Darwin's theory" as his exclusive reliance on "natural laws" to explain the development of life on Earth, from a primordial germ to humans. And he argued that Darwin, by denying "design in any of the organisms in the vegetable or animal world," including the eye, had brought his system "into conflict not only with Christianity, but with the fundamental principles of natural religion." Although Hodge had never attached great apologetical weight to natural theology, and denied that "the knowledge of God derived from his works [was] sufficient to lead fallen men to salvation," he strongly condemned Darwin's rejection of teleology. More important, Hodge failed to "see how the theory of evolution [could] be reconciled with the declarations of the Scriptures." In his opinion, "the grand and fatal objection to Darwinism" was its antibiblical denial of God's role in "the production of living organisms." Hodge concluded his tract with one of the most memorable phrases to come out of the nineteenth-century debates over evolution: "What is Darwinism? It is Atheism."[38]

This blunt verdict did not represent an obscurantist distortion of Darwin's views. It more accurately reflected the British naturalist's own feelings than did the sugarcoated versions of his theory presented by Christian evolutionists such as Gray. The religious press in America overwhelmingly applauded Hodge's effort. As one Methodist author aptly noted, the Princeton theologian's "spirit is courteous, his statements accurate, his logic conclusive." The most negative assessment came from Gray, who worried that Hodge's little book would "not contribute much to the reconcilement of science and religion" — and that it would undermine his own efforts to convince the reading public of the compatibility between Darwinism and theism. Even Gray, who privately complained to Darwin of

38. Hodge, *What Is Darwinism?* pp. 26, 40-41, 52, 141, 168, 177. For Hodge's assessment of natural theology, see his *Systematic Theology*, vol. 1, p. 25. See also Jonathan Wells, *Charles Hodge's Critique of Darwinism: An Historical-Critical Analysis of Concepts Basic to the 19th Century Debate* (Lewiston, ME: Edwin Mellen Press, 1988). On the writing of *What Is Darwinism?* see Noll and Livingstone, Introduction, p. 28. For a contrasting view, which highlights Hodge's philosophical as opposed to biblical concerns, see David N. Livingstone, *Darwin's Forgotten Defenders: The Encounter between Evangelical Theology and Evolutionary Thought* (Grand Rapids: Eerdmans, 1987), pp. 102-3.

the "uphill work I have in making a theist of you," grudgingly conceded the accuracy of Hodge's description of Darwinism. That was sufficient to satisfy the aging Hodge. "Gray admits that I have stated Darwin's position fairly," he told his grandson. "I don't care about the rest."[39]

Hodge's uncompromising opposition to Darwin's theory stands in stark contrast to his openness toward Laplace's nebular hypothesis. Both ideas originated with men notorious for their disavowal of Christianity; both promoted creation by natural law; both contradicted what had long been regarded as clear teachings of Scripture; and both, as countless Christian apologists had shown, could be harmonized with natural and revealed religion. Why, then, did Hodge go out of his way to portray Darwin's theory, but not Laplace's, as atheistic? In contrasting the nebular hypothesis and Darwinism, Hodge stressed Darwin's denial of all design. But Laplace, too, had denied design. The difference, I think, can be traced to the implications of Darwinism for the place of humans in nature. Early in *What Is Darwinism?* Hodge quoted Thomas Huxley as saying "The question of questions for mankind — the problem which underlies all others, and is more interesting than any other — is the ascertainment of the place which Man occupies in nature and of his relation to the universe of things." Hodge could not have agreed more. As he pointed out, the "grand conclusion" of Darwinism, found in *The Descent of Man,* was that "man (body, soul, and spirit) is descended from a hairy quadruped, furnished with a tail and pointed ears, probably arboreal in its habits, and an inhabitant of the Old World." Though the quotation was Darwin's, the parenthetical commentary was Hodge's, added to heighten the contrast between Darwin's views and those of the Bible.[40]

Timing also proved important. Hodge had labored for years to grant science its due, even when it meant abandoning cherished readings of the Bible. He had defended science and scientific men. As a theologian, he had adopted the methods of science. However, as he observed in *What Is*

---

39. "Philosophy, Metaphysics, and General Science," *Methodist Quarterly Review* 64 (1882): 586-92, quotation on p. 592; [Asa Gray], "What Is Darwinism?" *The Nation,* May 28, 1874, pp. 348-51; reprinted in Gray, *Darwiniana;* Asa Gray to Charles Darwin, June 16, 1874, quoted in Noll and Livingstone, Introduction, p. 33; William Berryman Scott, *Some Memories of a Paleontologist* (Princeton: Princeton University Press, 1939), p. 49. Positive reviews of *What Is Darwinism?* appeared in the following journals: *Catholic World* 19 (1874): 429-30; *American Church Review* 26 (1874): 316-19; *Unitarian Review and Religious Magazine* 3 (1875): 237-50; *Methodist Quarterly Review* 41 (1874): 514-16; *Presbyterian Quarterly and Princeton Review,* new ser., 3 (1874): 558-59; *Baptist Quarterly* 8 (1874): 374-75.

40. Hodge, *What Is Darwinism?* pp. 2, 39-40.

Darwinism? the rules of engagement had changed. Interpreters of the Bible and interpreters of nature no longer relied on a common inductive method; they now employed "different rules of evidence" that inevitably led to "different conclusions." To Hodge's way of thinking, the "main root of the trouble" between science and religion could be traced to this epistemological shift:

> If science be the knowledge of the facts perceived by the senses, and scientific evidence, evidence addressed to the senses, then the senses are the only sources of knowledge. Any conviction resting on any other ground than the testimony of the senses, must be faith. . . . Now as religion does not rest on the testimony of the senses, that is on scientific evidence, the tendency of scientific men is to ignore its claims.

The very word *science* was "becoming more and more restricted to the knowledge of a particular class of facts, and of their relations, namely, the facts of nature or of the external world." Theology thus lost its scientific status, and its practitioners, such as Hodge, found themselves increasingly regarded as objects of suspicion. To make matters worse, Hodge noted bitterly, scientific men tended to denigrate metaphysicians and theologians. In such strained circumstances, Hodge felt disinclined to continue granting men of science the benefit of the doubt in their encounters with religion. Though he desired peace, he feared it would prove elusive. Religion, he sadly concluded, was in a "fight for its life against a large class of scientific men."[41]

41. Hodge, *What Is Darwinism?* pp. 126-28, 134-35, 140-42.

Hodge, the Seminary, and the American Theological Context

E. BROOKS HOLIFIELD

Anyone who knows anything about Charles Hodge knows that in 1872, after fifty years of teaching, he announced that no new idea had originated at Princeton Seminary. To later generations the announcement seemed naive, and it is palpably unjust to dredge it up one more time, but if we move slightly beneath the surface we can see it displays Hodge's self-understanding as an American theologian anchored in the ethos of a nineteenth-century seminary. What was revealing in the statement was its depiction of a seminary as a school of thought, a unity, a corporate mind. This underlying assumption is more interesting than the surface meaning, and it suggests something about Hodge's location within the broader context of nineteenth-century American theology.

When Hodge went to Princeton Seminary, first as a student in 1819 and then as a tutor in 1822, he was entering a new American institution. Despite varied foreshadowings, the country had no theological seminary in the modern sense until 1791, when Catholics opened St. Mary's in Baltimore. Protestants looked to Andover, founded in 1808, as their first enduring institution with a multiple faculty devoted solely to teaching ministerial students. Princeton Seminary in 1822 was only a decade old; the seminary as an institution in America was only slightly older.

It turned out to be a potent agency for the churches and a formative place for Hodge. The seminary setting fashioned his outlook on theology in America, isolating him from some currents of thought, immersing him in others. It both limited and enhanced his work and influence. He waited until 1871 to begin publishing his three-volume *Systematic Theology*, for example, mainly because the seminary trustees worried that potential students might not choose Princeton if they had access to his lecture material elsewhere. The three volumes still read like seminary lectures, filled not only with doctrines but also with summaries and critiques of other options, historical and contemporary, that seminary students needed to know about. Furthermore, Hodge did his most incisive writing in essays in *The Biblical Repertory and Princeton Review* directed largely at other theologians in other seminaries. He was a full-time professional seminary theologian in a time when that was a new thing for an American to be.[1]

Unlike most earlier parish theologians or self-appointed amateurs, Hodge, as a seminary professional, had the training and resources to address almost any theological question that might arise. The seminary setting encouraged versatility; he had to know something about biblical exegesis, moral philosophy, and the history of doctrine as well as systematics, and his office required a vigilant watch over the American theological terrain. There he found four great principles competing for allegiance in the American churches: he labeled them the evangelical, the mystical, the churchly, and the rationalist. They comprised the greater part of the theological questions of Hodge's era, and he engaged them all.

I. The Seminary Culture

By 1822 theology in America was subject to the two competing trends of professionalization and democratization. The two could overlap, at least rhetorically, but for the most part the professionals and democrats looked askance at one another. The Shakers Benjamin Youngs and Calvin Green spoke for the popular theologians when they wrote in 1808 that the gospel belonged to "common people," not to "learned doctors" with their "subtle and obscure erudition." The friends of Andover spoke for the professionals when they called for highly trained experts who could specialize in hermeneutics and exegesis, natural and revealed theology, ethics, and metaphysics. The two parties disagreed especially about the need for educated theologians.[2]

---

1. Leonard J. Trinterud, "Charles Hodge (1797-1878): Theology — Didactic and Polemical," in *Sons of the Prophets,* ed. Hugh T. Kerr (Princeton: Princeton University Press, 1963), p. 37.

2. Benjamin Youngs and Calvin Green, *Testimony of Christ's Second Appearing,* 4th ed. (1st ed. 1808; Albany: Van Benthuysen, 1856), pp. viii, xiii, 134; A Society of Clergymen, "Thoughts on the State of Theological Science and Education in our Country," *Bibliotheca Sacra* 1 (1844): 741, 757.

Charles Hodge was not entirely averse to democratizing impulses, but he was no theological democrat. Depending on the opponent of the moment, he could insist as much as any religious populist that "the gospel was intended for plain people." He once said that "ordinary Christians" guided by common sense and sanctified feeling were more likely to grasp Christian truths than were learned scholars attracted to philosophical systems. He could write winsomely for a popular audience, as he did in *The Way of Life* (1841), published by the American Sunday School Union. Yet Hodge also believed that "the mass of the people" were "incompetent to judge in doctrinal matters," that democratization had ruined New England Congregationalism, and that when "uneducated, undisciplined men" ventured into deep theology, the "consequences were disastrous."[3]

Hodge taught at a time when the professionals were beginning to assert themselves. Having graduated from both Princeton College (1819) and Princeton Seminary (1822), he stood at a far distance from the ethos of self-trained, self-appointed theologians. Though he was not among the handful with European doctorates in theology, his two years at Halle and Berlin made him part of a tiny elite who had received graduate-level training beyond seminary at European universities. He returned to America in 1828 as one of the nation's best-educated linguists and biblical scholars. *Bibliotheca Sacra* observed in 1844 that America had "but a limited class of theologians in the technical sense of that word," teachers devoting themselves entirely to theological study and taking no part in "the practical duties of the ministry." Hodge loved to preach, but he was one of the few theologians "in the technical sense."[4]

By 1840, the churches had founded at least thirty-seven seminaries, with seven — Andover, Princeton, Union, General, Yale, Auburn, and Oberlin — standing out with high numbers of both faculty and students.

---

3. Charles Hodge, "Finney's Lectures on Theology" (1847), in *Essays and Reviews Selected from the Princeton Review* (New York: Robert Carter, 1857), p. 248; Hodge, "The Latest Form of Infidelity," *The Biblical Repertory and Princeton Review* (hereafter *BRPR*) 12 (1840): 36; Hodge, "Regeneration" (1830), in *Essays and Reviews*, p. 2; Hodge, *The Constitutional History of the Presbyterian Church in the United States of America*, 2 vols., (Philadelphia: William S. Martien, 1839), vol. 2, p. 72; Hodge, "Suggestions to Theological Students," *Biblical Repertory and Theological Review* (hereafter *BRTR*) 5 (1833): 112; Hodge, J. W. Alexander, and Albert Dod, "Transcendentalism of the Germans and Cousin," *BRPR* 11 (1839), in Perry Miller, ed., *The Transcendentalists* (Cambridge: Harvard University Press, 1950), p. 232.

4. Glenn T. Miller, *Piety and Intellect* (Atlanta: Scholars Press, 1990), p. 113; Alexander A. Hodge, *The Life of Charles Hodge* (London: T. Nelson, 1881), p. 99, 115, 143, 153; Clergymen, "Thoughts," p. 736; Hodge, *Princeton Sermons* (1st ed. 1879; London: Banner of Truth Trust, 1958), p. xiv.

The schools created a distinctive culture, a community of shared meanings and values. At its heart was the conviction that theology mattered — the schools were "the houses that theology built." Their critics claimed that they paid homage to "the idol of a learned rather than a spiritual and useful ministry," but Hodge believed that theological learning was a vital part of a "practical faith." He certainly agreed that piety also mattered. He prayed and sang with Princeton's students weekly in chapel, and his papers from the school's Sunday afternoon "conferences" reveal a deep interest in devotional exercises. But he never accepted the notion that piety could dispense with theology; truth and piety, he said repeatedly, were "intimately related." Religious opinions always bore the imprint of religious feelings, and doctrine affected the heart. The joining of theology and piety marked the everyday life of the seminary.[5]

The seminary culture was fragile. Its critics feared it as "an engine of political power" and accused the faculties of being out of touch with the local church. The schools also competed with each other. Hodge worried about Princeton's competitors, and they in turn tried to "break the charm" of the "Princeton ascendancy." He viewed Andover as dedicated to making "Old-School doctrines appear ridiculous and odious" and Yale as an enemy of orthodoxy, and he had his doubts even about some of the other Old School Presbyterian seminaries, whose faculties on occasion moved behind the scenes to embarrass their competitors. Seminaries represented schools of thought — visions of truth — and theological movements often received institutional labels: When Philip Schaff published in 1848 an essay on "Princeton and Mercersburg," or a Methodist reviewer in 1886 discussed "Princeton versus Danville," every knowledgeable reader would have known from the titles that they were comparing theologies, not describing institutions.[6]

---

5. Miller, *Piety and Intellect,* p. 3; Elwyn Allen Smith, *The Presbyterian Minister in American Culture* (Philadelphia: Westminster, 1962), p. 183; A. A. Hodge, *Life,* p. 373; Hodge, "Inquiries Respecting the Doctrine of Imputation," *BRTR* 2 (1830): 428; Hodge, "Introductory Lecture Addressed to the Students of the Theological Seminary," *Biblical Repertory* 1 (1829): 90, 94; Hodge, "God in Christ" (1849), *Essays and Reviews,* p. 443; Hodge, "Responsibilities of Boards of Missions" (1849), *Essays and Reviews,* p. 424; Hodge, "Beman on the Atonement," *BRPR* 17 (1845): 85; W. Andrew Hoffecker, *Piety and the Princeton Theologians* (Grand Rapids: Baker, 1981), p. 89; Mark Noll, ed., *The Princeton Theology 1821-1921* (Grand Rapids: Baker, 1983), pp. 33-34.

6. David F. Wells, "Charles Hodge," in *The Princeton Theology,* ed. David F. Wells (Grand Rapids: Baker, 1989), p. 59, n. 1; B. M. Palmer, *The Life and Letters of James Henley Thornwell* (Richmond: Willett and Shepperson, 1875), p. 90; Hodge, "Presbyterian Reunion," *BRPR* 40 (1868): 61; E. Brooks Holifield, *The Gentlemen Theologians* (Durham, N.C.: Duke University

II. Hodge and His Predecessors

As a theological seminary possessed with its own vision of truth, Princeton constructed a normative history of theology in America — one that served the theological aims of its faculty. In Princeton's version, the seventeenth-century New England Puritans dropped largely from view; Hodge knew them mainly through John G. Palfrey's *History of New England* and Cotton Mather's *Magnalia Christi Americana,* and he noticed them either to criticize their views of the church or to praise them for their allegiance to Calvinist ideas about salvation. He invested heavily in the same covenant theology that attracted the New England writers, but he developed its themes by drawing more on his beloved Francis Turretine in Geneva than on any American predecessors.[7]

He had a far deeper knowledge of eighteenth-century Reformed thought in America, and his *Constitutional History of the Presbyterian Church in America* (1839), published to support the position of the Old School party in the denomination against its New School opponents, tried to show that in the eighteenth century both the revivalist New Side Presbyterians and the confessionalist Old Siders had shared a common allegiance to Presbyterian polity and the Westminster Confession. On the disputed points, his sympathies lay with the Old Side theologians: he agreed with them that the Spirit did not always prepare the unregenerate for regeneration by convicting them dramatically of their sin; that assurance of salvation did not belong to the essence of faith; and that the faithful had no direct Witness of the Spirit making them indubitably aware of their salvation and able to recognize each other. He thought that the revivalists had put excessive stress on overheated feelings. But the important point for him was that both sides accepted the form of orthodoxy defended by Princeton.[8]

When he turned his attention to eighteenth-century New England, he discovered cause for worry — "repeated and extended defections" from Calvinist doctrine, which helped explain why the 1801 Plan of Union between Congregationalists and Presbyterians had weakened doctrinal in-

---

Press, 1978), p. 204; Philip Schaff, "Princeton and Mercersburg," *The Weekly Messenger of the German Reformed Church* 13 (July 7, 1848): 2650; Anon., "Danville Versus Princeton," *The Southern Methodist Review* 1 (1886): 145.

7. Hodge, *Constitutional History,* vol. 1, p. 73; Hodge, *Systematic Theology,* 3 vols. (New York: Scribner, Armstrong, 1871-73), vol. 2, pp. 354-77; vol. 3, pp. 545-48.

8. Hodge, *Constitutional History,* vol. 1, pp. 170, 190, 205; vol. 2, p. 79; Hodge, *Systematic Theology,* vol. 2, p. 106; vol. 3, pp. 32, 69, 107.

tegrity. The New Englanders were a problem for him and for Princeton, and no one was more problematic than Jonathan Edwards. Hodge claimed the true Edwardsean legacy, insisting that Edwards had refuted all "the main principles" that Princeton's opponents were now espousing. But Edwards was an unreliable ally.[9]

Reading Edwards through Princetonian lenses, Hodge liked much of what he saw. He shared Edwards's sense of divine sovereignty and human depravity and his conviction that the telos of creation was the divine glory. Edwards had taught, in a way that Hodge found satisfying, that dispositions of the soul preceded voluntary actions, and so he had been able to say, again happily for Hodge, both that a depraved human nature underlay evil volitions and that regeneration implanted a new principle that preceded holy exercises. He had shown that freedom — and moral responsibility — did not require a self-determining will, and he had overcome the argument that sinners were responsible for their sin only if they had the power to resist it. Furthermore, Edwards had sometimes spoken well of the doctrine that God imputed the guilt of Adam to all humanity and the righteousness of Christ to the elect. These, for Hodge, were no small truths.[10]

More often, though, Edwards had gotten it wrong. Hodge disliked Edwards's metaphysical idealism, and he felt wary of the assertion — characteristic of Edwards — that religion consisted in holy affections. He thought that Edwards's doctrine of continual creation blurred the distinction between creation and preservation; that his metaphysical doctrine of God veered toward pantheism; and that his distinction between the sinner's natural ability but moral inability to repent subverted the truth that the unregenerate had no ability whatever to change their hearts. Hodge disliked Edwards's definition of true virtue as disinterested benevolence, and he thought that the treatise on the *Freedom of the Will* both failed to make elementary distinctions — between willing and desiring, for example — and too loosely threw around terms like "necessity." Even on imputation, Edwards had, in one disastrous section of his book on *Original Sin*, speculated that God imputed Adam's guilt to humanity only because everyone, united

9. Hodge, *Constitutional History*, vol. 2, p. 71, n. 2, 72, 123; Hodge, "Professor Park and the Princeton Review," *BRPR* 23 (1851): 694; Hodge, "Narrative of the Visit to the American Churches," *BRPR* 7 (1835): 619; Hodge, "Clap's Defence of the Doctrines of the New England Churches," *BRPR* 11 (1839): 399.

10. Hodge, "Professor Park and the Princeton Review," pp. 685, 694; Hodge, "Regeneration," p. 18; Hodge, "Inquiries Respecting Imputation," p. 454; Hodge, *Systematic Theology*, vol. 2, p. 198; vol. 3, p. 116.

with Adam by a divine constitution, had shared in the committing of the primal sin. In Hodge's mind, this was no small error.[11]

He had even greater misgivings about the disciples of Edwards — the Edwardsean or New Divinity theologians like Joseph Bellamy, Samuel Hopkins, and Nathaniel Emmons. Impressed by Edwards's notion that piety and true virtue required a selfless love for the divine beauty, the Edwardseans had tried to deprive sinners of every excuse for their selfishness. Hodge approved the goal but not the theology that promoted it. He disagreed with a host of Hopkinsian theses: that the sinful shared in Adam's sin only by consent to it (and implicitly that all sin therefore consisted in sinning); that God imputed guilt to sinners only because they had thus sinned; that depravity resided in the will but not the understanding; that all sin was selfishness; and that the unregenerate would not profit by means of grace like sermons and prayers because they would use them only with selfish ends in mind. He did not share Hopkins's belief that in the order of salvation, repentance came before faith, or a love for God before justification, and he deplored the Hopkinsian claim that true piety required a love for God and neighbor so selfless that the Christian would be willing to be damned for God's glory. He thought it wrong to say that such disinterested benevolence was the only moral good, in any case. He also disagreed with the Hopkinsian view that Christ died for everyone and with the doctrine of some Hopkinsians that the atonement merely made it possible for God to forgive sinners without abandoning principles of moral government that required punishment for sin. Finally, Hodge could never accept Hopkins's explanation that God permitted sin as a necessary means of the greatest good.[12]

He found a few redeeming qualities in the Edwardsean tradition, but for the most part he saw it as a series of mistakes. Hopkins had at least been willing to speak (unlike Emmons) of a principle — a "taste" — that underlay sinful choices, and the distinction that Hopkins popularized between regeneration as a divine act imperceptible to the sinner and conversion as the sinner's consequent turn toward the divine beauty proved useful in Hodge's own theology. But Hodge often used the theology of Emmons, who carried Edwardsean ideas to the limits, as an example of speculation run wild. Hodge's comfort was that he saw the New Divinity

11. Hodge, *Systematic Theology,* vol. 2, pp. 192, 207, 220, 225-26, 285, 289, 303, 319; Hodge, "Free Agency," *BRPR* 29 (1857): 118; Hodge, "Clap's Defence," pp. 394-95; Hodge, "Inquiries Respecting Imputation," pp. 436, 451, 454.

12. Hodge, "Barnes on the Epistle to the Romans," *BRTR* 7 (1835): 289.

as a spent force: "Where are the Hopkinsians and Emmonites of former days?" he asked in 1835. Their doctrines, he answered, are "fast sinking." And happily the third generation of Edwardseans, like Leonard Woods at Andover, had by 1835 been long united with Old Calvinists of New England against the errors of Yale, and it was in Princeton's interest to minimize the Hopkinsian danger. Nonetheless, as late as 1873 the Edwardsean Enoch Pond at Bangor Seminary still complained about Hodge's misrepresentations.[13]

Hodge stood, as he repeatedly said, for "Old Calvinism." He had in mind chiefly the Calvinism of the late sixteenth- and seventeenth-century confessions, but on occasion he linked Princeton's Calvinism with the Old Calvinist party in eighteenth-century New England — Moses Hemmenway, James Dana, Jedediah Mills, and others — even though he seems never to have seriously read them. He and they shared a common distaste for the Edwardsean innovations, but Hodge never accepted their favorable estimation of self-love as an innocent "natural principle" that drew the sinner, desiring happiness and dreading misery, to take religion seriously. Hodge agreed with Edwards that religion prompted by self-love was nothing more than refined selfishness: "If the [sinner's] motive which prompts the choice have reference to himself," Hodge wrote, "then the only obligation which he fulfills, is to himself."[14]

He could draw on Edwards, he could even borrow an idea from Hopkins, and he could recognize his affinities with the Old Calvinists of eighteenth-century New England, but finally Hodge belonged in a different American tradition. Even though he regretted some of the Old Side actions in the Presbyterian Old Side–New Side schism between 1741 and 1758, he stood in closer proximity to the Old Side party and their spiritual heirs in the Presbyterian church than to anyone else among his American predecessors. They had throughout the eighteenth century resisted the introduction of Hopkinsian errors into the denomination; they had opposed the excesses of revivalism; and they had battled for the authority of the Reformed confessions. In these battles Hodge could find resonances of his own.[15]

13. Hodge, "Barnes on Romans," p. 289; Enoch Pond, "Dr. Hodge and the New England Theology," *Bibliotheca Sacra* 30 (1873): 371-81.

14. Hodge, "Narrative of the Visit," p. 212; Hodge, "Clap's Defence," p. 383; Moses Hemmenway, *Remarks on Mr. Hopkins's Answer* (Boston: J. Kneeland, 1774), p. 25; Hodge, "Regeneration," p. 32.

15. Hodge, *Constitutional History,* vol. 1, pp. 160, 219, 209.

III. Hodge and His Contemporaries

Hodge mined the eighteenth-century Calvinist traditions, largely ignoring other colonial movements and figures. Yet no one could accuse him of any narrowness of theological interest. In his own era, no one engaged a broader set of issues or took on a more distinguished array of opponents. As a professional theologian, he had interests that extended across the whole spectrum of disciplines and issues, and when he wrote on the four great principles that he saw as being at stake in the nineteenth-century debates — the evangelical, mystical, churchly, and rationalist — he displayed a remarkable breadth of involvement with the larger American theological context.

A. Evangelical

At the center of the evangelical principle for Hodge was the concept of "representation," which he saw pervading "the whole Scriptures" and defining "the dispensations of God from the beginning of the world." The concept had a prominent place in his thinking by 1830, and by the time he published his *Systematic Theology* he described it as one of the pillars of the covenant theology. It meant simply that one person — whether Adam or Christ — could properly represent others in a legal relationship. His defense of the idea drew him into a multi-sided debate over sin and depravity, freedom, regeneration, atonement, and theodicy.[16]

In the background of the debate over sin and depravity stood the liberal objection to the idea of original sin, epitomized for Hodge's generation in William Ellery Channing's 1819 sermon on "Unitarian Christianity." Channing's denial that a moral God would bring his creatures into the world depraved and accountable for it led to interminable polemics between the Harvard Unitarians and the Calvinists at Andover and Yale, with Leonard Woods at Andover declaring that both depravity and divine morality were scriptural "facts," even if they could not be reconciled, while Nathaniel William Taylor at Yale, disappointed at Woods's weak rebuttal, contended that Calvinism had no doctrine of original sin that fit Unitarian caricatures. Taking his cue from Edwardseans who said that sin was sinning, not a quality of human nature antecedent to volition, Taylor con-

---

16. Hodge, *Systematic Theology,* vol. 2, pp. 198, 354; Hodge, "Inquiries Respecting Imputation," p. 437.

cluded that moral depravity meant no more than "the free choice of some object rather than God, as [one's] chief good." To say that depravity was "by nature" meant only that human beings would sin and only sin in every relevant circumstance unless God interposed saving grace.[17]

Taylor developed his ideas by combining themes from both Old Calvinist and Edwardsean traditions, supplemented by ideas derived from Joseph Butler in England. His theology of "moral government" taught that the fallen will retained a free agency, a "power to the contrary" by which it could have always chosen other than what it chose; that sin and holiness both consisted in choices; and that regeneration, though the result of a "supernatural influence of God," was also a choice, an elective preference, that changed the governing purpose or controlling disposition of the mind. Like the earlier Old Calvinists, he discovered in human nature a morally neutral principle of self-love — a desire for happiness — that could serve as a motive for repentance. One corollary of his theology was that even God could not have prevented sin in a moral system populated by free agents. Another was that the aim of life was the "highest happiness of the sentient universe," human and divine. What the gospel offered was "perfect happiness" to the obedient.[18]

In advancing his case, Taylor dismissed the idea of imputation and claimed that for years no reputable theologian in New England had tried to resurrect it. By the 1830s proponents of the doctrine were indeed on the defensive. Unitarians ridiculed it; many Congregationalists rejected it, as did New School Presbyterians. Hodge claimed that Lutherans joined Calvinists in affirming it, but the revivalist Lutheran Samuel Schmucker argued against it, and the confessional Lutheran Charles Porterfield Krauth said that he could not recall "a single passage" in any Lutheran confession alluding to the imputation of the guilt of Adam's sin. Most Wesleyans also said that the imputation of guilt awaited the onset of moral agency. Even Old School Presbyterians disagreed among themselves, some contending for a "mediate imputation," consequent upon a prior native depravity, others sharing Hodge's belief in an "immediate imputation" of Adam's guilt, from which depravity followed.[19]

---

17. Leonard Woods, *Letters to Unitarians* (Andover: Flagg and Gould, 1820), pp. 26-27; Nathaniel William Taylor, "Concio Ad Clerum," in Sydney Ahlstrom, ed., *Theology in America* (Indianpolis: Bobbs-Merrill, 1967), pp. 217, 222.

18. Nathaniel William Taylor, *Lectures on the Moral Government of God,* 2 vols. (New York: Clark, Austin, and Smith, 1859), vol. 2, pp. 21-22, 196, 197, 210; Bruce Kuklick, *Churchmen and Philosophers* (New Haven: Yale University Press, 1985), pp. 94-111.

19. Taylor, "Concio ad Clerum," 235; Benjamin B. Warfield, "Imputation," *The New*

For Hodge immediate imputation was a battle line not to be breached. He first explained why in 1830: Just as Adam's disobedience as a federal representative resulted in the imputation of guilt, so also Christ's obedience resulted in justification. If no imputation — of guilt *and* righteousness — then no redemption. The analogy would reappear in debates over Romans 5:12 with Moses Stuart at Andover; over New School theology with the Philadelphia minister Albert Barnes; over justification with E. A. Park at Andover; and over the sacraments with John Williamson Nevin at Mercersburg. Imputation was the prime example of the concept of representation and the core of the evangelical principle.[20]

Hodge thought that the whole of the seventeenth-century federal theology, to which he ardently subscribed, rested on the idea of representation. To take it seriously meant to reject a host of errors circulating at Yale, Andover, and Harvard. Hodge deplored the New Haven definition of regeneration as a voluntary exercise of the mind; he described it rather as the immediate work of the Spirit, transforming the disposition that lay behind voluntary exercises. He disliked Yale's redefinition of freedom to mean that the will had the power, theoretically, to control the inclinations and create a disposition contrary to the prevailing one — that men and women had not only the freedom to will as they willed or act as they willed but also the "ability or power to obey God." Hodge argued rather that their freedom lay merely in the fact that their volitions proceeded from who they were, though they had not the slightest power to change their disposition — to change who they were — by willing it.[21]

He could not accept, moreover, Yale's governmental theory of atonement, the view that Christ died so that God could pardon the sinful while sustaining the authority of the divine law. Hodge saw the atonement as an act of satisfaction performed by a representative who bore the sins of the elect and accepted the punishment due them. Finally, Hodge disliked

---

Schaff-Herzog Encyclopedia of Religious Knowledge, 12 vols., ed. S. M. Jackson (New York: Funk and Wagnalls, 1909), vol. 5, p. 467; Samuel S. Schmucker, *Elements of Popular Theology* (New York: Leavitt, Lord, 1834), p. 128; Charles P. Krauth, *The Conservative Reformation and Its Theology* (Philadelphia: J. P. Lippincott, 1875), p. 382; Nathan Bangs, *The Errors of Hopkinsianism* (New York: John C. Totten, 1815), p. 93; Wilbur Fisk, *Calvinistic Controversy* (1st ed., 1835; New York: Lane and Scott, 1851), p. 178; James H. Thornwell, "Theology: Its Proper Method and Its Central Principle," *The Collected Writings of James Henley Thornwell,* 3 vols. (Richmond: Presbyterian Committee of Publication, 1871), vol. 1, p. 478.

20. Hodge, "Inquiries Respecting Imputation," pp. 431, 468.

21. Hodge, "Regeneration," p. 35; Hodge, "Remarks on Dr. Cox's Communication," *BRPR* 3 (1831): 518; Taylor, *Lectures,* vol. 2, p. 135; Allen C. Guelzo, *Edwards on the Will* (Middletown, Ct.: Wesleyan University Press, 1989), p. 251; Hodge, "Free Agency," p. 118.

Yale's theodicy — Taylor's suggestion that God could not prevent sin in a genuine moral system populated by free agents. Hodge saw sin and suffering as penal afflictions resulting from Adam's fall as the representative of the race. All of Yale's errors he interpreted as a failure to understand representation.[22]

The living proof of the seriousness of such errors — if more than biblical proof were needed — was the revivalism of Charles Grandison Finney. Hodge first attacked Finney in print in 1835, linking Finney's revivalist techniques to Taylor's "new divinity." The more extended critique came in 1847 when Hodge reviewed Finney's *Lectures on Systematic Theology.* Finney's theology — the Oberlin theology — strayed even more than Taylor's. Like Taylor, he assumed that inability was incompatible with obligation, equated liberty with ability, and taught that benevolence was a disposition to promote and religion a means to attain happiness. But Finney went further, reducing morality to good intention (rather than conformity to the will of God) and proposing that men and women with the right ultimate intention were as "perfectly holy" as it was possible to be. For Hodge none of this had any relation to a piety formed by the conviction that sinners could not save themselves and that the aim of the gospel was a love and obedience to God for the sake of God's "infinite excellence" and not the happiness of moral agents.[23]

Countering powerful tendencies in American theology — tendencies shaped by a sense of freedom, individualism, personal responsibility, and the attainability of happiness — Hodge set himself against the view that happiness was the highest good, the grand end of creation. A proper happiness was good, but it was not the end for which God created the world. When Hodge clashed with Edwards A. Park at Andover in the early 1850s, the two rehearsed the familiar arguments over free agency, the voluntary nature of sin, imputation, and atonement, but by that time Hodge had decided that the theological revisionists sought a "human-centered" rather than a theocentric theology dedicated to the glory of God. The end of the creation, he said, was "not the happiness of the creatures, but the infinitely higher end of divine glory." This end could be pursued only by adhering to the evangelical principle — and that meant adhering in theology to the concept of representation.[24]

22. Hodge, "Beman on the Atonement," pp. 109, 112, 116; Taylor, "Concio ad Clerum," p. 238; Hodge, "Narrative of the Visit," p. 167; Hodge, "Clap's Defence," p. 386.

23. Hodge, "Narrative of the Visit," p. 614; Hodge, "Finney's Lectures," pp. 247, 258, 283.

24. Hodge, "Clap's Defence," p. 386; Hodge, "Regeneration," p. 31; Hodge, "Professor Park's Remarks on the Princeton Review," *BRPR* 23 (1851): 309, 313, 318.

It is hard to know exactly why the concept of representation became so important to Hodge. It clearly served varied purposes in his thought: it seemed to capture the heart of Paul's letter to the Romans; it addressed the problem of theodicy by making a human flaw, not a divine purpose, the explanation for sin and evil; and it guarded against any compromise of the doctrine of justification by grace through faith. But there is another possibility as well. Hodge liked simplicity, clarity, and lucidity; his theology resembled the clean and angular lines of the seminary chapel in which he worshipped at Princeton. There was something clean and sharp in Hodge's parallel between the imputation of a representative's guilt and the imputation of a redeemer's righteousness, and it reflected a style of thinking that was characteristic of him.

B. The Mystical Principle

The stakes were equally high for Hodge in a second round of disputes about "mystical" interpretations of religion, which he defined expansively to include any systems teaching the identity of God and humanity (or God and the world), the possibility of an "immediate intuition of the infinite," or the theory that the feelings, rather than the intellect, were the source of religious knowledge. He associated mysticism with Hegel and Schleiermacher in Germany, Cousin in France, Quakers in England, and Transcendentalists in America, but he also saw mystical tendencies in American seminaries and pulpits, and it was the seminary disputes that led to his most extensive discussions.[25]

The first came in 1839 in an essay he co-authored on "Transcendentalism," directed against German Kantians, French Eclectics, and Ralph Waldo Emerson. The essay gave Princeton's response to Emerson's Divinity School Address at Harvard, which the Princetonians dismissed as "nonsense," especially dangerous because it had gained a hearing in a seminary by "young men about to go forth as preachers of Christianity." Emerson had taught them pantheism, immediate revelation, and trust in "sentiment" rather than intellect. And he had done it not with reasoned arguments but by "endless assertion." The following year Hodge reviewed Andrews Norton's critique of Emerson and found himself agreeing with Harvard Unitarians at least to the extent of defending the historical truth of the New Testament and the necessity for belief in miracles. But the es-

25. Hodge, *Systematic Theology,* vol. 2, p. 61.

say also turned the question back to the Calvinist seminaries: the real danger was "the treason of friends" who used the language of a faithless philosophy in treating of the mysteries of God. Hodge observed in passing that Park at Andover sometimes implied that "our higher nature accords with the Spirit of the Bible" in a way that also located religious truth within the self.[26]

Hodge would return to the Transcendentalists in a mordant review of the French philosopher Victor Cousin, but his more important encounters over the mystical principle came in his critiques of other seminary theologians and of Horace Bushnell's lectures at Yale, Harvard, and Andover. In 1845 he turned his attention to the tiny German Reformed seminary in Mercersburg, Pennsylvania, where Friedrich Rauch, Philip Schaff, and John Nevin had introduced German idealism. For the most part he liked Schaff's controversial inaugural address of 1844 — *The Principle of Protestantism* — but he complained of its Germanic "indefiniteness of language," and he fretted about Nevin, whose subsequent essay on sacramental theology — *The Mystical Presence* (1846) — would alarm him. Nevin had been an Old School ally, but Hodge now saw him as a captive of "the mystical system."[27]

Nevin argued that the divine-human Christ was present in the Lord's Supper in such a manner that believers could unite there with the whole of his "theanthropic life." He linked this sacramental doctrine with a larger claim that the divine-human life manifest in the Incarnation had redeemed humanity in principle and created the church as a living organism through which the faithful were saved by being drawn into union with Christ's continuing life. Hodge thought that the whole idea rested on a psychology permeated by the mystical idea of identity; Nevin had lost the difference between the divine and the human.[28]

For the next twenty-eight years, Hodge kept up the criticisms of Nevin, deeply alienating both Nevin, who resented the implication that he taught pantheism, and Schaff, who once quipped that Princeton would be the "one dry place to flee to at the next deluge." Hodge disavowed any intention to mislead, and Schaff eventually spoke well of him, but Hodge

26. Hodge, et al., "Transcendentalism," pp. 238-39; Hodge, "Latest Form of Infidelity," pp. 31, 37.

27. Hodge, "Schaf's Protestantism," *BRPR* 17 (1845): 627, 629; Hodge, "What Is Christianity?" *BRPR* 32 (1860): 121.

28. J. W. Nevin, *The Mystical Presence* (Philadelphia: J. P. Lippincott, 1846), pp. 146-77; Hodge, "Doctrine of the Reformed Church on the Lord's Supper," in *Essays and Reviews*, p. 374.

continued to complain that Nevin's theology left no place for imputation, atonement, justification by faith, or any real distinction between the human and the divine.[29]

He distrusted, moreover, the way Nevin and Schaff talked about history, especially about historical development in the church. By the 1850s several seminary theologians, including W. G. T. Shedd at Andover and Union and Henry Boynton Smith at Union, were discovering in the idea of historical development both a form of Christian apologetic and a way of understanding doctrine. Hodge was wary. He could concede a growing knowledge of Christianity, but he denied that the essential doctrines had undergone development. For Hodge, conceptions of historical development overemphasized tradition, intimated relativism, and suggested German notions of the self-evolution of the Absolute. He therefore defended a conception of Christianity not as a developing "life" but as a system of truth recorded in Scripture "in a definite and complete form for all ages."[30]

To think of Christianity as a developing "life" seemed to him to coincide with the theory that "feeling" trumped doctrinal truth, and the elevation of feeling suggested a theory of language as metaphorical or poetic. Hodge's criticism of the mystical principle led him into the labyrinths of religious language, and when he read Horace Bushnell's three addresses to the students and faculty of Harvard, Yale, and Andover, published as *God in Christ* in 1849, he concluded that the book's preface on language reduced Christianity to poetic feeling.

He read Bushnell as a "mystic" who made the feelings the subjects of immediate divine impression and rendered the intellect, along with clear doctrine, unimportant. Bushnell believed that all abstract language had roots in sensory experience and therefore bore always a metaphoric, figurative quality. Hodge agreed that conceptual language was usually symbolic and in certain ways inadequate, but he refused to abandon the claim for the rational truth of religious propositions. If there were no doctrinal propositions — cognitive statements conveying to the intellect ideas that

29. George H. Shriver, "Passages in Friendship: John W. Nevin to Charles Hodge, 1872," *Journal of Presbyterian History* 58 (1980): 121; Stephen R. Graham, *Cosmos in the Chaos* (Grand Rapids: Eerdmans, 1995), pp. 94-95; Philip Schaff, *Theological Propaedeutic* (1st ed., 1892; New York: Charles Scribner's Sons, 1894), p. 394; Hodge, "What Is Christianity?" p. 149; Hodge, "History of the Apostolic Church," *BRPR* 26 (1854): 151; Hodge, "Nature of Man," *BRPR* 37 (1865): 128; Hodge, *Systematic Theology*, vol. 2, pp. 201, 202, 210, 446-47; vol. 3, p. 655.

30. Hodge, "History of the Apostolic Church," pp. 159, 166, 171; Walter H. Conser, Jr., *God and the Natural World* (Columbia: University of South Carolina Press, 1993), pp. 37-64.

could be true or false — religious truth claims did no more than express emotion.[31]

The previous year Hodge had given a more favorable verdict about Bushnell's *Christian Nurture*. He approved of its sense of Christian piety as organic, communal, and covenantal, and he liked its emphasis on parental nurture and its wariness of revivalism. But he worried about its implicit rationalism and naturalism, and after the publication of *God in Christ* he adjudged Bushnell an incompetent theologian who had dissolved the atonement into subjective feeling, misunderstood Christology, and defined the Trinity away. When Bushnell tried to restate his views in 1866, Hodge pronounced that effort also a failure. Bushnell's dissertation on language had convinced Hodge that he was "a poet, and neither a philosopher nor theologian."[32]

The question of language surfaced again in the debate with E. A. Park, who in 1850, responding partly to Bushnell, suggested that some religious language, whether in Scripture or in systems of theology, expressed and addressed the feelings and should not be taken literally, but that the theologian could translate such language of feeling into precise and accurate doctrines of the intellect, ironing out its contradictions and rescuing it from offensiveness or exaggeration. It turned out that prominent among the emotive expressions were traditional Calvinist doctrines about inability, imputation, and atonement. Hodge smelled mysticism. He believed that figurative language could be as definite in meaning as any other; that the feelings demanded a truth that satisfied the intellect; and that figures had their own cognitive meanings that could not be explained away or construed as expressions of feeling. He resisted any theological position that seemed to rob theology of its cognitive content.[33]

C. The Church Principle

Philip Schaff wrote in 1846 that "the great central theme of the Present, around which all religious and theological movements resolve, is the

31. Hodge, "History of the Apostolic Church," p. 171; Hodge, "God in Christ," pp. 440, 448.

32. Hodge, "Bushnell on Christian Nurture," in *Essays and Reviews,* pp. 302-9; Hodge, "God in Christ," 436, 453, 471; Hodge, "Bushnell on Vicarious Sacrifice," *BRPR* 38 (1866): 172-84.

33. E. A. Park, "The Theology of the Intellect and that of the Feelings," *Bibliotheca Sacra* 7 (1850): 533-69; Hodge, "The Theology of the Intellect and that of the Feelings" (1850), in *Essays and Reviews,* pp. 538-40, 549.

Church question." The struggle included disputes over polity, clerical office, liturgical ritual, and soteriology, and it preoccupied theologians throughout the century. Nevin spoke of a "silent war" in "almost every denomination" over the nature of the church — "the great question of the age." Hodge therefore could not ignore the question, and he battled along with everyone else. Of his roughly 140 articles in the *Biblical Repertory and Princeton Review,* at least 32 — or almost a fourth — dealt entirely or in part with questions about the church, its order, its ministry, or its sacraments, always in opposition to what he called "the church system" or "high churchism."[34]

Hodge defined the visible church as an organized society professing the true religion, united for worship and discipline, and subject to the same form of government and tribunal. The invisible church consisted of all the elect, wherever they might be. These definitions placed him in opposition not only to high church movements but also to other traditions of Reformed piety. It distinguished him, for example, from the old Puritan idea that the visible church should consist, as far as possible, of the regenerate. Hodge would admit new members — along with their children — whenever they made a credible profession of true religion and promised obedience to Christ. The visible church could not "read the heart" and treat applicants according to their state in the sight of God.[35]

He felt, with some dismay, that the "Puritan view," which he also associated with Edwards and the Edwardseans, had "gained ascendancy" among evangelical Protestants, "even, to a great extent, among Presbyterians." He felt far greater concern, however, about "high church" movements, by which he meant different things, depending on the opponent of the moment.[36]

When he was opposing the American Episcopal proponents of the English Oxford movement, "high church" referred to any theology that defined the Church as the "storehouse and direct channel of grace" or made

34. Philip Schaff, *What Is Church History?* (Philadelphia: Lippincott, 1846), p. 9; J. W. Nevin, "Thoughts on the Church," *Mercersburg Review* 10 (April 1858): 181; Nevin, "Introduction," *The Principle of Protestantism* (Chambersburg, Pa.: Publication Office of the German Reformed Church, 1845), p. 26; Hodge, "Responsibilities of Boards," p. 397; Hodge, "Bishop Doane and the Oxford Tracts," *BRPR* 13 (1841): 456.

35. Hodge, "Is the Church of Rome a Part of the Visible Church?" in *Essays and Reviews,* p. 229; Hodge, *Systematic Theology,* vol. 3, p. 545; Hodge, "The Visibility of the Church," *BRPR* 25 (1853): 682; Hodge, "The Tecnobaptist: The Church Membership of Infants," *BRPR* 30 (1858): 349-50.

36. Hodge, *Systematic Theology,* vol. 3, p. 545.

the sacraments the principal means of saving grace. Hodge condemned the Oxford movement in 1838 and then again in 1841 in a polemic against the "church system" of the New Jersey Episcopal Bishop George Washington Doane, arguing that this form of high church thought substituted the church for Christ and sacramental piety for justification by faith. When he opposed the other American Episcopal high church movement, linked to Bishop John Henry Hobart and General Seminary in New York, the term referred to any theology that made a "particular form," like the apostolic succession of the clergy, essential to the definition of the church. To Hodge, the Hobartians confused the church as the body of Christ, the company of believers, with "an external society" and its practices. He even criticized his evangelical Episcopal friend and ally, Charles Pettit McIlvaine, Bishop of Ohio, president of the seminary at Kenyon College, and foe of both forms of Episcopal high church theology, when McIlvaine contended that bishops perpetuated the authority of the apostles. All three forms of Episcopal teaching were, for Hodge, "too close to Rome."[37]

Even Presbyterians, as Hodge saw it, could fall into a false "high churchism," and he especially bemoaned the fall of the southern Old Schoolers Robert Breckinridge, John Adger, and James Henley Thornwell. His dispute with them began in 1837 when he defended the right of the denomination to create boards to oversee missions. Thornwell took the position that such boards lacked scriptural warrant. By 1860, when Hodge and Thornwell had their great debate at the General Assembly, Hodge had decided that Thornwell was guilty of "superlative high churchism" by virtue of having claimed that Scripture prescribed the details of Presbyterian order, that every form required Scriptural warrant, and that prescribed forms were essentials. Hodge believed that Scripture had laid down the general principles of the Presbyterian order — the parity of the clergy, the right of the people to help govern, and the unity of the church — but the church had wide discretion to alter its forms, for its prerogatives came from the indwelling Spirit, not from a detailed biblical blueprint. Even *de jure* principles could not be considered essential to the being of the church if they were not essential to salvation.[38]

37. Hodge, "Tracts for the Times," *BRPR* 10 (1838): 87, 105; Hodge, "Responsibilities of Boards of Missions," p. 397; Hodge, "Idea of the Church," *BRPR* 25 (1853): 340; Hodge, "The Church of England and Presbyterian Orders," *BRPR* 26 (1854): 380; Hodge, "On the Permanency of the Apostolic Office," *BRPR* 28 (1856): 11.

38. Palmer, *Life and Letters of Thornwell*, p. 222; Hodge, "Voluntary Societies and Ecclesiastical Organizations," *BRPR* 9 (1837): 102; Hodge, "Presbyterianism," *BRPR* 32 (1860): 546, 553, 564.

The archetype of high church doctrine for Hodge was Roman Catholic ecclesiology. He had no direct debates with American Catholic theologians, though he did favorably review Thornwell's arguments against Bishop Patrick Lynch of Charleston on the authority of the church and the Apocrypha. He more often argued with classical authors like Cardinal Robert Bellarmine or with confessions like the canons and decrees of Trent. In his mind, the Catholics had defined the church as essentially an external organization, formed by outward profession and ritual, subject to papacy and priesthood, and claiming to possess exclusive sacramental channels of saving grace. He thought that such doctrines of grace usurped the place of justification by faith; that the elevation of priestly power contradicted biblical principles; that history disproved the church's claim to infallibility; that Catholic devotion to Mary and the saints was idolatry; and that Catholic appeals to tradition denigrated the sole authority of Scripture. For all these reasons, he deemed "Romanism immeasurably more dangerous than infidelity."[39]

Yet he resisted powerful currents of anti-Catholic teaching in his own denomination. When the General Assembly in 1845 denied the validity of Catholic baptism and pronounced Catholics "outside the visible Church of Christ," Hodge opposed the majority. He argued that the Roman communion included professing believers and that it taught enough about God, Christ, and the Spirit to convey saving truth; the papacy was outside the visible church, but many ordinary Catholics were within it. The ultra-Presbyterians — led by Thornwell and Breckinridge — pronounced Hodge's conclusion a disaster and launched another campaign to check the influence of Princeton, but Hodge refused to relent.[40]

Questions about sacraments surfaced not only in his writings on Rome but also in his disputes with the Mercersburg theologians, Episcopalians, Lutherans, and Baptists. Hodge viewed the sacraments in conventional Reformed terms as seals of the covenant of grace. This meant that baptism confirmed a child's status within the parental covenant while the Lord's Supper sealed the covenant by offering believers a means of grace

39. Hodge, "Thornwell on the Apocrypha," *BRPR* 17 (1845): 282; Hodge, "Idea of the Church," p. 277; Hodge, "Visibility of the Church," p. 670; Hodge, "Church of England," p. 380; Hodge, "The Church — Its Perpetuity," *BRPR* 28 (1856): 694; Hodge, "Tracts for the Times," p. 87; Hodge, "Theories of the Church," in *Essays and Reviews*, pp. 211, 213, 219; Hodge, "Rule of Faith," *BRPR* 14 (1842): 611; Hodge, "Schaf's Protestantism," p. 630.

40. Hodge, "Church of Rome," pp. 221, 237; Palmer, *Life and Letters of Thornwell*, p. 290; J. H. Thornwell, "The Validity of the Church of Rome" (1846), in *Collected Works*, ed. B. M. Palmer (Edinburgh: Banner of Truth Trust, 1979), pp. 283-412.

in which the Spirit conveyed the "virtue and efficacy" of Christ's saving work. He opposed the doctrine of baptismal regeneration, the belief in either a corporeal or a "mystical" presence of Christ's body and blood in the Lord's Supper, and the notion that the sacraments conveyed a grace not obtainable elsewhere.[41]

In 1838, therefore, he opposed high church Episcopal doctrines of baptismal regeneration on the grounds of their incompatibility with justification by faith; in 1848 he began the long dispute with Nevin, convinced that Nevin's views distorted the Reformed consensus that grace came through the Spirit, not the sacraments; in 1858 he defended infant baptism while trying to confute the Catholic and Lutheran doctrine that the sacrament admitted infants into the church (rather than recognizing a prior covenantal membership) and conveyed a sacramental rebirth.[42]

Sacramental issues provoked some of Hodge's relatively infrequent criticisms of Lutheran theology. He saw the Lutherans and the Reformed as "the two great branches of the Protestant church," and he maintained friendly relationships with Lutheran traditionalists like Charles Porterfield Krauth at the Lutheran seminary in Philadelphia. Krauth praised the *Systematic Theology*. He also noted Hodge's view that all who died in infancy were probably saved, and he approved his movement away from the "horrors" of a Calvinism that consigned many dying infants to damnation. On sacramental matters, though, Hodge and Krauth continued ancient Lutheran and Reformed disputes, with Krauth holding baptism ordinarily necessary for salvation and Hodge denying it. Hodge had maintained earlier that "no doctrine can be more radically opposed to the spirit and teaching of the New Testament than the doctrine of baptismal regeneration," and the doctrine remained for him a prime symbol of the "ritualism" that he always decried.[43]

As a professional seminary theologian, he had frequent occasion to address other practical matters of ecclesiology: Hodge wrote on discipline in the church; on the office of ministry; on the relationship between church and state; on the church's proper response to slavery and slaveholders; on Thornwell's argument that the church should address only spiritual, not

41. Hodge, "Doctrine of the Reformed Church," pp. 359, 362; Hodge, "Tracts for the Times," pp. 86, 105.
42. Hodge, "Tracts for the Times," p. 87; Hodge, "Doctrine of the Reformed Church," p. 387; Hodge, "Tecnobaptist," pp. 373-79.
43. Hodge, *Systematic Theology*, vol. 3, pp. 245, 604; C. P. Krauth, *Infant Baptism and Infant Salvation in the Calvinistic System* (Philadelphia: Lutheran Book Store, 1874), pp. 10, 13, 73; Hodge, "Tecnobaptist," p. 385.

social, matters (Hodge disagreed); on the church's duty to the poor; and on questions of Presbyterian unity and disunion. Krauth criticized the *Systematic Theology* for its inattention to the church, but no other single topic so consistently engaged Hodge throughout his career.[44]

D. Rationality

The topics for which Hodge is most often remembered by historians — his definition of biblical inspiration and his critical comments on Darwinism — had a relatively minor place within the overall sweep of his writing, but he did see the principle implicit in those topics — the principle of author-ity — as one of the decisive questions of the nineteenth century. He re-turned from his studies in Germany with a worry that rationalism — the assigning of "undue authority to reason in matters of religion" — jeopar-dized the vitality of Christian faith, and he never changed his mind about that. Yet Hodge also thought that whatever was contrary to reason could not be true and that what he sometimes called the "first truths of reason" were of divine authority. He walked a narrow line.[45]

On questions of authority, Hodge subscribed to a consensus some-times designated as "rational orthodoxy" or "supernatural rationalism" or theological "Baconianism." A few isolated thinkers — Nevin, Bushnell, and the Catholic convert Orestes Brownson, for instance — questioned the ra-tional orthodox premises, but almost all of Hodge's allies and his oppo-nents, whatever their denomination, took them for granted. Hodge laid them out in his *Systematic Theology:* Truth was a unity, and the truths of theology had the same logical status as the truths of science or philosophy, except that theology depended on an authoritative revelation. The revela-tion was addressed to reason; it therefore presupposed reason, which had the task of judging the revelation's credibility by assessing evidences.[46]

American theologians, following older European models, commonly

---

44. Hodge, "The Revised Book of Discipline," *BRPR* 30 (1858): 692-98; Hodge, "De-mission of the Ministry," *BRPR* 31 (1859): 361; Hodge, "Are There Too Many Ministers?" *BRPR* 34 (1862): 147; Hodge, "The Church and the Country," *BRPR* 33 (1861): 322; Hodge, "Emancipation" (1849), in *Essays and Reviews,* p. 513; A. A. Hodge, *Life of Charles Hodge,* p. 612.

45. Hodge, *Systematic Theology,* vol. 1, p. 52; vol. 3, p. 83.

46. Holifield, *Gentlemen Theologians,* p. 72; Conrad Wright, *The Liberal Christians* (Boston: Beacon Press, 1970), pp. 10-15; Theodore Dwight Bozeman, *Protestants in an Age of Science* (Chapel Hill: University of North Carolina Press, 1977), pp. 3-31; Hodge, *Systematic Theology,* vol. 1, p. 53.

assumed two kinds of evidences — external and internal. By the external they meant miracles and prophecies, both of which proved the divine authority of a revelation. By internal evidences they referred to the Bible's consistency: its internal consistency and its consistency with other truths, with the highest ethical insights, with the yearnings of the heart, and with religious experience. Hodge used all of these evidences, but as early as 1841 he was emphasizing the internal, especially the consistency of the Bible with "all the facts of consciousness, all the truths which our moral and religious nature involve." The ultimate foundation for confidence in the Bible remained for him the testimony of the Spirit — an emphasis that counterbalanced his employment of the external evidences — but in his appeals to the evidential tradition he proved himself a typical antebellum American theologian.[47]

Rational orthodox theology taught that after reason verified the revelation it had to submit to it. The Bible revealed truths that were above reason (though never in conflict with it), and reason lacked the authority to bring each biblical teaching before its tribunal. Once it demonstrated that the Bible was a divine revelation, it then had to accept biblical doctrines that it could not comprehend.

One of those doctrines was biblical infallibility. Hodge's defense of plenary inspiration and inerrancy has been called "the essential and most fateful feature of the Princetonian legacy." Again, however, in distinguishing between revelation (the communication of knowledge) and inspiration (the ensuring of its infallibility), in arguing that the Bible claimed to be an inspired and inerrant revelation, and in differentiating the errorless autographs of the Bible (no longer recoverable) from the later manuscript copies that departed, in trivial ways, from the original texts, Hodge restated commonplace ideas. His distinction between *autographa* and later manuscript copies may have departed subtly from most of Hodge's seventeenth-century authorities, who were more accustomed to distinguishing between the copies and the *apographa* (the earliest accessible Greek and Hebrew texts), but in antebellum America numerous Protestant theologians from varied denominations affirmed the doctrine — independently of Hodge — in the way that Hodge defined it, and a sizable number still joined in him affirming it in the 1870s.[48]

---

47. Hodge, "The Way of Life" (1841), in *Charles Hodge: The Way of Life*, ed. Mark Noll (New York: Paulist Press, 1987), pp. 56, 59, 64-76; Hodge, *Systematic Theology*, vol. 1, pp. 38-39.

48. Ahlstrom, *Theology in America*, 253; Randall Balmer, "The Princetonians and Scripture: A Reconsideration," *Westminister Theological Journal* 44 (1982): 354-62; Hodge,

The assertion of biblical authority and infallibility imposed a check on reason, but the rationalist side of Hodge's rational orthodoxy reasserted itself in his discussions of biblical interpretation. Because he believed in the unity of truth, he thought that reason and revelation would never conflict. This meant, among other things, that interpretive practices would change in accord with changing scientific knowledge, and Hodge adopted familiar solutions for reconciling texts like the creation narrative in Genesis with the findings of modern geology, speculating that the seven days in the Genesis account might have been eons or that an immense time might have elapsed between the creation of the universe and the creation of Adam and Eve. Hodge expressed the rational orthodox consensus: Whatever the scientist discovered — if it were truly a discovery — would prove consistent with the Bible, properly interpreted, even if this meant that a scientific discovery could alter generations of interpretation. In this sense, reason and science carried an implicit authority in Hodge's rational orthodoxy — as they did in most other American theologies of the day.[49]

His views of reason and science coincided with two other assumptions that placed Hodge within the consensus of American Protestant theologians. The first was that reason prepared the mind to accept revelation by means of a natural theology that pointed toward the higher revealed truth. Nature and human nature manifested God's existence; with countless other American religious writers, Hodge marveled at the descriptions of design in nature in the writings of natural theologians like the English archdeacon William Paley. The second was that philosophy confirmed biblical theology, especially the philosophy of the British common sense tradition.[50]

American theologians in the Reformed, Anglican, and Wesleyan traditions invested heavily in the Scottish Realism of Thomas Reid and Dugald Stewart in Edinburgh, and the Scots, in turn, popularized the inductive methods of Sir Francis Bacon to such an extent that Scottish philosophy was labeled "Baconian." Hodge admired the Scottish philosophers; he also admired Bacon, and Hodge's preference for an "inductive" reading of the Bible — the gathering, classifying, and synthesizing of biblical facts or

---

"Lochmann's New Testament," *BRTR* 6 (1834): 269-70; Hodge, "Inspiration," *BRPR* 29 (1857): 660-98; Hodge, *Systematic Theology*, vol. 1, pp. 151-88; Richard A. Muller, *Post-Reformation Reformed Dogmatics*, vol. 2: *Holy Scripture* (Grand Rapids: Baker, 1993), p. 433.

49. Jonathan Wells, "Charles Hodge on the Bible and Science," *American Presbyterians: The Journal of Presbyterian History* 66 (1988): 160; Hodge, *Systematic Theology*, vol. 1, p. 171.

50. Hodge, *Systematic Theology*, vol. 1, p. 25.

truths — had its inspiration in Bacon's theories of science. He also used Reid and Stewart in other familiar ways. He remained convinced, for instance, that they had discovered the "laws of belief" implicit in all reasoning and that those laws ensured the reliability of cognition within its proper sphere. Like other proponents of rational orthodoxy, he was less happy with the later Realist Sir William Hamilton, who combined Reid with Kant in a way that cast doubt on the ability of the mind to know the Infinite. Hodge believed that Hamilton had set rationality against itself. The rationalist side of Hodge could not abide that paradox.[51]

The main debt that American theologians owed the Scots displayed itself in their incessant "appeal to consciousness." The Scots had urged an introspective examination of consciousness as a way of discovering the universal and necessary principles of belief implied in particular acts of knowing and willing. Their followers used the method for an even greater array of tasks. Like others, Hodge often equated the "facts of consciousness" with the manifest content of ordinary experience, and he appealed to such facts to support a variety of claims. The doctrine of inability, for example, was "a plain fact of consciousness" because people were aware that they could not change their hearts simply by willing it; or the "facts of consciousness" contradicted materialism because people universally distinguished thinking, feeling, and willing, on the one hand, from bodily processes on the other. By the 1870s the appeal to consciousness had become little more than an assertion of self-evidence for whatever position one was arguing, but Hodge's continued use of it would not have been unusual among the seminary theologians.[52]

Hodge worried about scientific overreaching, but like most other antebellum American theologians he saw science and theology as partners. He thought that science itself, for instance, properly used, would confute the speculations of Josiah Nott, Louis Agassiz, and other ethnographers who denied that humanity was a single species with a common origin. Even his critique of Darwinism in 1874 reflected the admiration for science ingrained in the seminary theologians. Hodge referred far more in *What Is Darwinism?* to scientific than to religious critics of Darwin, and he conceded that some forms of evolutionary theory might be consistent with theism. His objection was that Darwin permitted no reference to teleol-

51. Hodge, *Systematic Theology,* vol. 1, pp. 10-15, 25, 60; Hodge, "Can God Be Known?" *BRPR* 36 (1864): 131; Hodge et al., "Sir William Hamilton's Philosophy of the Conditioned," *BRPR* 32 (1860): 472-510.

52. Hodge, "Professor Park's Remarks," p. 330; Hodge, *Systematic Theology,* vol. 1, pp. 276, 344.

ogy and therefore advanced an atheistic theory. The theologian, he said, could not dispute any "scientific fact," but scientific explanations were another matter, and he thought that Darwin's explanation for the variety of species crossed the line into the realm of metaphysics.[53]

The seminaries eventually adapted to Darwin — even Hodge's successors at Princeton found ways to accept evolutionary ideas — but they had to insert teleology where Darwin could not find it. Hodge let Darwin speak for himself. To this extent his reading of Darwin was more tough-minded and realistic than the more optimistic assessments of harmony between Darwinian science and traditional theology.[54]

Far more important than science or philosophy as hermeneutical lenses for Hodge, of course, were the Reformed confessions — especially Westminster — and in his confessionalism he diverged from American commonplaces. It differentiated him from pietist and revivalist strands of Protestantism, and it drew him into conflict with both New School revisionists and Old School traditionalists within his own denomination. Against the revisionists he argued that it made no sense to subscribe to the confessions merely for "substance of doctrine," for he saw no way to separate the substance from the form. Against at least some of the traditionalists, he argued that subscription did not mean accepting "every proposition contained in the Confession," for the church in America had never explicitly demanded this and the Synod of Philadelphia had itself not adopted the clauses relating to the power of the magistrate in religion. He thought that one should accept the Confession as containing "the system of doctrine" taught in Scripture — a system that corresponded with Princeton's version of Calvinist orthodoxy — and as providing the best guide to the deeper meaning of the Bible.[55]

Hodge's confessionalist traditionalism pulled him away from some of the big, popular questions that preoccupied segments of the Protestant world. He remained leery, for example, of prophetic schemes that presumed to find in the Bible a detailed guide to future events. On prophetic chronologies, he announced, he was "no expert" — one of the few topics that elicited such an admission — and while he had no misgiving about laying out the details of the second advent, he resisted efforts to link them

53. Hodge, "The Unity of Mankind," *BRPR* 31 (1859): 130; Hodge, *What Is Darwinism?* (London and Edinburgh: T. Nelson, 1874), pp. 141, 176-77; John W. Stewart, *Mediating the Center: Charles Hodge on American Science, Language, Literature, and Politics* (Princeton: Princeton Theological Seminary, 1995), pp. 36-44.

54. Hodge, *What Is Darwinism?* p. 123.

55. Hodge, "Adoption of the Confession of Faith," *BRPR* 30 (1858): 682, 689.

to world history, or to set dates, or to postulate a thousand-year millennial reign of Christ on earth before the end of the world. About such speculative matters professional theologians did not speak — at least not at Princeton.[56]

IV. Conclusion

After the reunion of the Old and New School Presbyterian churches in 1870, Hodge became less the voice of Presbyterian orthodoxy and more the theologian of one party within the Presbyterian church. Nonetheless, it was a party with wide appeal. The publication of his *Systematic Theology* made him the standard conservative federal theologian among the English-speaking Reformed churches, despite continuing criticisms from southerners like Robert L. Dabney, John Adger, and Robert W. Landis. Theologians at several Presbyterian and Baptist seminaries kept the book in use throughout the nineteenth century and beyond.[57]

Increasingly, though, as many of the older issues faded from view, Hodge's legacy narrowed. In the battles between liberals and fundamentalists in the early twentieth century, he became the great theologian of inerrancy, and his reputation waxed or waned in accord with the changing alignments of that struggle. Hodge the professional, the theologian who tackled just about every big issue of the nineteenth century, was, in both history books and theological polemics, pushed into the tight boundaries of the Darwinian and infallibility debates. When viewed in the broader context of nineteenth-century American theology, however, Hodge exemplified the nascent ideal of the professional theologian as an incisive and broad-ranging thinker able to comment on any question of theology that might arise. Within the theological world constructed by the antebellum American seminaries, Hodge had something to say about almost everything.

---

56. Hodge, *Systematic Theology,* vol. 3, pp. 790-843.
57. Trinterud, "Charles Hodge," p. 38; Ralph J. Danhof, *Charles Hodge as Dogmaticist* (Goes, The Netherlands: Oosterbaan and le Cointre, 1929), pp. 151-62.

Charles Hodge and the Europeans

B. A. GERRISH

The taste for German writers on dogmatic theology is factitious,
alien to the genius of the Anglo-American mind.

CHARLES HODGE

By way of a preface, two disclaimers are perhaps in order, though they may later seem to have been too obvious to mention. In the first place, I am not a Charles Hodge scholar, or even a specialist in American church history. You might say that I speak for the Europeans; at any rate, my competence is mainly in European religious thought from the time of the Protestant Reformation. But I have had a long-term interest in Hodge: he was the first theologian I ever became acquainted with by more than name. Even before I attended seminary, my circle of student friends in London and Cambridge used to pore over a worn set of Hodge's three-volume *Systematic Theology,* and our quest for theological wisdom led us as well to his *Commentary on the Epistle to the Romans.* As I recall, our liveliest interest was not in the Princeton doctrine of plenary inspiration (though we talked about that, too), but in the great soteriological themes at the beginning of volume three. We were all staunch Calvinists, worried that the Arminians were dictating the methods of evangelism; and we nodded approvingly when we found in Hodge that conversion is the effect of regeneration, which is an act of God alone and therefore not to be credited to the evangelist's powers of persuasion or the sinner's own choice.[1] But I

---

1. See Charles Hodge, *Systematic Theology* (hereafter *ST*), 3 vols. (1871-72; reprinted Grand

do not believe I have ever "dismissed" Hodge on *any* theme, and my subsequent attraction to his Mercersburg adversary John W. Nevin only quickened my old interest in him.[2]

My second disclaimer follows from the first. I cannot address my assigned topic out of the full range of the Hodge sources and secondary literature, as a specialist would. This certainly makes mine a high-risk contribution, but still, I hope, a contribution to our discussion even where it may prove to require additions or corrections. A pattern repeatedly appears in the sources I have used; it is not likely to need radical revision in the light of other sources that I have *not* used. With the theme of "Charles Hodge and the Europeans" in mind, I have gone through the *Systematic Theology* and A. A. Hodge's biography,[3] and I have picked out what sound like pertinent titles from the *Biblical Repertory and Princeton Review*.[4] It is possible that I have missed some other interesting material. I am told, for instance, that archival sources for Hodge's European tour in 1826-1828 still remain insufficiently explored, particularly letters to his wife that were not reproduced in the biography.[5] As for the secondary literature, as far as I have been able to ascertain, it is thin at just the point where my own interest is strongest: Hodge's attitude to Friedrich Schleiermacher (1768-

---

Rapids: Eerdmans, 1981), 3:3-40; cf. 2:684-89. Wherever possible, my references to *ST* are inserted in the main body of this chapter. The pagination has remained the same in all the various printings of this work. In my own copy (the 1981 reprint) the eighty-one-page index, paginated separately, is placed at the beginning of volume one.

2. This is meant as a (very mild) protest against John Stewart's statement that "Brian A. Gerrish dismissed Hodge as being uninteresting, except in Hodge's controversy with John Nevin and the Mercersburg theology." John W. Stewart, *Mediating the Center: Charles Hodge on American Science, Language, Literature, and Politics* (Princeton: Princeton Theological Seminary, 1995), p. 2, n. 5.

3. Archibald Alexander Hodge (1823-1886), *The Life of Charles Hodge, D.D., LL.D., Professor in the Theological Seminary, Princeton, N.J.* (New York: Charles Scribner's Sons, 1880); hereafter *LCH*, with page references mostly in the body of the text.

4. Hereafter *BRPR*. Unfortunately, this series is not readily available to me. I am grateful to Christine Deming for promptly sending me photocopies of *BRPR* articles I requested from the library of Princeton Theological Seminary. Wherever possible, I give references to the reprints in Charles Hodge, *Essays and Reviews* (hereafter *ER*; New York: Robert Carter and Brothers, 1857), or to the extracts in Mark A. Noll, ed., *The Princeton Theology, 1812-1921: Scripture, Science, and Theological Method from Archibald Alexander to Benjamin Breckenridge Warfield* (Grand Rapids: Baker, 1983).

5. Stewart reports, presumably on the basis of the archival evidence, that Hodge "actually attended Schleiermacher's *seminars* and preaching in Berlin in 1828" (*Mediating the Center*, p. 4, n. 10 [emphasis mine]; cf. p. 11) and "apparently conversed at length with the famed Berlin theologian" (p. 12).

1834), very different as it was from the attitude of the recent graduate (Nevin) who stood in for him during his European tour.

We must not make too much of the European tour, fascinating though his reports of it may be. They tell us about Hodge's impressions of the Europeans during two years at the very beginning of his career. They tell us also a good deal about how his impressions were formed. But the time span between his sojourn in Berlin and publication of the *Systematic Theology* is more than forty years. It cannot be presumed that between the earliest sources and the last he did not have any second thoughts about the Germans, though it cannot be presumed that he *did* either. The point to note is that in 1827-28 he was a novice instructor in Bible (Professor of Oriental and Biblical Literature since 1822) and in 1871-72 had become one of America's foremost systematic theologians (Professor of Exegetical and Didactic Theology since 1840, of Polemic Theology since Archibald Alexander's death in 1852).[6] Might he, one wonders, even have spent his time in Berlin differently had he been already a systematician?

I

The triangular relationship between theologies in Britain, America, and Continental Europe is still less thoroughly researched than one might expect. Claude Welch reminded us in 1972 that studies of nineteenth-century religious thought have been written as regional histories even when their titles have seemed to offer something more. Karl Barth's *Protestant Theology in the Nineteenth Century,* for example (first published in German: Zurich, 1946) was in fact concerned exclusively with the Germans. "A general history of nineteenth-century Protestant theology," Welch says, "has not yet appeared." His own two-volume work seeks to close the gap. He grants that nineteenth-century theology was not as obviously international as the religious thought of the Enlightenment, but he nonetheless proposes the thesis that national or linguistic boundaries are not the "primary grids" for interpreting the nineteenth century, and he looks for a measure of international unity in "concerns, tendencies, and problems" shared by Protestant theologians everywhere.[7]

6. Hodge was born December 28, 1797. He was twenty-eight when he left for Europe.

7. Claude Welch, *Protestant Thought in the Nineteenth Century,* 2 vols. (New Haven: Yale University Press, 1972-85), vol. I, pp. 1, 4, 15-16. If the approach is by examining responses to common problems, then one might question Welch's assertion that "it would be too much to ask for a combined study of Protestant and Roman Catholic thought" (vol. I, p. 1).

Claude Welch's project is not, of course, identical with an inquiry into the actual exchange of critical appraisals and constructive proposals between Britain, America, and the Continent. Throughout the nineteenth century, a traffic in theological ideas went on, often couched in chauvinistic talk about "the Teutonic mind," "the Anglo-Saxon character," or some other ethnological watchword; and this invites interesting questions about what Stephen Sykes calls "theological diplomacy." Sykes hopes to see eventually a "thorough and detailed history of the theological relations between England and Germany," a history that will take account of the manner in which the interpretation and reception of "foreign" ideas simultaneously transforms them.[8] Such a history, now lacking, could be very illuminating. How much more intriguing, albeit more complicated, it might be if Scotland and North America were allowed their place among the English-speaking theologians!

Whatever issues of theological diplomacy between England and Germany remain mooted or unexplained, it is commonly agreed that by the end of the eighteenth century the dominant flow of the intellectual traffic among the Europeans had been reversed: no longer from Britain to France and Germany, it was now from Germany to France and Britain. An interesting testimony to the change of direction can be found in the editorial introduction to a brief English translation from Johann Gottfried von Herder (1744-1803) that appeared in a Boston journal in 1820:

> The language and literature of the Germans have not till lately been much attended to by foreigners. It is a singular fact, that while scarcely a work of note, either in letters or the sciences, appears in English, without soon issuing in translation from the German press; our own language has been put in possession of little in return....

The editor then adds, however, that "men are beginning to believe that there is not science in the whole circle, which does not owe great obligations to German genius and research."[9]

When the tide turned, English churchmen greeted the theological scholarship of Germany with horror as something alien to the native good sense of Englishmen, although the Germans might be said to have been repaying with interest a debt they owed to England. Against the com-

8. Stephen W. Sykes, ed., *England and Germany: Studies in Theological Diplomacy,* Studies in the Intellectual History of Christianity, vol. 25 (Frankfurt am Main: Peter D. Lang, 1982), p. 1.

9. *The Christian Disciple,* n.s. 10 (1820): 233.

mon assumption that biblical criticism began in Germany in the late eighteenth and early nineteenth centuries, Henning Reventlow has shown that it actually began earlier in England, in the period between the Reformation and the Enlightenment, and was occasioned by the effort to harmonize the Scriptures with the new scientific and moral outlook that seemed to undermine their veracity. Reventlow traces the story to its climax in the subversive writings of the English deists.[10] In the nineteenth century, however, the hostility of English divines to German theology in general and German biblical criticism in particular showed no trace of penitence for the stimulus Germany had formerly received from England: the evil was assumed to be foreign. It is amusing to find Connop Thirlwall (1797-1875), Schleiermacher's first English translator, remarking defensively: "It would almost seem as if at Oxford the knowledge of German subjected a divine to the same suspicion of heterodoxy which we know was attached some centuries back to the knowledge of Greek."[11] Admittedly, Thirlwall was a Cambridge man, as was his friend Julius Hare (1795-1855), who tried harder than anyone to help his countrymen understand Martin Luther as well as the more recent German theologians.[12] But Thirlwall and Hare were lonely prophets even in their alma mater. Only a few weeks after publication of Thirlwall's translation, H. J. Rose (1795-1838) delivered his notorious four "sermons" at Cambridge attacking German rationalistic theologies, including Schleiermacher's.[13]

Charles Hodge (1797-1878), an almost exact contemporary of Thirlwall, maintained a lively interest in the progress of theology in France, Britain, and Germany throughout his career. He found himself thrust into the bitter controversy over the new German theology and German biblical criti-

10. Henning Graf Reventlow, *The Authority of the Bible and the Rise of the Modern World*, trans. John Bowden (Philadelphia: Fortress Press, 1985).

11. Friedrich Schleiermacher, *Luke: A Critical Study*, trans. Connop Thirlwall (1825; reprinted, with further essays and emendations by Terence N. Tice, Schleiermacher Studies and Translations, vol. 13, Lewiston, New York: Edwin Mellen Press, 1993), translator's introduction, p. ix.

12. See N. Merrill Distad, *Guessing at Truth: The Life of Julius Charles Hare (1795-1855)* (Shepherdstown: Patmos Press, 1979).

13. Hugh James Rose, *The State of the Protestant Religion in Germany* (Cambridge, 1825; 2d ed., titled *The State of Protestantism in Germany, Described*, London, 1829). Hodge quotes Rose in *ST*, vol. 1, pp. 45-46, on "Wolf" (i.e., Christian Wolff [1679-1754]). Rose was a high churchman, a precursor of the Oxford Tractarians. It is interesting that E. B. Pusey (1800-82), then studying biblical literature in Bonn, undertook to correct Rose's distortions of German theology. Pusey could not help admiring Schleiermacher even though he was not to become an advocate of German theology. See Sykes, *England and Germany*, pp. 149, 156.

cism. Unlike some, he took pains to master the dreaded German language;[14] but, like most, he was inclined to lard his observations on the theological situation with conventional wisdom (not to say prejudices) about the French, the English, and the German "minds." In general, he sided with the English mind against the German mind; and he aligned the French with the Germans, and the Americans with the English. The English are clear and sensible; the Germans obscure and speculative. German writers are seldom intelligible: they cannot discern the limits of knowledge and so are unable to distinguish between truth and "the phantoms of their creative imaginations," whereas the English mind rests content within the sphere God has assigned to it.[15] Germans of the Transcendental School may find the Anglo-Saxon race "dull, terrestrial, and shallow," but their own defect is equally unfortunate: they lack the faculty for recognizing nonsense when they see it.[16] And so on. The English writers reminded Hodge of those admirable qualities that made Francis Turretin (1623-87) and other orthodox divines highly favored at Princeton:

> After all the alleged improvements in theological research, we never feel so much disposed to take down one of the old Latin dogmatic writers of the seventeenth century, as immediately on closing a fresh work from Germany. . . . They have one obvious claim upon our preference, that they accord in their chief peculiarities with the characteristic of the American, or what is the same thing, the British mind.[17]

14. Hodge found the German language difficult to get into. During his stay in Germany, he was not always sure he understood what was said to him (*LCH*, pp. 115, 119-21). Later, however, he was more likely to blame the author than himself when he failed to comprehend a German text.

15. Hodge, "Schaf's Protestantism," *BRPR* 17 (1845): 626-36; see pp. 626, 634-35 (Noll, *Princeton Theology*, pp. 157, 163).

16. Hodge, "Transcendentalism," *BRPR* 11 (1839): 87.

17. Hodge, "Neander's History," *BRPR* 16 (1844): 155-83; see pp. 182-83 (Noll, *Princeton Theology*, p. 116). My epigraph at the head of my essay is taken from the same source (p. 183; Noll, *Princeton Theology*, p. 116). Hodge's negative perception of the German mind, it should be added, never blinded him either to the excellence of German learning or to the warmth of the German character (see, e.g., *LCH*, pp. 117, 131, 188, 207). Moreover, some of his German friends saw the national mind much as he did. August Neander (1789-1850) spoke appreciatively to Hodge of "the wonderful contrast between the practical common sense of the English, and the speculative spirit of the Germans" (*LCH*, p. 184; see also the letters to Hodge from Ludwig von Gerlach [1795-1877] and Otto von Gerlach [1801-49] in *LCH*, pp. 213, 221). Ernst Wilhelm Hengstenberg (1802-69) was convinced that if Strauss's *Life of Jesus* (see n. 22 below) had been published in England, it would have been forgotten in a couple of months. See Hodge, "The Latest Form of Infidelity" (*BRPR* 1840), *ER*, p. 110.

But now, to sharpen the focus a little: Of whom was Hodge talking when he pronounced his global verdicts on the British and the Germans? And where do the French fit in? My concern is only with European thinkers of the eighteenth and nineteenth centuries who were Hodge's immediate predecessors and contemporaries. He died in 1878, and this must obviously be my cut-off date. The victorious advance of the Ritschlians in and beyond Germany had barely started: the great three-volume system of Albrecht Ritschl (1822-89), *Justification and Reconciliation* (1870-74), came off the press at about the same time as Hodge's own *Systematic Theology*. In the Netherlands, the revival of Dutch Reformed theology under Abraham Kuyper (1837-1920) and Herman Bavinck (1854-1921) was also just beginning: it was left to B. B. Warfield (1851-1921) to represent Princeton in engagement with the Dutch theologians, notably on the question of apologetics and a scientific theology.[18] But a large field remains, and the extent of Hodge's knowledge of it is remarkable.

As we would expect, the *Systematic Theology* has plenty of references to the Scottish philosophers: David Hume (1711-76), Thomas Reid (1710-96), Dugald Stewart (1753-1828), Thomas Brown (1778-1820), William Hamilton (1788-1856), James McCosh (1811-94). Hodge also refers to Scottish churchmen and theologians such as Thomas Chalmers (1780-1847) and John Tulloch (1823-86). The index to the *Systematic Theology* is by no means exhaustive: some names mentioned by Hodge (such as Tulloch's) are not included at all, and some others that are included are mentioned more often than the index records. But it is not my intention to supply missing references, only (at this stage) to give some indication of which Scots and other Europeans Hodge had chiefly in mind, and of this the index is usually a reliable guide. As for Princeton's attraction to the Scottish "common sense" school, it has been the subject of considerable scholarly research, and I can safely leave it to others who know more about it than I do.[19]

18. See Noll, *Princeton Theology*, pp. 302-7. Close in thought to Kuyper and Bavinck was the neglected reviver of Calvinism in Calvin's own country, Auguste Lecerf (1872-1943). But his contributions lay even further in the future.

19. For a brief guide to the literature, see Noll, *Princeton Theology*, pp. 30-33. Hodge was particularly interested in William Hamilton, who tried to combine the common sense tradition with the critical philosophy of Immanuel Kant (1724-1804). See, for example, the excursus in *ST*, vol. 1, pp. 346-65, and Hodge's critical essay "Philosophy of the Conditioned," *BRPR* 32 (1860): 472-510.

When we note Hodge's references to men of learning south of the border, in England, it again comes as no surprise to discover a host of exact references to writers on scientific subjects. He was immensely interested in developments in the natural sciences and the ways in which they impinged on Christian beliefs. His confidence in the inerrancy of Scripture never wavered, but he admitted that "it is unwise for theologians to insist on an *interpretation* of Scripture which brings it into collision with the *facts* of science" (*ST,* 1:56, my emphasis; cf. 1:170-71). Darwinism was the main problem; Hodge took it seriously, but only as a *theory* that could not be endorsed by anyone who was even more serious about the facts of the Bible.[20] Besides Charles Darwin (1809-82) himself, he engaged Charles Lyell (1797-1875), William Benjamin Carpenter (1813-85), A. R. Wallace (1823-1913), T. H. Huxley (1825-95), and others. Hodge and natural science is also a theme that has been well explored in the secondary literature.[21] I can move on to some of the more properly theological developments in England that caught his attention.

He was particularly attentive to English writers on natural theology. Indeed, it should not be overlooked that the necessity for systematic theology, argued so forcefully by Hodge (*ST,* 1:2-3, 18-19), is something that on the whole eluded the English, who were preoccupied with preliminary questions of religious epistemology. Hodge mentions the famous Bridgewater Treatises (*ST,* 1:217), the *Natural Theology* (1802) of William Paley (1743-1805), the doubts of philosopher John Stuart Mill (1806-73) concerning the need for an ultimate explanation of natural sequences. What catches his eye in the controversial *Essays and Reviews* (1860) is the protest Baden Powell (1796-1860) leveled "in behalf of men of science" against belief in miracles as interruptions of natural law (*ST,* 1:619).[22] These are all issues in philosophical theology that border on Hodge's scientific interests. More strictly philosophical were the Bampton Lectures of 1858, in which H. L. Mansel (1820-71) relentlessly dismantled every claim to *theoretical* knowledge of God's nature and then commended the Scriptures as our only source of *regulative* knowledge concerning the way we ought to conduct ourselves in relation to

20. See especially *ST,* vol. 2, ch. 1.
21. For guidance, see Stewart, *Mediating the Center,* ch. 2.
22. Publication of the *Essays and Reviews* in England (London, 1860) has sometimes been compared to the appearance of David Friedrich Strauss's (1808-74) *Life of Jesus* (1835) in Germany as the pivotal event that forced the problem of faith and secular learning to the forefront of theological discussion. See Ieuan Ellis, *Seven Against Christ: A Study of "Essays and Reviews,"* Studies in the History of Christian Thought, vol. 23 (Leiden: E. J. Brill, 1980).

the unknown Absolute.[23] Hodge devotes one of his longest excursuses to Mansel; indeed, the chapter on "The Knowledge of God" in volume one of the *Systematic Theology* (part one, chapter four) is a running debate with the kindred views of Mansel and Hamilton. Hodge's acute criticisms show him at his argumentative best. But if the theory of Hamilton and Mansel is "suicidal . . . an incongruous combination of sceptical principles with orthodox faith" (*ST,* 1:363), and if Darwin's theory is as incredible as "the Hindu mythology and cosmology" (*ST,* 2:20), Hodge surely risks shattering our faith in British good sense.[24]

We shall not expect him to have thought any more highly of the theologians of the "Oxford School." The contexts in which he would have occasion to refer to the Tractarians in the *Systematic Theology* are predictable. Tract 85 is mentioned on tradition and authority (1:106, 127). John Henry Newman (1801-90), "one of the richest prizes gained by the Romanists from the Church of England in this generation" (3:454), is quoted by name on the teaching authority of the church (1:124, 126-27), ecclesiastical miracles (3:454), relics (3:459-461), and the Protestant identification of the pope with the Antichrist (3:818-19, 822). E. B. Pusey, who assumed the leadership of the Oxford movement after Newman's defection, is quoted for his objections to "the cruel invention of purgatory" (3:752-53, 756). The doctrine of baptism provides the occasion for mentioning William Palmer (1803-85) on the church (3:543). Presumably, we would hear much more about the Tractarians if Hodge had reached the fifth part of his system, which was to have been devoted to ecclesiology — oddly located after eschatology. (The inclusion of baptism and the Lord's Supper in part three is also, to say the least, unusual.) Hodge thought the *Tracts for the Times* could be regarded as "among the most important ephemerical [*sic*] productions of the day"; he judged their content to be a case for popery without the pope. The "second reformation" that the Tracts called for would be a step back to the system against which the sixteenth-century Reformers, not least the English Reformers, had struggled and protested: that is, the church understood as the storehouse of grace and the sacraments, dispensed by episcopally ordained clergy, as the instruments for

---

23. Henry Longueville Mansel, *The Limits of Religious Thought Examined* (London, 1858).

24. Hodge considered the strand in British religious thought represented by Samuel Taylor Coleridge (1772-1834) to be largely derivative. He did not have much to say about him in the *Systematic Theology,* though he mentioned (*ST,* vol. 1, p. 180) the views on inspiration held by Coleridge and his "friends and followers" Arnold, Julius Hare, and F. D. Maurice (1805-72). By "Dr. Arnold" Hodge meant Thomas Arnold (1795-1842), who was one of the leading "broad churchmen," better known as the headmaster of Rugby.

conveying it to individuals.[25] "The Reformed churches have ever considered Christ and justification by faith in his merits, as the great center of the Christian system. The Oxford Tract writers make the church the main point: the church as an ordinance for conveying life to all its members by means of the sacraments."[26]

The virtues of the British mind notwithstanding, Hodge found much to criticize in its characteristic theological products. But he retained his respect even in disagreement. A noticeable difference of tone pervaded his observations on French religious thought, and I can consider them much more briefly before turning to the Germans. The two French thinkers of whom he had most to say were Victor Cousin (1792-1867) and August Comte (1798-1857). Cousin he saw as an unoriginal pantheist (*ST,* 1:63, 301), and he was plainly piqued by his Gallic personality. He did not believe Cousin had done much more than transmit German pantheism to France, and he thought the French language ill suited to the task. In his *Introduction to the History of Philosophy* (Eng. trans., 1832), Cousin had found no reason to consider England or Scotland, Germany and France being taken for the only countries worthy of notice. Hodge quoted him as saying: "England, gentlemen, is a very considerable island; in England *everything stops at certain limits,* nothing is there developed on a great scale." The remark needed no refutation; it was sufficient to describe it as a "truly French statement."[27]

Comte's positivism earned a long excursus in the *Systematic Theology* (1:254-62) with copious quotations from the condensed English version of the *Philosophie positive* by Harriet Martineau (2 vols., London, 1853; New York, 1855). Naturally, Hodge alluded to Comte's "religion of humanity," in which the object of public worship was to be humanity itself, and he supposed that merely to state its leading features was sufficient to establish its absurdity. He gave rather more space, albeit not one bit more credence, to Comte's law of human development. Comte believed that the human race as a whole and each individual passes through three distinct stages, in which events are respectively attributed to supernatural causes (the theological stage), referred to invisible forces (the metaphysical

---

25. Hodge, "Oxford Tracts," *BRPR* 10 (1838): 84-119, a review of *Tracts for the Times,* by members of the University of Oxford, 2d ed., 3 vols. (London, 1837); see pp. 84, 93, 99, 116, 118. Also pertinent are "Bishop Doane and the Oxford Tracts," *BRPR* 13 (1841): 450-62; and "Theories of the Church," *BRPR* 18 (1846): 137-58, reprinted in *ER,* pp. 201-20.

26. Hodge, "Oxford Tracts," p. 88.

27. Hodge, "Transcendentalism," *BRPR* 11 (1839): 37-101; see p. 54n. And yet Hodge himself began this article with the admission that "metaphysical research" in Britain was at a standstill and had been so longer in England than in Scotland (pp. 37-38).

stage), or simply connected with one another in relations of resemblance and sequence (the positive stage). Theories of development seem always to have made Hodge nervous; Comte's theory he dismissed partly by enlisting the aid of infidel T. H. Huxley, who had exposed it as unscientific. Of Comte's system, then, Hodge concluded triumphantly: "Among the advanced men of science in England, there is scarcely one so poor as to do it reverence" (*ST,* 1:262).[28]

3

References to the contemporary German theologians are scattered throughout Hodge's *Systematic Theology,* and they cover the entire range of the Protestant "schools": rationalist, right-wing Hegelian and left-wing Hegelian, confessionalist, and mediating schools as well as the schools of Tübingen and Erlangen. There is no need to call the entire roll.[29] Hodge did not merely drop names but often gave exact quotations. Some of his favorites may at first glance seem surprising. There are several references to D. F. Strauss's dogmatics, for instance — more than the index lists.[30]

28. Charles Cashdollar has shown that positivism reached its peak relatively late, in the 1870s and early 1880s — that is, after Comte's death — and that it was perceived in both Britain and America as the most serious challenge of the time to religious belief. See Charles D. Cashdollar, *The Transformation of Theology, 1830-1890: Positivism and Protestant Thought in Britain and America* (Princeton: Princeton University Press, 1989). Cashdollar's book is an outstanding historical achievement, and it proves that Hodge underestimated positivism. But it is a bit unfair to him to give the impression that he opposed Comte only with the Book of Genesis (p. 278). He thought positivism had been discredited as bogus science.

29. Hodge also read the Roman Catholics, particularly Johann Adam Moehler (1796-1838), "the ablest and most plausible of the modern defenders of Romanism" (*ST,* vol. 3, p. 718). Some of the weightier German Protestants with whom he entered into conversation were F. C. Baur (1792-1860), K. G. Bretschneider (1776-1848), Karl Daub (1765-1836), Wilhelm DeWette (1780-1849), I. A. Dorner (1809-84), J. H. A. Ebrard (1818-84), E. W. Hengstenberg (1802-69), J. C. K. von Hofmann (1810-77), Philipp Marheineke (1740-1846), Julius Müller (1801-78), F. A. Philippi (1809-82), Schleiermacher, Alexander Schweizer (1808-88), F. J. Stahl (1802-61), D. F. Strauss, August Tholuck (1799-1877), August Twesten (1789-1876), Karl Ullmann (1796-1865), and J. A. L. Wegscheider (1771-1849). The list could be extended, especially if it included biblical scholars such as Franz Delitzsch (1813-90) and church historians such as August Neander (1789-1850) and Karl August von Hase (1800-90). It is a list that would stand up well in a history of theology; it is astonishing in a work of systematic theology.

30. Hodge usually quotes Strauss's dogmatic work as *Dogmatik.* The German title was *Die christliche Glaubenslehre,* etc. (2 vols., 1840-41).

139

The explanation lies partly in Hodge's characterization of him as "the most candid of the recent philosophical theologians" (*ST,* 1:414). Strauss made no effort to conceal the departure of much German theology from traditional Christian beliefs, and Hodge loved to marshal the troops of honest antitheologians and unbelievers against theological positions he considered pretentious but unstable (*ST,* 3:77).

The foundation of Hodge's extensive knowledge of the German theologians was laid during the European journey. His travels took him from France to Germany, and on the way home he stopped in Switzerland, France, and Britain. The visit to "old England" evoked some deep emotions from him. He wrote to his wife (27 June 1828): "You may suppose it was with a swelling heart I trod upon the soil of the mother country, which, with all her faults, is the most wonderful and admirable the world has ever seen" (*LCH,* p. 200). But it was vacation time; the visits to London, Cambridge, Oxford, and Edinburgh were without opportunity for theological exchange, though Hodge was delighted to hear the leader of the Cambridge evangelicals, Charles Simeon (1759-1836), preach a sermon. Only the stay in Germany can be considered an important influence on Hodge's theological formation.[31]

Hodge did not go to Europe to learn about theology. In Paris he worked on his French, Arabic, and Syriac. He moved on to Halle because he heard it was the outstanding university for the study of biblical literature. The main attraction was the reputation of orientalist Wilhelm Gesenius (1786-1842). Hodge had also been drawn by reports of August Tholuck's ability to combine learning and piety, and he took Tholuck's introduction to theology, "principally," as he said, "to gain an acquaintance with the theological literature" (*LCH,* p. 117). This, however, was not the sort of course we today would call "Introduction to Theology," meaning contemporary systematic or constructive theology. It was a course in so-called theological encyclopedia: the aim, he wrote to his mentor Archibald Alexander (1772-1851), was "to give the character of the most important works belonging to each department" (*LCH,* p. 117; cf. p. 119). Hodge kept his focus on Scripture and languages — now including German.

In Berlin, as in Halle, he sought out classes pertinent to his interest in

---

31. Hodge stayed in Halle for a little over seven months (28 February-10 October 1827) and in Berlin for about a month less (12 October 1827-30 April 1828). The principal sources of information on his sojourn in Germany are Hodge's journal and letters home; his son used the letters selectively in his biography (ch. 6), on which I am depending.

the Scriptures, regularly attending lectures by Neander,[32] occasionally lectures by Hengstenberg and the philologist August Böckh (1785-1867). Entirely in keeping with what we know of him, he also obtained permission to sit in on the instruction Alexander von Humboldt (1769-1859) was then giving on physical science.[33] But A. A. Hodge gives no indication that his father might have seized the opportunity to sit at the feet of G. W. F. Hegel (1770-1831) or Friedrich Schleiermacher, whom he had met briefly while still in Halle.[34] (And Schleiermacher, it should be remembered, lectured regularly on the New Testament.) He did hear Schleiermacher read a short paper before the Royal Academy of Sciences on "Kings as Authors" (*LCH*, pp. 170-71), and his biography gives a journal extract recording a visit to the Trinity Church — apparently because he could not think of anywhere better to go. "I went to hear Schleiermacher, not knowing of any more evangelical preacher who had service in the morning" (*LCH*, p. 152). Hodge thought the sermon, on the first and great commandment, "peculiar" and the ideas "vague and indefinite." He was not too sure that he managed to follow it, but his outline of the "drift" sounds plain enough: in brief, Schleiermacher said that the commandment is fulfilled with a willing heart through the work of Christ in renewing our nature. The visit, to be sure, came at the start of his Berlin residence (14 October 1827). In an aside in the *Systematic Theology* (2:440, n. 1), Hodge later tells us that he "often attended Schleiermacher's church." The biography gives no account of the other visits; it does not tell us whether they may have proved more edifying than the first, but it does document Hodge's preference for the "evangelical" preachers G. F. A. Strauss (1786-1863, the court preacher), and Emil Gustaf Lisco (1819-97, pastor of the Marienkirche).

His understanding of the German theological situation did not come, however, from lectures and sermons so much as from the personal friendships he formed with Tholuck in Halle and with the circles of Hengstenberg and the von Gerlach family in Berlin. Tholuck, who was frequently with Hodge also in Berlin, was especially important.[35] He warned Hodge that the variety of German theological opinions defied classification (*LCH*, p. 121). The influence of the old "neologists" had given way not

32. The notes Hodge took down on Neander's lectures on the Corinthian letters have survived (*LCH*, p. 153n.).

33. The biography reports that Hodge kept full notes on these lectures too, but does not say if they survived (*LCH*, p. 162).

34. The meeting appears to have been casual and without significance. It is reported in Hodge's journal entry for 18 April 1827 (*LCH*, p. 128).

35. See Hodge's tribute to Tholuck in *ST*, vol. 2, pp. 451-52n.

only to a new philosophy but to a spiritual awakening as well.[36] Professors and students alike were being identified as "pious" or "religious" if they had experienced awakening, and the awakened frequently reaffirmed traditional beliefs that had long been under assault.[37] "Pious" and "orthodox" were not necessarily identical terms. Tholuck certainly believed that "very few of those not religious were orthodox," but apparently the connection was not entirely reversible since he reported that converted neologists could not shake off their old skepticism, especially with regard to the Old Testament (*LCH*, pp. 121-22).

Tholuck's remarks about the role of "vital religion" in German theology are very interesting, and Hodge later echoed them (as we will see), extending Tholuck's reflections beyond the German context. It has often been pointed out that what was sometimes called "the new pietism" departed from the old (the pietism of Philip Jakob Spener [1635-1705]) in making itself the guardian of correct belief rather than the critic of orthodox formalism. Always one of the *Herrnhutter* at heart, Schleiermacher found the new pietists very different: in an uncharacteristic show of anger, he described them as uncharitable to the point of defaming others, painfully addicted to a handful of formulas by which they divided everyone into black or white, and resistant to open-minded inquiry.[38] But the reli-

36. By the "neologists" Tholuck presumably meant those among the theologians of the eighteenth-century *Aufklärung* who held that revelation could confirm but not add to the truths of reason, and who understood the task of biblical interpretation in this light. It is not entirely clear to me from Hodge's reports how Tholuck perceived the relationships between neologists, deists, and rationalists. The affinity of the neologists with such English deists as Matthew Tindal (1655-1733) is evident. By the German rationalist school is usually meant Bretschneider, Wegscheider, H. E. G. Paulus (1761-1851), and their friends. Their dominance could certainly be assigned to the period 1790-1815 or 1817, in which Tholuck placed "the prevalence of Rationalism in Germany" (*LCH*, p. 137), whereas the heyday of neology was earlier. See Horst Stephan, *Geschichte der deutschen evangelischen Theologie seit dem deutschen Idealismus*, 2d ed., revised by Martin Schmidt (Berlin: Alfred Töpelmann, 1960), pp. 9-13. Tholuck credited the 1817 theses of Claus Harms (1778-1855) with initiating the revolt against the rationalists, but they hardly played dead; Schleiermacher attended lectures by Wegscheider at Halle (*LCH*, pp. 120-121).

37. Other terms used to designate evangelical ministers were "positive" and "believing." By now "evangelical," once the banner of the Protestant churches in general (both Lutheran and Reformed), was claimed as the name for a party within Protestantism. In one passage in his journal (23 March 1828), Hodge even distinguished "Christians" and "liberals" and assigned Schleiermacher to the liberals (*LCH*, p. 178).

38. Friedrich Schleiermacher, *On Religion: Speeches to its Cultured Despisers*, trans. John Oman, from the 3d German ed. of 1821 (1894; reprinted New York: Harper & Row Publishers, 1958), pp. 144-145.

gious awakening was by no means confined to one party. Tholuck told Hodge that even the new philosophy had nurtured a "deep religious feeling" in contrast to the system it displaced (*LCH*, p. 120). What, then, are we to understand by the new German philosophy?

From Tholuck Hodge learned that Hegelian speculation had eclipsed not only Kant's critical idealism but the systems of J. G. Fichte (1762-1814) and F. W. J. von Schelling (1775-1854) as well. The speculative spirit seduced even the biblical theologians, unless the influence of religion on their hearts restrained them. A journal entry for 6 March 1827 shows Hodge still struggling a bit to understand his new friend and teacher, but beginning to grasp the main point: German religious thought had become pantheistic.

> The reigning philosopher of the day is Hegel. Schleiermacher has a system of his own. The present systems are all Pantheistic. Hegel and Schleiermacher both deny the personality of the Deity and the individuality of the soul of man. The universal principle with them is God, and, according to Hegel, the world itself is the Realität of the Deity, and all it contains, the different races of men, and the animals in their various orders, are all modes of existence of this one universal principle. This, at least, is the idea I got from Tholuck's description. (*LCH*, p. 119)

The catchword from then on, whenever Hodge thought of German religious thought, was "pantheism," represented not by the Hegelians alone but also by Schleiermacher. Indeed, Hodge felt that even Tholuck himself, who denied the dualism of matter and spirit, was not unaffected by the new philosophy (*LCH*, p. 119; cf. p. 140).

The next day (8 March 1827), Tholuck put in a good word for Schleiermacher: "His authority stands so high," he said, "that the respect which he manifests for the Bible, and the reverence with which he speaks of Jesus Christ, has [*sic*] great influence." Tholuck testified that Schleiermacher had been the "means of awakening the attention to religion of many young men," including Neander, and that he himself owed "much of his religious feeling to Schleiermacher's influence" (*LCH*, p. 120).[39] On a subsequent occasion (14 March 1827), Tholuck told Hodge

---

39. Later, in Berlin, Neander pointed out to Hodge the shift in Schleiermacher's thinking from the *Speeches* to his dogmatics, evident in his later affirmation of the personal existence of the soul after death (*LCH*, p. 184). As the religious parties became increasingly polarized, Neander himself moved closer to Schleiermacher's side (see Otto von Gerlach to

that Schleiermacher rejected "the appellation of Pantheist" (*LCH,* p. 122), and he read him a few passages from Schleiermacher's dogmatics. "But," says Hodge, "they seemed to me to darken counsel by words without wisdom" (*LCH,* p. 123). Just a few days later (20 March), Tholuck mentioned that Schleiermacher, who belonged to the Reformed Church, was an outspoken champion of some of the distinctively Reformed doctrines (*LCH,* p. 123).

In sum, Tholuck gave Hodge a warning about the complexities of the German theological situation in general and painted a complex portrait for him of Schleiermacher in particular. Upon his return to Princeton, however, Hodge felt himself equipped by his journey to present his students with a simple classification of German theologians into three main parties: orthodox, rationalist, and pantheist. And he echoed Tholuck's sentiments on the connection between vital piety and orthodoxy.[40] On the whole, then, he seems to have fulfilled the prayer and the wish of Archibald Alexander for him: "I pray God to keep you from the poison of Neology! I wish you to come home enriched with Biblical learning, but abhorring German philosophy and theology."[41] We must ask next whether the increasing complexity of the German scene, with which he tried to remain in touch, moved Hodge to make some adjustments to his classification scheme for the German theologians, or to think again about Friedrich Schleiermacher's place in it.[42]

4

A decade after the European trip, Hodge knew well that Schleiermacher's prestige had waned. His was no longer the most influential voice in German theology, and his followers were no longer the leading

---

Hodge, 28 February 1834, *LCH,* p. 184). It is also worth noting that even Neander was willing to defend the expression that worried Hodge, "Alles Seyn ist das Seyn Gottes" (*LCH,* p. 181).

40. Hodge, "Lecture Addressed to the Students of the Theological Seminary" (*BRPR* 1829), in Noll, *Princeton Theology,* p. 111.

41. Alexander to Hodge, 27 July 1827, in *LCH,* p. 161. Alexander's use of the term "neology" seems anachronistic.

42. One indication of problems in Hodge's scheme is that, whereas he saw Schleiermacher as pantheist, he classified his disciple Twesten (who eventually succeeded to his chair at the University of Berlin) as orthodox (*LCH,* pp. 142-43). This surely presumed an opposition between them that neither one would have acknowledged, whatever their differences.

school. The prevalent system was Hegel's, and it had "diffused itself" to a remarkable degree among the educated of all classes: not reclusive professors and speculative theologians only, but also statesmen, poets, scientists, and journalists. It had become, as Hodge nicely put it, the form in which the German mind then existed and exhibited itself to other nations. The Hegelian school had divided into the right and the left, and the left had divided again into center left and extreme left. At the extreme Hodge perceived a breakdown not only of truth, but of public decency too (that is, a flaunting of the embodied, sensual side of human nature). Still, Hegelianism remained one school; and it was, in a word, "pantheism."[43]

Relying on the authority of some of Hegelianism's most vociferous critics — Hengstenberg, Tholuck, and Heinrich Leo (1799-1878) — Hodge piled his own scorn on top of theirs. D. F. Strauss's *Life of Jesus* was now the focus of theological contention, creating "a sensation almost without parallel" in Germany. Strauss denied the existence of a personal God: the Infinite Spirit had reality only in the finite spirits of humanity, in whom it attained self-consciousness; and they in turn found their reality — and their only immortality — in the Infinite Spirit. The incarnation of God did not occur once and for all in Christ; it was occurring constantly in the endless succession of individuals in the human race. Christ's person and fate were simply the occasion of awakening the consciousness of humanity to the truth of its identity with God, and the gospel "history" was in the main a mythological byproduct of the consciousness of this truth. Patent surrender of fundamental Christian truths was covered up by the argument that there was no dishonesty in freely using the language of the imagination *(Vorstellung);* the philosopher, at least, knew what the language really meant.[44]

> Such, then, is this Latest Form of Infidelity. It knows no intelligent or conscious God but man; it admits no incarnation, but the eternal in-

43. Hodge, "The Latest Form of Infidelity" (*BRPR* 1840), in *ER,* pp. 87-127; see pp. 101-2. Later in this article (p. 126), Hodge asserted that the Germans managed to isolate their philosophy, so that when the Hegelian Marheineke turned his hand to writing on the German Reformation, the result was good, plain history. How this observation is to be harmonized with the alleged Hegelianizing of every aspect of German culture, Hodge did not explain.

44. Hodge, "The Latest Form of Infidelity," pp. 110, 108. Hodge's summary clearly had Strauss chiefly in mind, though not exclusively. Note that Strauss, too, was guilty of some duplicity in his adoption of the Hegelian contrast between *Vorstellung* and *Begriff,* even though Hodge could make use of him to unmask the duplicity of others.

carnation of the universal spirit in the human race; the personality of men ceases with their present existence, they are but momentary manifestations of the infinite and unending; there is neither sin nor holiness; neither heaven nor hell. Such are the results to which the proud philosophy of the nineteenth century has brought its followers.[45]

Hodge conceded that the overthrow of deism had given pantheism a semblance of truth: in place of an absentee deity, pantheism affirmed a God who was ever present and ever active. And it was winning its advocates beyond Germany — in France, England, even America. Coleridge was an Englishman, preserved from excess by his native disposition and familiarity with the Bible. Cousin, on the other hand, was a vain Frenchman, on whose mind the Scriptures had left no strong impress. In America, Hodge expected the progress of pantheism to be stemmed by the power of true religion and the national character inherited from the English: "A sanity of intellect, an incapacity to see wonders in nonsense, is the leading trait of the English mind. The Germans can believe anything." It is this "want of adaptation" — this happy inability of the Anglo-American mind to adapt to German ways of thinking — that makes Hodge find Ralph Waldo Emerson's trancendentalism so ludicrous and profane.[46]

In 1846, only a few years after his scornful reflections on the latest German infidelity, Hodge described a Hegelian empire that was not just divided but crumbling, and he could see no new cultural force taking its place. Pantheism or self-deification was still "the prevailing form of German infidelity," but the centrifugal forces had thrown everything into confusion. The simple, three-fold classification of German theologians had begun to dissolve in what Hodge called "a state of active fermentation." Alongside the rationalists and the confessionalists, he now wrote of "the German Catholics." To be sure, these were the three now identified as the leading parties, "or the principal elements in the struggling mass." But their subdivisions were almost endless.[47] Greeted initially as advocates of reform within the "Romish" Church, the German Catholics quickly proved that they did not want emancipation from the errors and oppression of Rome, but from the gospel. They believed that the church's

45. Hodge, "The Latest Form of Infidelity," p. 119.
46. Hodge, "The Latest Form of Infidelity," pp. 120-26; quotation on p. 125.
47. Hodge, "Religious State of Germany," *BRPR* 18 (1846): 514-46; see pp. 527, 545, 514. The article is a review of the 1845 volume of Hengstenberg's *Evangelische Kirchenzeitung*.

day — the day of doctrinal Christianity — was over and that the state "should set forth the vaguest possible confession of faith, and require all to submit to it."[48]

Among the Protestants, Hodge reported, the extreme left of the rationalists was styled "Protestant Friends" or "Friends of Light." There was nothing novel in their attack on church dogma, but they generated a good deal of excitement because they made their appeal directly to the masses. Academic rationalism, in fact, was now represented in the theological faculties only by a few old men, except at Giessen. Indeed, the ranks of the Friends of Light actually included advocates of pantheism, who had similarly moved philosophy out of the classroom into the pulpit and the popular press; and this had brought about a determined reaction from the growing number of the friends of evangelical doctrine. Pastors who popularized atheism should not be tolerated in the church; they should be deposed.[49]

Clearly, Hodge was no longer talking only about theological disagreement. As the old boundaries between "schools" eroded in the flood, "parties" became determinative: that is, coalitions formed to win the populace and influence the ecclesiastical and civil authorities. Declarations in Hengstenberg's *Evangelische Kirchenzeitung,* signed by hundreds of clergymen of the evangelical party, denounced other, unbelieving clergy by name. Moderates and even many of the evangelicals themselves were appalled and protested against the declarations. "Thus," wrote Hodge, "three parties were formed": Hengstenberg's confessionalists, the Friends of Light, and "this middle party composed chiefly of the followers of Schleiermacher."[50] The painful record of fragmentation and polarization continued as Hodge wrote that the Schleiermacherian center itself fell into two divisions. One was "composed of those who by his [Schleiermacher's] influence were brought to Christ, and then from Him, the

48. Hodge, "Religious State of Germany," p. 522. Hengstenberg also took account of a more conservative group calling itself "the Protestant or Christian Catholics," which was itself split into two (pp. 524-25).

49. Hodge, "Religious State of Germany," pp. 525-28. Strauss is credited in part with bringing the Hegelian philosophy down from the ivory tower of the universities (p. 527). "Feuerback" (i.e., Ludwig Feuerbach [1804-1872]) is also named in a quotation (p. 528), but Hodge does not pursue Feuerbach's declaration that theology is anthropology, and religion illusion.

50. Hodge, "Religious State of Germany," pp. 528-30. Hodge described Hengstenberg's party as "the advocates of the standards of the church" (p. 514). The opposition called them "pietists," "strict orthodox," or — less politely — "the church magazine party." They called themselves "church minded" or "friends of the confession" (p. 531n.).

only true Master, learned the truth." The other consisted of "mere disciples," committed to Schleiermacher's hopeless program of harmonizing church doctrine and rationalism, but without the inspiration of his personality.[51]

I cannot delay over Hodge's summary of Hengstenberg's case against the theology of Schleiermacher's school.[52] (I shall come back to Hodge's own case shortly, which echoes Hengstenberg's.) Nor is there any point in looking into the acrimonious trading of insults between Schleiermacher's party and Hengstenberg's.[53] Fourteen years later, in an interesting essay titled "What Is Christianity?" (1860), Hodge offered a further glimpse of the picture he entertained of the theological situation in Germany and beyond, and I will turn to it for my final testimony. The breakup of Schleiermacher's school, we learn, continued. The numerous divisions all "depart[ed] more or less from the great master whose authority they recognize[d]." Though he might have continued to speak of "the Schleiermacher system" from its acknowledged author, the designation had really become too restrictive in view of the modifications it had undergone since it had left his hands. He now, in fact, distinguished three groups within the school of Schleiermacher: those who like him were pantheists at heart; those who were theists but not trinitarians; and "those who sincerely endeavour[ed] to bring their theory into harmony with the doctrine of the Bible, and especially with the doctrine of the Trinity." It was not possible anymore to hold one disciple responsible for the teaching of an-

51. Hodge, "Religious State of Germany," pp. 530-31. Hodge used "Rationalism" loosely with reference to Schleiermacher's program; he knew that the champions of the rationalist school were among Schleiermacher's most vigorous adversaries ("The Latest Form of Infidelity," p. 98). Among the "personal friends and pupils of Schleiermacher" Hodge elsewhere named Friedrich Lücke (1787-1855), Ullmann, and Twesten ("The Latest Form of Infidelity," p. 101). In his journal, he said of Lücke: he "appears to be a great friend of Schleiermacher, although reckoned as belonging to the orthodox party" (LCH, p. 191). And in a later article he singled out Twesten as belonging to "the most moderate and orthodox class of Schleiermacher's disciples," "The Theology of the Intellect and That of the Feelings, II" (BRPR 1851); in ER, p. 599, n. 1. See further ST, vol. 2, pp. 532-33, where Hodge suggested that if Schleiermacher did not strictly found a school, he did introduce an influential method.

52. Hodge, "Religious State of Germany," pp. 531-41.

53. Schleiermacher's friends have always seen him as gentle and irenic, never speaking a harsh word unless provoked beyond human endurance. Hengstenberg insisted that the first provocation actually came when Schleiermacher announced (with Hengstenberg's party in mind): "The ground is heaving beneath our feet, and miserable worms are crawling out from religious crevices, who regard all speculation, beyond the circumvallation of the ancient letter, as satanic" (quoted in Hodge, "Religious State of Germany," p. 531). This outburst Hengstenberg judged worth an article in reply.

other. Most of them were theists, even though "the substratum of Schleiermacher's system was Pantheism."[54]

From Tholuck Hodge had learned that Schleiermacher repudiated the charge of pantheism. Over the years, however, Hodge had evidently become increasingly convinced that a pantheistic philosophy underlay Schleiermacher's theological program, although some of his disciples had managed to overcome it. Hodge had nothing against philosophy: "Every theology is in one sense a form of philosophy. To understand any theological system, therefore, we must understand the philosophy which underlies it, and gives it its peculiar form."[55] The trouble was that Schleiermacher picked a bad philosophy — a philosophy "almost entirely foreign to the ordinary modes of thought among Americans and Englishmen." The conclusion at which German speculation had arrived in the hands of Hegel and Schelling was "the unity of the divine and human, of God and man," and Schleiermacher's philosophy, in Hodge's opinion, "was scarcely less avowedly pantheistic than that of Spinoza or Hegel." Schleiermacher's Moravian training had induced him to try presenting philosophical ideas alien to the church in a Christian garb. But he had failed, bequeathing to his more orthodox successors the problem of bringing the deification of man, which is the worst form of atheism, into harmony with theism and the gospel. Hodge did not believe that the disciples had any better success than their teacher.[56]

Hodge was fascinated by German theology, but what he said of it seems always to have sounded a note of warning. "Few parts of the world present so much to interest the Christian," he said, "as Germany in its present state. Its elements of power for good or evil are immense."[57] As he surveyed the entire world of European theology at the end of the second third of the nineteenth century, he saw the Germans bewitched by a pantheistic philosophy that was extending its pernicious influence to the French and the Anglo-Saxon peoples. Actually, he thought, the doctrine of Schelling and Hegel had by then been recognized in Germany, by

54. Hodge, "What Is Christianity?" *BRPR* 32 (1860): 118-61; ostensibly a review of books by William Cunningham (1805-61), Ullmann, and Robert Wilberforce (1802-57), but largely directed against Nevin. See pp. 121, 131n., 138.

55. Hodge, "What Is Christianity?" p. 121.

56. Hodge, "What Is Christianity?" pp. 121-23.

57. Hodge, "Religious State of Germany," p. 545. I recall only one issue on which Hodge drew attention to an influence going the other way: in this same essay, he said it was obvious that the German controversy over church polity ("the church question") drew on the Free Church controversy in Scotland (p. 543).

friends and foes alike, as irreconcilable with Christianity.[58] As for Schleiermacher's followers, they had become hopelessly divided, though they were all frantically engaged in the same impossible task of mediation: they were "reduced to the sad necessity of either holding a philosophy in conflict with their theology, or of explaining away the plainest teachings of the Bible." In the eyes of the Germans themselves, the mediating theology *(Vermittelungstheologie)* had already passed away. Sadly, it survived elsewhere as an item of export. "It is unfortunate," Hodge complained in his best Olympian tone, "that the sun does not rise on America until it begins to set on Germany. . . . [The mediating theology] served for a while to occupy the German mind, and then was shipped to America."[59]

5

Schleiermacher was something of an enigma to Hodge, and it is with this intriguing facet of the theme "Charles Hodge and the Europeans" that I wish to conclude. Hodge did not question the man's stature. "Schleiermacher," he wrote, "is regarded as the most interesting as well as the most influential theologian of modern times" *(ST,* 2:440). However, "he was not and could not be self-consistent." Hodge's point was that Schleiermacher could not be consistent as he went about the attempt to reconcile contradictory doctrines. But he immediately went on to state the inconsistency as a disharmony between Schleiermacher's personal religion and his theological speculations, not between one doctrine and another. From the Moravians he learned a "reverence for Christ" that he retained all his life. In a footnote Hodge offered this warm testimony:

58. Hodge, "What Is Christianity?" p. 122. In his *Systematic Theology (ST,* vol. 1, p. 533, n. 1), Hodge observed that for a new generation in Germany, the philosophy of Schelling, Hegel, and Schleiermacher had itself become a thing of the past. A new materialism had taken its place: "The German mind has swung round from making spirit everything, to making it nothing."

59. "What Is Christianity?", pp. 135, 157. See also *ST,* vol. 2, pp. 452-54. The journal *Theologische Studien und Kritiken* was founded in 1828 as the organ of the mediating program, which sought to harmonize biblical faith and modern thought. Its advocates looked to Schleiermacher's dogmatics as the model of the mediating ideal. But in their ranks are usually included, besides such Schleiermacherians as Twesten and Schweizer, some of the "awakened" or "pectoral" theologians (Tholuck, Neander, Müller) and the more speculative Dorner and Richard Rothe (1799-1867), who were as much indebted to Hegel as to Schleiermacher. Hodge believed that Schleiermacher's mediating program was inherently unstable; those who thought to further it were bound either to move on to something worse (Hegelian atheism) or else to turn back to the Bible ("The Latest Form of Infidelity," p. 125).

When in Berlin the writer often attended Schleiermacher's church. The hymns to be sung were printed on slips of paper and distributed at the doors. They were always evangelical and spiritual in an eminent degree, filled with praise and gratitude to our Redeemer. Tholuck said that Schleiermacher, when sitting in the evening with his family, would often say, "Hush, children; let us sing a hymn of praise to Christ." Can we doubt that he is singing those praises now? To whomsoever Christ is God, St. John assures us, Christ is a Saviour.[60]

Sadly, in Hodge's opinion, the Moravian piety never found an adequate expression in Schleiermacher's doctrines; his theology and his religion were two very different things (*ST*, 1:452, 534). Perhaps Hodge had Schleiermacher in mind when he remarked in general: "It is a great mercy that, at least in some cases, those whose philosophy forbids their believing in the personality of God, believe in the personality of Christ, whom they regard as a man invested with all the attributes of the Godhead, and whom they love and worship accordingly" (*ST*, 1:439).[61]

Recall Tholuck's belief that spiritual awakening promotes correct doctrine. Hodge echoed it in the lecture he gave to his Princeton students after his return from Germany: reverence for the Redeemer, he assured them, is the vital piety that preserves the soul from infidelity when all else has failed.[62] If reverence for the Redeemer did not keep Schleiermacher from holding incorrect beliefs, he must have been an exception. "As a general rule, a man's faith is the expression of his inward life" (*ST*, 2:443). Hodge could exercise a judgment of charity when *vital piety* was made the measure of a theologian — that is, finding in Christ the object of highest devotion. "Every true worshipper of Christ," he wrote, "must in his heart recognize as a Christian brother, wherever he may be found, any one who loves, worships, and trusts the Lord Jesus Christ as God manifest in the

---

60. Hodge, *ST*, vol. 1, p. 440, n. 1. A passage in "The Latest Form of Infidelity" (*ER*, pp. 98-99) also mentions Schleiermacher's fondness for hymns, both at home and in church, that Hodge could endorse as "of correct sentiment." Hodge described Schleiermacher as "a very extraordinary man," who "made Christ the centre of his mystical system," and was, in fact, "a worshipper of Christ." Later in this same article, Hodge wrote approvingly of Schleiermacher's contempt for Pelagians as well as for rationalists (pp. 124-25).

61. On one traditional doctrine, the soul's survival of death, Hodge observed, "There is good reason to believe that . . . Schleiermacher sacrificed his philosophy, *as he certainly did in other points,* to his religion" (*ST*, vol. 1, p. 303; my emphasis).

62. Hodge, "Lecture to Theological Students," in Noll, *Princeton Theology*, pp. 111, 113 (cf. *LCH*, p. 204).

flesh and the only Saviour of men" (*ST,* 3:136). But Hodge found dogmatic security in the old ecclesiastical formulas, which in his view were to be resolutely repeated, not examined critically and revised as needed. Hence he warned: "The man should tremble, who ventures to say: I believe in Jesus Christ our Saviour, unless he believes in his true and perfect Godhead, for only on that assumption is he a Saviour or an object of faith."[63] Here the relation between piety and theology seems to be reversed: the measure of the theologian — indeed, the test of piety — is *correct belief.* And where does that leave Schleiermacher?

The theological points at issue between Hodge and Schleiermacher are subtle, not to be disposed of with a naive formula or two. They are also important and fascinating, and if I excuse myself from a full discussion of them, it is only because the task would demand much more detail than my allotted space allows. Hodge rightly wrote, "His [Schleiermacher's] doctrine concerning Christ is so implicated with his peculiar views on anthropology, on theology, and on the relation of God to the world, that it can neither be fully presented nor properly appreciated except as an integral part of his whole system" (*ST,* 2:442). My modest purpose is simply to note the main points at which Hodge introduced criticisms of Schleiermacher in the *Systematic Theology* and at least to open the question, Do the criticisms appear to rest on a sound understanding of him? This, of course, will leave the historical agenda open and will postpone to another day entirely the more properly theological question, Which of the two (if either) was right on the disputed issues — Hodge or Schleiermacher?

The index to Hodge's *Systematic Theology* lists twenty-nine references to Schleiermacher, one more than the references to Calvin. (Augustine earns still more, Turretin fewer.) I would not wish to infer too much from this perhaps surprisingly generous number of references to Schleiermacher — beyond noting that they afford solid evidence of a continuing preoccupation with this "very extraordinary man." They vary in length; some of them overlap; and the index is in any case selective. But what are the theological issues that led Hodge to refer to Schleiermacher's views, whether the references were included in the index or not? A closer look discloses, first of all, four excursuses that appraise Schleiermacher's "theories" on the dogmatic themes under discussion: three shorter ones, on the "mystical" theory of religion (*ST,* 1:65-66), revelation and inspiration (1:173-79), and sin (2:138-40); and a much longer one (already referred to) on the person and work of Christ (2:440-54; cf. 3:211-12). Second, there are a number

---

63. Hodge, "Religious State of Germany," p. 520.

of scattered allusions to Schleiermacher's understanding of the divine attributes (1:370, 376, 395, 398, 401-2, 411, 417, 428),[64] secondary causation in relation to the feeling of absolute dependence (1:592-94, 604), and the doctrine of the Trinity (1:481, 534; 2:445).[65] Third, reference is made in passing to his thoughts on theological method (1:9; cf. 2:532), historical development (1:118-19), the soul's survival of death (1:302-3; 2:57), miracles (2:448), grace (2:731-32), the unity of body and soul (3:19), the unity of God and the world (3:20), and humanity as the existence form of God on earth (3:20; cf. 1:176).

Each of the points at issue deserves more careful attention than I can offer here. But simply to locate Hodge's references to Schleiermacher under their several dogmatic rubrics, which often overlap, does not in itself pinpoint the springs from which his criticisms came. I think it can safely be said that Hodge traced all Schleiermacher's mistakes to two sources: his defective theological method and his commitment to a pantheistic philosophy. The two were closely connected in Hodge's mind. It would not be mistaken to say, more simply, that he discovered but one source of error in Schleiermacher's theology: the imposition of a pantheistic idea of God on everything else in the system.[66] But I will comment first on the question of method.

Hodge's objection to Schleiermacher's theological method was that it allegedly negated biblical authority by deriving doctrines from the reli-

64. Hodge conceded that for the seventeenth-century divines, both Lutherans and Reformed, the divine simplicity made it impossible to allow any real distinctions between one attribute and another; and he evidently recognized that this put Schleiermacher on the side of orthodoxy, whereas he himself wanted to take the distinctions between various divine attributes in Scripture at face value (*ST*, vol. 1, pp. 394-96). It does not seem to have occurred to him that this might call for second thoughts on Schleiermacher's relation to the dogmatic tradition.

65. Cf. Hodge, "What Is Christianity?" p. 160. Though he admitted that the ecclesiastical doctrine of the Trinity could not be "adequately proved by any citation of biblical passages" (*ST* vol. 1, p. 446), Hodge thought it well enough established by construction from the several constituent elements attested in Scripture that the church "has always refused to recognize as Christians those who reject this doctrine" (p. 443). The Trinity was important to Hodge because (he believed) it provided a foothold for belief in God's personality (vol. 2, p. 392).

66. The connection between the two sources of error becomes plain in Hodge's remarks on revelation and inspiration: for the mystic or pantheist, revelation cannot be "the communication of new truth" (*ST*, vol. 1, pp. 65-66), and "if the supernatural be impossible, inspiration is impossible" (vol. 1, p. 168). Revelation and inspiration, as Hodge understood them, require a personal, extramundane God who may act directly, not only mediately through fixed laws (vol. 1, p. 173).

gious consciousness, whereas we ought rather to "find in the Bible the norm and standard of all genuine religious experience" (*ST,* 1:11, 16).[67] Sometimes the warmth of Hodge's convictions led him to state the accusation incautiously: he was simply wrong to assert that Schleiermacher allowed the Scriptures no authority as a rule of faith (1:66); or that he made all theology consist in what the sense of dependence teaches us (1:376); or that he weaved a whole system of theology "out of the materials furnished by *his own* religious consciousness" (2:441; my emphasis). It may not be wrong, but it misses the point to say that Schleiermacher's "appeals to the Scriptures in support of his peculiar doctrines are extremely rare, and merely incidental" (2:443). The point, which wholly eluded Hodge, is that it falls to *exegetical* theology to judge whether doctrinal propositions are genuinely Christian, whereas the task of *dogmatic* theology is to present Christian doctrines systematically in their distinctively evangelical form. Hence the proximate court of appeal in Schleiermacher's dogmatics, *The Christian Faith,* is of necessity provided by the confessions of faith — another point that Hodge seems never to have noticed.[68] And this carries with it the obligation always to formulate doctrines in relation to the official teachings *(Lehrsätze)* of the church.[69]

In his more circumspect moments, however, Hodge (following Hengstenberg) put his finger on precisely the real issue: it is about the *nature* of the Bible's canonical authority (*ST,* 2:443).[70] For Hodge, the Scriptures have their authority as a "storehouse of facts" (1:10), or of truths and doctrines, supernaturally communicated (revelation) and preserved from error (inspiration) — except for a few minor mistakes that the Christian need not worry about (1:56, 155, 170, 176-77; 2:441). For Schleiermacher, the Scriptures of the New Testament both mediate and norm Christian faith in the present insofar as they contain Christ's self-testimony and the origi-

67. See also Hodge, "The Theology of the Intellect and That of the Feelings" (*BRPR* 1850), in Noll, pp. 204-5.

68. Friedrich Schleiermacher, *The Christian Faith,* translated from the 2nd German ed. of 1830-31, ed. H. R. Mackintosh and J. S. Stewart (Edinburgh: T&T Clark, 1928), §27. Given the fact that *The Christian Faith* is a work of dogmatic, not exegetical, theology, the index of Scripture references might even be considered generous.

69. Hodge therefore missed the mark once more, at least so far as Schleiermacher himself was concerned, when he said that the mediating theology does not "pretend to be founded on the Bible" or "profess allegiance to the Church doctrine" (*ST,* vol. 1, p. 453). See also Hodge, "The Religious State of Germany," pp. 533-34; and Hodge, "What Is Christianity?" pp. 121, 131.

70. Cf. Hodge, "Religious State of Germany," p. 532, where Hodge stated Hengstenberg's criticisms of the school of Schleiermacher.

nal preaching of Christ by his first disciples.[71] To be sure, Hodge's statement even of the real issue is hostile. He identified the *experience* of the Apostles and early Christians as Schleiermacher's theological norm and added, "He denies that the interpretation which they gave of their experience has normal authority for us, that is, he says that we are not bound to believe what the Apostles believed" (2:443). In fact, as I have indicated in his own words, Schleiermacher spoke of the apostolic *preaching* as the norm; but he held that the way Christians think today need not be restricted to the actual language of the apostolic norm.[72] Still, Hodge evidently recognized the issue: not whether, but why the Scriptures are authoritative.

As for the pantheistic philosophy, Hodge believed that it had brought about a revolution in theology (*ST,* 2:730, 3:650). He was convinced that it was the foundation of everything else in Schleiermacher's dogmatics: his thoughts on revelation, historical development, Christ, humanity, miracles, sin and grace, prayer (3:695), the Lord's Supper (3:656-57), and the afterlife (3:715). Hodge took pains to say what he understood by "pantheism" or "monism": not a naive identification of the world and God, but the affirmation of their essential unity (2:444), in particular of the essential unity of God and humanity (2:731).[73] God and world are correlative concepts: one of the most familiar aphorisms of the German philosophers is "Without the world there would be no God; and without God there would be no world" (1:301).[74] According to pantheism, "in its most rational form, all power, activity, and life, are the power, activity, and life of the one universal mind" (1:276).[75] Humanity is accordingly a mode of

71. Schleiermacher, *The Christian Faith,* §§128-29.

72. It is self-evident that the difference between Hodge and Schleiermacher on what makes Scripture authoritative must entail divergent estimates of the Old Testament, to which Schleiermacher allowed no dogmatic authority (see n. 68 above). A further consequence is that although they both claimed scientific status for their methods, Schleiermacher's "facts" were empirical (open to direct experience), while Hodge's were contained in reports that had to be taken on faith (*ST,* vol. 1, pp. 9, 11, 20-21). See further my essay, "Friedrich Schleiermacher" (1985), reprinted in Gerrish, *Continuing the Reformation: Essays on Modern Religious Thought* (Chicago: University of Chicago Press, 1993), pp. 147-77, especially pp. 152-54.

73. The main discussion in *ST,* vol. 1, pp. 299-334, presents in some detail a characterization, a history, and a critique of pantheism. My other references will be mostly supplementary. Hodge expressly indicated that in his account of pantheism he was thinking chiefly of Fichte, Schelling, and Hegel (*ST,* vol. 1, p. 331).

74. Cf. Hodge, "What Is Christianity?" p. 125.

75. It is this line of thought that made pantheism, in Hodge's judgment, inevitably deterministic (*ST,* vol. 1, p. 327; vol. 2, p. 281) and therefore anti-supernaturalist: the continu-

the divine existence (2:441, 449, 453, 731), the impersonal God come to consciousness (1:176, 393; 2:444).[76] Consequently, it matters little that Christ is said to be divine: that is not meant to set him apart from other men. The divine is human, the human divine (2:445). Against all these monstrous speculations, Hodge affirmed his theistic belief in an extramundane, personal God — "God" in the only legitimate sense of the word (1:204, 242, 284). The incarnation of God (the Son) in Jesus Christ was a unique union of the divine and human natures — without confusion — for the sake of our redemption (2:389, 455).

So, was Schleiermacher a pantheist? Hodge knows that Schleiermacher defined the concept "pantheism" with care,[77] and from Tholuck he had learned that Schleiermacher rejected the name. Nevertheless, one half of Germany thought him pantheistic;[78] and though Hodge sometimes professed himself willing to leave the question open,[79] his entire critique of Schleiermacher's doctrines presupposes that he had made up his mind.[80] The metaphysical issues are, if anything, even more difficult to sort out than the methodological ones. But two brief comments are in order. First, it is hard to suppose that Schleiermacher confused God and the world, or failed to distinguish them adequately, as long as critics from the other side, so to speak, saw his God as so "wholly other" that no contact between God and world was thinkable.[81] Second, Schleiermacher surely

---

ous divine activity admits no interruption. This certainly posed a difficulty for Schleiermacher, who, as Hodge pointed out, wanted to make the appearance of the Redeemer supernatural (vol. 1, p. 173; vol. 2, pp. 448, 453). I have addressed this problem elsewhere; see Gerrish, "Errors and Insights in the Understanding of Revelation: A Provisional Response," *Journal of Religion* 78 (1998): 64-88; see pp. 81-83.

76. Cf. Hodge, "What Is Christianity?" p. 126.

77. Hodge, "What Is Christianity?" p. 126. The "avowed Pantheists" in *ST,* vol. 1, pp. 481-82, are presumably the Hegelians.

78. Hodge, "What Is Christianity?" p. 123.

79. Hodge, "The Latest Form of Infidelity," p. 98.

80. Hengstenberg, by contrast, deliberately avoided this presupposition in his criticisms of Schleiermacher. See Hodge, "Religious State of Germany," p. 542.

81. More precisely, the question concerns the relationship between divine and natural *causality.* While Schleiermacher described them as coextensive, he insisted that they are wholly antithetical in kind (*The Christian Faith,* §51), as must clearly be the case if the divine causality is absolutely timeless (§52) and spaceless (§53). "No God without the world" certainly cannot denote an ontological relationship of mutual dependence any more than an identity of substances. It is rather an epistemological assertion that the dogmatic theologian cannot *say* anything about God apart from God's relationship to the world (see, e.g., §172.1). The point is, of course, commonplace in the tradition and has been echoed, for instance, by John Calvin (*Institutes,* 1.2.2).

avoided any talk of deifying humanity precisely by asserting that the distinctive presence of God to humans is through consciousness of God, which in Christ is a perfect — and therefore unique — consciousness.[82] Though Hodge wrote that, in that case, "the only difference between Christ and other men was that the *Gottesbewusstseyn* . . . determined in him all his activity from beginning to end," it must be noted that the *only* is his, not Schleiermacher's.[83] Schleiermacher believed he was offering a way to reconceptualize nothing less than the church's belief in the union of God and "man" in the Incarnation.

What happened, it seems to me, is that Hodge did not adequately distinguish Schleiermacher's philosophy from Hegelianism. He recognized that within the one new philosophy was a great diversity of individual systems, some closer to pantheism, others to theism (*ST,* 3:650). But they melted together in his mind as "the modern German theology" (3:651). He was grieved to learn, he said, that John Nevin, his friend of more than forty years, had taken offense when he read the first volume of the *Systematic Theology* and found his position confused with Hegel's, whose system he abhorred. Hodge's solution in volume three leaves much to be desired: to avoid any further danger of misrepresentation, he said, he had described the principles of the modern theology as far as possible in the language of its advocates, but he added: "No reference to names is given, so that no one is made responsible for the views expressed" (3:655, n. 1). Obviously, this will not do unless the generalizations are followed by a close reading of individual texts when individual theologians are under discussion. I have not found persuasive evidence that Hodge ever worked through Schleiermacher's *Glaubenslehre* as carefully as he appears to have read Strauss. He tended to fall back on books about Schleiermacher or publications critical of him. On one of the interpreters of German religious thought, J. D. Morell, he remarks: "Those who wish to understand the theory which he presents, would do well to study it in the writings of its authors."[84] Good advice, which all of us should take to heart.

82. Schleiermacher, *The Christian Faith,* §94.2.

83. Hodge, "What Is Christianity?" p. 130. Cf. *ST,* vol. 2, p. 447.

84. Hodge, "The Theology of the Intellect," pp. 540-41n. (cf. p. 601). Among Hodge's favorite interpreters of Schleiermacher were C. J. Braniss and F. W. Gess in Germany, Morell in England, and Nevin in America. He also relied heavily on Dorner for Schleiermacher's Christology and Müller for Schleiermacher on sin. When he did offer quotations from Schleiermacher, they sometimes came to him secondhand (e.g., *ST,* vol. 1, p. 302; "What Is Christianity?" pp. 124, 126). More often he simply referred to what others said about Schleiermacher (e.g., *ST,* vol. 2, pp. 446-47).

*   *   *

Charles Hodge stood for a way of doing theology that is in danger of extinction. He saw himself as a participant, along with others, in a grand enterprise that had a history of nearly 2,000 years behind it and deserved the best intellectual resources he could bring to it. The reader is continually amazed at the wealth of quotations and exact references that Hodge's erudition could marshal on every one of his dogmatic themes. They range over the history of theology, the (then) contemporary theological discussions, and the systematic theologian's continuing dialogue with conversation partners in philosophy and the sciences. His intention to bring the advocates of alternative positions into the discussion and to deal fairly and honestly with them is evident in the painstaking descriptions of their positions and the forthright enumeration of his objections. If I, as at least in part what Hodge called a "naturalized German" (see *ST,* 2:731, n. 2), complain that his usual learning and fairness came short in his treatment of Schleiermacher, that is only to say that I do not think the enterprise he engaged in is finished. A part of Hodge's legacy may be the comfort he brings to anyone who fails to take Schleiermacher seriously as an evangelical theologian. But he has left, in addition, a powerful testimony for those who continue to regard his style of systematic theology as a serious intellectual enterprise, which ought still to have its institutional home in both the seminary and the university.

Charles Hodge, Womanly Women, and Manly Ministers

LOUISE L. STEVENSON

C harles Hodge is known as nineteenth-century America's great defender of biblically based Calvinism. He protected the Reformed tradition of Protestantism against corrosion from the religious and social
philosophies of those who argued for an individual's power to affect his or
her ultimate destiny and those who applied German idealistic philosophy
to Protestant thought. Hodge's broad intellectual range and engagement
with the central political and theological controversies of his day have
drawn numerous positive and negative interpretations. Some scholars
credit Hodge with maintaining the intellectual integrity of the Reformed
tradition; others charge him with introducing theological methods leading to unbelief, or they find his writings a chief source of proslavery
thought.[1] Yet none of the scholarly analysis of recent years has recognized
that Hodge understood his world in the gendered terms of his day. So far
only one scholar has attempted to understand what Hodge thought about

---

1. For a recent summary of contemporary scholarship on Hodge, see John W. Stewart,
Mediating the Center: Charles Hodge on American Science, Language, Literature, and Politics
(Princeton: Princeton Theological Seminary, 1995), pp. 1-2. For positive assertions of
Hodge's intellectual impact on theology, see various pieces by Mark A. Noll, including, "In-
troduction," *Charles Hodge: The Way of Life* (New York: Paulist Press, 1987), pp. 1-44, and "In-
troduction: Charles Hodge and the Definition of 'Darwinism,'" in Charles Hodge, *What Is
Darwinism? and Other Essays*, ed. Mark A. Noll and David N. Livingstone (Grand Rapids:
Baker Book House, 1994). Larry E. Tise makes the proslavery argument, due to an incom-
plete reading and understanding of Hodge's writings, in *Proslavery: A History of the Defense of
Slavery in America, 1701-1840* (Athens, Ga.: University of Georgia Press, 1987), pp. 277, 282, 327.
See also James Turner, *Without God, Without Creed: The Origins of Unbelief in America* (Balti-
more: Johns Hopkins University Press, 1985), pp. 185-86.

the silent majority of nineteenth-century Presbyterianism — women — and to Hodge scholarship this article remains an interesting aside. Although contemporary historians consider themselves sufficiently aware and sophisticated to stand beyond their subjects' race- and class-based assumptions, many remain naively complicit with the gendered assumptions of the nineteenth century. Scholars who wish to analyze and explicate mid-nineteenth-century Old School Presbyterian thought would do well to account for the assumptions of gender upon which it rests. In this paper, I would like to raise to visibility Hodge's thinking about womanhood and manhood and to suggest that some present-day controversies continue those of Hodge's day. This paper opens by describing Hodge's ideal of womanhood, and then it shows how he modified his ideal in his public role as editor of the *Biblical Repertory and Princeton Review* and in his private roles as husband and father.[2]

To begin, let us ask a Hodge-like question: Who was Charles Hodge? and then answer with an essential fact: he was a man. Hodge belonged to the theological, educational, and publishing enterprises centered in and about Princeton Theological Seminary from the 1820s through the 1860s. Hodge was a man educated by men who taught men and wrote for men. To emphasize the obvious, had he been a woman, he would not have prepared for college, studied at the College of New Jersey (Princeton), prepared for the ministry, served as a Presbyterian minister, taught at the seminary, or edited and written for the *Biblical Repertory and Princeton Review*.

At the semi-centennial celebration of Hodge's professorship at the Princeton Theological Seminary in 1872, he made the often quoted and misunderstood statement that he was proud of the fact that the Seminary and the *Repertory* had generated no new ideas during his years of service. He meant that his colleagues and co-editors had done nothing to change the meaning of the Bible. Hodge believed that they had merely drawn on

---

2. Ronald Hogeland's pioneering article is "Charles Hodge, The Association of Gentlemen and Ornamental Womanhood: 1825-1855," *Journal of Presbyterian History* 53 (1975): 239-55. A work that preceded the current wave of gender scholarship is Barbara Leslie Epstein, *The Politics of Domesticity: Women, Evangelism, and Temperance in Nineteenth-Century American Thought* (Middletown, Ct.: Wesleyan University Press, 1981). For other periods see Susan Juster, *Disorderly Women: Sex, Politics, and Evangelicalism in Revolutionary New England* (Ithaca, N.Y.: Cornell University Press, 1994); and Susan Curtis, "The Son of Man and God the Father: The Social Gospel and Victorian Masculinity," in *Meanings for Manhood: Constructions of Masculinity in Victorian America*, ed. Mark C. Carnes and Clyde Griffen (Chicago: University of Chicago Press, 1990), pp. 67-78; Ivy Schweitzer, *The Work of Self-Representation: Lyric Poetry in Colonial New England* (Chapel Hill: University of North Carolina Press, 1991).

methods and knowledge gained from American and Continental biblical scholarship to explicate Biblical propositions. At the Seminary, the books of the Bible that became Hodge's special province and area of scholarship were the epistles of Paul. He lectured on these texts to seminary students and published commentaries on Romans, I and II Corinthians, and Ephesians between 1835 and 1857. Reviewing Hodge's sermons and Sunday afternoon talks to seminary students, one can gain a sense of Paul's central place in Hodge's thought. He referred to verses from Paul more than verses from the rest of the Bible, and he often mentioned to students that they should model themselves on the example of Paul.[3]

For Christians, Paul's epistles have always been an important source on the nature of women and women's social role. Consider, for example, one man who was particularly important in Hodge's life and in the history of Princeton Presbyterianism. Ashbel Green served as head pastor of the Hodge family's Philadelphia church when Hodge was a boy, then served as president of the College of New Jersey while Hodge was a student there; and when Hodge was editor of the *Biblical Repertory,* Green was a member of its editorial board (then called an association of gentlemen). Green's writings on womanhood furnish a starting point for study of his student ideas. In 1825, Green addressed the Female Society of Princeton on *The Christian Duty of Christian Women*. According to Paul, Green argued, women's public activities should never violate standards of womanly modesty and evoke negative comment. This limited women's public activities to charitable or benevolent work. Green assured the women of the Princeton society that their raising funds to support a school for women in India could earn only approbation, since they were seeking to educate and convert.[4]

In his writings on Paul and womanhood, Hodge never disagreed with his teacher. Still, Hodge's extensive commentaries gave him ample opportunity to understand the teachings of the Apostle more fully and to grapple with the potential complexity of their message. In his address, Green had argued for women's subordinate station and exclusion from public political and economic life by selecting Biblical verses that

3. A collection of his talks to students may be found in Charles Hodge, *Conference Papers or Analyses of Discourses, Doctrinal and Practical; Delivered on Sabbath Afternoons to the Students of the Theological Seminary, Princeton, N.J.* (New York: Charles Scribner's Sons, 1879). Many more manuscript sermons and talks are in Charles Hodge Papers, Archives and Special Collections, Luce Library, Princeton Theological Seminary (hereafter PTSL).

4. Hogeland, "Charles Hodge"; Ashbel Green, *The Christian Duty of Christian Women . . .* (Princeton: Princeton Press, 1825).

insist on sexual difference and hierarchy. He did not mention other passages in the Epistles that antebellum commentators read as implying equality. For his student Hodge, Galatians 3:28 was key. Here, Paul wrote that people — Jew or Gentile, men or women, slave or free — are one or equal in God's eyes. Hodge realized that this verse seemingly conflicts with others from Corinthians, Ephesians, and Romans. His reconciliation of these two messages lies at the core of his thinking about how people relate to God.

As a writer of the antebellum period, Hodge often explained human relationship to God by drawing on the vocabulary of slavery and freedom, equality and inequality. Hodge thought God offers either salvation or damnation in the next life on equal terms to all, no matter what their sex or station in this life. In the plan of salvation, whether one was slave or free in this world mattered little. Actual slavery in the mundane world, such as that of the American South, implied nothing about freedom in a divine or ultimate world. The slavery that did matter in an ultimate sense was that which enslaved the spirit and the soul to concerns of this world. In this sense, an enslaved African American or a white Southerner might be a slave if either did not realize the nature of true freedom, which resided in dependence on God. As Hodge said in an ordination sermon, "slavery to Christ is consummate and perfect liberty."[5]

Belief in the promise of ultimate freedom in the next world has two possible corollaries: either one can consider inequalities in this world inconsequential, or one can consider them consequential and part of God's plan. Like most Old School Presbyterians, Hodge took the latter tack and argued that God had organized the world with people in unequal relationships. As a nineteenth-century follower of Scottish realism or common sense philosophy, Hodge believed that the natural world and human world followed divine laws. As a divine creation, the logic of the human mind replicated the logic of the universe and thus could recognize its demonstrated truths. Hodge looked at the natural and human world of his day and saw hierarchies, including those of animals and plants, men and women, masters and slaves, and reasoned that "order and subordination pervade the universe." From the assumption that God was benevolent, he concluded that these unequal relationships were "essential to its being." While as subjects of God all people were equal in an ultimate sense, each man or woman, master or slave had his or her

5. Conference Talk, "The Liberty Wherewith God has Made us Free," 11 March 1867, PTSL.

particular place in the order of this world, which, Hodge knew, a benevolent God had created.[6]

One of the consequential unequal relationships God had created was that between men and women, and Hodge found the essence of that relationship explained in Corinthians. Paul wrote that man shows God's glory and woman shows the glory of man: "The head of every man is Christ; and the head of the woman is the man; and the head of Christ is God."[7] Thus the woman could not reflect the glory of God as ruler, since the supposed facts of her creation as told in Genesis show that she was meant to and did reveal the "glory of the man." She revealed what there is "of majesty in him" and always assumed his position in life, for better or for worse.[8]

For husband and wife, Hodge thought, God had created a hierarchy in which each had an equal relationship with God. Because obedience to her husband was a divine commandment, serving God meant a wife had to follow this dictum. She should have a "sense of his superiority out of which trust and obedience involuntarily flow." This subjection was to be cheerful, Hodge thought, since Paul had meant that a woman should be a man's companion and ministering angel. Those whom God had invested with authority — whether husband, master, or slaveholder — had a directive from God to follow his commandments exclusively. Husbands especially were commanded to love their wives as themselves.[9]

Hodge thought that Paul had commanded women in society to behave and dress in ways that denoted their subjection to and honoring of men. When Hodge observed customs in various parts of the world, the conclusion appeared that God had allowed for different ways of showing subjection. In some societies, such as those of the Middle East, a veil might indicate subjection; in others, long hair. To remain true to Biblical teachings, Hodge thought, it was not necessary to insist on male superiority in all areas of life. Women might be superior in those areas that did not entitle the man to authority. In short, what Paul meant was that women should do nothing that denied their subordinate status and that vitiated their being objects of "honor and affection." With regard to behavior, Hodge

6. "Charge to Ordinand: Edward B. Hodge," 28 April 1864, ms., PTSL; Charles Hodge, *An Exposition of the First Epistle to the Corinthians* (New York: R. Carter, 1857), pp. 11, 3.

7. Hodge, *First Epistle to the Corinthians,* pp. 11, 3.

8. Hodge, *First Epistle to the Corinthians,* p. 210.

9. Peter Lesley, Notes on Charles Hodge's Lectures on Ephesians, ms., PTSL, pp. 5, 23; Charles Hodge, *Commentary on the Epistle to the Ephesians* (New York: R. Carter and Brothers, 1856), pp. 354, 313, 353.

highlighted Paul's injunctions about women keeping silent in church or public, and said that Paul meant that women should not publicly prophesy. Hodge took care to point out that Paul had said nothing about private prayer or prophesying, so that women could use any means consistent with their nature to pursue their education in private, including prayer and prophesying. In fact, Hodge conceded, women might even be superior to men in some ways, as long as those ways were not essential to overall male superiority.[10]

In his commentaries, Hodge's methods of arguments went beyond those of his teachers and drew on scholarly means acquired in part during his 1826-28 studies in France and Germany. He could rely upon his knowledge of the original scriptural language, refer to other passages of the Bible from either Testament, introduce the opinions of other commentators from Luther to the present, or draw conclusions from observation in the natural and social worlds. For example, Hodge appealed to the facts of Creation recorded in Genesis to confirm Paul's arguments about woman's subservience to man. He also drew on his knowledge of early church history to show that the practice of early churches confirmed the validity of Paul's prohibition against women's praying and prophesying in public.

When Hodge cited facts from the social world as the basis of these conclusions, these facts might be observations from the white professional middle-class community in which he lived. For instance, Hodge observed that women derived their "power and usefulness" from being "objects of admiration and affection." Then he concluded that anything "which tends to excite the opposite sentiments should for that reason be avoided." He observed that the male had "those attributes which enable and entitle him to command: He is larger, stronger, bolder; he has more of those mental and moral qualities which are required in a leader. This is just as plain from history as that iron is heavier than water." Frequently, Hodge's so-called empiricism resulted in statements that he saw as universal truths but that modern scholars recognize as generalizations derived from class and gender interest. My favorite example of this is Hodge's argument that Paul had not intended to say that virgins are holier than wives. Rather, in Hodge's reasoning, Paul had meant that virgins could better devote themselves to the service of God; undistracted by husbands, they presumably had more time. Should well-meaning reformers overthrow God's laws for women as found in history,

10. Hodge, *First Epistle to the Corinthians*, p. 304.

society, and nature, Hodge promised gender anarchy, which would de-
grade both men and women, "making the one effeminate and the other
masculine."[11]

Hodge's discussion of women and their role in his commentaries de-
parts from his treatment of other subjects in two significant ways. While
discussing marriage, salvation, slavery, and slaveholding, Hodge usually
names the opponents of his arguments by name or group, whether abolitionists or slaveholders, Catholics, Arminians, or antinomians. Yet, his arguments about women in the commentaries never mention directly any
adversary or opposing theory, even though in his day America of was full
of opposing theories and theorists. Abolitionists Sarah and Angelina
Grimké argued that since men and women equally shared God's dispensation, they shared the duty of combating sin that they found on earth.
They concluded that women had the duty to speak in public against the
sin of slavery. Moral reformers opposed to prostitution acted publicly to
humiliate men arriving at brothels by dropping onto their knees in prayer
in front of them. In the 1848 Declaration of Rights at Seneca Falls, Elizabeth Cady Stanton and the hundred other women and men who signed
the document protested the strictures of the Bible that made women subordinate. During the 1850s, woman's rights conventions and temperance
conventions in New York, Pennsylvania, Ohio, and Massachusetts rehearsed arguments of women's moral agency and social responsibility.[12]
Since Hodge read several newspapers daily, and current events supplied a
staple for conversation in the Hodge household, he had to know of these
opposing ideas.

His silence on other commentators' theories about women and wom-

11. Hodge, *First Epistle to the Corinthians*, p. 304; Hodge, *Epistle to the Ephesians*, p. 312;
Hodge, *First Epistle to the Corinthians*, pp. 7, 34. Hodge's social thought follows the pattern de-
scribed by Theodore Dwight Bozeman in "Inductive and Deductive Politics: Science and
Society in Antebellum Presbyterian Thought," *Journal of American History* 64 (1977): 704-22.

12. See Sarah Grimké, *Letters on the Equality of the Sexes and Other Essays* (New Haven: Yale
University Press, 1988), esp. pp. 31-34; Carroll Smith-Rosenberg, "Beauty, the Beast, the Mili-
tant Woman: A Case Study in Sex Roles and Social Stress in Jacksonian America," *American
Quarterly* 23 (1971): 562-84; Nancy A. Hewitt, *Women's Activism and Social Change: Rochester,
New York, 1822-1872* (Ithaca, N.Y.: Cornell University Press, 1984). Hodge did write against
theories of woman's duty common among followers of William Lloyd Garrison, including
the Grimké sisters, in an 1838 review in the *Biblical Repertory and Princeton Review* (hereafter
BRPR): "If our women are to be emancipated from subjection to the law which God has imposed upon them . . . we shall soon have a country over which the genius of Mary
Wolstonecraft would delight to preside, but from which all order and virtue would speedily
be banished." Hodge, "West Indian Emancipation," *BRPR* 10 (1838): 604.

anhood may be explained by consensus within the scholarly discourse on those subjects. Since he usually referred to scholars who disagreed with him and never to scholars who agreed with him, his omission of conflicting opinions on women suggests that no one whom Hodge recognized as a scholar had a significantly different interpretation. The reason Hodge did not mention opposing social and political theories becomes apparent with analysis of articles by and about women in the *Biblical Repertory and Princeton Review* from 1825 to 1871.

Paul's Epistles and their admonitions to women on public prophesying and teaching served Hodge and his editorial board in their efforts to constrict women's influence. The *Repertory's* writers always disapproved of women authors setting forth original views on questions of theology and philosophy. The first review of a woman's book ever to appear in the *Repertory* set boundaries that never changed. The 1836 review of Catharine Beecher's *Letters on the Difficulties of Religion* (1836) by Hodge's senior colleague, seminary professor Archibald Alexander, described "Miss Beecher" as "inclined to meddle with too many things, and with things out of her reach." Alexander was glad that Paul had proscribed women's speaking in church and recommended that women avoid theological debate and controversy, leaving those issues to experts who had formally studied theology and metaphysics. Controversy, or warfare as Alexander called it, was not a fit activity for women and should be left to men, who felt it their duty. Phoebe Palmer's efforts to justify women's public religious activities caused another *Repertory* reviewer to remind readers of Corinthians and its "entire prohibition of public prophesizing" presented "in words too plain for the most desperate ingenuity to wrench into any other meaning." Near the end of the period in question, the *Repertory* proposed that most persons regretted "to see ladies of so much ability" as Caroline Dall wasting their time attempting the impossible: "the laws of nature cannot be altered." No man or woman could alter what God had made. It was "a cruel folly to attempt to make a gazelle do the work of a dray horse." According to the *Repertory*, Dall had done so in *The College, the Market and the Court* by arguing that women and men should have equal intellectual opportunity in education and employment.[13]

Repertory reviewers approved of women writing on subjects on which

---

13. Review of Catharine E. Beecher, *Letters on the Difficulties of Religion*, BRPR 8 (1836): 545; review of Phoebe Palmer, *Promise of the Father: or a Neglected Society of the Last Days*, BRPR 31 (1859): 624; review of Caroline H. Dall, *The College, the Market and the Court; or, Woman's Relations to Education, Labour and Law*, BRPR 41 (1869): 676, 677.

they were expert, namely those that educated their own sex. If women authors wanted to address both men and women, reviewers recommended two possible paths. They could become popularizers and write histories, biographies, and philosophies adapted to general readers who presumably did not have "the time or ability to consult more extended works" or the attention to study truths "presented abstractly and systematically." Or women authors could follow the example of the English moralist Hannah More, who addressed issues of ethics, practical piety, and Christian manners in books that enjoyed broad sales on both sides of the Atlantic. As a consequence of these directives, *Repertory* readers might find favorable mention or a several-sentence notice of non-fiction works by Hartford poet Lydia H. Sigourney and Susan Warner, author of the first blockbuster bestseller of the century, *The Wide, Wide World*. Or they might learn of books, forgotten in our present day, such as Mrs. Mary I. Torrey's *Ornament; or the Christian Rule of Dress* . . . (Boston, 1838); *A Mother's Tribute to a beloved Daughter, or a Memoir of Malvina Forman Smith* (New York, 1842); and Catherine M. Trowbridge's *George Morton and his Sister* (Philadelphia, 1864). Reviewers noted that these authors displayed piety, intelligence, soundness of judgment, delicacy of taste, and a "pure strain of spiritual feeling."[14]

Despite the consistent posture of opposition to certain kinds of women's intellectual activity in the public sphere, Hodge and his fellow editors made significant, tacit concessions by accepting any publishing by women. In his first-century travels, Paul had obviously not been troubled by women publishing, for he had forbidden merely women prophesying in public and in church. In his 1825 pamphlet, Green also had not mentioned women writing and publishing. Though *Repertory* editors never made any explicit statement about the principle of whether or not women should be authors, in practice they accepted women as their junior and subordinate allies in their struggle against infidelity and worldliness. Women authors thus assumed a sort of lady auxiliary status comparable to the status of Presbyterian women that joined in benevolent or charitable causes to ameliorate the condition of the so-called needy poor, especially widows and orphans. Benevolent women's reform activities coexisted with their churches. Like the Princeton Female Society, they attributed poverty to unfortunate circumstance and relied upon clergymen and prominent male parishioners to help them gain support and funds. In contrast, women temperance reformers, moral reformers, and

14. BRPR 29 (1857): 550; BRPR 39 (1867): 319; BRPR 8 (1836): 545; BRPR 11 (1839): 242.

abolitionists often challenged businesses and churches to purify themselves by ceasing to trade with or to cast out those whom they thought to be sinners — most often non-abolitionists.[15]

Ironically from the perspective of those who associate biblical literalism with conservative action, it was the Princetonians' insistence on biblical literalism that permitted their limited acceptance of women's writing and publishing. Hodge always argued that an activity was not sinful unless the Bible called it a sin. Since the Bible did not explicitly prohibit women from writing, it was logical that they should be able to do so, as long as their doing so remained consistent with other Biblical teachings. As Hodge pointed out in his commentaries, Paul's cautions on womanly behavior did not restrict women from pursuing their own education and self-improvement in private. Reading and writing were obvious means for pursuing that self-improvement.

The major restraint on women's writing stemmed from Paul's insistence on their subordinate status. Women's writing had to show honor to men as women's superiors, and writings that claimed women's equality in areas that the editors felt themselves and all men superior drew the Princetonians' censure. Within the intellectual context of the mid-nineteenth century, men maintained their superiority through specialized education and training, such as that acquired in theological seminaries. Thus women were warned from intruding into areas where specialized knowledge prevailed. Male authors were chastised for faulty philosophical premises, sloppy arguments, and hasty conclusions, but unlike the women who committed these same errors, men never became targets of ad hominem, gender-based arguments. The Princeton reviewers blamed women's superficial thinking on biology, not on women's exclusion from institutions of higher learning.

Hodge may not have mentioned conflicting theories of womanhood in his commentaries because to do so would have been to recognize women as worthy opponents in the public world of ideas. To leave opponents unnamed was a way of confirming the author's superiority. Maintaining the absence or silence of women was an essential means of making the Princeton enterprise a masculine endeavor — one that would retain

15. See Hewitt, *Women's Activism,* for comparison of various women's reform activities, and Lori D. Ginzberg, *Women and the Work of Benevolence: Morality, Politics, and Class in Nineteenth-Century America* (New Haven: Yale University Press, 1990), p. 39. Hodge's son would not let abolitionists speak in his church because he would not allow his people to be "vilified." See Caspar Wistar Hodge to Charles Hodge, 23 December 1857, in Papers of Charles Hodge, Special Collections, Firestone Library, Princeton University (hereafter PUL).

the respect of other men and one that could remain at the center of nineteenth-century American learned discourse.

The *Biblical Repertory* accepted women authors into auxiliary status probably because of the challenge that Presbyterians recognized in the publishing explosion of the antebellum period. As technological advances such as the Hoe steam printing press made book production cheaper and steamboats, canals, and railroads created larger and larger territories for book distribution, the Presbyterian General Assembly worried about the implications of these changes for the world's improvement. Books, pamphlets and newspapers seemed to spread theories and notions at odds with Presbyterian doctrine and social philosophy. So in 1839 the Board of Publication changed its name from the Board of Publication of Tracts and Sunday School Books and broadened its purpose. It would now publish all sorts of works "adapted to promote sound learning and true religion." Despite these new efforts, Presbyterian leaders continued to see ungodliness and ungodly literature growing stronger and more prevalent and lamented in 1849 "the deluge of fictitious narratives and sentimental religionism pouring in upon our children from every quarter." The Board of Publication noted that it had decided to try to stem this flood by accommodating itself to the market and publishing books with more market appeal. Its recent products had lower prices, more illustrations, and more interesting bindings.[16]

Still, there was one more marketing strategy that the Board of Publication left unmentioned in its 1839 policy statement. Without any fanfare, it began to publish more books by women, as testified to by the increasing number of notices of books by women appearing in *Repertory* short reviews and notices. The *Repertory* editors and members of the Board of Publication used the same criteria to evaluate the works of women authors. The board never accepted for publication books by women that poached on men's self-defined areas of expertise, and when other firms published them, *Repertory* reviewers noticed them unfavorably.

Just as necessity could encourage Presbyterian men to take as allies in public life those whom Paul had deemed subordinate, so too the complexities of real-life situations could cause Hodge to modify Biblical lessons. The letters of Charles Hodge, his wife Sarah Bache Hodge, and their relatives reveal that Charles revered Sarah and that they enjoyed a warm and

---

16. *BRPR* 11 (1839): 438; *BRPR* 21 (1849): 152. For a discussion of the ties between organized religion and the antebellum literary marketplace, see R. Laurence Moore, *Selling God: American Religion in the Marketplace of Culture* (New York: Oxford University Press, 1994), ch. 1.

physically close relationship. After her death, he wrote his brother that he visited her grave at least twice weekly. He turned his "heart towards her with much the same feelings with which a Roman who stops short of idolatry looks up to his patron saint." Like many mid-century men and women, Charles's attitude toward motherhood fed his powerful feelings. He explained these when he thought about the birth of his first son, Archibald Alexander Hodge ("Arch" to family members). As he watched his newborn son, he said that he was stunned as he found the feelings of a parent overtaking those of a husband. Years afterwards, on the birth of his first grandchild from his favorite and first-born daughter, he shared his feelings with his wife. Mary "now knows the peculiar joy of a mother's heart, a joy so great, as our blessed saviour says, to obliterate the recollection of the anguish by which it is purchased." To this pious man of the nineteenth century, women were above all mothers, and he objectified woman in maternal terms. His perspective is reflected in his remarks upon his first night away from his wife as he departed for a two-year journey. Writing to his "darling," he told her that

> I have a lock of your hair and one of dear Alexander's but none of sweet little Mary. . . . My heart is full of longings after them and you. My lonely couch last night long refused me sleep. I pictured to myself, your room and you with one dear treasure on each arm with tearful love embracing them alternately. O could I see you — could I hear dear Alexander's silver voice and Mary's infant cry "Papa" how willingly would I give up all other pleasures.[17]

Looking at the physical side of the Hodge's marriage, we realize that the couple did not share our modern assumption that reverence for motherhood implies lack of delight in the physical aspect of marriage. Between 1823 and 1840, Charles Hodge and Sarah Hodge produced five boys and three girls, even with his absence in Europe for two years. Charles and Sarah were out of step with most of their fellow white Americans. From 1800 to 1850, roughly the years of Sarah's lifetime, the average number of births per white woman surviving to menopause declined from 7.04 to 5.42. Letters dating from Charles's 1826-28 trip to Europe testify to the fulfillment each derived from their relationship. The pair often lamented their separation. He would write of his lonely couch, while she described their letters as

17. Charles Hodge (hereafter CH) to Sarah Bache Hodge (hereafter SBH), 6 June 1851, 30 July 1849, 30 September 1826, PUL.

the only intercourse now left to those so tenderly attached except that more holy one that gives me so much consolation. Indeed, my Charles, I had no expectation of being able to feel as I do on this subject of our separation. . . . I feel that we are now actuated by higher motives than those that have usually governed me and this of itself is not divested of comfort. I feel assured that your spirit is guided to heavenly sources of satisfaction and that your self-denial will be abundantly rewarded.[18]

When Sarah died unexpectedly on Christmas day in 1849 after a three-month illness, probably with a cancerous tumor, Charles often recalled their relationship in letters to his brother. She never "evinced warmer love to me," he remembered, "than during the last two months of her life." On the afternoon or evening of her death, he remembered that he was lying beside her when "she began to sink." The next month he recalled that his "habit of caressing and fondling her kept alive" the feelings that they shared "so that to the last she was like a girl in her love."[19]

Their love had its intellectual and spiritual dimensions as well. While he was in Europe and she was living with relatives in Philadelphia, she attended chemistry lectures at the University of Pennsylvania. Her letters to Charles often commented on current events. Together they opposed Jackson's policies toward the Cherokees and the United States Bank, and she kept Charles up to date on the doings of the Unitarians or Quakers. On religion she looked to him as a teacher for herself and her children. She referred to her husband as "her pious friend." Before they were married Charles gave her Dodderidge, and she thanked him for directing her attention "to serious things."[20]

When it came to education of the Hodge children, Sarah appears to have left Charles in charge of the big picture while she took care of the day-to-day practice. She said that Charles's wish would be her command, and she home-educated all their children for their first years. When Arch (who later replaced Charles in his teaching position at the seminary) was

18. Daniel Scott Smith, "Family Limitation, Sexual Control, and Domestic Feminism in Victorian America," *Feminist Studies* 1 (Winter-Spring 1973): 40-57; SBH to CH, 23 October 1826, PUL. On love and marriage see Karen Lystra, *Searching the Heart: Women, Men and Romantic Love in Nineteenth-Century America* (New York: Oxford University Press, 1989).

19. CH to Hugh Lenox Hodge (hereafter HLH), 15 January 1850, 25 December 1849, 26 January 1850, PUL.

20. SBH to CH, 20 January 1827, 14 February 1827, 20 January 1828, 28 March 1828, PUL. Also one letter with no date: SBH to CH in Box 8, folder 2, PUL. Based on the content, it is probably misfiled and dates from before their marriage.

four, she taught him Isaac Watts's infant catechism and hymns and the Sunday School primer. When Arch told a lie, she reported to Charles that she had "whipped him in the most conscientious manner I was able." Troubled about the incident, she asked Charles for advice. In reply, Charles never mentioned the physical punishment or whether he approved of what she had done. Instead, he guided her toward another way to discipline by telling her how to "enlighten" children's consciences. When their moral feeling weakened it needed strengthening by

> inculcation of the great simple moral principles which find in every human heart a witness to their truth, and by a uniform manifestation of disapprobation of all that is evil. Children's characters are formed more by the silent influence of example than by the best precept. . . . Let a child see the devout reverence of a Parent for God and divine things and he will feel that reverence too. Let us, my dear love, never forget that it is only by being good that we can hope to make our children good. . . . There is as much difference in the original moral feelings of children as in their talents, dispositions, or anything else.

And to Arch he wrote that he had wept at news of his behavior and told him that he must realize "how wicked it is to tell a falsehood." "Your dear saviour cannot love you if you do not speak the truth and the Holy Bible tells us that *liars* cannot go to heaven."[21]

Though Sarah had yielded to Hodge when he wished to go to Europe, leaving her with their infant daughter Mary and toddler Arch, she did not always do so. Later in the senior Hodges' marriage, when Mary was about to have her first child, Sarah expressed her desire to assist at the delivery. Her daughter and husband lived in a boarding house in Danville, Kentucky, and had no servants. The daughter had told her mother that in a slave state it had been impossible to hire help during her pregnancy and would also be impossible after the delivery. Charles advised against Sarah's going to Danville because the great cholera epidemic of 1849 was then sweeping up the Mississippi and turning afflicted cities and neighborhoods into what Charles called "charnel houses." Even Mary did not want her mother to come, especially if she did so against her father's wishes. Even though Charles felt Sarah should not go, he felt that he could not impose his authority. As he asked his brother, "where did duty lie?" On the one hand, his daughter had no nearby friends or family to

21. SBH to CH, 14 February 1827; CH to SBH, 9 April 1827, PUL.

help with the delivery and newborn, and she had had been sickly for some months. When thinking of "my dear Mary," Charles confided, "my heart trembles." On the other hand, should his wife leave her husband and six other children, he worried, "to encounter certain danger?"[22]

Sarah decided the matter for herself and went, taking along one of her sons. Undertaking an arduous journey by train, canal boat, river steamer, and stagecoach, made even more arduous by the necessity of skirting cholera-stricken areas, she arrived in Danville in time to deliver her daughter of a redheaded son on July 23, 1849. Unfortunately, the new mother developed puerperal fever, which was often life threatening, and then an abscess on her breast. In August, with the cholera approaching Danville, Sarah organized removal of the new mother and child to the estate of family friends in Lexington. After recovering a bit, Mary insisted that her mother not return with her to Danville, while Sarah insisted that her daughter was unfit to care for herself and the baby. A compromise was reached, for in early September, grandmother, mother, and child surprised their friends in Princeton with their arrival. During their absence, Charles had considered his wife's willfulness and written her that he rejoiced that she had "followed the 'instinctive judgment,' the gift of your sex, rather than the advice that the wisdom of men dictated." Later in the fall, when Mary's husband protested her absence, Charles commiserated with him with a jest that ignored the painful discussions that must have preceded Mary's western trip. Charles wrote that since he "had all my life been forced to submit to my wife, he had no right to be surprised at finding himself very small game in her hands."[23]

At times, the apostle Paul's teachings could help Charles deal with separation from his children. When confronting his beloved daughter Mary's moving to Danville with her new husband, he had written that when a daughter marries, she "acquires a higher obedience than that to her parents." A husband, therefore, had a right to take his wife anywhere he pleased. He lamented that Mary "not now and never can be to us what she once was." Although Charles dreaded his daughter living in a slave society threatened by rebellion and with public morals so low that white men shot one another in the street, he did nothing to urge his son-in-law to move east.[24]

<hr/>

22. SBH to CH, 5 August 1849; Mary E. Scott to CH, 7 July 1849; CH to HLH, 27 June 1849, PUL.
23. CH to HLH, 6 September 1849, PUL.
24. CH to HLH, 14 September 1848, PUL.

Regardless of Paul's words and women's intention to subordinate themselves, sometimes they unintentionally made men follow them. In 1847, Arch took his new wife Elizabeth with him to Allahabad, India, where he was to be a teaching missionary in a Presbyterian school. On the lengthy voyage, Elizabeth suffered from a prolonged bout of seasickness, or possibly morning sickness. Delivering two children within her first two years of marriage, she became so debilitated after a year in India that doctors recommended her return to the United States to save her life. Since Hodge had had his own missionary career thwarted by a rheumatic hip twenty-five years previously, he felt his son's loss as if it were his own. The elder Hodge lamented his son's disappointment by commenting that having so "feeble a wife" was "a dreadful drawback to his usefulness." If Elizabeth died, Charles first imagined, Arch could stay in India. But then he remembered that Arch would have to return even if she did die, for "how else to take care of two infants on a ship?"[25]

As Hodge's family life illustrates, even a literal reading of Paul might lead to conflict and uncertainty. A daughter's obedience to her husband might cause pain to her father. A daughter-in-law might obediently follow her husband, but her physical condition might mean that her husband had to follow her needs and return to the United States. And when duty called in two directions, women might decide that the stronger call led away from husbands. In these instances and others, the Hodge women carved out small, private areas of responsibility and self-determination. Nevertheless, the narrowness in scope of these areas shows that Presbyterian theology contained no lode of empowering messages for women. Although the Hodge women could count on circumstance to present them with opportunities to decrease their dependence on men in private and public life, circumstance would not bring them autonomy from the biblical strictures and Old School thinking that decreed their subordination.

Though Hodge's ideas on women and womanhood seem very far from those of the present and those of nineteenth-century woman's rights advocates seem much closer, Hodge's ideas were more widely shared in his own day than those that are more congenial in the present day. To the present-minded analyst, it might seem as if Hodge spoke for traditional womanhood. But the womanhood that he spoke for had not existed before his mother's generation. He had married a woman well educated for her day, who was his intellectual companion. Further, he allowed individual wishes, rather than family considerations, to govern his children's

25. CH to HLH, 14 September 1847, 22 August 1848, 28 August 1849, PUL.

marriage choices. Arch married a woman who had few resources and his daughter Mary married a man of whom the family might have been expected to disapprove. Her husband William Scott grew up as a farmer on the Midwestern frontier, and he was a Democrat (and possibly belonged to the most radical reformist wing of the party, the "Locofocos"). Still, Charles allowed his daughter to marry Scott. Hodge could not say no to a man who "who loves and fears God, who is delicate in his feelings, amiable in disposition, and possessed of promising talents for usefulness."[26]

Within the context of his time, while far from the vanguard of the woman's rights movement, Charles Hodge occupied a place in its very rear guard, in the company of such prominent antebellum women educators as Catharine Beecher, Emma Willard, and her sister Almira Lincoln Phelps. In his commentaries on Paul's epistles, Hodge validated women's self-development and education and so would have supported the founding of the women's educational institutions for which these women were noted. Beecher's writing for women and Willard's and Hart's publishing textbooks for secondary schools fall well within the publishing strictures for women established by the *Biblical Repertory*. Like them, he disapproved of women's public political reform activities. He once said that women had better things to do than collect signatures for a petition to Congress protesting President Andrew Jackson's removal of the Cherokees from Georgia. Aware of their fellow Americans' racial prejudice and sharing it to a lesser degree, all these educators opposed abolitionists and supported the movement to colonize former slaves in Africa. Whereas the women educators have benefited from women historians' praise of their educational efforts and silence on their racial attitudes, men with similar attitudes have not.[27] Such discrimination creates women heroines while limiting our understanding of the broad consensus for reform in the antebellum period. Comparing Hodge to Beecher, Willard, and Phelps deepens our understanding of the place of each in antebellum America. Hodge's biblical writings meant that the women could pursue their educational goals free from clerical sanction, and the women's tacit alliance

26. CH to HLH, 1 January 1846, PUL. On marriage changing, see Lystra, *Searching the Heart*, pp. 227-28.
27. The definitive work on Beecher is Kathryn Kish Sklar's *Catharine Beecher: A Study in American Domesticity* (New Haven: Yale University Press, 1973); a revisionist view of Willard can be found in Nina Baym, "Women and the Republic: Emma Willard's Rhetoric of History," *American Quarterly* 43 (1991): 1-23. I derived my understanding of Hart from reading published catalogues and records of the Patapsco Female Academy, Maryland, at the Library Company of Philadelphia.

with Hodge confirms their position as conservative reformers who wished to expand women's sphere of public action while not challenging women's dependence on men.

At the heart of Hodge's theological belief and thinking about women were two propositions involving dependency. The first proposition involves God's promise of salvation and people's inability to save themselves. Hodge often told prospective converts and ministers that they could do nothing better to win their salvation than to feel their dependence on God.[28] Cultural historians following Ann Douglas's *Feminization of American Culture* have argued that nineteenth-century theologians' insistence on dependence on God belonged to the feminization of Protestantism and the larger culture. Evidence from reviews of women's books in the *Biblical Repertory* and Hodge's discussion of the ministry with future ministers suggest that little feminization was going on among Old School Presbyterians of Princeton. Although Hodge and his colleagues on the *Repertory* did accept women as their allies in publishing, they made acceptance conditional on strict conditions. To make sure that ministers stayed physically manly, the seminary offered gymnastics on its grounds "according to the most approved methods for sedentary men."[29]

Hodge explicitly invoked images of manliness in weekly Sunday afternoon talks and ordination sermons for Seminary students. In informal but structured conversations, Hodge explained the duties of a minister and the biblical grounds for faith. He larded these talks with mention of manliness for several reasons. By insisting that ministerial work was manly, he assured students that their prospective roles were not effeminate. Study would give them the wisdom of men, not, as Hodge had told his wife, the "instinctive" knowledge of women. Hodge's words also reveal his effort to cast being a minister as a masculine endeavor requiring bodily strength as well as mental effort. This effort did not so much separate ministers from other men but join them to other men in an active life of work. To describe the mastery of personal sin, he used a language of battle and conflict and he filled his sermons and talks to students with mentions of the minister as a workman or soldier fighting the good fight, although softer images of the minister as shepherd did come up rarely. Hodge also stressed the active life that a minister led. He told ordinands that they would be active and busy, since they had to overcome the seven

28. Hodge, *Conference Papers*, pp. 7, 83, 280; Alexander A. Hodge, *The Life of Charles Hodge* (1881; reprinted New York: Arno Press, 1969), p. 58.
29. Catalogue of Princeton Theological Seminary, 1871.

deadly sins as well as teach the gospel, instruct the young, comfort and teach, and visit the sick. For everyone, bringing one's self to the eternal world was a great work requiring great effort, for people had to fight "to preserve the inward life of the soul." Presbyterian ministers might wait upon God's deliverance, but that waiting took effort and work.[30]

While describing the ministry as a manly profession, Hodge guided ministerial students by word and example away from some activities antebellum Americans associated with manliness. He argued that ministers should not be embarrassed by making money but should avoid its pursuit. He wanted them to enjoy the world and its things but deemed certain activities and certain novels too worldly. He played croquet and cards and read novels, although he delayed reading Henry Fielding's *Tom Jones* until the months before his death. He also warned ordinands from dancing or attending dances and the theater, and in private life he forbade his children and grandchildren from doing so as well. Rather than seeing nineteenth-century culture in dualistic terms of masculine and feminine, Hodge's had a more nuanced vision. To him there were at least four categories — men and women who owned God as their savior and men and women who did not. Those who did followed reformed gender roles that required their eschewing certain pleasures in this world for the promise of perfected life in the hereafter.[31]

The second part of this vision derived from Paul and said that dependence on God and Christ brought perfect freedom. Therefore, inequality in this world neither denied nor vitiated equal participation in God's plan of salvation. Thus society comprised a series of covenants between unequal individuals, and social fabric of interlocking covenants guaranteed social order. This understanding of the world as a collection of covenants has taproots extending into seventeenth-century Calvinist thought. In the nineteenth century, this thinking flowered especially among the allies of Whig politicians found in Unitarian, Presbyterian, and Congregationalist seminaries and their allied churches. Of course, professors cannot always

30. See "Charge to Ordinand: John Mitchelmore, 27 April 1825"; "Charge to Ordinand: Francis B. Hodge, 9 May 1863," Charles Hodge Manuscript Collection, Department of Archives and Special Collections, Princeton Theological Seminary Libraries (heretofore PTSL); Hodge, *Conference Talks,* p. 279.

31. Hodge, *Conference Talks,* pp. 277, 278; "Charge to Ordinand: Edward B. Hodge, April 28, 1864," PTSL; Sermons: ns 32 — "They which preach the gospel should live the Gospel," 21 February 1847, PTSL. For a description of Hodge's home life, see William Berryman Scott, *Some Memories of a Palaeontologist* (Princeton: Princeton University Press, 1939), esp. p. 75 for the reading comment.

influence their students on every subject, as the Democratic party loyalties of Hodge's student and son-in-law testify.[32]

By the second decade of the twentieth century, this sort of covenant thinking was no longer applicable to the American political system. Extension of the suffrage to all native-born white male citizens during the first third of the nineteenth century, then passage of the thirteenth, fourteenth, and fifteenth amendments to the Constitution during and after the Civil War, enfranchised about 50 percent of American adult citizens. Finally, ratification of the nineteenth amendment in 1920 ended the correspondence between a political theory of dependence and the American political system while introducing one based on the individual. After constitutional amendments prohibited limiting suffrage on the basis of sex, race, national origin, and former condition of servitude, all adult individuals who were citizens had equal standing in American political life, at least in theory. In practice, African American citizens in the South remained disenfranchised until the Civil Rights Act and Voting Rights Act of the 1960s, and women were a protected and unequal class in the American economy until recent court decisions.

After 1920 no politician would again argue that husband and wife were the fundamental *political* unit in American life. Still, politicians and ministers continued to debate the relationship of women and men in American *social* life. Battles arose in the 1920s and persist to the present day concerning the role of women within the church and its work. Margaret Lamberts Bendroth, a historian of religious fundamentalism, distinguishes between those who find justification for women's subordination in Eve's creation from Adam and others who find justification in Paul's pronouncements. In the late nineteenth century and early twentieth century, both groups of male churchmen assumed what Bendroth calls a "self-consciously masculine posture" and avoided making common cause with women's religiously inspired reform efforts, such as the Women's Christian Temperance Union. They hoped instead for a united crusade under male leadership. In the twenties, conservative Calvinists associated with Princeton Seminary often argued that the seminary and Presbyterianism were meant to be essentially masculine endeavors, and opposed women's church leadership and ordination. In making their arguments, Ethel-

32. See Daniel Walker Howe, *The Political Culture of the American Whigs* (Chicago: University of Chicago Press, 1979), esp. ch. 2. I have described the political theory of the Princetonians' Congregationalist parallels in *Scholarly Means to Evangelical Ends: The New Haven Scholars and the Transformation of Higher Learning in America* (Baltimore: Johns Hopkins University Press, 1986).

bert D. Warfield, Finley D. Jenkins, and others were among those who relied less on the biblical story of creation and Eve's inferiority to Adam and more on injunctions about women found in the New Testament, especially those in the Epistles of Paul. As Hodge had opposed Sarah Grimké and like-minded antebellum abolitionists' and women's rights advocates' use of perfectionist doctrine to claim Biblical sanction for their expanded role, so did these conservative Calvinists oppose what they termed "ecclesiastical feminarchy."

Bendroth finds that in recent years conservative Calvinists pose the most challenging arguments in opposition to women's increasing role in the church. They use Paul's emphasis on order and hierarchy and argue that it is consistent with the order of a divinely created universe. Women's subordination and men's lordship, both rightly understood, must exist for this world to reflect God's excellence.[33] With their reliance upon Paul and his insistence on order and subordination, present-day Calvinists descend from Hodge and the Princeton reviewers, who, we have seen, buttressed the church and academic ministry as male preserves. Since the gender issues and arguments that the Princetonians marginalized 150 years ago appear at center stage today, we may assume that the nineteenth-century solution to women's expanding role in the public world remains a contested issue.

---

33. The discussion in this and preceding paragraphs relies heavily upon Margaret Lamberts Bendroth, *Fundamentalism and Gender, 1875 to the Present* (New Haven: Yale University Press, 1993), pp. 29, 40, 41, 124-25. For a discussion of submission and order, see Susan Foh, *Women and the Word of God: A Response to Biblical Feminism* (Phillipsburg, N.J.: Presbyterian and Reformed Publishing Co., 1980), ch. 9. A brief introduction to the current debate is Randall Balmer, "American Fundamentalism and the Ideal of Femininity," in *Fundamentalism and Gender,* ed. John Stratton Hawley (New York: Oxford University Press, 1994), and extended discussions are found in John Piper and Wayne Grudem, eds., *Recovering Biblical Manhood and Womanhood: A Response to Evangelical Feminism* (Wheaton, Ill.: Crossway Books, 1991).

Charles Hodge as an Expositor
of the Spiritual Life

MARK A. NOLL

This paper is a sympathetic account of a failure. The failure was
Charles Hodge's effort to describe Christian faith as an integrated reality constituted by an objective ground of truth in the Scriptures and a
subjective experience of Jesus Christ. The paper is sympathetic because it
concludes that Hodge's full lifetime of theological exposition, even if it
never offered an entirely cohesive account of Christian existence, nonetheless still revealed a surprisingly supple understanding of spirituality —
perhaps, regarded in the round, the most satisfying version propounded
by any American theologian of his era.

All efforts to judge the adequacy of spiritual exposition must depend
in considerable measure on the theological standards of the adjudicator,
and this paper is no exception. As a Protestant with great sympathy for
the theology of the Reformation, I am predisposed to appreciate Hodge's
efforts. Yet as one who also thinks that better accounts of subjective and
objective aspects of Christian faith were provided by early Protestants (for
example, Calvin himself) and by more recent Reformed voices outside of
the United States (for example, Abraham Kuyper in the Netherlands) than
by any nineteenth-century American, I am predisposed to find fault. Personal perspective notwithstanding, however, this paper tries to root
Hodge's writing securely enough in its contexts to make a historical con-

I am pleased for this opportunity to thank Randall Balmer, Allan Fisher, Earl William
Kennedy, George Marsden, and David Wells for early assistance of various kinds in the
study of Charles Hodge, along with William O. Harris and Bradley Gundlach for more
of the same in recent years.

tribution for those who do not share my standards of judgment as well as for those who do.[1]

The subject of Hodge's spiritual vision has a general historical importance because of how widely he was respected in his own day. Just as a considerable range of opponents seemed to feel that their views could not be established unless Hodge's were overturned, so also a wide circle of admirers held up his expression of the Christian faith as a model. When in 1844 Robert Baird published the first full history of Christianity in the United States, he singled out Hodge's *The Way of Life* (1841) for special recognition. According to Baird, that volume exhibited "the great doctrines of the gospel as held by all evangelical Christians" and was read with "entire satisfaction" by "all the evangelical Christians throughout the land."[2] Little more than a decade after Baird published these words, Philip Schaff visited president-elect James Buchanan at his home in Lancaster, Pennsylvania. Buchanan, who had been born in the nearby Mercersburg of Schaff and J. W. Nevin, was reading a copy of this same book.[3] The extent to which Hodge's influence extended is indicated by the fact that Daniel Alexander Payne, the Lutheran-trained stalwart of the African Methodist Episcopal Church, called Hodge "the greatest theologian which America has yet produced."[4] Although Hodge never gained the kind of Continental recognition enjoyed by his contemporary Henry Boynton Smith, he was the only American theologian of his age with a substantial reputation in Canada,[5]

1. The argument of this paper draws upon my earlier efforts to assess Hodge's exposition of the spiritual life in the Introduction to *Charles Hodge, The Way of Life,* Sources of American Spirituality (New York: Paulist, 1987), 32-44; and headnotes to documents in *The Princeton Theology, 1812-1921* (Grand Rapids: Baker, 1983), especially pp. 61-62, 107-8, 117-18, and 185-86. The most helpful secondary account of the subject is Andrew Hoffecker, *Piety and the Princeton Theologians* (Grand Rapids: Baker, 1981), pp. 44-94. A recent monograph by John W. Stewart points the way to better understanding of Hodge by its effort to situate him concretely in his historical situation; see *Mediating the Center: Charles Hodge on American Science, Language, Literature, and Politics* (Princeton: Princeton Theological Seminary, 1995).

2. Robert Baird, *Religion in the United States of America* (Glasgow: Blackie & Son, 1844), p. 606.

3. David S. Schaff, *The Life of Philip Schaff* (New York: Charles Scribner's Sons, 1897), p. 206.

4. Daniel Alexander Payne, *Recollections of Seventy Years* (orig. n.d.; reprinted New York: Arno, 1969), p. 248.

5. See awareness of the *Biblical Repertory and Princeton Review* (hereafter BRPR) in *The Home and Foreign Record of the Canada Presbyterian Church* 2 (Jan. 1863): 83; 2 (Mar. 1863): 138; and an especially full commendation in 4 (Sept. 1865): 11. See also Richard W. Vaudry, "Canadian Presbyterians and Princeton Seminary, 1850-1900," in *The Burning Bush and a Few Acres of Snow: The Presbyterian Contribution to Canadian Life and Culture,* ed. William Klempa

Scotland,[6] and Ireland.[7] Largely because of Hodge, Princeton was the only American seminary of the era to which considerable numbers of students came for study from outside the country.[8] Further testimony to the reach of Hodge's influence is provided by a thematic bibliography of American theological quarterlies in the era of the Civil War prepared by August Wenzel. This bibliography shows that Hodge was the only theologian of the period whose views on more than one theological topic were subject to widespread debate, and the only one whose works were exciting comment in more than one region of the country. Even as the war unfolded and Hodge's opinions on the conflict were queried by the Lutheran *Evangelical Quarterly* and the *Southern Presbyterian Review,* his views on ecclesiastical politics were under fire from the New School *American Presbyterian and Theological Review,* and the broader theological positions he had staked out over the preceding thirty years were being challenged by the Old School *Danville Quarterly Review,* the *Methodist Review,* and the *New Englander.*[9] A different kind of historical significance is suggested by the fact that Hodge is one of only two American theologians of his period — the other is Charles Finney — whose works continue to be read outside of the academy at the end of the twentieth century.[10] In short, an examination of Hodge's

---

(Ottawa: Carleton University Press, 1994), pp. 224-27 (though Vaudry is mistaken in think-ing that Canadian students did not come to Princeton until 1860); and Craig I. Stevenson, "'Those Now at War Are Our Friends and Neighbors': The Views of Evangelical Editors in British North America toward the American Civil War, 1861-1865" (M.A. Thesis, Queen's University, Ontario, 1997), pp. 39-40.

6. See Patrick Fairbairn, "Prefatory Notice," *Theological Essays Reprinted from the Princeton Review. First Series* (Edinburgh: T&T Clark, 1856), p. i: "not a few of [these essays], those in particular which are occupied with the discussion of the more distinctive tenets of Calvin-ism [i.e., Hodge's], are of so high an order as to be fully entitled to a place in our permanent Theological Literature." In early 1873, Hodge noted that there were almost as many copies in print of the first two volumes of his *Systematic Theology* in Scotland as in the United States; Hodge to Hugh Lenox Hodge, 17 Feb. 1873, Papers of Charles Hodge, Manuscript Di-vision, Firestone Library, Princeton University (hereafter PUA).

7. See David N. Livingstone, "Darwinism and Calvinism: The Belfast-Princeton Con-nection," *Isis* 83 (Sept. 1992): 408-28; and A. A. Hodge, *The Life of Charles Hodge* (New York: Charles Scribner's Sons, 1880), p. 585 (hereafter AAH, *Life*).

8. Peter Wallace and Mark Noll, "The Students of Princeton Seminary, 1812-1929: A Re-search Note," *American Presbyterians* 72 (Fall 1994): 208-11.

9. August Wenzel, "Theological Implications of the Civil War" (Evanston, Ill.: Garrett Theological Seminary Library, 1971). Wenzel's annotated bibliography is by his own admis-sion incomplete.

10. *Books in Print 1996-97* (New Providence, N.J.: R. R. Bowker, 1996), shows thirty-six ti-tles in print for Finney, fifteen for Hodge, six for Bushnell, four for Schaff (plus volumes of

picture of the Christian life is important, not only for what it says about Hodge, but also for what it reveals about the spiritual convictions, or at least about religious questions that mattered, for a considerable range of Americans for a considerable period of time.[11]

Defining the Christian Faith

Charles Hodge characteristically spoke of Christianity in two ways at once: as a set of propositional doctrines that he felt were taught by the Scriptures, and as habits of personal being that he felt were given life by the Holy Spirit. A typical example occurred in 1860 in an essay entitled "What Is Christianity?" Ostensibly the paper was examining works from Scotland, Germany, and England, but it was in fact an extended polemic against J. W. Nevin's effort to adapt a Continental *Vermittlingstheologie* to an American context. As he eased into his argument, Hodge paused to answer the question of his title:

> Christianity is both a doctrine and a life, . . . the object of true faith is both a proposition and a person. . . . Christianity objectively considered, is the testimony of God concerning his Son, it is the whole revelation of truth contained in the Scriptures, concerning the redemption of man through Jesus Christ our Lord. Subjectively considered, it is the life of Christ in the soul, or, that form of spiritual life which has its origin in Christ, is determined by the revelation concerning his person and work, and which is due to the indwelling of his Spirit. In one sense, therefore, we may affirm that Christianity is a doctrine, and in another sense we may with equal truth affirm that Christianity is a life.[12]

Shortly after Hodge published these words, he provided a similar two-fold definition of religion in a Sunday afternoon meditation to the seminarians at Princeton. Significantly, in that context Hodge told the students which of the two forms of religion was more important:

---

the Early Church Fathers), one for J. H. Thornwell, and none for John Henry Hobart, J. W. Nevin, E. A. Park, Moses Stuart, and N. W. Taylor. This listing excludes Harriet Beecher Stowe, which is probably a mistake.

11. For other testimonies, some of them in superlative terms, to Hodge's importance, see AAH, *Life*, pp. 257-60, 585-87.

12. Hodge, "What Is Christianity?" *BRPR* 32 (Jan. 1860): 119.

There are two ways of conceiving of God, the philosophical and the religious, as he [God] stands related to the reason and as he stands related to the heart. According to the one method we regard God as the first ground and cause of all things. . . . According to the other, we regard him as a person to whom we bear the relation of creatures and children, of responsibility and dependence . . . , who has towards us the feelings of a father and to whom we can make known our joys and sorrows. Both these are right, so far as limited and determined by the Scriptures. . . . In the Bible both elements are harmonized; though the latter is the predominant, as it should be with us.[13]

Hodge repeated this twofold definition of true religion in several different forms and venues throughout his career. The most well-rounded statements came in his biblical commentaries, as in this reflection on Ephesians 3:17: "According to the Bible, religion is not a form of feeling to the exclusion of the intellect, nor a form of knowledge to the exclusion of the feelings. Christ dwells in the heart, in the comprehensive sense of the word. He is the source of spiritual life to the whole soul, — of spiritual knowledge as well as of spiritual affections."[14] Or this on II Corinthians 5:14: "A Christian is one who recognizes Jesus as the Christ, the Son of the living God, as God manifested in the flesh, loving us and dying for our redemption; and who is so affected by a sense of the love of this incarnate God as to be constrained to make the will of Christ the rule of his obedience, and the glory of Christ the great end for which he lives."[15]

Exact matters under consideration differed — whether the nature of Christianity, God, faith, or Hodge's general emphases as a seminary pro-

13. Hodge, "The Tender Mercies of God" (Ps. 146:9) conference for 11 March 1860, in *Princeton Sermons: Outlines of Discourses . . . Delivered at Princeton Theological Seminary on Sabbath Afternoons* (London: Thomas Nelson & Sons, 1879), p. 14.

14. Hodge, *Ephesians* (1856; reprinted Edinburgh: Banner of Truth, 1991), p. 129.

15. Hodge, *1 & 2 Corinthians* (1859; reprinted Edinburgh: Banner of Truth, 1994), p. 509. For other examples of definitions combining subjective and objective components, see Hodge, "Assurance," ms. conference for 16 Oct. 1853, Princeton Theological Seminary (hereafter PTS); Hodge, "Walk in Wisdom," ms. conference for 30 Sept. 1855, Charles Hodge Manuscript Collection, Archives and Special Collections, Luce Library, PTS; Hodge, *Commentary on the Epistle to the Romans* (2nd ed. 1864; reprinted Grand Rapids: Eerdmans, 1993), p. 35; and "Address of Rev. Dr. Hodge," *Proceedings Connected with the Semi-Centennial Commemoration of the Professorship of Rev. Charles Hodge . . . April 24, 1872* (New York: Anson D. F. Randolph, 1872), p. 51. Others often stressed the same combination; see Henry A. Boardman, "Address," *Semi-Centennial Commemoration,* pp. 46-47; and A. A. Hodge, "Preface," *Princeton Sermons,* p. vi.

fessor — but the pattern of his profession was constant. Hodge held that Christianity needed to be seen from two angles at once, from what on many occasions he called "objective" and "subjective" perspectives.

While there were problems — perhaps serious problems — in Hodge's dual characterization of Christian life, he yet was able to exploit this bipolar vision with telling effectiveness. In particular, this way of viewing the spiritual life allowed Hodge to expound traditional Calvinistic soteriology as an exercise in piety, rather than as a riddle to be solved by disinterested ethical reasoning (as it so often appeared among the New England Congregationalists of the period). Second, it enabled him to develop a theology of Christian life with a surprisingly large role for the work of the Holy Spirit, or at least to do so in his biblical commentaries, in non-polemical occasional writing, and in polemical essays aimed at opponents whom he considered rationalists. Third, the same two-sided picture also made it possible for Hodge repeatedly to speak of Christianity as primarily an affective, intuitive, and emotional reality. Exposition with these emphases was at least one of the things that made him such a widely respected figure in his day.

The close tie Hodge drew between the propositions of Calvinist dogma and the wellsprings of Christian piety allowed him to expound formal theology with unusual fervor. When, in his early seventies, he wrote a retrospective history of the *Princeton Review,* he paused to list the crucial Calvinist doctrines that he and his colleagues had defended in that journal. This list featured the dynamic work of the Holy Spirit. These doctrines were that "men are born into the world, since the fall, in a state of sin and condemnation; that this fact was due to the sin of Adam; that men are dependent on the Holy Spirit for their regeneration; and that it is due to the sovereign and supernatural interposition of the Spirit that one man is converted and not another." By contrast, Hodge characterized the doctrines combated by the *Princeton Review* as concerned more with the prerogatives of self than with the acts of God:

> that all sin consists in the voluntary violation of known law; that men, since the fall, are not born in a state of sin; that they are not chargeable with guilt or moral pollution until, having arrived at the years of discretion, they deliberately violate the divine law; that all men have plenary ability to avoid all sin; and, having sinned, to return unto God and do all that he requires at their hands; that God cannot prevent sin, or the present amount of sin, in a moral system; that he cannot effectually control the acts of free agents without de-

stroying their liberty; that in conversion it is man, and not God, who determines who do, and who do not, turn unto God; that election is founded on the foresight of this self-determined repentance on the part of the sinner.

For Hodge, dogmatic convictions about soteriology defined a living religion, whereas the assertions he held to undercut Calvinist orthodoxy violated "the vital principles, not of the Reformed faith only, but even of Catholic Christianity."[16]

Given his sense of living Calvinist propositions, it is not surprising that Hodge could wax lyrical at the end of even the driest theological demonstration. Thus, when in 1850 he concluded the first round of his important debate with E. A. Park on the nature of religious language, Hodge used an arboreal image, probably from the First Psalm, for the views he was defending, but a lifeless, mechanical image for what he considered the sub-orthodox views of Park:

> It will be a matter of deep regret to many to find Professor Park, with his captivating talents and commanding influence, arrayed against the doctrines repudiated in this discourse; and many more will lament that he should have prepared a weapon which may be used against one doctrine as easily as another. Our consolation is that however keen may be the edge or bright the polish of that weapon, it has so little substance, it must be shivered into atoms with the first blow it strikes against those sturdy trees which have stood for ages in the garden of the Lord and whose leaves have been for the healing of the nations.[17]

If Hodge's view of the spiritual life as both doctrinal fact and lived experience convinced him that the exposition of dogma was a pious experience, it also led him to develop a surprisingly expansive theology of the Holy Spirit.[18] This theology was developed primarily in his commentaries on the Pauline epistles, but it also influenced some of his polemical theology, especially in writing against errors he ascribed to rationalism. Thus,

16. Hodge, "Retrospect of the History of the *Princeton Review*," *BRPR: Index Volume* (Philadelphia: Peter Walker, 1870-71), pp. 12-13.

17. Hodge, "The Theology of the Intellect and That of the Feelings," *BRPR* 22 (Oct. 1850); quoted from *Princeton Theology*, p. 207.

18. For a full account of this subject, with dozens of citations to Hodge's works, see Steven L. Martin, "The Doctrines of Man, Reason and the Holy Spirit in the Epistemology of Charles Hodge" (M.A. Thesis, Trinity Evangelical Divinity School, 1984), pp. 178-225.

for Hodge, "Without being strengthened by the Spirit in the inner man . . . it is impossible to have any adequate apprehension of the gospel or of the love of Christ therein revealed."[19] Similarly, "the mere presentation of truth, apart from the influences of the Spirit, can neither renew nor sanctify the heart."[20]

Hodge often went out of his way to link the doctrine of the Holy Spirit to the truth-telling character of Scripture, as he did for example by urging against Horace Bushnell in 1849 that "all the operations of the Spirit are in connexion with the Word. . . . [T]hey involve an intellectual apprehension of the truth, revealed in the Scriptures."[21] But he was equally convinced that at the root of what he saw as the rationalism of New Haven theologians and Charles Finney was neglect of the Holy Spirit. The New Divinity "kept the Holy Spirit and his influences out of view."[22] Finney had abandoned the only sure way of knowing the truth: "turn to the scriptures and ascertain whether those doctrines are really taught therein. If satisfied on that point, and especially if he experience through the teaching of the Holy Spirit their power on his own heart, if they become to him matters not merely of speculative belief but of experimental knowledge, he will be constrained to make his philosophy agree with his theology."[23] Hodge never held back from describing the work of the Spirit in dogmatic terms, but just as thoroughly that work was for him a vigorous force in its own right.[24]

So deeply rooted, in fact, was Hodge's sense of Christianity as a lived reality that regularly throughout his career he pointed to Christian experience as a sufficient basis for an entirely adequate, broadly ecumenical theology. On such occasions, Hodge the dogmatist clearly gave way to Hodge the experientialist. Thus, in 1826, as a young man early in his tour of Europe, Hodge wrote to his wife about a generically Protestant service he had attended in Paris. It was shared piety that made Hodge delighted

19. Hodge, commentary on Eph. 3:18, in *Ephesians*, p. 131.
20. Hodge, commentary on Rom. 7:14, in *Romans*, p. 246.
21. Hodge, "Bushnell's Discourses," *BRPR* 21 (Apr. 1849): 273-74.
22. Hodge, "The New Divinity Tried," *BRPR* 4 (1832): 301.
23. Hodge, "Finney's Lectures on Theology," *BRPR* 19 (Apr. 1847): 241, quoted in Hodge, *Essays and Reviews: Selected from the Princeton Review* (New York: Robert Carter & Bros., 1857), p. 250 (hereafter *Essays and Reviews*); *Princeton Theology*, p. 170.
24. Hodge's stress on the importance of the Holy Spirit was particularly strong in the middle years of his career; see, as examples, "Zeal," ms. conference for 15 Oct. 1845, PTS; "Security of Believers," ms. conference for 28 Nov. 1852, PTS; "Assurance," ms. conference for 16 Oct. 1853, PTS; *1 & 2 Corinthians* (orig. 1857), p. 32; and especially "Dependence of the Believer & the Church on the Holy Spirit," ms. conference for 4 Sept. 1859, PTS.

to report that "the true religion is the same everywhere, that the experience of men of practical piety in Europe & America is perfectly in unison, that they both know the necessity of conviction of sin, of the renewal of the heart, & of faith in Jesus Christ, & they make all these exercises to consist in the same feelings." In fact, Hodge felt that the ability of different sorts of Protestants to practice the faith together was one of the greatest testimonies to the truth of Christianity: "There is to me few evidences of the reality of practical piety of greater strength than this. If there was not something in it, you could not find men in every quarter of the globe, when they come to compare their experiences on the subject so perfectly agreeing with each other."[25]

More than forty years later, Hodge repeated this same willingness to define Christianity broadly on the basis of shared religious experience in an unusual document. At the request of two General Assemblies, Hodge was asked to decline an invitation from Pope Pius IX that American Presbyterians send observers to the First Vatican Council. As might be expected, Hodge expostulated at some length on the doctrinal differences that rendered such attendance impossible. But at the end of his letter piety returned as the predominant note:

> [A]lthough we cannot return to the fellowship of the Church of Rome, we desire to live in charity with all men. We love all those who love our Lord Jesus Christ in sincerity. We regard as Christian brethren all who worship, love, and obey him as their God and Saviour; and we hope to be united in heaven with all who unite with us on earth in saying, "Unto him that loved us, and washed us from our sins in his own blood, and hath made us kings and priests unto God and his Father, to him be glory and dominion forever and ever. Amen."[26]

If, on the basis of a shared love of Christ, Hodge was willing to countenance a shared eternity with at least some Roman Catholics — whose beliefs he otherwise considered so erroneous — it is not surprising that at several points throughout his career he suggested that hymns and devotional writings from throughout the far reaches of the church could construct an entirely sufficient picture of true Christianity. Such suggestions came, for example, in 1845 when Hodge was arguing against Nathan Beman on the nature of the atonement, in 1850 when debating E. A. Park

25. Hodge to Sarah Bache Hodge, 5 Nov. 1826, PUA.
26. Hodge to Pius IX, 1869, PTS, as photocopied from PUA.

on the use of theological language, in several places in the *Systematic Theology*, and, most extensively, in 1876 in one of the last essays he published.[27] What Hodge seemed to be saying in these proposals was that systematic collection of the life experience recorded in hymns and devotional writings could yield a theology as fully satisfying as — and certainly more ecumenically comprehensive than — theology constructed by rational attention to revealed dogma.

In retrospect, it is a shame that Hodge himself never attempted to do what he said could be done — that is, to write a systematic theology on the basis of hymns and devotional writings. If he had done so, it might have saved him from some of the problems that others have seen in his more philosophical dogmatic expositions. To be sure, at various points throughout his life he seemed quite content with an experiential theology. As a young man he had delighted in the generic Christian experience of his fellow worshipers in Paris, so in the last days of his life it was hymnody to which he turned.[28] Yet these moments did not define his usual approach to exposition of the spiritual life.

Nonetheless, in Hodge's works there is a strand of theology defined much more by existential or presuppositional reasoning than by the requirements of propositions. That theology never quite received a full exposition, but it appeared in various forms throughout his life. After returning from Europe in 1829, he told students at the seminary that "man's religious opinions are the result and expression of his religious feelings."[29] Much of the opening section of *The Way of Life* in 1841 was devoted to showing that the Scriptures "everywhere represent faith as the effect and evidence of right moral feeling, and unbelief as the result of moral or spiritual blindness."[30] The same elaboration of how Christianity rests on the existential bond between the person and God, rather than on a strictly rational foundation, appeared frequently in his correspondence, biblical

27. Hodge, "Beman on the Atonement," *BRPR* 17 (1845), quoted from *Essays and Reviews*, p. 130; Hodge, "The Theology of the Intellect and That of the Feelings," *BRPR* 22 (Oct. 1850), quoted from *Princeton Theology*, pp. 201, 203; Hodge, *Systematic Theology*, 3 vols. (New York: Charles Scribner's Sons, 1871-73) vol. 1, p. 16; vol. 2, pp. 250, 525-26 (hereafter *ST*); and Hodge, "Christianity Without Christ," *Presbyterian Quarterly and Princeton Review*, new ser. 5 (Apr. 1876): 356-58.

28. AAH, *Life*, pp. 581-82. On Hodge's recourse to hymns as a tool of theological education for his family, see AAH, *Life*, p. 227.

29. Hodge, "Lecture Addressed to the Students of the Theological Seminary," *BRPR* 1 (Jan. 1829), quoted from *Princeton Theology*, p. 112.

30. Hodge, *Way of Life*, p. 60.

commentaries, meditations for the seminarians, *Princeton Review* essays, and even the *Systematic Theology*.[31] Had Hodge ever written a theology based on hymns and devotional works, it would have been a fitting summation to the affectional, pneumatic, and experiential picture of the Christian life that is marbled throughout his work.

As it is, however, Hodge did not write such a hymn-based work. Neither, in fact, did he ever satisfactorily show how the pietistically defined faith that bulks large in his work related to the propositionally defined Christianity about which he also wrote a very great deal. This inability to show how — in his words from 1860 — the "one sense" of "Christianity as a doctrine" and "another sense" of "Christianity [as] life" cohered — has been one of the reasons why later students of nineteenth-century American theology have been half right in their strictures on Hodge's thought. Because of the woodenness with which Hodge's attention to "Christianity as doctrine" was often expressed, and because his exposition of "Christianity as doctrine" sometimes simply overwhelmed his understanding of "Christianity [as] life," there is some justice in thinking that Hodge's work was marked by "dogged literalism" or "a literalistic view of scriptural inspiration," or that it was crippled by a "Thomist theological method" and "devotion to Protestant scholasticism."[32]

Tangled Connections between Doctrine and Life

When considering Hodge's work as a whole, however, these epithets are misguided, for Hodge's theology of pious experience was always part of his dogmatic Calvinism. However much "scholasticism" or "literalism" did show up, those elements were more than overwhelmed by his repeated evocation of existential piety. The difficulty with Hodge's view of the spiritual life was not a neglect of lived religious experience, of the person, or

---

31. As examples, see Hodge to Hugh Lenox Hodge, 4 Aug. 1827 (from Halle), PUA; "Suggestions to Theological Students," *BRPR* 5 (Jan. 1833): 101-05; "Beecher's Great Conflict," *BRPR* 26 (Jan. 1854): 138; "Sin of Unbelief," ms. conference for 30 Mar. 1856, PTS; *1 & 2 Corinthians*, 29; and *ST,* vol. 1, p. 52.

32. Bruce Kuklick, *Churchmen and Philosophers from Jonathan Edwards to John Dewey* (New Haven: Yale University Press, 1985), p. 204; Sydney E. Ahlstrom, *A Religious History of the American People* (New Haven: Yale University Press, 1972), p. 463; Jack B. Rogers and Donald K. McKim, *The Authority and Interpretation of the Bible: An Historical Approach* (San Francisco: Harper & Row, 1979), p. 296; Richard E. Wentz, *John Williamson Nevin: American Theologian* (New York: Oxford University Press, 1997), p. 145.

of the affections. It was rather his predilection for affirming Christianity both as a set of scriptural doctrines and as a living connection with Christ, while yet never finding a way to bring these two affirmations into cohesive unity.

Sometimes the problem appeared when Hodge defined Christian realities in different ways without seeming to be aware that he was saying different things. For example, in a late sermon on the question, "What must I do to be saved?" Hodge responded, first, "believe the record God has given of his Son — This found in Old & N. Testament." But then after talking about how that record was verified, he took off in another direction. To be saved, one must "trust in Him and in Him alone, renouncing all other grounds of confidence."[33] On other occasions Hodge blithely simplified the intellectual and spiritual factors at work in understanding the Bible, as when he told the seminarians in 1856 that it was "two things . . . perfectly distinct" to "know what [Scripture] teaches & to apprehend its spiritual power."[34]

But the sharpest examples of strain between doctrine and life appeared in the pages of the *Systematic Theology*. Right at the start, for example, Hodge defends the adequacy of Scripture as the grounds for theology, but also wants to suggest that lived experience, properly understood, has a positive role to play in theology as well. The result appears as contradictory, or at least conflicting, assertions within adjoining paragraphs:

> The true method in theology requires that the facts of religious experience should be accepted as facts, and when duly authenticated by Scripture, be allowed to interpret the doctrinal statements of the Word of God. . . . The true method of theology is, therefore, the inductive, which assumes that the Bible contains all the facts or truths which form the contents of theology, just as the facts of nature are the contents of the natural sciences.[35]

The way in which Hodge shifted between spirituality defined strictly by adherence to dogma and spirituality defined piously by a life's entire shape was illustrated most clearly in his discussion of faith. In a lengthy

33. Hodge, "What Must I Do to Be Saved?" ms. sermon, July 1877, PTS. An exposition on the nature of faith that does somewhat better at relating assent, trust, and reliance than this sermon appears in Hodge's commentary on Rom. 1:16; *Romans*, p. 29.

34. Hodge, "The Word of God as a Means of Grace," ms. conference for 30 Nov. 1856, PTS.

35. *ST*, vol. 1, pp. 16-17.

section where the internal tensions are actually not as stark as isolated quotations suggest, Hodge still was not able to align the objective and subjective aspects of Christianity, despite his manifest commitment to both. With an eye to the subjectivity (and also to the first chapter of the Westminster Confession) Hodge affirmed that "the ultimate ground of faith . . . is the witness of the Spirit." Yet only a few pages later he seemed both to reverse his perspective and set aside the Confession: "This witness of the Spirit is not an affirmation that the Bible is the Word of God."[36]

Similarly, Hodge's dual interpretation led to conflict rather than coherence on the critical issue of the nature of faith itself. On the one hand is an objective statement: "The faith of the Christian is the persuasion of the truth of the facts and doctrines recorded in the Scriptures on the testimony of God." On the other is a much more existential reading: "The special object of faith, therefore, is Christ, and the promise of salvation through Him. And the special definite act of faith which secures our salvation is the act of receiving and resting on Him as He is offered to us in the Gospel."[37] In a word, the ambiguity in Hodge's view of the spiritual life is an ambiguity between "persuasion of the truth of the facts" and "the act of receiving and resting on Him."[38]

Explanations for the tensions in Hodge's view of the spiritual life must be sought from a combination of sources that include intellectual difficulties, biographical circumstances, and the more general American situation. The intellectual difficulty in Hodge's spiritual vision was made up of at least three parts, with the latter two posing the most serious difficulties.[39] First was Hodge's occasional profession to treat the words of the Bible as unmediated facts of experience. Second was an assumption, informing much of his writing, that theological method could and should be disinterested. Third was a confusing commitment to common sense

---

36. *ST,* vol. 3, pp. 60, 69.

37. *ST,* vol. 3, pp. 67, 96.

38. Hodge does go on to say (*ST,* vol. 3, p. 96) that faith defined as "receiving and resting on Him" is "so clearly and so variously taught in the Scriptures as hardly to admit of being questioned." But this assertion does not amount to an explanation for how accepting scriptural "facts" becomes the "receiving and resting on" Christ.

39. General studies shaping my reading of Hodge at this point are George Marsden, "Everyone One's Own Interpreter? The Bible, Science, and Authority in Mid-Nineteenth-Century America," in *The Bible in America: Essays in Cultural History,* ed. Nathan O. Hatch and Mark A. Noll (New York: Oxford University Press, 1982), pp. 79-100; and Marsden, "The Collapse of American Evangelical Academia," in *Faith and Rationality: Reason and Belief in God,* ed. Alvin Plantinga and Nicholas Wolterstorff (Notre Dame: University of Notre Dame Press, 1983), pp. 219-64.

moral intuitions whereby Hodge defended the validity of ethical intuitions but arbitrarily limited such intuitions to those, and only those, that supported his dogmatic conclusions.

A Mechanical View of Scripture

The first and least serious of these problems was Hodge's occasional willingness to treat the Bible as a simple reservoir of facts. Jack Rogers and Donald McKim phrase this difficulty well: "Hodge had no sensitivity to the significant difference between a verbal statement and a material thing."[40] This weakness is of least importance because Hodge's massive lifelong reliance on the Bible usually did not drift in such a mechanical direction. Thus, *The Way of Life* from 1841 begins with standard defenses of the Bible as the Word of God, like arguments from fulfilled prophecy. But Hodge's main concern in 1841 was an appeal to the harmony between preexisting dispositions (either faith or unbelief) and attitudes toward Scripture.[41] Likewise in 1845, Hodge used a discussion of the Apocrypha to expand upon the human experiences that lead to belief in the Bible: "This is not a thing which, in the proper sense of the word, admits of proof. The only possible proof of the correctness of a moral doctrine, is to make us see its truth; its accordance with the law of God, the supreme standard, and with that law as written in our own hearts."[42] Later, in 1857, when Hodge defined the nature of biblical inspiration more exactly, he came closer to a mechanistic view of Scripture (and anticipated the analogy found in his *Systematic Theology* between biblical statements and facts of science). But that exercise in definition also included a full statement affirming the humanity of biblical writers that made way for a flexible, nuanced, and theologically self-conscious use of the Scriptures.[43]

40. Rogers and McKim, *Authority and Inspiration*, p. 297.

41. Hodge, *Way of Life*, p. 56: "It is . . . the positive internal evidence of a divine origin, which gives power and authority to the claims of the Bible. . . . When the mind is enlightened to see this holiness; when it perceives how exactly the rule of duty prescribed in the word of God agrees with that enforced by conscience; how the account which it gives of human nature coincides with human experience; how fully it meets our whole case; when it feels how powerfully the truths there presented operate to purify, console and sustain the soul, the belief of the scriptures is a necessary consequence."

42. Hodge, "Thornwell on the Apocrypha," *BRPR* 17 (Apr. 1845): 272 (reprinted as "Ground of Faith in the Scriptures" in *Essays and Reviews*).

43. Hodge, "Inspiration," *BRPR* 29 (Oct. 1857), in *Princeton Theology*, p. 140.

In fact, only occasionally in his lengthy corpus did Hodge treat the Bible as a simple bundle of facts. In an 1861 meditation on "The Truth," Hodge moved toward the analogy that he later fleshed out in the introduction to his *Systematic Theology:* "In the spiritual world the doctrines of the Bible have the authority that the laws of nature have in the external world. . . . The laws of the moral & spiritual government of God are just as immutable as the laws of nature."[44] But these occasions were rare, since Hodge's normal procedure was to read Scripture under the guidance of Calvinist doctrines and with attention to its grand narrative of human need and divine grace.

In a discourse on "method" in the opening pages of the *Systematic Theology,* however, Hodge did in fact define the Scriptures quite directly as a simple compendium of facts. These assertions have been frequently quoted:

> The Bible is to the theologian what nature is to the man of science. It is his store-house of facts; and his method of ascertaining what the Bible teaches, is the same as that which the natural philosopher adopts to ascertain what nature teaches. . . . [T]he duty of the Christian theologian is to ascertain, collect, and combine all the facts which God has revealed concerning himself and our relation to Him. These facts are all in the Bible.[45]

On the basis of these assertions, Hodge then went on to suggest that "The Theologian [is] to be guided by the same rules as the Man of Science."[46]

In these terms, the Bible was no longer a book of affection and mind together but of mind alone. To be sure, Hodge's exposition of this notion was somewhat more complex and somewhat closer to classical Reformed expressions than first appeared, when, for example, he phrased the authority of Scripture in comparative terms:

> It may be admitted that the truths which the theologian has to reduce to a science, or, to speak more humbly, which he has to arrange and harmonize, are revealed partly in the external works of God, partly in the constitution of our nature, and partly in the religious experience of believers; yet lest we should err in our inferences from the works of God, we have a clearer revelation of all that nature re-

44. Hodge, "The Truth," ms. conference for 29 Sept. 1861, PTS.
45. *ST,* vol. 1, pp. 10-11.
46. *ST,* vol. 1, p. 11.

veals, in his word; and lest we should misinterpret our own consciousness and the laws of our nature, everything that can be legitimately learned from that source will be found recognized and authenticated in the Scriptures; and lest we should attribute to the teaching of the Spirit the operations of our own natural affections, we find in the Bible the norm and standard of all genuine religious experience.[47]

Yet his bold statement remains: the Bible is a "store-house of facts." On such a trajectory, the next stop was fundamentalism.[48]

It is doubtful whether a major American thinker ever published anything that so seriously damaged his intellectual reputation as these pages on method in the *Systematic Theology*. Taken at face value, Hodge's account of theological method overrode the need to think about relationships between words and experiences, flattened out the multifaceted understanding of "truth" that had always existed within Christianity, and exploited a chimerical ideal of scientific investigation as the standard for theological reasoning.

The curiosity that most of Hodge's earlier theological exposition — as well as much of what followed in the *Systematic Theology* — proceeded in blithe disregard of these methodological counsels cannot erase the effect of his words. Although they define a theological method that Hodge himself rarely followed, he was the one who chose to open the summary work of his career in this way. The difficulty Hodge's comments on method pose for the interpreter of his theology as a whole constitutes a problem internal to his thought, not one foisted upon it from the outside.

The result for Hodge's exposition of spirituality was to suggest that the life of piety amounted to a mechanical application of disembodied truths. If this suggestion flies in the face of most of Hodge's other exposition of the Christian life, it reflects a difficulty. Even if that difficulty appears larger than it really was — since Hodge so often disregarded his own counsel — it nonetheless remains.

47. *ST,* vol. I, p. II.

48. See, for example, R. A. Torrey's *What the Bible Teaches* (1898), which followed Hodge's advice quite literally, but which Hodge's successor B. B. Warfield panned as a mockery of true induction; Warfield, *Presbyterian and Reformed Review* 39 (July 1899): 562-64.

Theological Method as Disinterested

Hodge's exposition of the spiritual life was also complicated by the constantly recurring assumption that theological method could and should be disinterested. This aspiration to disinterestedness was as much a part of the era's infatuation with Baconian science as was the analogy between theological science and natural science with which Hodge began his systematics.[49] It also reflected the particular responsibility assumed by all major thinkers at Princeton from the late eighteenth century to the early twentieth — from John Witherspoon, Samuel Stanhope Smith, Ashbel Green, Archibald Alexander, and Joseph Henry through B. B. Warfield, J. Gresham Machen, and Robert Dick Wilson, and especially Charles Hodge — to preserve a mutually beneficial interchange between theological and scientific discourses.[50] Again, it is the introduction to the *Systematic Theology* that puts the goal of disinterested theological inquiry in sharpest terms. Theology, Hodge averred, was to be sanitized from the theologian's own instincts, predispositions, attitudes, and preconceptions:

> [S]peculations on matters of science, unless sustained by facts, are worthless. It is no less unscientific for the theologian to assume a theory as to the nature of virtue, of sin, of liberty, of moral obligation, and then explain the facts of Scripture in accordance with his theories. . . . It is plain that complete havoc must be made of the whole system of revealed truth, unless we consent to derive our philosophy from the Bible, instead of explaining the Bible by our philosophy. . . . It would be easy to show that in every department of theology, . . . men, instead of taking the facts of the Bible, and seeing what principles they imply, what philosophy underlies them, have adopted their philosophy independently of the Bible, to which the facts of the Bible are made to bend. This is utterly unphilosophical. It is the fundamental principle of all sciences, and of theology among the rest, that theory is to be determined by facts, and not facts by theory.[51]

49. The essential study is Theodore Dwight Bozeman, *Protestants in an Age of Science: The Baconian Ideal and Antebellum American Religious Thought* (Chapel Hill: University of North Carolina Press, 1977).

50. See Mark A. Noll and David N. Livingstone, Introduction to Charles Hodge, *What Is Darwinism? and Other Writings on Science and Religion* (Grand Rapids: Baker, 1994), pp. 12-23.

51. *ST,* vol. I, pp. 13-14.

Unlike the assertions concerning the character of Scripture, Hodge's desire for disinterested theological method recurred frequently throughout his career. Hodge's polemical essays were often intellectually forceful, subtle in their use of Scripture, and even sometimes compelling in historical argumentation. Yet in many of these performances Hodge at critical moments evoked not so much a citation from Scripture as a statement concerning what all disinterested readers must agree the Scriptures were teaching. Thus, the authority of "the doctrines of the Bible" was what Hodge missed in Finney's theology; "the great doctrines of the Bible" and "the express declarations of Scripture" were enough to silence E. A. Park; and "the declarations of the Scripture" provided the light necessary to repel Darwin.[52] In arguing like this, Hodge was only doing what virtually all theologians had been doing since the sixteenth century: appealing, in different ways in the different theological traditions, to the simple declarations of Scripture. However widespread the practice, it still created problems.

The difficulty for Hodge's view of the Christian life in the assumption that theology flowed easily from a disinterested application of Scripture was twofold. First, as we have seen, he had himself developed in many places a picture of theological commitment resting on moral persuasion, spiritual standing, individual decision, and other interested circumstances. Where in the *Systematic Theology* he contended that "theory is to be determined by facts, and not facts by theory," earlier he had written in *The Way of Life*, "It is the experience of true Christians in all ages and nations that their faith is founded on the spiritual apprehension and experience of the power of the truth."[53] The problem was not that Hodge kept affirming these two stances toward theological truth — disinterested and interested — but that he did not seem to realize that his dual assertion meant the task remained to indicate how the two could be maintained together.

Second, Hodge's own life, especially during the Civil War, provided precisely the kind of real-life experiences necessary for modifying, or at least nuancing, his strong statements about the disinterested character of theological formation. This awareness had existed earlier, for Hodge had often noted that where a person stood geographically, culturally, racially, or denominationally affected that person's interpretation of facts. For example, he was willing to be indulgent in his early reviews of the work of

---

52. Hodge, "Finney's Lectures on Theology," *BRPR* 19 (Apr. 1847), in *Princeton Theology,* p. 169; Hodge, "The Theology of the Intellect and that of the Feelings — Article III," *BRPR* 23 (Oct. 1851), in *Essays and Reviews,* pp. 613, 619; and Hodge, *What Is Darwinism?* p. 138.

53. *ST,* vol. I, p. 14; Hodge, *Way of Life,* p. 63.

Philip Schaff, because he realized that Schaff's education had been so very different from the kind on offer in Britain and America.[54] During the Civil War, however, Hodge's awareness of how an individual's location influenced judgments on facts and morals reached a new level. At the dawn of the war he was pushed in this direction by reactions to his writings that seemed, at first, far out of proportion to what he had said. Especially that a longtime Southern friend could "evidently approve of what I consider great crimes, and disapprove of what I consider the plainest principles of truth and justice" revealed to Hodge that "the difference is in the medium through which we look at the same truth, and the bearing we give it in present circumstances."[55]

By the end of the war, in his remarkable series of *Princeton Review* essays from 1865, Hodge had fully developed an understanding of how context shaped conviction. To be sure, Hodge mostly employed this insight to account for the errors of pious, well-meaning Southerners. Thus "a man's character, his opinions, feelings, and conduct are determined in part by the inward principles of his nature, and largely by the external influences to which he is subject."[56] But at least in one instance he broadened the insight reflexively to include the North and himself. It was a remarkable judgment:

> It would betray great self-ignorance and self-conceit to assume that we here at the North . . . are free from the operation of this law [of being swayed by "outside pressure, and made the organs of the spirit around them"]; that we can rise above these disturbing elements, and think, speak, and act simply under the guidance of right principles, and of correct feeling. . . . [Rather] we and our ecclesiastical bodies are as much swayed by the spirit of the time and of the community, as our brethren of the South. . . . It is easy to say that we are right and they are wrong. This in the present case is, no doubt, in a great measure, true. But it is not because we are right, that we go with those

54. Hodge, "Dr. Schaff's Apostolic Church," *BRPR* 26 (1854): 150-53. For an excellent treatment of this exchange, see Gary K. Pranger, *Philip Schaff (1819-1893): Portrait of an Immigrant Theologian* (New York: Peter Lang, 1997), p. 117. Hodge also had no difficulty admitting that the "tastes & dispositions" bestowed by God often played a major role in determining which churches people chose as their own; Hodge to Hugh Lenox Hodge, 16 Sept. 1865, PUA.

55. Hodge to John Leighton Wilson, 20 Dec. 1860, The John Leighton Wilson Papers, Presbyterian Department of History, Montreat, N.C., as quoted in Stewart, *Mediating the Center*, p. 92.

56. Hodge, "President Lincoln," *BRPR* 37 (July 1865): 451; and for a similar analysis, Hodge, "The Princeton Review on the State of the Country and of the Church," *BRPR* 37 (Oct. 1865): 645.

around us, any more than it is because the South is wrong, that Southern ecclesiastical bodies go with the people of whom they form a part. It is largely in both cases, because every man, and every body of men, are more or less subject to the controlling influence of public opinion, and of the life of the community to which they belong.[57]

Hodge's insight, shaped painfully by the events of the war, deserted him when the issue at stake was not the nature of the Union but the nature of the atonement. That Hodge's opponents on the latter question — as well as Hodge himself — could have been shaped by "the controlling influences of popular opinion" does not seem to have crossed his mind. This was a serious lapse. Hodge the commentator on the war saw what Hodge the expounder of theological method did not.

The lapse was significant for Hodge's view of the spiritual life. During the Civil War, he had made real progress in bringing together arguments for the moral superiority of Northern positions and empathic consideration of how assertions about the conflict reflected the life circumstances of Northerners and Southerners. As a theologian, Hodge was primed to make similar progress, for he had developed in many places a picture of how belief (or unbelief) contextualized an apprehension (or rejection) of Christian faith. Yet as a theologian Hodge did not take the step he took as a commentator on the war. The result was a lingering tension between his lifelong stress on the interested effects of piety and the summative formal statements of his career on the disinterested character of theological exposition.

Common Sense Moral Intuition

A third problem weakening Hodge's exposition of the spiritual life was his tangled commitment to common sense moral intuitions. The confusion at this point is complex, because it touched so many of Hodge's controversies as well as so much of his constructive efforts. The situation can be outlined as follows:

(a) Hodge regularly asserted that every theological proposition had to conform to the revelatory truth of Scripture.

(b) In parallel, he also insisted that, when we let our "philosophy" or "our preconceived theories" influence our theology, the result is "complete havoc."[58]

---

57. Hodge, "The General Assembly," *BRPR* 37 (July 1865): 506.
58. *ST,* vol. 1, p. 14.

(c) Yet, alongside the facts of Scripture, Hodge on many occasions spoke as well of the facts of human experience or of common sense moral intuitions that were in their own way as authoritative as the Bible. Hodge's exact wording for these extra-biblical authorities varied, but their weight was unmistakable. Thus, in 1847 he could appeal to "Scripture, experience, and the common consciousness of man" as coordinate authorities.[59] In 1859, it was "the authority of the Bible, and . . . the facts of our mental, moral and spiritual nature."[60] In the *Systematic Theology* he averred that to trust the Bible for all the facts of theology was "perfectly consistent . . . with the admission of intuitive truths, both intellectual and moral, due to our constitution as rational moral beings; and . . . with the controlling power over our beliefs exercised by the inward teachings of the Spirit, or, in other words, by our religious experience."[61]

(d) In fact, it is hard to imagine that Hodge could have operated without putting some kind of stock in truths derived from moral intuitions, since he lived in an America where intellectual life was dominated by such assumptions. Edwards Amasa Park, whom Hodge was so eager to confront on questions of dogma, nonetheless spoke for Hodge as well as for almost all other publishing theologians of his day when he hailed "the philosophy of Reid, Oswald, Campbell, Beattie, Stewart . . . *the philosophy of common sense*" as helping theologians "to develop 'the fundamental laws of human belief'" and so aiding "our writers in shaping their faith to these ethical axioms. . . ."[62] Hodge only rarely cited authorities for his employment of universal moral intuitions, but otherwise they functioned for him nearly as forcefully as they did for Park and others who traced the Scottish pedigree of this ethical common sense.

(e) Difficulties arose in the application of these ethical axioms. On issues where the deliverances of moral conscience supported his conclusions (or where he thought they agreed with his understanding of the Bible), Hodge was more than willing to employ common sense fully. Thus, in an early essay where he avowed to "recognize no authoritative rule of truth and duty but the word of God," Hodge came to final conclusions on issues of race by adducing truths "on all hands admitted" and an "ac-

---

59. Hodge, "Finney's Lectures on Theology," *BRPR* 19 (Apr. 1847), in *Princeton Theology*, p. 175.

60. Hodge, "Unity of Mankind," *BRPR* 31 (1859): 149.

61. *ST*, vol. 1, p. 15. For examples from the many other places where Hodge made the same juxtapositions, see "Beecher's Great Conflict," *BRPR* 26 (Jan. 1854): 101; "Salvation by Grace," ms. conference for 20 Mar. 1853, PTS; and *ST*, vol. 1, p. 53.

62. E. A. Park, "New England Theology," *Bibliotheca Sacra* 9 (Jan. 1852): 191.

knowledged right" of states to treat African Americans differently than whites.[63] In an essay from 1862, Hodge made the same move. It was not so much the Bible as intuitive knowledge of the "moral and physical nature of man" that could "easily refute all the speculation that has been advanced . . . in favour of a separate and independent origin for his several races or varieties."[64] Similarly, Hodge rested much of his argument in 1874 against what he took to be the ateleology of Darwin's natural selection on "intuitions which are infallible, laws of belief which men cannot disregard any more than the laws of nature . . . the testimony of consciousness and . . . the intuitions of reason and conscience."[65] In other words, on some questions Hodge was more than willing to look to his own moral nature, instead of to the Bible, as a final adjudicator.

The theological issue where this propensity appeared most clearly was Hodge's account of the connection between Adam and the rest of the human race.[66] Hodge's defense of a classical doctrine of the imputation of Adam's sin was foundational to his theology. But when it came to how Adam was connected to the whole human race, such that all humanity bore the guilt of Adam's sin, Hodge mostly gave up the Bible for common sense. In particular, several times in his career he took pains to rebut Jonathan Edwards' theory of imputation, which had posited a kind of Platonic unity of human nature acting in Adam. Against this view, Hodge offered almost no scriptural argument. Rather, as he put it in the *Systematic Theology*, "This doctrines denies the existence of substance. The idea of substance is a primitive idea. It is given in the constitution of our nature. It is an intuitive truth, as proved by its universality and necessity."[67] Thus, on some critical issues, Hodge was in fact eager to use "preconceived theories" to construct his theology.

(f) If Hodge was willing to employ common sense moral intuition to defend doctrinal propositions he thought were correct, he also wanted to rule out the moral intuitions of others when their conclusions contradicted his own. At this point, the difficulty was severe for someone who wanted both to defend traditional Calvinism and to maintain the truth-

63. Hodge, "Slavery," *BRPR* 8 (1836), in *Essays and Reviews*, pp. 479, 503.

64. Hodge, "Diversity of Species in the Human Race," *BRPR* 34 (July 1862): 462.

65. Hodge, *What Is Darwinism?* p. 137.

66. On the exceedingly complex issues of imputation as they were argued in the nineteenth century, I have benefited greatly from George P. Hutchinson, *The Problem of Original Sin in American Presbyterian Theology* (Nutley, N.J.: Presbyterian and Reformed, 1972), with pp. 28-35 on Hodge.

67. *ST*, vol. 2, p. 219.

telling character of moral intuitions, since it was primarily on the basis of what were asserted to be universal moral sentiments that Hodge's opponents adduced their most devastating arguments. So it was when the *New Englander* in 1862 took Hodge and his Princeton colleagues to task for maintaining a whole host of dogmas that contradicted what the author considered universally perceived moral intuitions:

> Let him take it to a popular audience, or to the common sense of men, anywhere, and say that all sin is decreed of God before the foundation of the world, and is but the Divine method of the universe according to God's plan; that it is the necessary means of the greatest good . . . that men act freely in sinning as they do, yet "without power to the contrary." . . . With such a doctrine no wonder that we have Universalists, and Infidels, and Nothingarians, and Unitarians, not to speak of others nearer the truth than they. The position does in truth annihilate a moral system, and take the life of virtue.[68]

So it was also in 1874 when the *Methodist Quarterly Review* took note of Hodge's *What Is Darwinism?* The reviewer applauded Hodge's conclusions on Darwin but then pointed out that he "repeatedly . . . appeals to our 'intuitions' as the conclusive stronghold against his materialist opponents." This use of intuition the reviewer thoroughly approved. But then came what, given Hodge's profession about common sense intuitions, could only have been an embarrassing series of questions:

> But how can Dr. Hodge's own theology stand before the judgment-seat of our own intuitions? Certain it is, that in the contest between Arminianism and Calvinism, one great power of the former has been in an appeal to the intuitive pronunciation against the view presented by the latter of the Divine government. How far can we base our Christianity on intuitive assumptions, and then reject the intuitive negative upon our special theology?[69]

(g) Hodge's standard response to such arguments followed a dual course. Characteristically he held that the Bible supported what his opponents controverted and also that moral intuition, properly grasped, did too. The latter assertion was the problem, for Hodge himself on several occasions did precisely what he accused his opponents of doing — he used

---

68. Anonymous, "The Princeton Review and Rev. Dr. Squier," *New Englander* 21 (April 1862): 303-04.

69. Anonymous, *Methodist Quarterly Review* 56 (July 1874): 516.

his common sense intuitions of the way things must be to guide his inter-pretation of Scripture. Thus in his commentary on Romans 5:12 Hodge brought his exposition of the phrase, "as by one man sin entered into the world . . . ; so death passed upon all men," to a close with an unabashed appeal to moral intuition: "It is a monstrous evil to make the Bible con-tradict the common sense and common consciousness of men. This is to make God contradict himself."[70]

The fact that E. A. Park could not have said it better did not trouble Hodge. Nor did the fact that Jonathan Edwards, less than a century be-fore, had argued for the position that Hodge rejected on the basis of both exhaustive scriptural exegesis and what Edwards considered to be truths "plainly acknowledged . . . evident . . . undeniable in fact . . . [conforming to] an established law of nature . . . [and exhibiting] an apparent manifold analogy to other constitutions and laws, established and maintained through the whole system of vital nature in this lower world."[71]

(h) The conclusion must be that Hodge held contradictory positions. Against those who brought their philosophy of common sense to the Scrip-tures, he quoted the Bible, except when his own common sense intuitions dictated to him how the Bible must be read. It is an arguable judgment that Hodge performed this legerdemain less frequently than his New School, New Haven, and Finneyite opponents. But the fact that he did it at all — that on occasion he simply allowed his own religious experience to come first in determining the meaning of Scripture — gave the lie to his formal statements about theological method, compromised his contention that the doctrines for which he argued represented simply the church's historic Augustinianism without variation, and made instinctive assertions stand in for self-conscious exposition in the construction of his theology.

By extension, the peculiar place of common sense moral intuitions in his theology also undercut Hodge's exposition of the spiritual life. That

---

70. Hodge, *Romans*, p. 151. George Hutchinson points out how heavily nineteenth-century sentiment about the innocence of children bore down upon Hodge at this point. As a classical Calvinist Hodge had to preserve human unity in Adam, but as a sensitive Victo-rian, he had somehow to get dying infants into heaven. The result was a theory of imputa-tion that made an ingenious distinction between imputed sin (which only grace could over-come) and actual sinning (which condemned people to hell). That Hodge found in Scripture a theology of covenant to support his new position suggests how complicated the exchange of social conventions and objective research actually was for biblical exegesis. See Hutchinson, *Problem of Original Sin*, p. 33.

71. Jonathan Edwards, *Original Sin*, ed. Clyde A. Holbrook (New Haven: Yale University Press, 1970), pp. 394, 398, 409, 397, 406.

effort was riven, divided between an effort to re-present classical Calvinist spirituality and to defend a certain set of common sense moral intuitions. Despite his own obvious intentions, his spiritual vision strained under an effort to incorporate what Hodge saw as subjective and objective parts of Christian life, for "objective" turned out to mean not only the dogmas of Scripture, but also the facts of universal moral consciousness; and "subjective" turned out to mean not only the self-authenticating witness of the Holy Spirit, but also the intuitions of the moral sense.

Despite his well-publicized claims, a new theological idea had indeed arisen at Princeton. That idea was the selective, random, and unacknowledged functioning of Hodge's own moral intuitions as a guide for theological reasoning.

To summarize: Hodge's exposition of the spiritual life was weakened intellectually for at least three reasons. On occasion he spoke of the Bible as a mechanical repository of facts while neglecting the question of how those facts related to the sources of faith in experiential piety that he otherwise promoted so vigorously. More frequently Hodge defended theology as a disinterested science despite the fact that his own writing concerning the effects of piety and his own experience in the Civil War testified to the power of interest in all intellectual activities. Finally, Hodge's ad hoc use of common sense moral intuition as a building block of his theology represented a nineteenth-century innovation at odds with his own profession to root spirituality exclusively in the narrative of Scripture.

Hodge in His Times

A grasp of the weaknesses in Hodge's exposition of the spiritual life, at least as those weaknesses appear from one angle more than a century after his death, is one thing. Contextual, historical understanding of these weaknesses, as well of the considerable strengths of that exposition, is another. For the latter purpose both comparisons with his contemporaries and biographical explanations take us much further toward understanding Hodge than examination of his work alone.

Comparison

The main comparative point to make is that, if Hodge's exposition of the spiritual life lacked coherence at certain points, he was in good company.

Excluding advanced thinkers like Emerson, who turned their faces deliberately away from the Christian tradition and who must be evaluated by other criteria, the field of moderate and conservative theologians of the first two-thirds of the nineteenth century as a whole labored under singular difficulties. Almost all of them carried willingly the burden of a superannuated Christendom — formal in Britain, informal but just as powerful in the United States. That burden promoted confusion by demanding that speech in and to the church function also as speech to and for society as a whole. Intellectually, and for different reasons in Britain and America,[72] theologians as a whole also suffered from the even greater burden of a singular psycho-social pressure. That pressure was the demand for a Paleyite form of natural theology to fulfill the "modern" felt need for clear, thoroughly understandable, and universally valid explanations for God's ways with the world. The process that James Turner describes in *Without God, Without Creed* was fully underway, whereby the burden of proof for the existence and goodness of God had shifted from unbelievers to the church.[73] In consequence, theologians were straining to meet the challenge of theodicy, but most of them simply accepted the intellectual standards of the age as the criteria by which to judge their success. Some theologians — like Hodge, N. W. Taylor, Finney, and the self-conscious descendants of Jonathan Edwards — attempted to fulfill these demands by Christianizing the Newtonian ideals of the Enlightenment. Others, like James Marsh, J. W. Nevin, H. B. Smith, and admirers of Samuel Taylor Coleridge more generally, sought to Christianize the organic impulses of romanticism.[74] Only a few from the vast middle and right of the theological spectrum realized how important it was to query the basic social and intellectual con-

72. Compare the moral crises described by Boyd Hilton, *The Age of Atonement . . . 1795-1865* (Oxford: Clarendon Press, 1988); Robert Hole, *Pulpits, Politics and Public Order in England, 1760-1832* (New York: Cambridge University Press, 1989); and David Hempton, *Religion and Political Culture in Britain and Ireland: From the Glorious Revolution to the Decline of Empire* (New York: Cambridge University Press, 1996); with those pictured in Robert H. Wiebe, *The Opening of American Society: From the Adoption of the Constitution to the Eve of Disunion* (New York: Knopf, 1984); Nathan O. Hatch, *The Democratization of American Christianity* (New Haven: Yale University Press, 1989); and Gordon S. Wood, *The Radicalism of the American Revolution* (New York: Knopf, 1992).

73. James Turner, *Without God, Without Creed: The Origins of Unbelief in America* (Baltimore: Johns Hopkins University Press, 1985).

74. For a revealing exchange early in Hodge's career that showed why his cautious appreciation for Coleridge would be overwhelmed by his worry that Coleridge transferred too much of the divine prerogative to the self, see James Marsh to Hodge, 4 Nov. 1830; and Hodge to James Marsh, 22 Nov. 1830, PTS (photocopies from the University of Vermont).

ventions of the era in order to secure integrity for theology. Apart from John Henry Newman, theologians in Britain and America during the nineteenth century were almost uniformly willing to work out their convictions about God and humanity within the intellectual framework provided by the assumptions of the age. There were, in other words, few who tried to do what disparate figures like Nicolas Malebranche, Jonathan Edwards, Soren Kierkegaard, or Karl Barth attempted in other times and places, which was to critique an era's entire way of thinking as a prolegomenon to theological construction.

In a theological situation restricted by these self-imposed burdens, Charles Hodge was a giant. Only ahistorical judgments can suggest otherwise. For example, to label Hodge "unimaginative"[75] is only possible if one forgets what it took to make a persuasive statement of Calvinistic predestination in a republican American inebriated with visions of personal right. The same must be said for other analyses of Hodge that extract him from his times, like Frank Hugh Foster's cunning judgment that Hodge could "be safely left by the historian of a progressive school of theology to the natural consequences of his own remark that during the many years of his predominance at Princeton that institution had never brought forward a single original thought."[76] Hodge was not a paragon and Frank Hugh Foster was far from a fool, but it is certain that after the passage of two hundred years, there will be no more ongoing interest in Frank Hugh Foster and his progressivism than there is in Hodge and his conservatism. It is the same with loose talk about Hodge as a "scholastic" or with simplistic, unqualified judgments, of which I have myself been guilty, that Hodge was dominated by the Scottish philosophy of common sense. Apart from the fact that, if Hodge was scholastic or dominated by Scottish realism, so were virtually all of his significant peers, such judgments badly underestimate the vigor that different forms of scholasticism and the Scottish philosophy sustained into the nineteenth century.[77]

One especially important requirement for a proper historical understanding of Hodge is the proper placement of his *Systematic Theology*. In

75. Kuklick, *Churchmen and Philosophers*, p. 79.
76. Frank Hugh Foster, *A Genetic History of the New England Theology* (Chicago: University of Chicago Press, 1907), p. 432.
77. For a thorough deconstruction of negative connotations of "scholasticism" for Hodge's own tradition, see Richard A. Muller, *Post-Reformation Reformed Dogmatics*, 2 vols. (Grand Rapids: Baker, 1987, 1993). For indications of the vigor of Scottish thinking, see Alasdair MacIntyre, *Whose Justice? Whose Rationality?* (Notre Dame: University of Notre Dame Press, 1988), pp. 323-33.

contradiction to what it has been called by otherwise shrewd observers like Leonard Trinterud, this work was not "the capstone of his long career."[78] Despite the continuity between these three stout volumes and his thinking before 1871, Hodge wrote the *Systematic Theology* as if it were, in the words of David Wells, "a piece of eternal wisdom," much of it "gathered from European divines, which could be deposited in any age or place with equal ease." In contrast, Hodge's much more characteristic stance — from his commentary on Romans in 1835 through his two-volume *Constitutional History of the Presbyterian Church* in 1840 and the thousands of impassioned pages in the *Princeton Review* to *What Is Darwinism?* in 1874 — was intense engagement with, again as Wells puts it, the pressing circumstances of a "time of dramatic social and intellectual change."[79] No account of Hodge's work is complete without considering his *Systematic Theology*, but neither is any account adequate without recognition that this work was no more than a caboose — stately, impressive, and hard to miss though it may be — at the end of a very long train.

Once Hodge has been reinserted into his own times, comparison with his peers adds much to judicious assessment of his work. On questions of the church and sacraments, for example, Hodge was not only shallower than J. W. Nevin, but also far less a follower of Calvin. Yet much more effectively than Nevin, Hodge communicated in an America far different from sixteenth-century Geneva or Wittenberg the liberating beauty that Luther and Calvin had found in the vicarious atonement.[80] Bruce Kuklick has shown in a well-considered judgment that N. W. Taylor was the premier philosophical mind among leading American theologians of his era.[81] But by comparison with Taylor, Hodge preserved a far better understanding of the rootedness of evil in the human heart. It may be due to the fact that Taylor did not live through the Civil War, that conditions in New England and among Congregationalists shifted rapidly after his death, or that his

78. Leonard J. Trinterud, "Charles Hodge (1797-1878): Theology — Didactic and Polemical," in *Sons of the Prophets: Leaders in Protestantism from Princeton Seminary*, ed. Hugh T. Kerr (Princeton: Princeton University Press, 1963), p. 38. Similar judgments inform the analyses of Bozeman, *Protestants in an Age of Science*, pp. 153-55; and Rogers and McKim, *Authority and Interpretation*, pp. 289-98.

79. David F. Wells, "Charles Hodge," in *Reformed Theology in America*, ed. D. F. Wells (Grand Rapids: Eerdmans, 1985), pp. 55, 37.

80. For helpful comparative reasoning from Nevin's perspective, see B. A. Gerrish, *Tradition and the Modern World: Reformed Theology in the Nineteenth Century* (Chicago: University of Chicago, 1978), pp. 60-70.

81. Kuklick, *Churchmen and Philosophers*, pp. 94-105.

theology contained the seeds of self-destruction that Hodge perceived, but whatever the explanation, later developments proved Hodge prescient in predicting the decline of Taylor's particular theology, although the rapidity of that decline, I think, would have surprised even Hodge.

The most interesting comparison for Hodge is with Horace Bushnell. Hodge's review of Bushnell's *Christian Nurture* in 1847 conceded, in effect, that if the theology of Schleiermacher could be nudged toward orthodoxy, Bushnell was the only one who could do it.[82] This grudging respect for Bushnell suggests, I think, that Hodge sensed his own understanding of the foundational character of piety needed to be fleshed out — if not as Bushnell had done it, nonetheless with the seriousness that the Hartford pastor had expended in placing lived religion at the foundation of an entire theological system. Hodge's other essays on Bushnell, which were much harsher, showed that Hodge was almost completely lacking in the theological creativity that has made Bushnell such an interesting figure for American academics in the second half of this century.[83] Yet where Hodge gave way to Bushnell in willingness to try out new ideas, Bushnell as thoroughly gave way to Hodge in seeing the potential in historic theological formulas. And if Bushnell was provocative on some questions of theological construction in ways that Hodge was not, Hodge was profoundly measured on the moral meaning of the Civil War and painstakingly discriminating on the meaning of evolution in striking contrast to Bushnell's atavistic blood-lust on the war and his anti-intellectual carping against Darwin.[84]

Similar judgments could be drawn in comparisons between Hodge and moderate or conservative theologians throughout the Atlantic world, whether Orestes Brownson, Charles Finney, John Henry Hobart, Daniel Alexander Payne, Philip Schaff, Henry Boynton Smith, Harriet Beecher Stowe, or James Henley Thornwell in the United States, Thomas McCulloch, Nathanael Burwash, or George Monro Grant in Canada, or John McLeod Campbell, Thomas Chalmers, Henry Cooke, Thomas Erskine, John Keble, or Charles Simeon in Britain. Hodge was never as willing to launch beyond the safe boundaries of the Westminster Confession

---

82. Hodge, "Bushnell on Christian Nurture," *BRPR* 19 (Oct. 1847).

83. For example, "Bushnell's Discourses," *BRPR* 21 (Apr. 1849): 259-98; and "Bushnell on Vicarious Sacrifice," *BRPR* 38 (Apr. 1866): 161-94.

84. See Bushnell's sermon delivered in New Haven in July 1865, "Our Obligations to the Dead," in Bushnell, *Building Eras in Religion* (New York: Charles Scribner's Sons, 1881); and Bushnell, "Science and Religion," *Putnam's Monthly Magazine* (1868), as quoted and discussed in Jon H. Roberts, *Darwinism and the Divine in America* (Madison: University of Wisconsin Press, 1988), p. 44.

as the more creative of such theologians. He was never as insightful about the historical dynamics of the faith as those who were busy refurbishing historic confessions in opposition to free-market drift. And he was never as shrewd on the power of the affections as the thorough sentimentalists. But, at least with respect to the American situation, Hodge internalized the Bible (or at least a classical understanding of the Pauline Epistles) better than any publishing theologian of his generation. He was in person as attractively pious as any public figure of his day.[85] He did a better job than anyone in the English-speaking world at the difficult task of both preserving traditional Calvinism and speaking it into a largely anti-Calvinist intellectual climate. And he kept alive the ideal of a unified field of divinely enabled knowledge — embracing especially scientific and theological research — with more vigor than almost any of his contemporaries.

A historical assessment of Hodge's exposition of the spiritual life depends in considerable measure on such comparisons. They do not obviate or excuse the problems that weakened Hodge's account of spirituality. But they do show that the problems Hodge could not overcome were, at least in part, the problems of an era. Within that era, and by comparison with how others approached the issues that mattered most at the time, Hodge's forceful insistence on a spirituality fully objective and fully subjective was a substantial contribution, even if he was not alert to the ways in which his promotion of the objective undercut his commitment to the subjective, and vice versa.

Biography

Historical assessment is not, however, the same as historical explanation. The nature of Hodge's strengths as well as weaknesses in expounding the

85. The testimony of Hodge's grandson, William Berryman Scott, who became a paleontologist at Princeton University where he taught a version of evolution that Hodge had condemned, is particularly germane. Scott spent many of his childhood years in Hodge's home and wrote these words as an old man: "It is the fashion nowadays to decry the Calvinistic theology and to paint its professors as gloomy and austere fanatics. Whatever may be true of other communities, I can truthfully say that never, in any part of the world, have I met such sunny, genial, kindly and tolerant people as my Grandfather and his children. He stands in my memory as the ideal of a perfect saint and gentleman, in whom I could see no flaw. The whole community revered and honoured him, but I can give no conception of the position which he held, or of the selfless, unconscious way in which he held it. He never talked of himself. . . ." Scott, *Some Memories of a Palaeontologist* (Princeton: Princeton University Press, 1939), p. 8.

spiritual life can, in fact, be at least partially understood by attention to the circumstances of his life. For Hodge's philosophical and method-ological commitments, as well as his place in the broader history of the-ology in America, the course of Hodge's life makes some things reason-ably clear.

Why, first, did Hodge stumble the way he did across the border be-tween philosophy and theology? The probable answer is that Hodge loved his teachers with filial or fraternal intensity, and his teachers taught him the philosophical method to which he was always committed. Many com-mentators have noted the intensity of Hodge's affections for Archibald Al-exander, Alexander's sons Addison and James, his seminary classmates like Bishop John Johns, the teachers like August Tholuck who befriended him in Germany, his wife Sarah Bache, his children, and his many grand-children.[86] Hodge also early recognized the importance of such ties, as when he wrote his wife from Halle in 1827 that "From my disposition I cannot be happy without having some body near me whom I really love. . . . Here Tholuck is the happy man. — & of course is my all & every thing."[87] It sheds much light on the nature of his thought to realize that Hodge was instructed in notions of Baconian method and common sense moral intuitions by three of the individuals to whom he felt the strongest possible human bonds.

Ashbel Green was the pastor in Philadelphia who baptized Hodge, buried his father, catechized him, supported his widowed mother through difficult days, in 1812 became president of the College of New Jer-sey just as Hodge entered as a student, and in the winter of 1814-15 guided the awakening during which Hodge made public profession of his faith. Green's major academic accomplishment as president of the college was to restore John Witherspoon's text in moral philosophy as the college's in-tellectual foundation. Reciting its pages, Hodge learned about "the prin-ciples of duty and obligation . . . drawn from the very nature of man" and was exposed to Witherspoon's hope that "a time may come when men, treating moral philosophy as Newton and his successors have done natu-ral, may arise at greater precision."[88]

Looming even larger in Hodge's formation was Archibald Alexander, whom the young Hodge heard deliver his inaugural address as the first

86. For example, Henry A. Boardman, *Discourses Commemorative of the Life and Work of Charles Hodge* (Philadelphia: Henry B. Ashmead, 1879), pp. 60, 64.

87. Hodge to Sarah Bache Hodge, 4 June 1827, PUA.

88. For details, see Mark A. Noll, *Princeton and the Republic, 1768-1822* (Princeton: Prince-ton University Press, 1989), pp. 41, 272-91.

professor of Princeton Seminary in the summer of 1812, whose preaching sustained the revival of 1814-15, who selected Hodge personally to join the seminary faculty, whom Hodge came to consider a replacement for the father he had never known, and who at his death movingly bestowed upon Hodge the blessing of Elijah. Among the first lectures Hodge heard from Alexander when he entered seminary in 1815 was a disquisition on the "Nature and Evidence of Truth." In that lecture, Alexander explained the sort of "self-evident propositions . . . self-evident truths . . . intuitive truths" that humans could use to "prove [God's] existence" and so pursue "the object of Theological Science," which is "the discovery of truth."[89] One of the last acts Hodge performed for Alexander was to oversee the posthumous publications of the latter's *Outlines of Moral Science* (1852), the text that had grown over the years from the lecture on truth that Hodge had attended, and which deviated not at all from the Baconian common sense of Alexander's first approach to the subject.[90]

The bonds of affection that linked Hodge so personally to the views on method expounded in the opening pages of the *Systematic Theology* received unexpected reinforcement during his time in Germany. Hodge's relationship with August Tholuck may be said to have vindicated his decision to go to Europe. Tholuck, a brilliant linguist, pietist convert, and tireless writer, went out of his way to befriend the young American early in Hodge's stay in Halle. In Tholuck, Hodge found not only an expert teacher, but also a warm friend. Little matter that Tholuck's theology was far closer to the Mercersburg views that Hodge could never accept in the United States. Far away from home, almost certainly troubled by guilt at leaving a young wife and two small children, in financially straitened circumstances, frequently subjected to Alexander's conflicted advice to benefit from his studies but not fall from the faith, the clarity of Tholuck's teaching and the warmth of his friendship could only have been a godsend. In those personal circumstances, it is significant that Hodge heard Tholuck begin a historical overview of eighteenth-century German theology with these words: "All human knowledge, is derived from two sources, Reflexion & Experience. — These cannot be separated. Experience must supply the facts and Reflexion must arrange & systematize these facts. — He therefore who is in search of knowledge must first direct his attention

89. Alexander, "Nature and Evidence of Truth," in *Princeton Theology*, pp. 63, 64, 65, 62.
90. For Alexander's difficulty in squaring his Calvinism and his common sense moral philosophy, see D. H. Meyer, *The Instructed Conscience: The Shaping of the American National Ethic* (Philadelphia: University of Pennsylvania Press, 1972), pp. 55-56.

to the collection of facts."[91] The composition was not precisely what Hodge had heard from Green and Alexander, but the timbre was the same.

When the circumstances of Hodge's career after returning from Europe are also considered, the account of his methodological commitments becomes even clearer. The Princeton theologians of Hodge's generation were probably better philosophers than they pretended to be, but for a group that exhibited so much brilliance in so many areas, their lack of concern for formal philosophy was striking. Hodge once wrote of the precocious Joseph Addison Alexander, "If, when reading a book he came across any philosophical discussion, he would turn over the leaves until he found more congenial matter."[92] For formal philosophical essays, the *Princeton Review* turned to the Maryland lawyer Samuel Tyler and Lyman Atwater, a student of N. W. Taylor at Yale who eventually joined the Old School Presbyterian church, the faculty of the College of New Jersey, and the editorial board of the *Princeton Review*.[93] Atwater, especially, was Princeton's philosophical hit man. He was an able casuist, particularly in pointing out how New England theological developments, purportedly in the spirit of Edwards, actually contradicted what Edwards actually defended. Yet Atwater's unwavering commitment to Baconianism, his penchant for reading innovative sallies by various New Englanders as great eruptions of heresy, and his inability to see that the "self-evident excellence and obligation of first moral truths" were not, in fact, equally self-evident to all, meant that he was a much better critic than constructive theologian.[94] Despite his relative weaknesses, Atwater was left by Hodge and his colleagues to carry the philosophical burden for Princeton as a whole, at least until 1868 and the arrival of James McCosh as president of the college.

The character of Hodge's formative personal attachments and the constitution of his collegial circle, along with the intensity of his affections for both, offers the clearest explanation for the ambiguities, contradictions, and confusion that are now so apparent in Hodge's understand-

---

91. Hodge, "The History of Theology in the Eighteenth Century by Dr. Aug. Tholuck, Professor of Theology in the University of Halle — June 1827," ms., PTS. A slightly different version of this manuscript was published in *Biblical Repertory* 4 (1828): 9-57.

92. Hodge, *A Discourse Delivered at the Re-Opening of the Chapel, September 27, 1874* (Princeton: Chas. S. Robinson, 1874), p. 15.

93. For their contributions, see *BRPR: Index Volume*, pp. 94-96, 308-9.

94. Atwater, "Dr. Taylor's Lectures on the Moral Government of God," *BRPR* 31 (July 1859): 496.

ing of the theological task, but which he did not, and probably could not, see. To see them would have been to violate the most intimate personal relations of his life.

But what of the broader intellectual landscape? What can we say about the world in which Hodge lived that will bring clearer insight into the nature of his theology? An indication of that larger picture is found in a revealing exchange between Hodge and R. L. Dabney on the eve of the Civil War. Early in 1860 Hodge had tried to persuade Dabney to leave Union Seminary at Hamden-Sydney, Virginia for a position at Princeton. Those negotiations failed, but they did establish rapport between the two Old School theologians. After the election of Abraham Lincoln, the correspondence resumed as Dabney and Hodge solicited each other's opinions on what they were publishing about the crisis of union. Though they were ultimately unable to agree, their correspondence remained cordial. At the end of a lengthy letter in January 1861, Dabney closed by thanking Hodge for his "instruction in sound presbyterian and republican principles."[95]

Dabney's linking of republican and Presbyterian principles was insightful, for Hodge was always more than a theologian of the Old School. In antebellum America, all Christian thinkers who exerted an influence were also, to one degree or another, republicans as well as theologians. The perceptive judgment of D. H. Meyer explains the situation well: "The philosophy of human nature had to keep pace with the ever-increasing potential of men living in a commercial and democratic society. The nineteenth-century Christian moralist . . . had to balance his theological commitments over against his 'Baconian' spirit and his social concerns."[96] Hodge's standing as the leading theologian at one of the leading centers of higher learning of any kind in mid-nineteenth-century America had much to do with his ability to "speak American." That he did so with determinative set purpose as a Westminster Calvinist does not alter the fact that he mastered the American conceptual idiom. That idiom, after a generation of ideological confusion following the Revolution, had emerged by the 1830s as an amalgam of evangelicalism, republicanism, common sense Baconianism, and free market capitalism.[97] Situating inherited theological vocabularies in

95. Dabney to Hodge, 23 Jan. 1861, Dabney Papers, Historical Foundation of the Presbyterian and Reformed Churches, Montreat, North Carolina.

96. Meyer, *Instructed Conscience,* p. 54.

97. Outstanding treatments of this ideological mixture are Daniel Walker Howe, *The Political Culture of the American Whigs* (Chicago: University of Chicago Press, 1979); Richard J. Carwardine, *Evangelicals and Politics in Antebellum America* (New Haven: Yale University Press, 1993); and John G. West, Jr., *The Politics of Revelation and Reason: Religion and Civic Life in the*

such an ideology had allowed Christian theologians of several varieties both to rescue intellectual self-respect and to assert the centrality of the churches in the dynamically expanding culture of the early republic. Hodge's strategy for making Calvinism understood in the antebellum intellectual marketplace was different from strategies pursued by Finney, Taylor, and others. But not to make the effort was to be silent. For Hodge, the standard ideological idiom was the only way that traditional Calvinism, a theology of election tending toward sectarianism and an ecclesiology of hierarchies tending toward oligarchy, could still resonate at the center of an American society defined by republican equality.

Hodge became a widely respected American theologian precisely because he could communicate the power of traditional Calvinism by using an American vocabulary defined by almost magical respect for the Bible, incredible hermeneutical optimism, Baconian understandings of theory formation, and a common sense trust in moral intuitions. The surprise is not that an ambitious individual who wanted his ideas to count used that vocabulary, but that in using it Hodge maintained as well as he did the integrity of pre-Revolutionary Calvinism.

Conclusion

A full exploration of reasons for the fractures in Hodge's view of the Christian life would require the kind of situated biographical treatment that to date he has not received. Hodge as bogey to exorcise or as champion to vindicate has always, and regrettably, received more attention than Hodge in his times. The reason for this relative lack of serious historical attention is plain. Hodge held a critical place in the history of Calvinism in the United States; confessional Calvinism has been America's one fully functioning system of hegemonic theology; thus, Hodge's ideas have been much more attractive as targets (or, for a bypassed minority, as icons) than as inducements for historical investigation. Yet attention to

---

New Nation (Manhattan: University Press of Kansas, 1996). I have tried to show how the amalgamation was promoted by, and then affected, evangelical Protestantism in "The American Revolution and Protestant Evangelicalism," *Journal of Interdisciplinary History* 23 (Winter 1993): 615-38; "The Rise and Long Life of the Protestant Enlightenment in America," in *Knowledge and Belief in America: Enlightenment Traditions and Modern Religious Thought*, ed. William M. Shea and Peter A. Huff (New York: Cambridge University Press, 1995), pp. 88-124; and "The Bible and Slavery," in *Religion and the Civil War*, ed. Randall Miller, Harry S. Stout, and Charles Reagan Wilson (New York: Oxford University Press, 1998), pp. 43-73.

the human being, along with attention to the world in which he lived, is what it will take to answer the profoundest questions about the shape of Hodge's spiritual vision and why it enjoyed such great respect in America and other parts of the world.

Of course, biography as such will not fully explain that vision, for there were many who shared his theology but not his life experiences, and some who shared his experiences but not his theology. It is rather that the tone, conjunctions, organization, synapses, blind spots, and affectional emphases of Hodge's Calvinism will never be satisfactorily situated without full attention to his life in its times.

When such mature historical study is carried out, it is likely that a final assessment of Hodge's exposition of the spiritual life will agree with Robert Hastings Nichols, who in one of the first objective judgments of Hodge suggested that Hodge's "most characteristic work" arose out of "his real and strongly emotional piety, the heart of which was vital apprehension of the love of God in Christ."[98] But it is also likely that such an assessment will agree as well with Charles Hodge himself, who in almost the last words he wrote noted that "men have often more of Christ in their religion than in their theology."[99]

98. Nichols, "Charles Hodge," *Dictionary of American Biography,* Vol. 9 (New York: Charles Scribner's Sons, 1932), p. 98.
99. Hodge, "Christianity Without Christ," p. 362.

Charles Hodge as Interpreter of Scripture

DAVID H. KELSEY

As a brief appendix to A. A. Hodge's biography of Charles Hodge, B. B. Warfield contributed reflections on "Dr Hodge as a Teacher of Exegesis."[1] Warfield recalled his former teacher of exegesis with great fondness, but not without reservations. According to Warfield, "[I]n questions of textual criticism he constantly went astray."[2] As Warfield remembered it, Hodge had "no taste for the technicalities of Exegesis. . . . His discussion of disputed grammatical or lexical points had a flavor of second-handedness about them. He appeared not to care to have a personal opinion upon such matters, but was content to accept another's without having made it really his own. . . . He seemed sometimes to be quite as apt to choose an indefensible as a plausible opinion."[3] The upshot "was that often texts were quoted in support of doctrines of which they did not treat; and a meaning was sometimes extracted from a passage which it was far from bearing."[4]

On the other hand, Warfield recalled, what Hodge was really good at was capturing and summarizing the overall movement and central thrust of a complex biblical text: "Dr. Hodge's sense of the general meaning of a passage was unsurpassed. He had all of Calvin's sense of the flow and connection of thought. Consequently the analysis of passages was superb. Nothing could surpass the clearness with which he set forth the general

---

1. A. A. Hodge, *The Life of Charles Hodge D.D., L.L.D.* (New York: Charles Scribner's Sons, 1880), pp. 588-591 (hereafter AAH, *Life*).

2. AAH, *Life*, p. 590.

3. AAH, *Life*, pp. 588-90.

4. AAH, *Life*, p. 590.

argument and main connections of thought. Neither could anything surpass the analytical subtlety with which he extracted the doctrinal contents of passages. . . . He seemed to look through a passage, catch its main drift and all its theological bearings, and state the result in crisp sentences, which would have been worthy of Bacon; all in a single movement of mind."[5]

"From what I have written you will see," Warfield continued, "that Dr. Hodge commanded my respect and admiration as an exegete, while at the same time I could not fail to recognize that this was not his forte. Even here he was the clear, analytical thinker, rather than a patient collector and weigher of detailed evidence. He was great here, but not at his greatest. Theology was his first love."[6]

Warfield added a comment about Hodge as teacher: "I have sat under many noted teachers, and yet am free to say that as an educator I consider Dr. Hodge superior to them all. He was in fact my ideal of a teacher. . . . I cannot hope to describe this mode of teaching or express my profound admiration of it. I can only say that in that room of Systematic Theology, I think I had daily before me examples of perfect teaching."[7]

Not only Hodge's commentaries, especially Romans,[8] but also his biblical interpretation in responses to other people's commentaries, in his polemical articles in *The Biblical Repertory and Princeton Review*,[9] and in his *Systematic Theology*,[10] all tend to confirm Warfield's general characterizations of Hodge as interpreter of the Bible. Of course, what we have access to now is not Hodge's practice of teaching exegesis but his practice of biblical interpretation in print. But Charles Hodge was to an extraordinary degree all of a piece. Warfield remarked that "the material of the lectures [in exegesis] resembles very much his printed commentaries."[11]

Hodge's actual practice of biblical interpretation was deeply informed by and consistent with his theology of the Bible as God's inerrant word, plenarily and verbally inspired. It is also deeply formed by his view of the nature of revelation, the nature of theology, and the relation between the

---

5. AAH, *Life*, p. 589.

6. AAH, *Life*, p. 590.

7. AAH, *Life*, p. 590.

8. Charles Hodge, *Commentary on the Epistle to the Romans*, ed. Alister McGrath and J. I. Packer (Wheaton, Ill.: Crossway Books, 1993).

9. Hereafter cited as *BRPR*, followed by volume number, year, and page number.

10. Charles Hodge, *Systematic Theology*, 3 vols. (New York: Scribner, Armstrong, and Co., 1872); hereafter cited as *ST*, followed by volume and page number.

11. AAH, *Life*, p. 589.

two. As we shall see, the result is that biblical interpretation for Hodge could not *not* be interpretation in the service of constructive theology; and that theology was done in service of forming the minds and the hearts of the faithful. There was a wonderful fit — Hodge surely would have said it was a providential fit — between his gifts for grasping a text's movement of thought and the main purpose (theological) of interpreting Scripture in the first place. So far as being an interpreter of Scripture is concerned, Hodge was a good systematic theologian; and so far as being a systematic theologian is concerned, Hodge was a splendid theological teacher in Christendom's church.

I. Interpretation: Theory and Rules

To characterize Hodge fairly as an interpreter of Scripture, we must place him in the larger intellectual history of biblical interpretation. The more immediate point of reference must be the history of controversies about biblical interpretation generated by "radical" scholarship, especially in Enlightenment Germany, from Hermann Samuel Reimarus (1694-1768) through David Friedrich Strauss (1804-74) and Julius Wellhausen (1844-1918). During the two years Hodge spent in Germany in his youth (1826-28), he acquainted himself with the claims of the more radical scholarship and with the principle strategies of theologically conservative rebuttals. It is clear that he found the theologically conservative position of F. A. Tholuck particularly congenial. He had heard Schleiermacher preach. He was aware of the controversies that churned in the wake of Strauss's *Life of Jesus* (1835).

Just how shall we place Hodge's own conservatism as an interpreter of Scripture? Does he simply repristinate Luther's and Calvin's interpretive practices? In comparison with the interpretive practices of the vast majority of biblical scholars today, no matter whether liberal or conservative, are his practices somehow inherently "precritical," or devoid of "historical consciousness," or "premodern"? Intuitively it seems clear that there is some sort of definite divide between Hodge's interpretive practices and those of the preponderance of contemporary scholarly interpreters of the Bible, whether they count themselves theologically evangelical or liberal. But the case of Charles Hodge sorely tests the clarity of such conventional classificatory terms as "modern," "critical," and "historical consciousness."

Hodge developed no theory of interpretation. In his *Systematic Theology* he did offer three very traditional "Rules of Interpretation":

1. "The words of Scripture are to be taken in their plain historical sense."

2. "If the Scriptures be what they claim to be, the word of God, they are the work of one mind, and that mind divine. From this it follows that Scripture cannot contradict Scripture. . . . Hence Scripture must explain Scripture. If a passage admits of different interpretations, that only can be the true one which agrees with what the Bible teaches elsewhere on the same subject. . . . This rule of interpretation is sometimes called the analogy of Scripture, and sometimes the analogy of faith. There is no material difference in the meaning of the two expressions" (*Systematic Theology*, 1:187, hereafter *ST*).

3. "The Scriptures are to be interpreted under the guidance of the Holy Spirit, which guidance is to be humbly and earnestly sought" (*ST*, 1:187-88).

These three rules come as the conclusion of the chapter in the first volume of his *Systematic Theology* devoted to "The Protestant Rule of Faith," doctrine *about* the Bible as word of God. For Hodge the force of these rules flows "from their own intrinsic truth and propriety" (*ST*, 1:187) because their conceptual home is that doctrine of Scripture. Hodge's doctrine of Scripture provides the warrants for his rules governing interpretation of Scripture.

The systematic placement of this chapter is important. The chapter on the doctrine of Scripture concludes the introduction to the system. "Theology proper" only begins in the following section, Part I of the system, on the doctrine of God. Hodge's introduction deals with formal matters: the method and nature of theology (chapters one and two), the relation to theology of reason and philosophy (chapter three) and to mysticism (chapter four), and a contrast between Roman Catholic (chapter five) and Protestant (chapter six) understandings of the "rule of faith," i.e., the word of God, which norms theological construction. These systematic features of Hodge's project are important because they bring out the fact that his doctrine of Scripture, which warrants his rules for interpreting Scripture, is itself ordered to and is in service of answering questions about the *formal* features of properly executed theology.

This paper will examine some of Hodge's actual practice of interpretation to see how these rules shape that practice, testing whether and how far his interpretive practices somehow count as pre-critical or devoid of historical consciousness or pre-modern.

II. "Plain Historical Sense": Pre-critical?

According to Hodge's first rule of interpretation, the words of Scripture "are to be taken in their plain historical sense." This is to interpret Scripture according to its "literal" meaning. It involves what is sometimes characterized as "grammatical-historical" interpretation. It is, Hodge says, "the sense attached to [the words of Scripture] in the age and by the people to whom they were addressed" (*ST,* 1:187).

This rule is warranted by the theological claim that biblical texts are infallible because the divine inspiration of their human authors is both plenary and verbal. In his *Systematic Theology,* Hodge characteristically wrote of the infallibility of Scripture for Christian faith and practice, not of its inerrancy. Hodge is clear that the claim about Scripture's infallibility follows *from* the claim about the inspiration of its human authors by the Holy Spirit (*ST,* 1:154). The claim of infallibility is not, as it were, an empirical generalization based on the independently tested accuracy of all biblical writings, from which the claim of inspiration is then inferred. Rather, the claim of infallibility is analytically entailed in the claim of inspiration. For its part, the claim of inspiration is grounded in Scripture's own teaching about itself (*ST,* 1:154, 157-163; *Biblical Repertory and Princeton Review* 29 [1857]: 679, hereafter *BRPR*).

The further claims that inspiration is both verbal and plenary are entailed, in turn, by the claim that the texts are infallible regarding all matters of faith and practice. The biblical writers were inspired so as to give an infallible record of divine revelation (*ST,* 1:164). Since "[t]he thoughts are in the words" (*ST,* 1:164), if the record is to be infallibly what the Holy Spirit wants it to be, the Spirit must inspire the writers with the words they write and not merely the with the thoughts they seek to express. This claim has mostly formal force in Hodge's thought. This doctrine of the verbal inspiration of Scripture claims that what is religiously important about a biblical text is what the words say; it does not have any material implications for what the content conveyed by those words will turn out to be.

Moreover, if the record is to be infallible regarding all that pertains to faith and practice, then its inspiration must be plenary rather than partial. This applies only to the "special purpose" for which the biblical writers were employed, i.e., as "teachers, and when acting as the spokesmen of God" (*ST,* 1:165). When they do fill that office, everything they write is equally inspired. The upshot, as Hodge pointed out, is that the doctrine of plenary inspiration has largely negative force. It "is opposed to the doctrine that some parts of Scripture are inspired, and others are not; or that a higher degree of inspiration belongs to some portions than to others; or that inspiration is confined to the moral and religious truths contained in the Bible, to the exclusion of its historical or geographical details" (*BRPR* 29 [1857]: 664).

Hodge considered the inspiration of biblical writers to be an instance of miracle. In contrast to the providential agency of God, which is everywhere at work as God the first cause works God's purposes through creaturely secondary causes, inspiration is a "supernatural influence" in which, as in all miracles, God acts "by immediate efficiency without the intervention of such [secondary] causes" (*ST,* 1:154). Strictly speaking, it is God who is the author of Scripture (*BRPR* 29 [1857]: 663). Hodge was certain that the metaphysical theory he employed here, including the distinction between "first cause" and "secondary causes," and the specific form of theism that brings with it, constitute "general facts or principles which underlie the Bible, which are assumed in all its teachings, and which therefore must be assumed in its interpretation" (*ST,* 1:153). Even with this theory in hand, however, Hodge claims that "we have no knowledge whatever of the mode of the Spirit's operation. We only know its effects" (*BRPR* 29 [1857]: 666).

Hodge saw two effects of the Spirit's inspiration. On one side, it renders the biblical writers infallible "as to all that they teach, whether of doctrine or fact," but *only* as they thus teach. God uses them "as his organs of communication" (*BRPR* 29 [1857]: 663, 666). On the other side, it preserves the biblical writers as free agents.[12] It is a misconception, Hodge wrote, to suppose "that verbal inspiration implies such a dictation as supersedes the free selection of his words on the part of the sacred writer. It is a fundamental principle of scriptural theology, that a man may be infallibly guided in his free acts." "Verbal inspiration does not suppose anything mechanical" (*BRPR* 29 [1857] 677-78). Hence "inspiration did not destroy the conscious self-control of its subjects" (*BRPR* 29 [1857]: 672) and "the individuality of its subject was fully preserved" (*BRPR* 29 [1857]: 673).

It is not necessary, I think, to charge his doctrine of inspiration with material self-contradictions between claims about the biblical authors' fully historical humanity and their divinely inspired infallibility.[13] Consider as an analogy a possible interpretation of one type of logical force

---

12. "Free Agency" is a technical term for Hodge, explained in his article "Free Agency," *BRPR* 29 (1857): 101-35.

13. For a different view see Jack B. Rogers and Donald K. McKim, *The Authority and Interpretation of the Bible* (San Francisco: Harper & Row, 1979), pp. 274-98.

the Chalcedonian formula has concerning the two "natures" of Christ. It is arguable that, among other uses, the formula has a formal force. In this respect it does not offer any theory as to how the "natures" are to be understood or how the relation between them is to be conceived. Rather, it provides a set of meta-linguistic rules about how best to talk about who Jesus Christ is, without specifying materially any particular conceptual scheme to use in doing so. The formula itself is cast in fifth-century metaphysical concepts, but they do not affect its content as a set of formal rules. The formula functions at least to "fence the mystery," ruling out misleading ways of talking about it. There is no reason to suggest that Hodge himself held any such view of the Chalcedonian formula. The only point here is to suggest an analogy with this interpretation of Chalcedon: Hodge's doctrine of inspiration may be seen to provide purely formal meta-linguistic rules for how to talk about the Bible as at once an infallible guide for Christian faith and practice and as the work of historically conditioned free agents. It yields two assumptions governing the interpretation of the Bible as Christian Scripture: (a) Always assume that its writers were finite and historically conditioned free human agents whose historicity requires, in turn, historical methods of biblical interpretation; and (b) always assume that correctly interpreted Scripture has the logical force of teaching, a teaching that is infallible in regard to belief and practice. His doctrine of scriptural inspiration fences one of what Hodge himself calls mysteries, "*musteria,* things concealed, unknown and unknowable, except as revealed to the holy Apostles and Prophets by the Spirit" (*ST,* 1:181) — in this case, a mystery concerning Scripture itself.

One might judge that Hodge's doctrine of inspiration is theologically unjustified, is not in fact "taught" by Scripture, is unnecessarily baroque in its complexity, or is an invitation to over-belief. But, I shall argue, it is difficult to see any way in which the doctrine necessarily commits Hodge to "pre-critical" practices of biblical interpretation.

Before we turn to the implications for biblical interpretation of the doctrine of inspiration, I want to bring out an important assumption implicit in Hodge's understanding the doctrine to imply rules governing interpretation of inspired Scripture. The obvious assumption is that precisely *as inspired* Scripture nonetheless *requires* interpretation — that is, the inspired words do not immediately and completely determine their construal. To the contrary, precisely as verbally inspired, the biblical texts' words underdetermine their meaning.[14] By contrast, consider the famous

---

14. I am indebted to Merold Westphal for pointing out the importance of this point

question, "Just which part of 'No!' do you not understand?" In this context, the words of the sentence fully determine the meaning of the sentence; no interpretation of it is required. But, for all of their being inspired, the words of Scripture apparently do *not* fully determine their meaning. The meaning of biblical texts is underdetermined by precisely their inspired words. That is why the doctrine of inspiration assumes that biblical texts require interpretation according to rules warranted by the doctrine of inspiration.

If they require interpretation, then it must be the case that the inspired words admit of more than one plausibly possible construal, one of which must be selected as the correct construal. And if one construal is to be selected in favor of other admittedly possible meanings, arguments must be given in defense of the chosen construal. The crucial point is this: if what is privileged is the "plain historical sense" of Scripture, then the arguments that are especially relevant are those made by historians, rather than, say, metaphysicians. It is historians' arguments that discipline biblical interpretation as properly historically-*critical* interpretation. If Hodge is to be charged with "pre-critical" interpretive practices, it must be because he fails or refuses to discipline his interpretive practices with the full array of appropriate historians' arguments, subject to properly historical criteria.

Turn now to the implications of the doctrine of the plenary verbal inspiration for the interpretation of Scripture. It implies one explicit and one implicit rule for interpretation of the Bible as the word of God. The explicit rule is: Base your interpretation on the plain meaning of the words of the text. The implicit rule is: Always practice interpretation with the *a priori* knowledge that the content conveyed by the plain meaning of the words of the text is coherent and true, and comes from God. Does this second, implicit rule so constrain interpretation practiced according to the explicit rule that the interpretation will inevitably be "pre-critical" in character?

I suggest that, in the case of Hodge's actual practice, the answer is perhaps yes, but in principle, probably not. Chronologically, of course, Hodge was not "pre-critical." Development of the complex research paradigm in biblical scholarship that has come to be called "historical-critical" was already well begun by his day. He lived in the era of genuinely "critical" bibli-

---

about inspired texts' lack of determination of readings of their meaning. See Westphal, "Post-Kantian Reflections on the Importance of Hermeneutics," in *Disciplining Hermeneutics,* ed. Roger Lundin (Grand Rapids: Eerdmans, 1997), pp. 57-69.

cal scholarship and was conversant with the work of many of its major practitioners. However, his own interpretive practices were so conservative as to raise the question of whether or not he was "pre-critical" not chronologically, but in principle. Do the principles governing his interpretive practices simply exclude key principles of properly "critical" interpretation and, at least *de facto,* commit him to the "pre-critical" paradigm of biblical study?

An answer must be governed by at least four dimensions of properly "critical" biblical scholarship.

1. Hodge, of course, found so-called "lower criticism" to be positively mandated by his first explicit rule for interpretation. Hodge was well aware that biblical texts have been subject to a history of scribal error.[15] Where it seemed to him important in the course of a commentary, he noted textual variants and gave reasons for choosing one. After all, if the words are inspired by God, one has a religious duty to work with the best critical edition of the text one can secure. And the relevant arguments in support of critical decisions are historians' arguments. The fact that one is dealing with the verbally inspired word of God in no way qualifies that.

Hodge's characteristically brief, perfunctory, and entirely conventional treatment of text-critical issues tends to support Warfield's dim view of Hodge's critical acumen. However, because of their relative infrequency, Hodge's uncertain treatment of critical issues did not tend to cause him to lose the woods of the text for the trees of grammatical and lexical details.[16]

2. Hodge's doctrine of inspiration also required that he interpret texts within horizons set by the cultural settings, personalities, and literary styles of the biblical authors. He was well aware that it is sentences, not individual words, that mean. That is why interpretation must be disciplined by a "*grammatical*-historical" method. The meaning of the inspired words is a function of their grammar in a broad sense of the term, i.e., their ruled use. And the grammar must be understood historically. It consists

---

15. For example, he notes that in Romans 3:22 ("the righteousness of God which is by faith of Jesus Christ unto all and upon all them who believe," in the King James Version) the words "*to all* are omitted in the manuscripts A, C, 20, 31, 47, 66, 67 in the Coptic and Ethiopic versions and by several of the Fathers. . . . [B]ut most modern critical editions retain them, both on external and internal evidence" (*Commentary on the Epistle to the Romans,* p. 85).

16. For a different view see Richard Lints, "Two Theologies or One? Warfield and Vos on the Nature of Theology," *Westminster Theological Journal* 54 (1992): 239, n. 17; and Lints, *The Fabric of Theology* (Grand Rapids: Eerdmans, 1993), p. 183, n. 93.

of the rules, formal and informal, governing use of words in the historical time and culture of those to whom the text was first addressed.

Moreover, Hodge's doctrine of inspiration held that the inspired writers remained children of their time, as culturally conditioned as anyone else. "The indications are abundant and conclusive," Hodge wrote, "that the sacred writers shared in all the current opinions of the generation to which they belonged . . ." (*BRPR* 29 [1857]: 669). "As to all matters of science, philosophy, and history, they stood on the same level with their contemporaries. . . . Their inspiration no more made them astronomers than it made them agriculturalists" (*ST,* 1:165). "Inspiration did not cure their ignorance" (*BRPR* 29 [1857]: 668). Biblical writers may have believed errors, but they did not teach them. But inspired writers "differed as to insight into the truths which they taught" (*ST* 1:165; *BRPR* 29 [1857]: 670). Hence, if one is to interpret biblical texts correctly, one needs to discipline interpretation with historical knowledge of the culture of which the biblical authors were part and by which they were shaped.

Hodge practiced this extensively.[17] He was flexible in this type of interpretive practice. He could argue against the apparent force of historical usage.[18] He could also argue for interpretation that went against the grammar of a passage.[19] It must be said, however, that he engaged in this dimension of properly "critical" interpretation in a very restricted way. With the exception of a very few references to ways in which certain rabbis used key terms, Hodge — guided, no doubt, by the second rule of interpretation, the "analogy of Scripture" — confined himself to study of word usage within the canon. He betrayed no awareness of how knowledge of changes over time in ancient cultures and language might nuance interpretation of ancient texts.

Hodge's doctrine of inspiration also claims that the inspired writers' peculiar personalities and literary styles are preserved. Verbally inspired, they used "the language of common life . . . founded on apparent, and not on scientific truth" (*ST,* 1:170), and they "were free to use such language, and to narrate such circumstances as suited their own taste or purposes" (*BRPR* 29 [1857]: 678). If one is to interpret correctly, interpretation must be informed by literary-critical criteria attentive to the authors' idiosyn-

17. See, for example, his careful explanation of why the word "reckoned" in Romans 4:3 (". . . Abraham believed God, and it was reckoned to him as righteousness") must be interpreted as "imputed," a terminological point of central importance to Hodge's theology.

18. For example, at Romans 3:25, regarding translation of *hilastērion* ("mercy-seat" or "propitiation"?).

19. For example, at Romans 5:18a.

crasies of personal style. Hodge illustrated this by pointing to the differences among the four Evangelists.[20]

3. Properly "critical" biblical interpretation also must take into account the socio-culturally conditioned character of the interpreter. In particular, that means taking into account the belief system in which the interpreter cannot help living.

Like most of us, Hodge was largely oblivious to his conditioning by cultural context.[21] He took it to be "self-evident" that children should be submissive to their parents and servants to their masters, that a mixture of races was injurious to the integrity of blacks and whites alike, and that principles of order and subordination pervade the universe. It may be, as Bruce Kuklick's paper in this volume points out,[22] that Hodge's philosophical commitment to Scottish Realism, especially as interpreted by William Hamilton, underwrote Hodge's appeal to common sense and self-evidence. In any case, such uncritical appeals deeply shaped Hodge's biblical interpretation of such passages as Ephesians 6:5-9. As we shall see, it had terrible consequences for his theological stand on the slavery question.

On the other hand, for a nineteenth-century interpreter, taking the interpreter's own socio-cultural conditioning into account critically in the course of biblical interpretation meant especially taking into account a new and possibly religiously threatening scientific worldview. This Hodge did famously. Far from being threatened, in his biblical interpretation Hodge was actively engaged in showing the compatibility of scientific truths and biblically revealed truths. Hodge pointed out that "Science has in many things taught the Church how to understand the Scriptures." Scientific facts have come into conflict with our interpretations of the Bible, but never with its record of revealed facts. Hodge cited changes in biblical interpretation following the shift from the "Ptolemaic system of the universe" to the "Copernican system," and possible changes in light of geology from the view that the earth "has existed only a few thousand years" to the view that it "has existed for myriads of ages" (*ST* 1:171). It has been pointed out[23] that the same view kept Hodge theologically non-defensive about theories of evolution and optimistic about their eventual harmoni-

20. See *BRPR* 29 (1857): 678.
21. Professor Daniel Migliore quite rightly pointed this out in his response to this essay.
22. Kuklick, "The Place of Charles Hodge in the History of Ideas in America," in this volume.
23. See Mark A. Noll and David N. Livingstone, "Introduction" to Charles Hodge, *What Is Darwinism? and Other Writings on Science and Religion*, ed. Noll and Livingstone (Grand Rapids: Baker, 1994).

zation with revealed facts, despite his opposition to Charles Darwin's version of evolutionary theory. Hodge's attentiveness to the theological import of truth from any quarter helps makes plausible the claim that his methods of biblical interpretation were not in principle incompatible with properly historical-critical methods.

4. Thus far Hodge's way of interpreting seem to be consonant in principle with properly "critical" interpretation of the Bible, although in actual practice he did so within such narrow boundaries that the results were nearly indistinguishable from "pre-critical" interpretation. There is, however, one further dimension of properly critical interpretation of the Bible today that seems to be wholly missing in Hodge. This is critical historical analysis of the editorial process through which the received biblical texts have gone. A naive concept of authorship (one text, one identifiable author) has given way to more nuanced notions of implied authors, editors, and redactors. The "historical" in "historical critical" has largely to do with interpretation critically disciplined by the results of historians' efforts to reconstruct the history of the development of the texts, mostly on the basis of internal evidence. In his commentaries Hodge never brought up problems raised by such historical study. However, it would perhaps be ahistorical on our part to expect more of him. Although more or less tentative hypotheses about such historical development of biblical texts had been proposed at least since the work of J. S. Semler a quarter-century before Hodge's birth, Julius Wellhausen's field-transforming documentary hypothesis concerning the Hexateuch was not published until 1899 *(Die Composition des Hexeteuchs und der historischem Buecher des Alten Testaments)* and his defense of the postulation of "Q" as a literary source for the Synoptic Gospels not until 1915.

Anticipations of full-fledged documentary hypotheses regarding the development of the canonical versions of many biblical books were known in Hodge's day and, so far as I can discover, Hodge never even polemicized against such historical reconstruction of the development of biblical texts. For example, discussing D. F. Strauss's *The Life of Jesus* in "The Latest Form of Infidelity,"[24] Hodge focused entirely on Strauss's Hegelian philosophical theology and not at all on the method or content of Strauss's New Testament criticism. He saw Strauss as the most important example of a movement in German theology that he believed to be especially misguided. It had already "set its cloven foot in America" (p. 121).

---

24. Charles Hodge, *Essays and Reviews: Selected from the Princeton Review* (New York: Robert Carter & Bros., 1857), pp. 87-129 (hereafter cited as *E&R*).

However, Hodge had no fear of its prevailing "either here or in England, as it does in Germany. . . . A sanity of intellect, an incapacity to see wonders in nonsense, is the leading trait of the English mind," Hodge opined. "The Germans can believe anything. Animal magnetism is, for them, one of the exact sciences" (p. 125).

At this juncture of his thinking, it appears that the metaphysical warrants for Hodge's doctrine of inspiration trump the historically interpreted biblical warrants. Judging from Hodge's polemic against it, what was misguided about the movement for which Strauss is the emblematic figure was its pantheistic doctrine of God and its misleading tendency to appear to accept Christian doctrine but only as a rhetoric whose true meaning is provided by Hegelian ontology (p. 115). At no point did Hodge take on Strauss's historical-critical, as opposed to philosophical, claims and method. It is as though Hodge did not see in them any distinctive challenge to his own interpretive practices. Nor were Strauss's arguments widely accepted at the time among Hodge's peers in biblical scholarship. It would be unjust to fault Hodge for not being so in advance of the relatively ahistorical conventions of his day that he could have seen the implications of the hypothesis of biblical texts' own historical developments for the practices of properly "critical" scholarship. I shall develop the theme of Hodge's ahistorical mindset and its consequences in the next section.

We can more fruitfully ask whether there is anything about Hodge's first rule for interpreting Scripture, or about the doctrine of inspiration behind it, that would in principle conflict with adopting this dimension of properly historical-critical analysis. I think there is none. In order correctly to construe the "plain historical sense" of the words of Scripture, all relevant *historical* arguments must be employed. That necessarily includes examination of the force of arguments about the historical development of biblical texts and the implications of that development for interpretation of those texts. The fact that Hodge did not subject the texts to such examination meant that his own practice of biblical interpretation was often *de facto* "precritical." But there seems to be no reason in principle why he could not have disciplined his construals of the "plain historical sense" of the words of Scripture in this historical way.

If that conclusion is correct, we may draw an important distinction between what is systematically warranted by Hodge's doctrine of Scripture on one hand and the consequences of his ahistorical mindset on the other. His doctrine of the plenary and inerrant inspiration of Scripture in principle warrants every dimension of historical-critical interpretation of the Bible. The doctrine of plenary inspiration may have suffered a kind of progressive sclerosis in his successors from A. A. Hodge through B. B. Warfield to J. Gresham Machen, but in Charles Hodge's hands it seemed flexible enough to be capable *in principle* of endlessly accommodating all new scientific and historical truth. I have suggested that this flexibility is rooted in the doctrine's largely formal status in Hodge's theological system. On the other hand, a consequence of Hodge's ahistorical mindset is that many possible ways of interpreting Scripture and of understanding Scripture's relation to Christian theology could never even appear within his mental horizon. This ahistorical orientation was a perfectly normal effect of Hodge's cultural conditioning by his own historical era. The point I wish to urge is that Hodge's ahistorical sensibility is not materially implied by his doctrine of the inspiration of Scripture. To the contrary, the various dimensions of properly historical-critical interpretation of the Bible that *are* warranted by his doctrine of inspiration could be expected to nurture a historical sensibility in place of an ahistorical mindset.

There are two major objections to this judgment, one related to Hodge's view of biblical authorship and the other related to his stand on the slavery question.

Hodge took for granted the naive view that there was one author for each biblical book and that that author is usually identifiable. Hodge assumed that David wrote the Psalms, Moses the Pentateuch, Paul all the letters attributed to him, and so on. Presumably he did so because those texts are attributed to those persons by certain biblical texts themselves. Historical examination of the process of textual editing rules out this assumption. Does this not conflict with Hodge's doctrine of inspiration?

Probably not. It is not essential to Hodge's doctrine of inspiration that the inspired writers be personally identifiable. Nothing in his doctrine of inspiration would need to be changed if it could be shown on historical grounds that the final inspired editor or writer of any given text is not personally identifiable. Personal identifiability of biblical writers is materially important only to Hodge's quite traditional explanation of the canon of the New Testament. There the personal identifiability of authors provides the note by which to select those and only those books that belong to the canon — namely, books written by identifiable Apostles (*ST* 1:153). (The note by which to identify the canon of the Old Testament was simply its acceptance as Scripture by Jews of Jesus' day.) It is plausible, however, to surmise that if historians' arguments made a convincing case that the historical Apostles did not author all the books attributed to them, Hodge could consistently accommodate himself to that finding.

He was perfectly capable of permitting traditional interpretations of other texts to be radically accommodated to convincing scientific arguments regarding geology and astronomy. His doctrine of inspiration would create no difficulties in cases where ascription of a text to a particular named author is demonstrably not itself part of the ancient and inspired text. Where ascription (or apparent self-ascription) of a text to a particular named author is part of an inspired text, such as Colossians, Hodge might be persuaded by historical arguments that it would be an egregious anachronism to consider such ascription as immoral[25] and therefore inconsistent with the author's inspiration. Such accommodation would involve a change in Hodge's account of the canon but not in his doctrine of inspiration or in his rules for biblical interpretation.

The second objection to the thesis of this section is based in Hodge's stand on the slavery question. At the end of Hodge's long, tortuous, and dismaying theological debate about the correct Christian assessment of slavery, he ended up in his last essay on the subject in 1872 repeating the position he had adopted in 1836: "The doctrine that slave-holding is in itself a crime is anti-scriptural, and subversive of the authority of the word of God" (*BRPR* 44 [1872]: 16). As Allen Guelzo shows in his essay in this volume,[26] there were a number of personal and cultural factors that helped shape Hodge's view. There were also theological factors shaping his view. One was a long-standing maxim in the Reformed tradition about the relation between Scripture and moral theology: what Scripture does not explicitly reject cannot be said to be a sin. Hence, since Scripture nowhere explicitly rejects slavery as against God's will, even though it nowhere enjoins it, slavery could not be said absolutely and in the abstract to be sinful. Hodge argued just that point in his commentary on Ephesians,[27] at 6:5-9, and in summary in his "analysis" of verses 1-9. Is it also the case that Hodge's doctrine of the inspiration and infallibility of Scripture closes off the possibility of other interpretations of Scripture on slavery and so inevitably leads to the same conclusion about slavery?[28] I will argue in the next section that Hodge's profoundly ahistorical sensibility obscured the historicity of the Bible, the historicity of doctrine, and the historicity of the relation between the two, thus closing off possible avenues for interpreting Scripture in relation to slavery and other topics.

25. See Alberto Manguel, *A History of Reading* (New York: Viking, 1996).

26. See Allen C. Guelzo, "Charles Hodge's Antislavery Moment," in this volume.

27. Charles Hodge, *Commentary on the Epistle to the Ephesians,* ed. Alister McGrath and J. I. Packer (Wheaton: Crossway Books), 1994.

28. Daniel Migliore suggested this in his response to this paper.

However, my point here is that neither Hodge's ahistorical sensibility nor its closing off of possible avenues for biblical interpretation is materially implied in the extraordinarily flexible way in which Hodge in principle understood and employed his doctrine of biblical inspiration, plenary and infallible.

Overall, Hodge's biblical interpretation seems to be just one more exercise in an entirely familiar biblical concept theology.[29] Whatever the inadequacies of biblical concept theology as a method, it continues to be practiced by scholars who do not subscribe to Hodge's doctrine of inspiration and whose credentials as fully "critical" scholars are impeccable. The inadequacies of Hodge's practice of this sort of interpretation seem to be the consequence of the scholarly limitations Warfield attributed to Hodge. Conservative as they are, they do not justify classifying Hodge's interpretive practices as *inherently* "pre-critical." That is, they do not seem to be a necessary consequence of either the rule of interpretation he was following nor the doctrine of the verbal plenary inspiration of the Scriptures that warrants the rule. There seems to be no reason rooted in the theology of Scripture warranting his first rule of interpretation why he could not in principle have followed the rule by practicing a more fully "critical" interpretation of Scripture.

III. One Divine Author:
Inadequate "Historical Consciousness"?

According to Hodge's second rule, Scripture must be used to explain Scripture according to "the analogy of Scripture" because, since "it is the work of one mind, and that mind divine," Scripture cannot contradict itself. This rule has two major implications for the way Scripture is construed. First, Scripture is to be construed as always and everywhere having the logical force of *teaching*. So the rule is, in interpreting, always focus on what a passage of Scripture may be said to be teaching, even when its manifest force is something else, such as praying to or glorifying or railing against God. The second implication, as Hodge put it in his essay on "Inspiration," is that Scripture is to be construed as being a systematic unity, the unity of "one grand concatenated system of truth" (*BRPR* 29 [1857]: 679). In the first volume of his *Systematic Theology* Hodge was careful to

---

29. See David H. Kelsey, *The Uses of Scripture in Recent Theology* (Philadelphia: Fortress, 1975), pp. 24-32.

qualify this theme. The "Scriptures do not contain a system of theology as a whole"; nonetheless, the truths they do contain in fact constitute a system (*ST,* 1:3). Hodge can call it an "organic unity" (*ST,* 1:166). So the rule becomes, of several possible construals of any text, always reject interpretations that can be shown to contradict other passages and always select as correct the interpretation that maximizes Scripture's systematic unity as a whole. In short, Hodge interpreted Scripture not only within the horizons of textual criticism, the cultural and historical context of the authors and original readers, and the authors' personal and literary styles; he also interpreted within the horizon of Scripture construed as a certain type of unified whole that teaches truths.

In doing this did Hodge show himself deficient in "historical consciousness"? I believe he did. "Historical consciousness" might be characterized as a sensibility that is acutely attentive to and perceptive about the contingency and socio-culturally conditioned character of all human artifacts, including truth-claiming. It is often vaguely named as the mindset that necessarily goes with a truly "critical" scholarly method in Scripture studies. The question is whether Hodge's picture of Scripture as teaching a "concatenated system of truth" thought by "one mind, and that mind divine" is incompatible with the way a genuinely historical consciousness could perceive the array of canonical texts. I suggest that there is such an incompatibility, and that Hodge's general take on the Bible exhibits a sensibility largely devoid of historical consciousness. (Whether or not that is a bad thing is a subject for another time.) This generally ahistorical sensibility is exhibited in several ways.

To begin, Hodge had a remarkably ahistorical understanding of the history of doctrine. Rogers and McKim rightly remark that "Hodge was not an historian of doctrine. He often erroneously asserted that the whole church held to a position that was actually peculiar to Protestant Scholasticism."[30] In particular, Hodge assumed that the theological positions defended by the Westminster divines and Francis Turretin were identical with what the whole church believed at all times and in all places.

Second, Hodge's relative lack of historical consciousness surfaced in the categories he used to describe the primary datum of biblical interpretation, the Bible. We do not need to be committed to historicism, either new or old, to acknowledge the force of the thesis that we only have data under some sort of description. There are no "pure" or "brute" data. Historical consciousness tends to consider biblical texts under descriptions

30. Rogers and McKim, *Authority and Interpretation,* p. 282.

that are characteristically historical, stressing the texts' historical contingencies. Hodge, by contrast, considers the texts as a single whole described in categories provided either by Christian dogma or by a metaphysical theism. The unity of the truths taught by the Bible as a whole is ahistorically identified with the unity of classical orthodox dogma. Thus, in his *Commentary on the Epistle to the Romans* at 1:3-4, Hodge simply assumed that Paul's uses of the phrase "Son of God" were identical with the uses of that phrase in Nicene trinitarianism. Hodge seems to have had no sense for the historical development of doctrine after the "Apostolic period."

The other set of categories Hodge used to describe the Bible as a whole were drawn from his metaphysical theism. Thus he claimed that there are "certain general facts or principles which underlie the Bible" and must be assumed in its interpretation. These boil down to a type of personalistic theism: God "is a Spirit, — a self-conscious, intelligent, voluntary agent, possessing all the attributes of our spirits without limitation, and to an infinite degree," who is creator, everywhere present and active, in ways both mediated through created secondary causes and immediate without secondary causes, who makes the Bible contain revelation (*ST,* 1:153-54).

There is another feature of Hodge's general approach to Scripture that betrays his ahistorical sensibility. Richard Lints's description of B. B. Warfield may be applied equally well to Hodge: "The *historicity* of the Scriptures was so significant for [him] that he may well have been unable to see the *historical flow* of the text."[31] It is no accident that Hodge wrote no commentaries on the Gospels. When he did attend to the Gospels he construed their narratives as strings of beads of historical facts and, unlike Calvin, for example, ignored the implications of the history-likeness of their narrative.[32]

It was, I suggest, this ahistorical sensibility regarding Scripture, not Hodge's formal and endlessly flexible doctrine of inspiration, that may have closed off possible alternative ways of interpreting Scripture. Thus, for example, an ahistorical picture of biblical texts (according to which they themselves underwent no historical process before reaching their canonical form), combined with an ahistorical picture of doctrine (espe-

31. Lints, "Two Theologies or One?" p. 250.

32. As Daniel Migliore pointed out in his response to this essay, it is fascinating to speculate what difference it might have made to Hodge's way of interpreting Scripture, and indeed to his entire theological project, if he had written commentaries on the Gospels in addition to the ones he wrote on Paul's Epistles, and if his discussion of the atonement had rested on exegesis of the Passion and resurrection narratives.

cially classical Reformed theology, according to which it undergoes no historical development), combined with an ahistorical picture of the relationship between Scripture and doctrine, taken together close off the possibility of challenging the long-standing maxim that what Scripture does not proscribe, such as the institution of slavery, cannot be called a sin. Further, they close off the possibility that Scripture's failure explicitly to condemn the institution of slavery might need to be interpreted for Christians in the light, say, of Galatians 3:28, "There is no longer . . . slave nor free . . . ; for all of you are one in Christ Jesus."

Finally, and perhaps most decisively for Hodge's systematic theology, the specific *way* in which he construed the unity of the biblical canon exhibited Hodge's relative lack of historical consciousness. The unity within whose horizon every text is to be interpreted is the systematic unity of a *plan* exhibited by a temporally extended sequence of events recorded in Scripture. The plan is the "plan of redemption." According to Hodge, the central question revelation answers is who is saved, and how? (cf. *ST,* 1:23-25). The plan of redemption provides the answer to that question and must norm all theological answers to all other questions.

The biblical *locus classicus* that teaches us that the very specific *structure* of this plan is the fifth chapter of Romans. Consequently, the interpretive adequacy of any exegesis of any other text and the theological adequacy of any theological proposal both turn on how well they comport with a correct exegesis of Romans 5. Implicitly, at least, Romans 5 functions for Hodge as a canon within the canon (not that Hodge would be happy with this characterization). That is, proper interpretation of Romans 5 provides the litmus test by which the theological adequacy of any New Testament exegesis and any interpretation of Christian belief must be tested. Other themes are probably more systematically basic for Hodge than Romans 5's statement of the basic structure of the plan of salvation, in particular the grounding of redemption in God's sovereign and eternal purpose (cf. Ephesians 1). But New Testament witness to God's eternal sovereign purpose in history, however grand, is vague. Romans 5, on the other hand, provides an outline of a detailed theology of history. It outlines the very *structure* of the plan grounded in God's eternal purpose. To be sure, Hodge's interpretation of Scripture is also controlled by the Westminster Confession and Catechisms. In Hodge's view, the Westminster standards provide the clearest and most accurate statement of the system of doctrine implicit in the Bible, and he was proud that, during his editorship of the *Princeton Review,* no article had ever appeared in the journal that opposed the system of doctrine contained in the Westminster standards (*BRPR* 43 [1871]: 9).[33] But what the Westminster divines got right, in Hodge's view, along with the entire Reformed tradition from John Calvin through Francis Turretin to Hodge himself, was the proper interpretation of the structure of the plan of salvation in Romans 5. It is that plan that gives unity to God's revelatory actions and to Scripture's report of them. Hence I suggest that, for Hodge, to practice biblical interpretation within the horizon of the unity of the canon meant to practice it in ways ruled by Hodge's very particular interpretation of Romans 5.

Several considerations support this judgment. We begin with Hodge's idea of revelation[34] and its relation to inspired Scripture. He distinguished between them emphatically. The aim of revelation is "the communication of knowledge," and its effect is to "render its recipient wiser." The aim of inspiration is "to secure infallibility in teaching," and its effect is "to preserve [the recipient] from error in teaching" (*ST,* 1:155). "Many have received supernatural revelations, who were not inspired to communicate them. . . . on the other hand many inspired men were not the subjects of any special revelations" (*BRPR* 29 [1857]: 665).

Incidentally, all of the Bible may be equally alive with the breath of God, but the revelations it records are not all equally important. As Hodge observed in his often quoted article on "Inspiration": even though "in the attribute of infallibility the sacred writers were on a par," nonetheless "[t]here may be a great difference in the importance and extent of the revelations imparted to different" writers (*BRPR* 29 [1857]: 668). The biblical texts are all equally inspired, but the revelations they record may vary in importance and extent. "Some members of the body are more important than others; and some books of the Bible could be far better spared than others. There may be as great a difference between St. John's Gospel and the Book of Chronicles as between a man's brain and the hair of his head; nevertheless the life of the body is as truly in the hair as in the brain" (*ST,* 1:164) and inspiration is as truly in the Book of Chronicles as in the Gospel of John. Inspired Scripture is always *about* revelation, but not all revelations are equally important. Hence not all books of the Bible are equally important. This clearly opens the door to privileging Romans as the most important book, and within it, Romans 5 as the most important chapter in the book.

---

33. I am indebted to Daniel Migliore for this citation.

34. In contrast to twentieth-century theology, it is striking that nowhere in the *Systematic Theology* is there a chapter, let alone an entire "Part," devoted to a material doctrine of revelation. The topic is confined to the introduction.

Hodge located revelation in history, and inspiration in the Bible. Both, he said, developed over time:

> The Bible is as obviously an evolution of the plan of redemption as an object of faith, as the history of our race is an evolution of the plan as a matter of experience. The two run parallel. . . . If there are unity and design in history, there are unity and design in the Bible. If the one is the work, the other is the word of God. (*BRPR* 29 [1857]: 663-664)

The plan is the plan of the redemption that God enacts in history and that unifies the inspired Scripture that records and teaches it.

This "plan of redemption" can be specified in more detail. It is defined by the typological pattern in which Adam and Christ are related as type and antitype according to Romans 5. The plan of salvation periodizes all of human history into two eras: one governed by God's covenant of works with Adam, in which humankind's relation to God is determined by Adam's "work"; and the other by a covenant of grace with Christ, in which elect humankind's relationship to God is determined by Christ's gracious sacrifice, appropriated in faith.

Thus are we led next to Hodge's interpretation of Romans 5, especially verses 12-21, in his *Commentary on the Epistle to the Romans*. The importance of Romans 5 to Hodge is signaled by the fact that his commentary devotes more space to it than to any other chapter of Romans. The crucial exegetical issue for Hodge is to understand correctly how we are related to Adam so that sin comes to us and death spreads to all (cf. Romans 5:12: "Therefore, just as sin came into the world through one man, and death came through sin, and so death spread to all because all have sinned . . ."). Hodge insisted that because Paul set up a typological relation between Adam and Christ, any adequate interpretation must be governed by the logic of the typology. In particular that means that "Adam was the cause of sin in a sense analogous to that in which Christ is the cause of righteousness" (p. 138).

Through a long, very complex, and extraordinarily clear exegetical argument whose "evidence is cumulative" (p. 171), Hodge contended that the typological relation between Christ and Adam requires that our relation to Adam be understood not as a relation of imitation, nor as a natural or organic relation, but as a "judicial" relation.[35] Adam's sin and its

---

35. Hodge repeated this three-fold menu of possible interpretations of Romans 5:12 several times in the course of his commentary on Romans (see, for example, pp. 138, 142-49, 162).

penalty, death, are imputed to us by God. We are "in Adam" in exactly the same sense that we are "in Christ" — namely, by God's judicial act. Just as our justification is a judicial act by God in which Christ's righteousness is imputed to us, as is warranted by the conventions established through the covenant of grace, so the sin of Adam is imputed to us by a judicial act of God, as is warranted by the conventions established through the covenant of works (cf. pp. 146-7 on 5:12b in relation to 5:13-14, "because all sinned"). Furthermore, the "sin" that is imputed to us, and its attendant penalty, is imputed to us as is grace, before we do anything. Hodge was prepared to entertain the possibility that there have been human beings who never actually sinned personally, such as those who die in infancy, to whom nonetheless the sin of Adam is imputed in the covenant of works (cf. *ST*, 1:26-27, 156). "God deals with men not merely as individuals but as communities, on the principle of imputation" (p. 147). That explains both how sin came into the world and how death spread. Correspondingly, the "death" that comes is "not a consequence of the original constitution of man" (p. 139), but must be interpreted judicially as all types of "penal evil" (pp. 150-51, 154).

For Hodge it was crucial that "in Adam" be interpreted in strict parallel with "in Christ," because the typological relation between them simply *is* the structure that unifies the plan of redemption that God works out in history. It was Hodge's view that the typological relation between the story of Adam and the story of Christ actually is the structure of human history that reveals God's purposes in history and the meaning of history and unifies the canon into a "grand concatenated system of truth." The typological relation is the precise structure of the temporally extended sequence of events that exhibit God's plan of redemption.

The central importance to Hodge of his "judicial interpretation" of the Adam/Christ typology in Romans 5 was reflected in the way it almost obsessively drove his choices of polemical subjects. We have been reviewing evidence that Romans 5 functioned as a canon within the canon for Hodge, and turn now for further evidence to some of his polemical targets: an exegete, a theologian, and two scientists.

Hodge's critique of Moses Stuart's *Commentary on the Epistle to the Romans* focused on the inadequacies of Stuart's interpretation of Romans 5:12-19. Hodge was lavish in his praise of Stuart's technical acumen: "We do him unfeigned homage as the great American reformer of biblical study, as the introducer of a new [truly "critical"?] era" (*Essays and Reviews* [hereafter *E&R*], p. 50). Alas, the problem was that "[t]he work is *too* theological" (*E&R*, p. 50; my emphasis). Stuart was so theologically muddled that he himself implicitly taught imputation (*E&R*, p. 71) in Romans 12–19, even though he denied that the juridical categories of "imputation" and "penal punishment" were appropriate interpretive tools and, in Hodge's view, did not understand them properly anyway (*E&R*, pp. 83-84).

Hodge's side of acerbic exchanges with theologian Edward A. Park turned on the same issue. Park had published a well-intentioned irenic theory that would have "value as a general solvent of all allowable creeds" (Hodge!), overcoming the bitter conflicts between New England and New Jersey theologians by showing that the formulas of the creeds were poetic expressions of general religious truths. Hodge would have none of it. The energy of his polemic was driven by the threat he perceived to the juridical categories he used in interpreting Romans 5. When the "creeds speak of the imputation of Adam's sin," he asked, "is that to be considered as only an intense form of expressing, 'the definite idea, that we are exposed to evil in consequence of his sin'?" (*BRPR* 23 [1851]: 308). Hodge thought not. In two essays he hammered the point that a "judicial interpretation" of Romans 5 had been the cornerstone of "the piety of the Church in all ages" (*BRPR* 23 [1851]: 319).[36]

As Hodge understood it, it is essential to the Adam/Christ typology in Romans 5 that humankind be one species, that it have one origin, and that that origin, Adam, be as truly a historical individual as was Jesus Christ. The surpassing theological importance of Romans 5 drove Hodge, who was interested in medicine anyway, to pay particular attention to current developments in the scientific study of human origins. One essay (1859) on J. L. Cabell's *The Testimony of Modern Science to the Unity of Mankind*

---

36. Hodge's 1847 critique of Horace Bushnell's *Discourses on Christian Nurture* hangs indirectly on issues about the interpretation of Romans 5. Hodge rejoiced in Bushnell's emphasis (against the dominant individualism, as Hodge saw it, of most New England theology) that God deals with us as communities, not as individuals, and even children are included in the community (for example, *E&R*, pp. 309, 322). There is the community of the unregenerate, parents and children, condemned to the punishment of penal death; and there is the community of those undergoing regeneration in the church, parents and children. However, Bushnell thought the relation between one generation and the next within each community is best understood in natural and organic terms (*E&R*, pp. 325-33) rather than in juridical terms. Bushnell was so theologically muddled that he saw no difference between the two forms of interpretation (*E&R*, p. 325). In Hodge's mind this was a serious theological mistake because it is parallel to Romans 5:12-21 on the relation between Adam and his natural children, on one side, and between Christ and his adopted children, on the other. Bushnell's was the most serious of theological errors in Hodge's eyes, I suggest, because it contradicts the very structure of the plan of salvation that unifies Scripture's "system of truth."

rejoices that "the highest class of scientific men" support the view that "all the arguments which prove the specific unity of men prove also their common parentage" ("The Unity of Mankind," *BRPR* 31 [1859]: 134). The bulk of the essay, however, attacks on conceptual grounds Agassiz's theory of several distinct species of humankind.

A second essay (1862) is a withering review of two works by a Dr. Morton, "Crania Americana," with an "Essay on the Varieties of Human Species," and "Crania Aegyptica." Morton argued for a diversity of human species on the basis of measurements of human skulls from various parts of the world ("Diversity of Species in the Human Race," *BRPR* 34 [1862]: 435-64). Hodge attacked Morton's astonishingly flawed methodology. The fact that Hodge took pains to review these books even though, as Hodge acknowledged, Morton's work was already out of date when it was published suggests the theological importance of the unity of the species for Hodge.

It is true that it was important to Hodge to establish the unity of the human species against those who were defending the institution of chattel slavery on the grounds that Africans belong to another species ("Slavery," *E&R*, pp. 480, 508-11). However, other matters hung on the unity of the species as well. What mattered theologically for Hodge was the compatibility of scientific truth with the revealed truth of the unity of the origin of the species. The typological relation between Adam and Christ, the very structure of the plan of redemption, requires the unity of the origin of the species. Hodge was careful not to overstate his argument. He did not pretend to prove scientifically the existence of the historical Adam. It was not even possible to prove scientifically a single origin of the species. He acknowledged that although the unity of origin implies the unity of the species, "the latter does not necessarily imply the former." However, "if men are of the same species they *may* have a common origin" (*BRPR* 31 [1859]: 108, 135; emphasis mine). It was the unity of the species that Hodge aggressively sought to demonstrate. He sought to show that the truths of science are at least compatible with the revealed truth of the unity of humankind. That at least shows that science does not rule out the unity of humankind's origin. That, in turn, shows that scientific truth is compatible with understanding Adam in Romans 5 as a historical individual. And that is essential to the structure of the plan of redemption reported in Romans 5.

We have reviewed a variety of types of evidence that Romans 5 functioned as a canon within the canon for Hodge, as the litmus test by which the adequacy of theological proposals as well as of exegeses of Scripture must be tested. Romans 5 is privileged in this way because it expressly teaches the structure of God's plan of redemption, which is exhibited in an extended sequence of historical events and ties the contents of inspired Scripture together in a systematic whole.

Even if Romans 5 did function for Hodge as a canon within the canon, what has that got to do with the claim that Hodge was largely devoid of "historical consciousness"? I suggest that Hodge's "judicial interpretation" of the typological relationship between Adam and Christ in Romans 5 makes the case against Hodge's "historical consciousness" even stronger. Earlier I characterized "historical consciousness" as a sensibility that is acutely attentive to and perceptive about the contingency and socio-historically conditioned character of all human artifacts, including truth claims. It experiences history as, among other things, a flow of interactions among agents for whom character and circumstance are interdependent. Confronted with Scripture's history-like stories, a historical consciousness could be expected to perceive a narrative mimetic of history's flow. The narratives' "unity" would be their plot, which is not so much illustrated or exhibited as enacted by the temporally extended series of interactions it narrates.

What Hodge perceived in biblical stories, by contrast, was a chronicle of a series of temporally extended events that exhibit a plan. A narrative plot is not a plan. Discovering a plan in history (even a revelatory plan) that gives Scripture its unity is not the same as finding a narrative plot in history (even a revelatory plot) that gives Scripture its unity. Hodge's interpretation of Romans 5 does not engage the typological relationship between Adam and Christ with the sensibility of "historical consciousness" that sees the typology as a plot line in history that is analogically *enacted* over and over again. Instead, it engages that typological relationship as a static pattern exhibited and *illustrated* by sequences of events. The contrast between the sensibility dubbed "historical consciousness" and Hodge's sensibility is a good example of the contrast Hans Frei draws between Calvin's practice of typological construal of Scripture's history-like narratives and the early Enlightenment's eclipse of narrative.[37] For all of his theological conservatism, on this issue Hodge belonged firmly on the side of the early Enlightenment.

---

37. Hans Frei, *The Eclipse of Biblical Narrative* (New Haven: Yale University Press, 1974), ch. 2-3.

IV. Guidance of the Holy Spirit: "Pre-modern?"

The third rule of interpretation is: "The Scriptures are to be interpreted under the guidance of the Holy Spirit." The implicit hermeneutical principle here is "like knows like." "Congeniality of mind is necessary to the proper apprehension of divine things." Given human sin, "The unrenewed mind is naturally blind to spiritual truth. His heart is in opposition to the things of God" (*ST,* 1:188). The requisite "congeniality of mind" must therefore be given by God the Holy Spirit.

What can this mean as a rule of interpretation? The role of a rule is to discipline a practice over which one can have some control. But one has no control over the Holy Spirit. What the rule means is that biblical interpretation is to be practiced as part of a Christian spiritual discipline. That is something one can control. Hodge briefly summarized the discipline as "humbly and earnestly" seeking the guidance of the Holy Spirit (*ST,* 1:187). Hodge would probably have called it a "devotional discipline." For Hodge, biblical interpretation is properly practiced only when it is practiced within the context of that discipline.

Does this rule classify Hodge's practices of biblical interpretation as "pre-modern?" Speaking descriptively in a sociological way, the answer is surely yes. A hallmark of distinctively modern biblical interpretation has been that Scripture is to be interpreted by the same practices used in interpreting any ancient text. Ancient texts in general do not require interpretation in the context of a Christian spiritual discipline, so Scripture does not either. The ethos of the modern community of biblical interpreters tends to remove practices of biblical interpretation from the context of any spiritual discipline.

However, we may rephrase the question. Does Hodge's third rule necessarily exclude him from the modern community of biblical interpreters, leaving him somehow "pre-modern" in principle? Probably not. Commitment to the third rule does not of itself exclude Hodge from practicing any aspect of properly critical biblical interpretation. What it does do is control two features of Hodge's interpretation: what he tended to focus on as most important and interesting in Scripture, and the larger purpose in whose service he interpreted the Bible.

Reasons for saying this lie in Hodge's view of the task of theology combined with his doctrine of illumination by the Holy Spirit, which warranted his third rule for interpretation. Hodge's view of theology has often been said to be "Baconian," but that is only part of it. The Baconian side was Hodge's claim that theology is a "science" in exactly the same sense of the word as the physical sciences. "In every science," he wrote, "there are two factors: facts and ideas" (*ST,* 1:1). "The Bible is to the theologian what nature is to the man of science. It is his store-house of facts" (*ST,* 1:10). The ideas concern the relations among the facts.[38] "[T]he man of science is assumed to understand the laws by which the facts of experience are determined. . . ." So too theology must offer "an exhibition of the internal relation of those [biblically revealed] facts, one to another, and each to all" (*ST,* 1:1). The principles governing the relations among facts are "derived from the facts, not impressed upon them" (*ST,* 1:13). However, God "does not teach us systematic theology" (*ST,* 1:3); it is a task we must do for ourselves. Scripture contains all the facts of theology, but these facts can and must be shown to be consistent with the facts discovered by science and known by intuition (*ST,* 1:15).

While it contains the revealed facts, the "Bible is not more a system of theology, than nature is a system of chemistry" (*ST* 1:1). However, Hodge added, "we have in the Epistles of the New Testament, *portions* of that system wrought out of our hands. These are our authority and guide" (*ST,* 1:3; emphasis mine). Hence the Epistles are the canon within the canon that guides us in our theological task. And, as we have seen, among the Epistles, Romans, and within Romans chapter 5, is the operative canon within the canon within the canon. In short, as Bacon characterized the scientific method, the proper method of theology is "inductive" (*ST,* 1:9-17), aiming to exhibit systematically the relations among revealed truths.

However, for Hodge the task of systematic theology went beyond this. Theology is done in service of understanding inspired Scripture as the infallible guide for faith and practice. For Hodge, both faith (as belief in revealed truth) and practice (both devotional and moral practice) were rooted in the renewed heart; only the renewed heart was capable of fully grasping the faith or caring to engage in the practices. "The question" orienting theology, he wrote, "is not first and mainly, What is true to the understanding, but what is true to the renewed heart?" (*ST,* 1:16). Hodge's own spirituality was unmistakably one of the horizons within which he practiced interpretation of Scripture. John Oliver Nelson suggested that

---

38. Hodge was not entirely clear about the relations among "facts" (= "truths"), "ideas," "theories," "interpretations" and "hypotheses." He was dismissive of "hypotheses," proposals that can be neither confirmed nor disconfirmed. The Hegelian system is a favorite example. "Theories" get assimilated to "interpretations." They can be revised or disconfirmed (the impact of Copernican astronomy on Biblical interpretation is a favorite example), whereas facts cannot. He did not clarify the difference, if any, between "theories" and "ideas."

Hodge not only had memorized, but had existentially appropriated both the Westminster Shorter and Longer Catechisms,[39] a truly astonishing act of spiritual heroism. Andrew Hoffecker has shown that concern for shaping the religious affections of his students and readers was as central to Hodge's theological project as was his concern for right doctrine.[40] Hodge himself was aware that the two easily come apart, so that "it is no uncommon thing to find men having two theologies, — one of the intellect, and another of the heart" (*ST,* 1:16), and Hoffecker acknowledges that Hodge did not consistently succeed in holding them together himself. Nevertheless, Hodge saw theology as a task to be done in the service of forming the renewed heart in its faith and practice. The task of theology is to teach Christians whose faith and practice flow from renewed hearts.

However, neither correct interpretation of Scripture nor systematic theology alone renews the heart — only the Holy Spirit does that. This work of the Spirit is called "illumination," and Hodge identified it with "religious experience," i.e., the experience of Christian people (*ST,* 1:16). Just as he firmly distinguished revelation from inspiration, so Hodge distinguished illumination from inspiration. "The subjects of inspiration are a few selected persons; the subjects of illumination are all true believers." The aim of inspiration is "to render certain men infallible as teachers" and it has "no sanctifying influence"; the aim of illumination "is to render men holy" (*ST,* 1:154-55; cf *BRPR* 29 [1857]: 665-66). Hodge construed "illumination" as the Spirit renewing the whole person, not merely (as it tended to be for Calvin) illuminating the mind. It is regeneration of fallen human nature. Proper interpretation of Scripture is oriented by and is in the service of illumination by the Holy Spirit.

Hodge stressed both the right and the duty of "private judgment" in biblical interpretation. Indeed, that right "is the great safeguard of civil and religious liberty" (*ST,* 1:185-86). God may deal with us "as communities, not as individuals," but the Spirit illumines us one by one. The sociality of covenant communities is a function of God's judicial decision and is extrinsic to our created natures. Hodge was a metaphysical individualist, and so is the Holy Spirit. Nonetheless, an individual's practices of interpretation must be undertaken in conversation with others, present and past, in the covenant community of grace. "If . . . the Spirit performs

---

39. John Oliver Nelson, "The Rise of the Princeton Theology" (Yale University dissertation, 1935), pp. 315-22.

40. Andrew Hoffecker, *Piety and the Princeton Theologians* (Phillipsburg, N.J.: Presbyterian and Reformed Publishing Co., 1981), ch. 2.

the function of teacher to all the children of God, it follows inevitably that they must agree in all essential matters in their interpretation of the Bible. And from that fact it follows that for an individual Christian to dissent from the faith of the universal Church (*i.e.* the body of true believers), is tantamount to dissenting from the Scriptures themselves" (*ST* 1:184).

Hodge's third rule points, then, not to a method for more adequate interpretation, but to one more horizon by which interpretation is to be oriented. This horizon does not in principle exclude any critical method in interpretation. It need not conflict with a "historical consciousness" on the part of the interpreter. What it does is orient Hodge's own biblical interpretation in two ways. It focuses particular *interests* in the text. In particular, it oriented Hodge's attention to the "plan of redemption" whose goal is spiritual illumination of the heart and attention to other revealed truths chiefly insofar as they are related to that plan. And it *orders* the practice of interpretation to the theological task of exhibiting the systematic connections among those truths in such a way as to be of service to deeper engagement of persons' hearts in Christian faith and practice. Such an orientation could be counted "pre-modern" only if it is inherently "pre-modern" to study Scripture in the service of forming Christian identity.

The Politics of Charles Hodge

RICHARD J. CARWARDINE

I n the last year of his life, Charles Hodge committed to paper the bright memories of his early years as a Philadelphia schoolboy. Vividly he described the infectious enthusiasm of an unconventional teacher, an amiable, Irish-American Swedenborgian who had no appetite for repetitive classroom drill. Instead, Hodge recalled, the teacher would gather half a dozen pupils around a large wall map of England, France, or some other country, point out the nation's main physical features, and then spiritedly describe "the elements of its population; the manners and customs of its people; its productions; its great men; mixing up geography, antiquities, history and statistics. He would linger around the battle-fields, describe the conflicts, taking part vehemently with one side against the other . . . [and] dubbing [his pupils] with the names and ranks of his heroes."[1] Here was only one of the influences that shaped the formidably varied intellectual interests of the mature Hodge. But in this early introduction to matters of economics, historical change, social tradition, physical geography, and statecraft, the young pupil confronted the complex forces whose interplay (what he would term "the operation of second causes") shaped political events, albeit under the control of an ever-present, "extramundane, personal God."[2]

---

1. A. A. Hodge, *The Life of Charles Hodge, D.D. LL.D.* (New York: Charles Scribner's Sons, 1880), p. 12.

2. Hodge, *Hodge*, p. 522; Charles Hodge, "President Lincoln," *Biblical Repertory and Princeton Review* 37 (July 1865): 435-36 (hereafter *BRPR*).

I am grateful to the participants in the Hodge Symposium and to my colleague Dr. Robert Cook for their comments on an earlier draft of this paper.

For a seminary professor whose lasting public contribution would lie chiefly in the field of theology and the world of the sacred, Hodge developed and sustained a remarkably deep interest in the secular politics of his day. Over the course of his eighty years, he saw the insecure and self-conscious republican polity created by the Founding Fathers transformed into a confident mass democracy. War and territorial purchase hugely extended the country's boundaries. The number of states grew from sixteen to thirty-eight, while the population increased tenfold, from five to fifty million. Through the combined effect of economic change, the rapid growth of a national market, the revolution in technology and communications, and — most important of all — the defining experience of the Civil War, plural states became a singular nation. Through most of this Hodge was no casual, detached observer but an engaged citizen whose sense of responsibility drove him to energetic efforts to shape the events through which he lived. As such he exemplifies a particular religious-political type, one whose significance in Early National and Civil War America it is hard to exaggerate: the politically engaged evangelical Protestant driven by a powerful sense of civic duty. Hodge was by no means the most prominent of those who comprised this constituency, but he was one of the most intelligent and lucid. The first part of the analysis that follows looks at his ideas concerning the political responsibilities of American Christians and the religious obligations of the state.[3]

Any exploration of Hodge's political practice and principles is also bound to concentrate on two other issues: his party allegiances and his Unionism. Both act as a prism for understanding the extent and limits of his conservatism and mediating bridge building in church and state. Hodge's political party progression from Federalism to Whiggery to Republicanism was, of course, a common path for northern evangelicals, but his choice of route deviated from the most conservative course available to him. Nor was his rarely faltering Unionism consistently the handmaid of intersectional emollience: through part of the period of the secession crisis and subsequent war, his nationalism pushed him into more hard-line positions than he was perhaps temperamentally equipped to hold, and from which he sought to retreat only with the coming of peace.

3. John W. Stewart, *Mediating the Center: Charles Hodge on American Science, Language, Literature, and Politics* (Princeton: Princeton Theological Seminary, 1995) provides a valuable introduction to the political discourse and engagement of Hodge, whose writings he justly lauds for their "lucid prose, scrutiny, wit . . . [and] passion" (p. 67). Also helpful is William S. Barker, "The Social Views of Charles Hodge: A Study in 19th-Century Calvinism and Conservatism," *Presbyterian: Covenant Seminary Review* 1 (Spring 1975): 1-22.

I

As a young man in the 1820s and 1830s Charles Hodge, along with many other evangelical observers, watched the United States move towards institutionalized two-party politics. The arrival of white adult male suffrage and popular elections for the presidency engendered a new breed of professional manager, incessant and exuberant electioneering, and a revised view of the function and value of political parties, which were increasingly regarded as essential and even moral elements in the polity. By 1840 the recognizable forerunner of the modern party system was in place, in which organized, even disciplined, parties competed for the support of a mass electorate in almost every state of the Union. Against this backdrop, Christians' reflections about their political duties and responsibilities, a common feature of their colloquy in the early Republic, became all the more urgent.

Evangelicals' views of their civic obligations tended towards one or other end of a spectrum that ran from what may be termed the "quietist" to the "Calvinist." Quietists, professing a more private Christianity, drawing on the perspectives of Pentecost and celebrating the inspiration of the Holy Spirit, were moved by a conviction that politics, whether in the legislative chamber or on the campaign stump, were in the main spiritually harmful, commonly divisive, and profoundly irrelevant. This was certainly the posture of many early Methodists, for whom the imminence of the kingdom and the concerns of Zion screened out the tawdry banalities of secular politics; it was all the more so for those premillennialist Adventists whose calculations told them that Christ's return made electoral computation wholly irrelevant. Quietists were to be found in all denominational families, but most commonly among Baptists, Disciples, and Methodists, especially in the South.[4]

More influential, however, in the early Republic and the antebellum years was a Calvinist, postmillennialist understanding of politics as a means of introducing God's kingdom. Most evangelicals, and especially those of the Reformed tradition, conferred a moral character on the state and concluded that the Christian's political duty was to ensure the virtuous conduct of civic affairs. The harmonizing of American republicanism and civil liberty with Protestant Christianity was, as Fred J. Hood and Mark A. Noll have eloquently reminded us, the distinctive contribution

---

4. Richard J. Carwardine, *Evangelicals and Politics in Antebellum America* (New Haven: Yale University Press, 1993), pp. 14-17.

made by Princeton to the young nation. Synthesizing Scottish common sense philosophy, Reformed theology, and the realities of American experience, John Witherspoon and Samuel Stanhope Smith provided an influential mental framework for many of the country's leading clergy and prospective statesmen. Their perception that, under the providential government of the world, national prosperity depended on virtue and healthy religion ensured that even though the federal Constitution outlawed a church establishment, the need for Christian rulers, a moral citizenry, and good laws was widely recognized. It was Protestant Christianity, celebrating the priesthood of all believers and the freedom of the individual to interpret the sovereign Scriptures, that sustained the civil and religious liberties of Americans and their republican institutions. Thus government had a duty to discourage irreligion and blasphemy, to recognize a Christian God, and to do nothing that obstructed the operations of the divine law. Citizens themselves were obliged to elect Christian rulers, monitor their government's acts, and turn out those magistrates who had been weighed in the balance and found wanting.[5]

Hodge was both heir and proponent of this Calvinist approach to political engagement, more or less consistently taking the position, as he put it to his brother, that "real politics, . . . when connected with morals and the character and interests of the country, is a subject second only to religion in importance." As a young man at Princeton he noted the surprise of a family acquaintance who found him "so much of a politician": "I was not aware of the gradual lapse into this character," he told his brother, "but I take the liberty to think & speak on questions of the day with more decision than perhaps becomes me."[6] He was a voracious reader of the daily political press, and readily proffered his thoughts on a range of national and international affairs. (This sometimes reached a point of amusing self-mockery: commenting on Robert Peel's role in the "bedchamber crisis" early in Victoria's reign, he told his brother, "The little Queen has my hearty approbation! Which she will no doubt appreciate duly.") He also enjoyed some access to the first and second tier of political and civic leaders, at least in the middle states, and through the dark days of the Civil War had in his brother-in-law, General David Hunter, both a source

5. Fred J. Hood, *Reformed America: The Middle States, 1783-1837* (University, Ala.: University of Alabama Press, 1980), pp. 7-112; Mark A. Noll, *Princeton and the Republic, 1768-1822: The Search for a Christian Enlightenment in the Era of Samuel Stanhope Smith* (Princeton: Princeton University Press, 1989); Carwardine, *Evangelicals and Politics*, pp. 17-30.

6. C. Hodge to H. L. Hodge, 8 Mar. 1825, 17 Sept. 1841, Papers of Charles Hodge, Firestone Library, Princeton University (hereafter cited as PCH).

of information and an entrée into the world of Washington politics.[7] It was entirely in character that under his editorial direction the *Biblical Repertory and Princeton Review* should admit essays and reviews, some from his own pen, that at times turned it into something of a polemical political journal.[8] He was a determined voter, and if — unlike several of his Presbyterian colleagues — he never aspired to political office, his reputation for political engagement and lucid exposition of political issues prompted one of his ministerial admirers (Cortlandt Van Rensselaer), at the approach of the 1852 election campaign, to put the not entirely whimsical question, "Won't you consent to be a candidate for the Presidency?"[9] Hodge was not blind to the merits of the piety of those political quietists like John Newbold, a college associate who took little interest in secular affairs, "except as they were connected with duty, or with the interests of religion," and whose conversation "was in heaven"; indeed, Hodge would subsequently hold up Newbold as an example to each generation of Princeton students, to show "how much good can be done, simply by being good." Nor was he in any doubt that the Christian ministry was a superior vocation to that of the politician, and was sure, as he told his mother, that "To gain this world is not what we have promised to aim at. . . . I have lately, in reading Bonaparte's Russian Campaign, and the Life of Sheridan, been very much struck with the truth of the remark how little they enjoy the world to whom the world is everything. . . . There is nothing lost, therefore, even as regards the present world, by seeking *first* the kingdom of God; that is, by making it the primary object of pursuit. . . ." But throughout his long life Hodge remained, in Henry A. Boardman's words, "so vigilant an observer . . . of events, that nothing of importance escaped his notice as he looked out through the loop-holes of his retreat upon the great Babel."[10]

7. Hodge, *Hodge*, pp. 233, 453; C. Hodge to H. L. Hodge, 29 Nov. 1832, 26 Sept. 1833, 4 Nov. 1847. Hugh Hodge got used to his brother's requests to send him the daily Philadelphia papers, especially at election time. C. Hodge to H. L. Hodge, 10 July 1820, 21 Nov. 1836, 28 Oct. 1840, PCH. Through Hunter, Hodge had access to military headquarters in Washington. Stewart, *Mediating the Center,* pp. 91-92.

8. For an estimate of the influence exerted by the *Biblical Repertory and Princeton Review,* see Mark A. Noll, ed., *The Princeton Theology, 1812-1921: Scripture, Science, and Theological Method from Archibald Alexander to Benjamin Breckinridge Warfield* (Grand Rapids, Michigan: Baker, 1983), pp. 22-23.

9. C. Hodge to H. L. Hodge, 21 Nov. 1836, PCH; C. Van Rensselaer to C. Hodge, 29 Dec. 1851, Charles Hodge Manuscript Collection, Princeton Theological Seminary Libraries (hereafter cited as CHMC-PTS).

10. Hodge, *Hodge*, pp. 37-38, 98, 109-10, 602.

When Hodge defined his personal political duties, he conceived of the nation as a moral being. He took the common Reformed view that the separation of church and state presented no barrier to conducting the Republic's public affairs on Christian principles; fusing pre-Enlightenment theocratic doctrine with newer contractual theory, he insisted that it was obligatory for the government both to follow "the will of God as revealed in the Bible" and to remember that it represented "a Christian people." He contemptuously dismissed "the radical and infidel theory of civil government" that the nation's rulers were obliged to be so completely neutral in matters of religion that the claims of non-Christians had to be upheld at the expense of believers' rights. Rather, it was quite proper for both federal and state governments, by convention and by law, to protect the teaching of the Bible in public schools; to maintain Christian chaplains in legislative bodies, the army and navy, hospitals, almshouses, penitentiaries, and other public institutions; to enforce the observance of the Sabbath; to demand the swearing of oaths in courts of law; to preserve Christian marriage by punishing polygamy or adultery; and to call for days of fasting or thanksgiving.[11] Confronting the objection that such laws infringed citizens' constitutional guarantees of religious freedom, Hodge proffered three lines of rebuttal, based on appeals to historical-cultural reality, to Christian conscience, and to constitutional justice.

In the first place, America was a Christian and a Protestant country, by both quantitative and qualitative measure. It was not simply that Protestant Christians made up the majority of the inhabitants, though they did so overwhelmingly, but that they constituted the "heart, soul, life, and essence" of the nation. For Hodge the clue lay in the early settlement of the North American colonies by Protestants whose practices and cast of mind provided defining elements in the country's cultural and political evolution. "As every tree or plant, every race of animals, so every nation has its own organic life," Hodge explained. "Every nation . . . has its

11. Charles Hodge, "Sunday Laws," BRPR 36 (Oct. 1859): 734, 738, 742. When the new president, John Tyler, called for a national fast to mark the sudden death of William Henry Harrison, Hodge wrote, "It ought to be responded to with gladness by all the friends of religion, because the strict constructionists of the constitution, & the wicked, will be but too ready to make it a topic of abuse. I think the measure does him and the government great credit." C. Hodge to H. L. Hodge, 19 Apr. 1841, PCH. For Hodge's explication of the "novel, yet sound doctrine" of the separation and independence of church and state, an American refinement of Reformed doctrine, see Charles Hodge, "Relation of the Church and State," BRPR 35 (Oct. 1863): 691-93.

peculiar character and usages," the outcome of that organic growth. The early settlers "formed themselves as Christians into municipal and state organizations. They acknowledged God in their legislative assemblies; they prescribed oaths in his name; they closed . . . all places under public control on the Lord's day. They declared the common law of England, of which Christianity is the basis, to be the law of the land. In this way we grew to be a Protestant nation, by the same general law that an acorn becomes an oak." America's historical evolution was an essential fact that the nation's rulers could not ignore. Taking, in effect, the conservative credo "what is, should be," Hodge adopted a starkly functional position: "It matters not . . . whether the Bible is the word of God or not. It is enough that the people believe it to be his word."[12]

Obliged to respect these fixed historical-cultural realities, Christians who held political office were also morally bound to bring their principles to bear on the business of government. "They must obey [Christianity] . . . as men, . . . as magistrates, as citizens, as legislators and executive officers. They cannot deliberately violate any of its injunctions without doing violence to their own conscience, and forfeiting their allegiance to God." The salient word here was conscience. Hodge had learned from his mentor, Archibald Alexander, that even the hardened hearts of the most wicked were vulnerable to the workings of conscience, which "could neither be silenced nor sophisticated." Conscience, understanding (or reason), and the heart (or feelings) were the three faculties that operated in moving men and women to action. In regarding conscience as the superior faculty, to be informed by understanding, Hodge kept faith with conventional moral philosophy (though in so defining its operations as to keep them in harmony with the enforcement of the law and respect for the powers that be, he placed himself firmly in the camp of the social conservatives, and at odds with the "higher law" absolutism of many New School Calvinists).[13]

12. Hodge, "Sunday Laws," pp. 757-60. For the widespread judicial opinion in the early republic that Christianity was a part of the common law, see Hood, *Reformed America,* pp. 89-96.

13. Hodge, "Sunday Laws," p. 760; Hodge, *Hodge,* pp. 26-27; Daniel Walker Howe, *The Political Culture of the American Whigs* (Chicago: University of Chicago Press, 1979), pp. 28-30. For examples of Hodge's appeal to conscience and his understanding of its operations, see Hodge, *Hodge,* p. 359; Charles Hodge, "The Princeton Review and the State of the Country and of the Church," *BRPR* 37 (Oct. 1865): 627, 638-41; Hodge, "Sunday Laws," p. 741. See Raleigh Don Scovel, "Orthodoxy in Princeton: A Social and Intellectual History of Princeton Theological Seminary, 1812-1860" (Ph.D. dissertation, University of California at Berkeley, 1970), pp. 201-2, for a discussion of Hodge's "inadequate" definition of conscience.

Conscience was not something Christians could leave at home or in church. They had to carry their principles into their workshops, banking houses, and civic offices: "The man who was at once a prince and a bishop, could not get drunk as a prince, and be sober as a bishop." Rulers who chose to defy their citizens' respect for the Bible as the revelation of God's will would effectively disfranchise all Christians, for in conscience none could serve in or hold office under a government that acted unscripturally. Only "Jews, infidels and atheists" would be left conscientiously to exercise power. "We should have a test act of a novel character," Hodge declared. "Not religion, but irreligion would be demanded as a necessary qualification for every post of trust or power. . . . If we banish religion as a controlling power, we thereby establish atheism."[14]

Hodge insisted that a government which acted on Protestant principles "in all cases in which Christianity affords a rule for . . . governmental action" did nothing to violate anyone's "constitutional rights or natural liberty." Since the Scriptures did "not prescribe any particular form of civil government, nor any definite principles of political economy," citizens were free to debate and alter the character of their polity, and enjoyed great latitude in establishing economic policies and programs. Neither did Christianity "invest civil government with authority over the faith of its subjects, nor over the performance of their religious duties." The scriptural requirement was "simply" that God's word be the rule for Christians "in all their relations and associations." Hodge shared in the Reformed orthodoxy that real civil liberty, "consistent with the existence of human society," was to be secured only in conjunction with Protestant Christianity, which abhorred tyranny, taught people "their essential equality before God," and removed "the yoke of superstition and the bondage of priests";[15] and that the Constitution was a true guarantor of that freedom. Indeed, he joined with others in judging that this interconnection of civil liberty, constitutional provision, and Protestant religion would be even more tightly bonded by a more overt recognition in the Constitution of Americans' dependence on the Almighty. At Princeton, both Samuel Stanhope Smith and Archibald Alexander regarded that document as defective for failing — unlike most state constitutions — to acknowledge God's existence and superintending providence. Hodge was known to hold similar views and during the Civil War lent his name to the efforts of

14. Hodge, "Sunday Laws," pp. 737-8, 760-5. Cf. Charles Hodge, "The American Quarterly Review on Sunday Mails," *BRPR* 3 (Jan. 1831): 127-31.

15. Hodge, "American Quarterly Review," pp. 106-7.

the National Reform Association, formed to secure a corresponding amendment to the preamble of the Constitution.[16]

The political activism that Hodge expected of individual Christian citizens, he did not automatically concede to, or expect of, the church itself. At the Presbyterian General Assembly of 1861, in relation to Gardiner Spring's pro-Union resolutions, and again in response to the "Pittsburgh orders" of 1865, which imposed church penalties on secessionists, Hodge famously declared that the church had exceeded its legitimate sphere; he took a similar approach to the *cause célèbre* of Samuel McPheeters, whose dismissal from his charge in St. Louis for disloyalty to the Union he regarded as an excess of partisan zeal over jurisdictional propriety. It is, however, easy to overstate the significance of Hodge's stance in these cases.[17] First, to the extent that principle was involved, it was not one of church abstention from all political questions. Where the word of God had a bearing on political matters, the church could and should speak out. In response to James Henley Thornwell's doctrine, presented in 1859, that the church was "a spiritual body, clothed only with spiritual powers for spiritual ends, that all intermeddling with anything not directly bearing on the spiritual and eternal interests of men was foreign to its office," Hodge complained that Thornwell had defined the term *spiritual* so narrowly that it pertained only "to what concerns the method of salvation, as distinguished from the law of God." It was a ploy to deny the church the right to proscribe unjust slave laws and practices, "as well as . . . rebellion and disloyalty." Hodge noted dryly that Thornwell and his allies had subsequently found it impossible to hold to their doctrine when tempted, in the crisis over secession, to preach on slavery and to rally support for the new confederacy.[18] Secondly, we may reasonably ask whether Hodge's just reflections on Thornwell's untenable position ("It is no disrespect to say that men adopt theories to suit their purposes") may be just as pertinently applied to his own views. Certainly, as we shall see below, Hodge's

---

16. Hodge, *Hodge,* p. 411. The proposed preamble read: "We, the people of the United States, humbly acknowledging Almighty God as the source of all authority and power in civil government, the Lord Jesus Christ as the Ruler among the nations, his revealed will as the supreme law of the land, in order to constitute a Christian government, and in order to form a more perfect union. . . ." James H. Moorhead, *American Apocalypse: Yankee Protestants and the Civil War 1860-1869* (New Haven: Yale University Press, 1978), p. 125.

17. Scovel, "Orthodoxy in Princeton," p. 327, refers to the "glaring incongruity" of Hodge's omission of the church from his efforts to revive theocracy.

18. Charles Hodge, "The General Assembly," *BRPR* 31 (July 1859): 607-18; Hodge, "Princeton Review on the State of the Country," pp. 645-47.

position over the Spring resolutions and the Pittsburgh orders was related to his concern of first preserving and then reestablishing national harmony in the church. Significantly, Hodge did not sustain the same objection to local church bodies declaring for the Union when there was no danger of dissent. Moreover, such pragmatism was entirely in keeping with the ecclesiastical realities and practice of the day. In an era of plural and proliferating denominations, vigorous party politics, and divisive and polarizing issues, it was a matter of institutional self-protection for churches to avoid taking a collective stance on political questions. The nasty experiences of church schism over abolition and slavery showed only too painfully the price to be paid for institutional declarations of purpose. Few churches judged it expedient to risk nailing their colors to a partisan mast or offering an election endorsement. With church affiliation the experience of the many, not the privilege of the few, congregations commonly ran the political gamut. It was sheer realism to leave politics to the conscience of the individual.

II

In his celebratory biography, Archibald Alexander Hodge extolled his father's lifelong political consistency, rooted in his temperamental conservatism and sustained in the face of changing times and party combinations. The man who was addicted to fixed routine in his personal life, who shunned quack diagnoses in medicine, and who resisted new measures and novel doctrine in religion was the man equally tenacious in sustaining "without a shadow of change absolutely the same principles . . . as to the relation of government to moral and religious questions . . . after the war as he did years before."[19] The implication is that, as Hodge advanced from Federalism to Whiggery and from there to the Republican party, he continued to champion a cluster of principles and values that took various programmatic forms but enjoyed an essential coherence. If the picture of unrelieved consistency is open to question, the broad claim, that through his changing political affiliations there remained a continuous spine of thought and ambition, is persuasive enough.

The young Hodge absorbed his Federalist opinions from his family, in

19. Hodge, *Hodge,* pp. 236, 241-42, 253. For most of his life Hodge used the same study chair, patronized the same tailor, and jotted down every morning the particulars of the weather.

whose religious orientation, economic circumstances, and social location we can discern several of the quintessential aspects of the party of George Washington and Alexander Hamilton. Hodge's paternal grandfather, Andrew, an immigrant from Ulster in the 1730s, had risen to become a leading figure in mid-century Philadelphia, a highly successful merchant with substantial property and a liberal founder of the Second Presbyterian Church, organized by the pro-revival "New Lights." Hugh, his fourth son and Charles Hodge's father, graduated from the College of New Jersey, acted as a surgeon in the Revolutionary War (during which he was captured by the British) and subsequently developed a socially well-connected medical practice. His premature death during a yellow fever epidemic in 1798 left the six-month-old baby Charles to the care of a godly mother who for some years drew a "comfortable" income from Andrew Hodge's commercial property. Several of Charles's cousins were well placed in law, commerce, medicine, and politics. They included Samuel Bayard, clerk to the United States Supreme Court, and James Ashton Bayard of Delaware, United States Representative and later Senator, who had played a key role after the 1800 election in the abortive Federalist scheme to deny the presidency to Thomas Jefferson.[20] There is little in these features of the Hodge family to surprise historians of Federalism, who have located its principal support in older, stable communities, oriented towards commerce; among the socially better off, especially the mercantile and legal professions, often anxious about their future in a changing social order; and among conservative Congregationalists and Presbyterians. Guided by a vision of a hierarchical society, and shivering at the tremors of emerging democracy, Federalists valued religion, education, and the law as the means of maintaining a harmonious and controllable social order.[21]

We may reasonably surmise that the increasingly straitened circumstances of the Hodge household in the first decade of the new century only served to energize the family's Federalist loyalties. The financial returns from the wharf, docks, and warehouses bequeathed by Andrew Hodge depended on the state of trade, and the Jeffersonian Republicans' non-intercourse act and embargo severely diminished that income. The

20. Stanley Elkins and Eric McKitrick, *The Age of Federalism: The Early American Republic, 1788-1800* (New York: Oxford University Press, 1993), pp. 746-50.

21. M. J. Heale, *The Making of American Politics* (New York: Longman, 1977), pp. 86-87, 104-5; Ronald P. Formisano, "Federalists and Republicans: Parties, Yes — System, No," in *The Evolution of American Electoral Systems*, ed. Paul Kleppner, et al. (Westport, Conn.: Greenwood, 1981), pp. 60-66.

war of 1812 saw a further suspension of business, and increased hardship. But instead of pressing her two sons to provide for themselves, Mary Hodge sacrificially met the expenses of their college and professional education through self-denial and by taking in lodgers. When Charles entered the College of New Jersey in 1815, he stepped into an institution whose authorities were stamped with the imprint of old-style, patrician Federalism. The death of the sainted Washington, Jefferson's accession to power on the back of "the deluded Multitude," and the subsequent "anarchy and confusion" of his "infidel" administration, and then the experience of war, had encouraged a bleak assessment of the political order.[22] The defining and dispiriting experience of student revolt in 1807 had its roots in the friction between the largely Federalist leadership under Stanhope Smith and a student body whose members included many from the South who were Jeffersonians in politics, wedded as much if not more to the values of honor than of evangelical religion, and ready to use Revolutionary ideology in their own way to challenge the college's synthesis of republicanism and Christianity. By the time of Hodge's arrival the college leadership, under first Smith's and then Ashbel Green's presidency, had retreated from public political involvement towards spiritual projects. They were, Mark Noll tells us, "no less eager to save the nation," but their weapons would now be "voluntary agencies, revival, and ministerial education." Privately, though, they continued to dispute the plebeian, Jeffersonian reading of America's republican destiny, and thus Princeton, from whose seminary Hodge graduated in 1819, and where he taught between 1820 and his departure for Germany in 1826, remained a powerful locus of deferential Federalism. This was the congenial setting in which Hodge initially celebrated John Quincy Adams's presidential victory in 1824 and then rebuked his neglect of Federalists — "that ancient and excellent order" — in his cabinet appointments.[23]

The precise steps in Hodge's journey towards the emergent Whig party of the early 1830s are not easily established, but some major landmarks rise clear of the historical mist. The Jacksonian revolution of 1828, even when hedged about by the caveats of modern historians, can properly be seen to have opened a new era in American political history. Within two months of Hodge's return from Europe in September of that year, a disciplined, pro-

22. The phrase is Elias Boudinot's. Noll, *Princeton and the Republic,* p. 250. For Samuel Miller's early endorsement and his subsequent repudiation of Jeffersonian politics, see Scovel, "Orthodoxy in Princeton," pp. 318-19.

23. Noll, *Princeton and the Republic,* pp. 214-43, 283, 295-96; C. Hodge to H. L. Hodge, 8 Mar. 1825, PCH.

fessionally managed, nationwide, and mass-based party carried its candidate into the White House on a tide of popular enthusiasm, signaling the death of the legislative caucus system and spurring further changes in party management and campaigning that would culminate in the legendary election of 1840. We can be sure that Andrew Jackson's lack of intellectual credentials and the populist nature of his campaign were not to Hodge's taste. He communicated some sense of this concern to Augustus Tholuck shortly before Jackson's inauguration: "Although I feel as deeply as ever the great advantages which our ecclesiastical liberty confers upon us, and think that we have reason to rejoice in the general prevalence of truth and piety in most sections of our country, I am now aware to a greater degree, than formerly, of the evils which attend even the best system." Given the unprecedented power of public opinion it was imperative to nourish the electorate's "vital piety" through revivals and other forms of missionary outreach.[24] Equally, Hodge's antipathy to the new political professionalism and institutional discipline that was maturing in the Democratic party of Jackson and Martin Van Buren is evident enough in his reflections on the comic writings of the pseudonymous "Major Jack Downing," which he commended as "a most excellent and useful book! not merely for excellent humor and point, but for a complete exhibition of the whole nature, machinery and chicanery of American politics."[25] Hodge grieved that the "collar discipline" of party demanded the sacrifice of "private opinion, conscience & every thing else" in the pursuit of office.[26]

Hodge's reactions remind us that opposition to Jacksonian populism and its organizational forms ran deep within much of Reformed Protestantism (especially Congregationalism and the continuing tradition of Federalist Presbyterianism). What is less clearly understood is the precise place of Reformed evangelicals in the disjointed and hesitant process by which Old Hickory's opponents began to cohere politically. Jackson's stance on the various questions of economic nationalism (that is, the scheme of federally funded internal improvements, protective tariff, and

24. Hodge, *Hodge*, pp. 210-11.
25. C. Hodge to H. L. Hodge, 9 Jan. 1834, PCH; Hodge, *Hodge*, p. 233. Several authors adopted the guise of "Major Downing." Hodge referred to Seba Smith's sharply satirical volume, *The Life and Writings of Major Jack Downing, of Downingville, Away Down East in the State of Maine* (Boston: Lilly, Wait, Colman & Holden, 1833), which promised to "tell folks more about politics, and how to get offices, than ever they knew before in all their lives" (p. vi), and which used homespun humor to reflect on a variety of issues of the day, including the Bank of the United States, nullification, and Indian removal.
26. C. Hodge to H. L. Hodge, 13 Dec. 1833, 17 Jan. 1834, PCH.

national bank that went under the name of Clay's American System) certainly put political water between him and his opponents, the National Republicans and their successors. Indeed, the issue of the recharter of the Second Bank of the United States would be the essential catalyst in 1832-33 in the emergence of a distinctive Whig opposition to "King Andrew" and his executive "tyranny." But before the bank issue arose, economic questions did not so cleanly divide the parties, nor can they satisfactorily explain the urgency and moral energy among the anti-Jacksonians during his first term. For this we need to turn to a much-neglected issue of early Jacksonian politics: the federal government's alleged complicit role in undermining the Christian Sabbath.

There is little doubt that the perception of the national government as a desecrator of the Sabbath, through its commitment to transporting mails and opening post offices every day of the week, including Sunday, prompted a massive and unprecedented mobilization of public opinion against their federal rulers. The issue first arose in 1810 when Congress required postmasters to open their offices, if so required by the public, on any day that mail arrived, including the Sabbath. In the consternation thus aroused throughout the Protestant community, the prior question of the propriety of transporting the mails every day of the week (as had occurred on some routes from before the existence of the federal government) itself became an issue, and for several years a coalition of church leaders, particularly the American heirs of the Reformed tradition, battled unsuccessfully with Congress to secure the repeal of the 1810 law and achieve complete adherence to Sabbatarian principles. Agitation entered a new phase in the mid-1820s, as improvements in transportation accelerated the commercialization of the Sabbath. Presbyterians took the lead in calling for the boycott of all companies who ran stagecoaches or steamboats on that day, and warmly supported the initiative of Josiah Bissell of Rochester, founder of the Sabbath-keeping Pioneer Line (an upstate New York stagecoach and canal packet company) in establishing the General Union for the Promotion of the Christian Sabbath in May 1828.[27]

27. Richard R. John, "Taking Sabbatarianism Seriously: The Postal System, the Sabbath, and the Transformation of American Political Culture," *Journal of the Early Republic* 10 (Winter 1990): 516-67. See also Hood, *Reformed America*, pp. 97-101; Bertram Wyatt-Brown, "Prelude to Abolitionism: Sabbatarian Politics and the Rise of the Second Party System," *Journal of American History* 58 (Sept. 1971): 316-41; Paul E. Johnson, *A Shopkeeper's Millennium: Society and Revivals in Rochester, New York, 1815-1837* (New York: Hill and Wang, 1978), pp. 83-88; John R. Bodo, *The Protestant Clergy and Public Issues, 1812-1848* (Princeton: Princeton University Press, 1954), pp. 39-43.

An avowedly nonsectarian, broad-based coalition of evangelicals, the General Union embarked on a massive exercise in public education or "consciousness raising" by making creative use of the burgeoning postal system and the new steam presses to distribute tens of thousands of documents and to appeal directly to the public. The petition campaign it coordinated from December 1828 consciously avoided abstruse theological issues but made concerted play of that Christian republican theory so closely associated with Hodge's Princeton — representing the Sabbath as essential to the piety and morality on which republics depend, insisting on the postmasters' right to the free enjoyment of religion, and representing the congressional law on the Sabbath as a form of religious test. The accumulation of signatures from all over the nation and right across the Protestant spectrum (though especially strongly represented in New England and the mid-Atlantic states, and within the Congregational-Presbyterian nexus) suggested that Sabbatarian activists had managed "to unite thousands of Americans in a common cause."[28]

Hodge was drawn publicly into the campaign quite late in the day, in January 1831, replying at length in the *Princeton Review* to an anti-Sabbatarian essay in the pages of the Philadelphia journal, the *American Quarterly Review*. By then Princeton, both seminary and community, had confirmed its reputation as a bastion of Sabbatarianism, not least by the town authorities' action in blocking the progress of a Sunday mail wagon (actually they had been tricked into doing so, but the public saw only the inhabitants' pious readiness to challenge federal law). By then, too, the anti-Sabbatarians had found their own activists and voices, most influentially in the shape of Richard M. Johnson, chairman of the Senate Committee on the Post Office and Post Roads. The senator from Kentucky, who was a friend of the anti-Sabbatarian Alexander Campbell and the brother of a Campbellite preacher, issued two reports, in 1829 and 1830, designed to respond in kind to the Sabbatarians' impressive mobilization of public opinion: they very effectively played on the widespread fear, inside and outside evangelicalism, that the Sabbatarians' insatiable appetite for "clerical tyranny" would reestablish the bonds between church and state, and that the federal government would be led to declare its opinion on a religious controversy (the true nature and location of the Sabbath) well beyond its proper sphere.[29]

28. John, "Taking Sabbatarianism Seriously," pp. 538-39, 543, 556. By May 1831, over 900 petitions had reached Congress, some containing several thousand signatures.

29. The reports were in fact the work of Johnson's Washington landlord and friend,

Much of Hodge's essay was an exercise in scriptural and historical exegesis, as well as a recapitulation of the familiar Reformed doctrinal triangulation of Sabbath observance, public virtue, and republican liberty. But in its culminating sections he addressed the anti-Sabbatarians' warnings about the "priestly" threat to religious freedom and the related *argumentum ad horrendum,* that a Sabbatarian victory would result in a "Calvinist"-inspired government acting to compel religious observance and "to prohibit all men from an attendance at an Unitarian or Catholic church." He impatiently noted the anti-Sabbatarians' inconsistency in accepting the government's ban on most Sunday trading, and the closure on the Lord's Day of the nation's legislative and judicial bodies — evidence that they conceded the constitutional principle underlying Sabbatarian demands — while still insisting on their "right" to receive mail. In calling for the protection of the nation's minority of non-Christians and those Christian groups convinced that Saturday was the Sabbath, Hodge judged that Johnson and other anti-Sabbatarians made a "grand mistake": "they think themselves heathen, whereas they are Christians; members of a Christian community, and bound to act accordingly." America's legislators might have no right to pass any law in support of religion, but equally "they are not authorized to make any, which interferes with it" — on which basis the law of 1810 was "oppressive and unjust." Hodge dismissed Johnson's principle of minority protection as "completely and radically revolutionary. It would change the whole practice of the government, and overturn it from its very foundations. Let Congress once announce to the people that they are to be treated as Atheists; that their most sacred rights and opinions are to be trampled in the dust, and our government is at an end." By contrast, the repeal of the 1810 law would end the violation of "the rights of Christians in a Christian country."[30]

The Sabbatarian question powerfully aroused and divided American public opinion, and, as historian Richard R. John has shrewdly argued, in a society where many people were so serious about their religion it is hardly surprising that, as the democratic era dawned, those who sought to mobilize political support should have exploited it to the full. It was no accident that the battle over the Sunday mails, and the bitterness over another issue with powerful religious ramifications, Antimasonry (which di-

---

Obadiah Brown, Baptist minister and post office clerk. John, "Taking Sabbatarianism Seriously," pp. 551-52, 559.

30. Hodge, "The American Quarterly Review on Sunday Mails," pp. 86-134; "Sunday Mails," *American Quarterly Review* 8 (Sept. 1830): 175-97.

vided the evangelical churches even more profoundly than did Sabbatarianism), marked the transition from the old caucus politics to the mass engagement of the "second party system." However, Sabbatarians did not fall immediately or neatly into line behind a single political party: in 1828 Jackson's Presbyterianism helped to keep them politically divided. But the Democrat Richard Johnson's reports helped give political party focus to the debate. The Sabbatarian forces became more insistently anti-Jacksonian, and in due course staunchly Whig. This is where Hodge had been located and would remain. It cannot be claimed that he played a defining public role in the campaign. He was no popularizer, in contrast to ministers like Lyman Beecher, the anonymous author of the mass circulation pamphlet *The Address of the General Union for Promoting the Observance of the Christian Sabbath*. Moreover, if the Sabbatarian movement was an important episode "in the democratization of American culture" (Richard John's judgment), this was despite, not because of, Hodge.[31] But there is much significance in the fact that Hodge's first public intervention on a political matter was an extended examination of the Sabbath issue. For him, as for many other evangelicals, it was deep anxiety over a question involving religion and public virtue that gave focus to his political allegiances in the critical formative stages of the emerging second party system and the era of mass politics.

Sabbatarian anxieties fused with outrage over Jackson's Indian policies to pull Hodge and like-minded evangelicals even more completely into the loose coalition of Old Hickory's opponents that would shortly cohere into the Whig party. A program of Christianizing and "civilizing" missions to various Indian tribes had been part of united evangelical (and especially Reformed) efforts over several years. Missionaries and reformers, guided by a benevolent paternalism, believed that Indians could be "redeemed" and assimilated, a conviction reinforced by the experience of the Cherokee Nation in Georgia. As literate Christians and settled agriculturalists, the Cherokees were widely seen to have earned the guarantees afforded them by federal treaty. But the state of Georgia, in the interests of land-grabbing cotton-growers, and with the support of the president, set about expelling them to Oklahoma, and in the process arrested two defiant white missionaries to the Indians. Hodge, who expressed himself "astonished" at Jackson's Indian policy and thought Southerners "hardly sane" over the issue, contributed to the explosion of anger and alarm within Reformed Protestantism and the evangelical united front. His "re-

31. John, "Taking Sabbatarianism Seriously," p. 556.

vering friendship" with Theodore Frelinghuysen, whom he had come to know ever more intimately over twenty years and whose political philosophy was similarly grounded in Reformed, Princetonian doctrine, gave him access to the most energetic of the Cherokees' supporters (and indeed Sabbatarians) in the Senate. From the moment it was clear that the Indian treaties were under threat Hodge feared for America's "national character," since such unchristian disregard among rulers for solemn obligations had chilling implications for the republic's prosperity and durability. Hodge, the usually consistent supporter of established authority, reacted to the "misconduct" of the "miserable" president in the case of the incarcerated Georgia missionaries with a remarkable confession to his brother: "Verily, I think I could join a rebellion, with a clear conscience, as I am sure I could with a full heart." When the United States Supreme Court under the Federalist John Marshall ruled Georgia's action unconstitutional, Hodge considered it the most important judgment in its history, one to be "cherished as long as good men live in America." But he was shrewd enough to expect powerful resistance to its enforcement, not least from Jackson himself. Regretting the failure of the incumbent's opponents to run only one candidate for president in 1832, Hodge favored William Wirt, the anti-Mason. It was an unsurprising choice in view of Wirt's role as the Indians' champion and the lawyer for the Cherokees, as well as his other links to the world of Reformed evangelicals.[32]

Hodge moved more or less smoothly into the ranks of the new Whig party, born out of the crisis over the rechartering of the Second Bank of the United States in 1832-33. He regarded this emerging anti-Jacksonian force, of whose early lack of cohesion he was deeply scornful, as the heir of the Washingtonian and Hamiltonian tradition, and subsequently alluded to the Democrats' opponents as "the Whig, Conservative, Federal" party, a vehicle by which for short periods "the mass of the intelligence & property of the country" could "get the upper hand."[33] Hodge saw in both Federalism and Whiggery the best means of promoting the nation's industrial and commercial development, and of protecting the propertied interests on whose energy and enterprise it depended. He was a typical Whig in fusing conservative social and political principles with a faith in economic and technological progress. He deeply admired Yankee enterprise and know-

32. Howe, *The Political Culture of the American Whigs*, 40-41; C. Hodge to H. L. Hodge, 15, 31 Dec. 1829, 22 Jan., 24 Mar., 26 Aug. 1831, 10 Mar. 1832, PCH; C. Hodge to A. Tholuck, 9 Feb. 1831, C. Hodge to H. L. Hodge, 1 Oct. 1831, Hodge, *Hodge*, pp. 217, 230-31. Marshall's death Hodge considered "a great national calamity." C. Hodge to H. L. Hodge, 7 July 1835, PCH.

33. C. Hodge to H. L. Hodge, 21 Mar. 1834, 15 Dec. 1842, PCH.

how. Thus he took great delight in discovering that the Prussian government had employed a young American engineer to develop their spinning and weaving machinery, and that in Berlin "[t]he American machines have displaced the English, and every year there is a complaint that one expensive machine is rendered useless by the Yankees inventing a better." He expected the socio-economic order to reward talent and ability.[34] He warmly endorsed the protective tariff as a means of cultivating American manufacturing and giving scope to the entrepreneurial spirit.

He also saw in a sound national banking system and the regulated growth of credit an essential mechanism for economic expansion and a protection against the worst fluctuations of boom and crash. From the first he had no confidence in Jackson's banking schemes ("an engine of corruption and tyranny"), but like many others he thought the President would not risk vetoing the recharter bill. When Jackson took the fight to Nicholas Biddle and removed the federal deposits, Hodge reached the boiling point. He understood the power of Jackson's appeals to hard money sentiment, given the "vast predominance of paper" liable to depreciation, and he especially feared the influence of the radical Jacksonians (the locofocos) after the onset of depression in the later 1830s. During the bank suspensions of those years in Philadelphia Hodge wrote bleakly of the "popular clamor against all banks and their advocates" and the likelihood of a withdrawal of bank charters that would threaten "a revolution of property," cause widespread financial ruin, and damage the seminary as well as his personal interests. "How many hundreds, who depend on bank dividends, will have no income, until they can get their money back and reinvested, should the banks prove ultimately able to pay their stockholders?" he asked his brother. This was no dry academic question. Hodge, who enjoyed only a modest income, held $500 of stock in the United States Bank of Pennsylvania. It made him particularly anxious over its falling value and the possibility that the battle between radicals and conservatives in the state legislature would end in the repeal of the Bank's charter.[35]

---

34. Visiting Dresden in 1827, Hodge wrote: "It is pleasant to see that talent in Germany, at least in the learned professions, has fair scope. Neander's father was a Jew, who trafficked in old clothes. . . . Tholuck's a silver-smith." C. Hodge, Journal, 4 Sept. 1827; Hodge, *Hodge*, p. 142.

35. Hodge's attention to banking and currency issues through the 1830s and early 1840s is a persistent feature of his correspondence with his brother. See especially C. Hodge to H. L. Hodge, 15 Dec. 1829, 16 Jan. 1832, 26 Sept. 1833, 22 Oct. 1834, 18 Apr. 1836, 8, 21 Feb., 4 Mar. 1840, 28 Jan., 23 Feb., 13 Mar., 19 Apr., 10 Nov. 1841, PCH; C. Hodge to H. L. Hodge, 10 Oct. 1839, in Hodge, *Hodge*, p. 245.

Hodge's concern to protect personal property and grasp the economic possibilities of the burgeoning national market was an important element in his approach to public issues, but we seriously misunderstand his Whig political thought if we explain it narrowly, or even principally, in these terms. His Sabbatarianism and stance on the Indian question sprang from his Christian republicanism, as did other essential strands in the broad skein of ideas that made up his Whiggery: notably the emphasis on discipline, improvement, and moral responsibility in both individual and society, and on the organic unity and underlying harmony of the American social order.[36]

Hodge's esteem for the self-improving, industrious individual driven by a strong sense of duty and aspiring to full self-control is evident from his earliest years. An earnest, Calvinistic mother, ambitious for her sons, taught the virtues of effort and persistence and demanded constant striving after the highest ideals. "[I]f you are not improved and polished Gentlemen it will be your own fault," she told them in January 1811 (when Charles was thirteen), pointing out the educational advantages that her energetic resourcefulness had secured.[37] She seems to have thought that Charles rarely did justice to his talents, and fell short in "diligence, ambition, or power of concentrated and sustained effort." In fact, the young Hodge was moved by a strong sense of duty and discipline, especially after his public profession of faith in 1815. When Mary Hodge proposed a further year's physical recuperation before starting his ministerial training, he protested that postponement would be time "even worse than lost. . . . [Y]ou know that it is necessary for the powers of the mind to be more or less concentrated in order to produce effects"; any intermission should be delayed to let him follow "three or four years of professional studies, when the mind will be more matured, the habits of study and attention more firmly fixed, the stock of information increased, and the capacity for improvement in every way enlarged." His wishes granted, he peppered her with letters from Princeton Seminary: "to be constantly occupied is to be happy, provided you are convinced that the occupation is important in itself, and proper for you," he wrote shortly before his twentieth birthday. "Accordingly, I have never been in better spirits than I have been in, all this session. Up before sunrise, and not to bed ever much before twelve." Eighteen months later he reflected with wry, self-mocking humor, "My character for diligence is better than for anything else, I am afraid. One of my fel-

36. Howe, *Political Culture of the American Whigs,* especially p. 21.
37. Scovel, "Orthodoxy in Princeton," p. 158.

low-students, who is quite fond of me, said the other day I must be a fool if I did not know a great deal, for I study so much." Such industriousness went hand-in-hand with the strictest self-control, and throughout his life Hodge enjoyed a reputation for the most rigorous command of his appetites, for temperance in food and drink, and for admirable cheerfulness in the face of the chronic pain and lameness that his inflamed hip and thigh occasioned. Diligence and control, of course, were not merely ends in themselves, but routes to a higher achievement: in each of Hodge's chief career decisions, a concern for moral self-improvement stands out above all else. His ministerial education at Princeton would, he said, be in the hands of talented teachers "devoted to the improvement of their pupils." Accepting a professorship at the seminary was to enter "decidedly the most eligible situation for improvement, for satisfaction, and for usefulness, which our church affords." The decision to spend two years studying in Europe from 1826, at no small family sacrifice, expressed even more dramatically his conviction that "my improvement should be paramount to all other conditions."[38]

To shape society in the image of the disciplined, self-improving individual required the energetic construction of a public education system. Hodge was a quintessential Whig in believing in the power of education to reshape human nature, and he looked to the state as well as to the churches to provide the moral, Protestant-based instruction essential to good citizenship. He had no time for those who declared that state schools should teach no religion (nor, indeed, for those fellow Presbyterians, like Thornwell, who would later deny the right of churches to engage in secular education). Of course, religious values and "vital piety" could be disseminated outside formal educational arrangements: one of the positive aspects of the religious revivals that otherwise elicited an ambivalent response in Hodge was their capacity for nourishing a healthy public opinion. But institutional instruction was indispensable to the work of fusing morality and intelligence. The world presented sobering examples of the price of defective education. Hodge reflected trenchantly on the sad lessons of the rise of Louis Napoleon: "It is so clear to me that liberty can exist only the foundations of intelligence and religion, that I have no hope for France, where the intelligent part of the population have no religion and the religious part no intelligence."[39]

---

38. Hodge, *Hodge*, pp. 32-33, 42-43, 56, 63, 91, 100-101.
39. Howe, *The Political Culture of the American Whigs*, p. 36; Hodge, *Hodge*, pp. 210-11, 395, 408-10.

Hodge's conception of social order and social process was, like that of his fellow Whigs, hierarchical (though not frozen) and organic. They judged that, whatever expressions of social conflict scarred the face of Jacksonian America, in essence its citizens were interdependent, and what united them was more important than their points of division. Elements of evangelical doctrine and practice did much to heighten the belief in social consensus. As Hodge explained during the season of burgeoning revivals in the early 1830s, Christian worship brought "friends and neighbours" regularly together, "to mingle their feelings before the throne of God," achieving a potent sense of unity. "The differences arising from wealth and other adventitious circumstances, here disappear. The high are humbled without being depressed; the low are exalted without being elated." Their fellow-feelings, he wrote, awaken "the consciousness of community of origin and of nature. They learn that God has made of one flesh all the dwellers upon earth; that he has breathed one spirit bearing his own image into them; placed all under the same benevolent laws; offers the same glorious immortality to all, and has thus bound them together as one great brotherhood." Such interdependence obliged all to reflect on their responsibilities to others, and required the socially fortunate to intervene in a spirit of paternalism to help those unable to fend for themselves. Hodge's earliest memories included that of his mother (a founder of the "Female Association for the Relief of Widows and Single Women of Reduced Circumstances") trudging through winter snows to deliver groceries to the destitute of Philadelphia. Such benevolence was a duty. His words of approval for Prince William of Prussia, who gave to the poor one sixth of his annual income, are revealing: such conduct was "remarkably correct."[40]

Hodge, then, in association with many of his Presbyterian colleagues, helped to establish the Whigs as the party of moral order, benevolence, respectability, and social harmony. Not that there was a uniform Presbyterian political allegiance. Many church members shared the politics of Andrew Jackson, himself a Presbyterian, and after the denominational schism of 1837-38 it is clear that Democrats were well represented in the ranks of the Old School, especially in the middle and southern states. That, in contrast, most New Schoolers were hearty Whigs might seem to suggest a neat division of New and Old School men into opposing political camps. But in fact the institutional and theological quarrels within

40. Howe, *Political Culture of the American Whigs,* p. 21; Hodge, "American Quarterly Review on Sunday Mails," p. 105; Hodge, *Hodge,* pp. 10, 162.

Presbyterianism in the 1830s did not translate so straightforwardly into the era's developing political alignments. Hodge, along with adherents of the Old School less reluctant than he, certainly had his doubts about the new revivalism and the challenge it represented to the old Calvinism, but he continued to line up politically alongside Albert Barnes, Lyman Beecher, Charles Finney, and other New School luminaries, as well as many from the ministerial elite of the Old School. No doubt this had much to do with the Whiggish social conservatism of traditionalists like Hodge, but it also had to do with a conviction shared across the Presbyterian divide that moral activism and social improvement were the business of Christian citizens and of the government they elected. Hodge and Whiggish Old Schoolers may have been alert to the dangers of reliance on an unchecked conscience, but they could have no faith in a party that seemed to dismiss respect for that conscience altogether.[41]

This was certainly the construction that Whigs themselves put on their opponents. Democrats loomed in Whig rhetoric as morally ambiguous demagogues who, remorselessly pursuing the spoils of office and neglecting orthodox Protestant interests, resorted to cheap egalitarianism and the language of social conflict. In fact, whatever Whigs might say about their own pedigree as "the Christian party," huge numbers of Protestant evangelicals continued to support the Jacksonians, notably members of the two largest denominations, the Baptists and Methodists. Inheriting the Jeffersonian Republicans' mantle as the party of laissez-faire and pluralistic tolerance, Democrats successfully played on the fears of religious "outsiders" (especially in the South and West) that church-and-state Whigs would act as the political arm of Yankee religious "meddlers" and moral imperialists.[42]

Hodge, though, provided a quintessential example of Whig evangelical disgust at the Jacksonian order. Though he found Jackson "very gracious" when he visited Princeton in June 1833 (and attended morning prayers at the college), this did nothing to moderate Hodge's contempt for Old Hickory's "folly & arbitrary disposition" nor prevent him from fantasizing that Congress might impeach the President, "find him guilty & send him to *Arabia*."[43] Much of this animus derived from Hodge's despair over the new system of rotation in office, "the most demoralizing and unhinging proposition which radical ingenuity ever devised." The spoils system

---

41. Carwardine, *Evangelicals and Politics,* pp. 122-24.
42. Carwardine, *Evangelicals and Politics,* pp. 97-132.
43. C. Hodge to H. L. Hodge, 15 Dec. 1829, 19 Sept. 1832, 14 June 1833, 14 Apr. 1834, PCH.

would deter "men of worth" from public service and ensure that the Jacksonian administration would be "held together by no principle, but desire of office & power." Personal gain would supplant concern for the public good. Van Buren's sub-treasury scheme, for example, would result in "all the loco-focos dipping their straws into the molasses hogsheads of the people's money, and smacking their lips at a great rate." Electoral changes ensuring "the ascendancy of the rabble" had freed the Democrats from the moral discipline of accountability to society's better sort. Hodge told his brother in the early months of Van Buren's administration, "If we could have a Republic with the right of suffrage restricted to householders, who can read and write, and have been at least ten years in the country, we could get along grandly. But democracy with universal suffrage will soon be worse than an aristocracy with Queen Victoria at the head." A little later he added, "I do not believe we can stand it much longer. We must get rid of universal suffrage or we shall go to ruin."[44]

Hodge's anxieties over the implications of an unrestricted suffrage turned to "grievous disappointment" as he brooded on the defeat in the 1844 presidential election of the Whigs' most luminous statesman, Henry Clay. He deeply admired the Kentuckian, "a praying man" who, he believed, "never had introduced a measure into Congress, without first kneeling down and invoking the guidance and blessing of God." That the defeat also marked the rejection of Hodge's friend and the champion of Reformed Protestantism, Theodore Frelinghuysen, the vice-presidential candidate, added a further cup of gall. Clay's buoyant hopes had been dashed, Hodge explained, repeating the commonplace Whig analysis, by the votes, often fraudulent, "of foreigners and Catholics, aliens and enemies really of the country." It was a judgment encouraged by the report, which Hodge declared authentic, that Archbishop John Hughes had confided to his Whig friend William Henry Seward that Romanists "could stand Clay; but we cannot stand Frelinghuysen." The Whigs' defeat seemed to Hodge to vindicate those who, like himself, had been calling for an alteration in the naturalization laws to prevent newly arrived immigrants from voting. "[W]hat right have the paupers of Europe to be citizens of America?" he asked rhetorically. "We must take care of ourselves, or we shall have all our affairs under the control of the mob of foreigners who swarm our cities."[45]

44. C. Hodge to H. L. Hodge, 15 Dec. 1829, 5 Dec. 1833, 17 Jan. 1834, 3 Apr. 1841, PCH; C. Hodge to H. L. Hodge, 10 Oct. 1839, 1, 17 Aug. 1837; Hodge, *Hodge*, pp. 233, 245.
45. Hodge, *Hodge*, pp. 15-16, 348-49; C. Hodge to H. L. Hodge, 30 Oct., 8 Nov. 1844, PCH.

Hodge denied that nativists who called for restrictions of this kind were necessarily trading in crude xenophobia or in religious bigotry. When in May 1844 John Hughes attacked the American party in New York on both counts, Hodge claimed that the archbishop confounded two very different things: "opposition to foreigners, as foreigners, governing the country, and opposition to Papists, as Papists. It is true that most of these objectionable foreigners are Papists, but the opposition to them is as foreigners. It also true that they are mostly Irish, but the opposition is not to them as Irish." Hodge's claim undoubtedly underestimated the strength of anti-Catholicism and crude prejudice within popular nativism, but as a projection of his own attitudes we need not question its sincerity. His sojourn in Europe in the 1820s may have played a part in broadening his attitudes; certainly it sparked a warmth of regard towards German immigrants. Moreover, his views on the Roman Catholic Church were interestingly subtle — or, at least, far more so than most of his fellow Presbyterians'. He agreed that the institution of the papacy was Antichrist. He also regretted the tendency of Romanist theology "to destroy the moral sense" and the absence in Roman services of Protestant simplicity: "the religion of the Catholics is, with the common people, so much a matter of feeling and so little of principle. And hence the glaring inconsistency, so often to be found among them, between their open immorality and austere devotion. Bandits and prostitutes being habitually religious."[46] But he insisted that the person of the pope was not Antichrist, and that the church's members did "profess the essentials of the true Christian religion." When by an overwhelming majority the 1845 General Assembly declared that Roman baptism was not valid, he issued a rebuke. To dismiss Catholicism as no church, in the extremist spirit of Robert J. Breckinridge and his nativist allies, was to commit the greatest of blunders: "What gives it [popery] its power," Hodge wrote, "what constitutes its peculiarly dangerous character, is that it is not pure infidelity; it is not the entire rejection of the gospel, but truth surrounded by enticing and destructive error."[47]

Nuanced as Hodge's position was, he was nonetheless at bottom a "British Whig" determined that the United States were, and should remain,

46. Hodge, *Hodge,* pp. 24, 107-9, 348; Hodge, "American Quarterly Review on Sunday Mails," p. 106.

47. Hodge, *Hodge,* pp. 340-42; Scovel, "Orthodoxy in Princeton," pp. 275-76. During an earlier public eruption of anti-Catholicism Hodge had reflected, "What an unhappy business this is of [Robert J.] Breckinridge's uniting . . . in public disputations against the Catholics. He is letting himself down amazingly I think." C. Hodge to H. L. Hodge, 28 Nov. 1833, PCH.

Protestant British in their essential character. His one and only visit to England, in 1828, confirmed his regard for what he called "the mother country," whose faults did not prevent her being "the most wonderful and admirable the world has ever seen."[48] He took enormous satisfaction in Britain's prestige and influence abroad, and her social and political stability at home, founded on Protestantism and constitutional defenses against tyranny and unrestrained democracy. Whereas many Whigs tempered their Anglo-Saxonism with a conviction of the justice of Celtic dissent, and greatly admired the Irish reformer Daniel O'Connell, Hodge — his Ulster Protestant ancestry asserting itself — rejoiced in O'Connell's conviction for creating disaffection in Ireland in 1844 ("If the law and justice would fully sustain the sentence, I think it would be a great good to give him a life estate in Australia"). Only Britain's high-Tory blindness to the virtues of American republicanism really irked him.[49] Through the mid- and later 1840s he remained chronically anxious over the possibility of war with the mother country, especially over the Oregon boundary. The quarrel would be folly on two counts. Hodge shared the common Whig hostility to westward expansion, convinced that the qualitative improvement of American institutions within manageable existing boundaries was far preferable to the quantitative growth prosecuted by James K. Polk and other Democrats; thus he opposed the annexation of Texas as "a great crime, & a great calamity," as well as urging the adoption of the forty-ninth parallel as a compromise boundary in the far Northwest.[50] Secondly, a "wicked" war with Britain would tragically divide the two nations on whom the world most depended for the defense of Protestantism and freedom. As his good friend and correspondent, the Scottish Free Church leader William Cunningham, put it to him in 1852, in the brewing fight between the British and the continental forces of "Popery and arbitrary power," Britain "would confidently expect the sympathy and assistance of the United States."[51]

48. C. Hodge to S. Hodge, 27 June 1828, in Hodge, *Hodge,* pp. 200, 234. "England has transmitted to us her Anglo-Saxon life. We are bone of her bone and flesh of her flesh. . . . What we are, is but the normal development of English life under new conditions." Charles Hodge, "England and America," *BRPR* 34 (Jan. 1862): 147.

49. Hodge, "American Quarterly Review on Sunday Mails," p. 108; Howe, *Political Culture of the American Whigs,* p. 77; Hodge, *Hodge,* pp. 347, 360 (C. Hodge to W. Cunningham, 29 Jan. 1845).

50. Howe, *Political Culture of the American Whigs,* pp. 20-21; C. Hodge to H. L. Hodge, 26 Mar. 1844, PCH; C. Hodge to H. L. Hodge, 17 Apr. 1846, in Hodge, *Hodge,* pp. 350, 364; Hodge, "Princeton Review and the State of the Country," p. 656.

51. W. Cunningham to C. Hodge, 16 Oct. 1852, in Hodge, *Hodge,* p. 426.

Hodge remained aloof from campaign extravagance; in 1840 he thought "the demoralizing influence" of the Log Cabin "hurrah" campaign damaging to all.[52] Nor did he allow his Whiggery to become an unthinking partisanship. When William H. Harrison's unexpected and calamitous death handed the presidency to John Tyler, and the Whig triumph of 1840 turned sour during the Virginian's administration, Hodge blamed not just the treachery of the second-rate Tyler ("weak, . . . dishonourable & dishonest") in vetoing sound Whig financial measures. He also lost faith in his own sometime hero, Daniel Webster, for not following his cabinet colleagues' example and resigning, as well as in the party leadership as a whole for subsequently failing "to give up personal objects for the general good" and for trying to make Tyler's administration "unpopular, & . . . as disastrous as possible" — even to the point of opposing tariff and currency measures that (Hodge believed) would have hastened the return of prosperity.[53] In all this Hodge gave expression to that "antiparty" mode of thought that remained characteristic of elements in Whiggery throughout the party's lifespan and which contributed to the organization's relative lack of robustness when confronted by the political crisis of the tumultuous mid-1850s.[54]

The process by which the political alignments of the second party system yielded to a new set of allegiances in the 1850s was highly complex and marked by considerable local and regional variation. Though historians are divided over the relative importance of the elements at work, it is fair to say that the foundations of the electoral system revolving around Whig-Democratic competition were eroded through the early 1850s by a mix of issues that can be reduced to two headings: slavery and nativism. The implications of the Mexican territorial cession for the future of slavery had begun a debate only partially silenced by the Compromise of 1850, while the mass immigration from the mid-1840s had focused attention on

52. C. Hodge to H. L. Hodge, 1 Sept. 1840, PCH. In the Clay-Polk campaign four years later, Sarah and Alexander Hodge went with Mrs. Dod to hear Daniel Webster at a great Whig meeting at Trenton. Charles disapproved. "I thought they were crazy. But it seems the ladies as usual knew best. Mr. Field got them seats in the council chamber with the ladies of the governor, chief justice &c & they had a grand time. They are all for Clay & Coons." C. Hodge to H. L. Hodge, 31 May 1844, PCH.

53. C. Hodge to H. L. Hodge, 28 Jan., 13 Mar., 8 June, 18 Aug., 17 Sept., 6 Dec. 1841, 15 Dec. 1842, PCH.

54. Ronald P. Formisano, *The Birth of Mass Political Parties: Michigan, 1827-1861* (Princeton: Princeton University Press, 1971), pp. 56-80; Howe, *Political Culture of the American Whigs*, esp. 43-68; John Ashworth, *"Agrarians" & "Aristocrats": Party Political Ideology in the United States, 1837-1846* (London: Royal Historical Society, 1983), pp. 205-18.

questions of citizenship, education, prohibition, and the integration of the newcomers, Catholics in particular. Free Soilers and nativist Know Nothings were already disaffected from the second party system before the explosion over the repeal of the Missouri Compromise in 1854 destroyed the Whigs and stunned the Democrats. Out of these pieces hesitantly emerged the Republican party, but only in the second half of 1856 did it become fully clear that it, and not the Know Nothing movement, would provide the principal opposition to the continuing, but now Southern-dominated, Democratic party.[55]

These years, from 1848 to 1856, were what Hodge's son described as his father's "least productive period," a time when his nervous system was buffeted by the deaths of his wife (in 1849) and of his surrogate father, Archibald Alexander, two years later.[56] He now began to take more recreation and rest, which may be why he wrote fewer political commentaries. This makes it difficult to trace the precise route that Hodge took in his political journeying, but the general direction is clear enough. Faced with a choice of new political homes, he followed a course that divorced him from one set of heirs of Whiggery, the American party, and united him with another, the Republicans.

Given Hodge's contemporary reputation for conservative views on slavery, this seems a remarkable development. Arguing from the premise that slavery enjoyed scriptural sanction, but that slaveholding practice should conform to the laws of God, he was roundly critical both of abolitionists who, blind to Scripture, condemned slaveholding *per se,* and of Southern defenders of the "abominations" of slavery, notably the inhumane regulations relating to the marriage, family integrity, and education of blacks. Hodge sought to mediate between these two extremes, calling for an improvement in slaves' "moral, religious, and intellectual culture" that would culminate in gradual emancipation as slaves were "elevated and prepared for liberty."[57] Thus he supported colonizationists' efforts to encourage the manumission and emigration of slaves, and endorsed the

55. William E. Gienapp, *The Origins of the Republican Party 1852-1856* (New York: Oxford University Press, 1987); Stephen Maizlish, *The Triumph of Sectionalism: The Transformation of Ohio Politics, 1844-1856* (Kent, Ohio: Kent State University Press, 1983); Tyler Anbinder, *Nativism and Slavery: The Northern Know Nothings & the Politics of the 1850s* (New York: Oxford University Press, 1992); Carwardine, *Evangelicals and Politics,* pp. 199-278.

56. Hodge, *Hodge,* pp. 369-71, 375-77, 383; Stewart, *Mediating the Center,* p. 82.

57. Hodge, "Slavery," *BRPR* 8 (1836): 268-305; Charles Hodge, "Abolitionism," *BRPR* 16 (1844): 545-81; Hodge, "The Princeton Review and the State of the Country," pp. 638-41; Charles Hodge, "Emancipation," *BRPR* 21 (Oct. 1849): 582-607; Hodge, *Hodge,* pp. 333-36.

abortive Kentucky plan of emancipation of 1849, advanced by his Old School colleague Robert J. Breckinridge and other gradualists. Radical antislavery measures were quite another matter. The conduct of Joshua Giddings and other Northern representatives during the furor over the congressional gag rule in the early 1840s he judged foolish in the extreme ("The fuss they make over the right of petition is just as unreasonable as the commotion about abolition"), and when the Liberty party's vote in New York cost Clay the presidency in 1844, he continued to lament the growing political momentum of "silly" abolitionism.[58] It was a creed all the more pernicious for springing from New School Calvinism and Yankee heterodoxy.[59] Though one of these New England "sinners," Lewis Tappan, seems to have detected in 1849 a hardening in Hodge's attitude towards the voluntary slaveholder's right to church membership, the Princetonian's alienation from the abolitionist temper could not have been more clearly stated than in his essay on civil government of January 1851. Designed to encourage acquiescence in the compromise measures of 1850, it confidently set out the case for the citizen's scriptural duty of obedience to laws in general and to the Fugitive Slave Law in particular.[60]

Faced with a choice in 1856 between the American party and the Republicans, many conservative evangelicals of Whig orientation opted for the former, attracted by its explicit nativism and by the candidacy of Millard Fillmore, seen as a sectional conciliator and a facilitator of the Compromise of 1850. For his part, John C. Frémont, the Republicans' nominee for president, standing on a platform of slavery restriction, defiance to the Slave Power, and the celebration of free labor, picked up the near-unanimous support of radical antislavery denominations and also did well amongst mainstream churches, notably Congregationalists and New School Presbyterians.[61] Given that conservative Old School Presbyterians furnished notable support to Fillmore (not least Hodge's intimate friend, James W. Alexander, and his own brother, Hugh) or chose to abstain (as did another close friend, John Hall),[62] and given Hodge's

---

58. C. Hodge to H. L. Hodge, 18 June 1841, 16 Dec. 1844, in Hodge, *Hodge*, pp. 344, 349; C. Hodge to H. L. Hodge, 23 Nov. 1833, 5 May 1846, PCH.

59. Hodge, *Hodge*, pp. 77-81, 271-72, 593.

60. L. Tappan to C. Hodge, 25 Nov. 1849, PCH; Charles Hodge, "Civil Government," *BRPR* 23 (Jan. 1851): 128 and passim.

61. Carwardine, *Evangelicals and Politics*, pp. 258-69, 273-75.

62. Hall made an election day jotting in his diary: "I did not vote for Fremont, because &c nor for Buchanan, because &c nor for Fillmore, because &c." John Hall, Journal, 4 Nov. 1856, Presbyterian Historical Society.

own predilection for mediation and compromise, and his nativist inclinations, his firm decision for Frémont calls for some explanation. He had, after all, welcomed earlier movements to control the naturalization of foreigners; he had rejoiced in the success of the Know-Nothings' forerunner, the American party, in New York in the mid-1840s; and his response to Clay's defeat in 1844 was to declare, "We shall all have to turn natives."[63] On the other hand, there were elements in Fillmore's Know-Nothings that he found unappealing: he was no ally of the legal prohibitionists who brought a temperance flavor to much of nativism, nor was he friendly to the movement's overt anti-Catholicism.[64] (We should also note that the Republicans' posture was able to embrace Hodge's brand of nativism. He would shortly address the "warts and excrescences on the body politic," those few immigrants who resisted assimilation into "the essentially British Protestant character of the nation," and would tell them bluntly that "if you cannot live with Christians, you must go elsewhere.")[65] It seems clear, though, that Hodge's chief reason for voting Republican lay in his belief that Frémont gave the best answers to the troubling questions thrown up by the Kansas-Nebraska Act.

Hodge saw the repeal of the Missouri Compromise as the dishonorable betrayal of a binding compact.[66] His immediate sense of the wanton violation of the sacred by proslavery Southerners, their northern allies, and the Pierce administration was subsequently compounded by the one-sided justice in bleeding Kansas.[67] He was outraged at the South's double standards and the meekness of a divided North: "If Ohio had done to Kentucky what Missouri has done to Kansas, the South would have risen as one man and redressed the grievance. And if the North had risen as one man and told the South that Kansas should have justice, we should have had no difficulty." In the face of the Democrats' commitment to the am-

63. C. Hodge to H. L. Hodge, 10 Apr., 31 May, 8 Nov. 1844, PCH.

64. Hodge did not consider drinking wine to be in its "essential nature sinful" (a remark made in 1853, at the height of the Maine Law movement); teetotalism was certainly not sanctioned by the word of God. Hodge, *Hodge*, p. 397. In February 1856 Hodge warmly welcomed Nathaniel Banks's election as speaker, which represented not only a defeat for the South but a Republican triumph over Know-Nothingism. Hodge was not sure his brother shared his pleasure. C. Hodge to H. L. Hodge, 11 Feb. 1856, PCH; Anbinder, *Nativism and Slavery*, pp. 197-202.

65. Hodge, "Sunday Laws," pp. 759, 767.

66. C. Hodge to H. L. Hodge, 15 May 1854, PCH; Charles Hodge, "The State of the Country," *BRPR* 33 (Jan. 1861): 4.

67. "I have got so anti-Pierce that I want to volunteer for Kansas." C. Hodge to H. L. Hodge, 11 Feb. 1856, PCH.

biguous platform of "congressional non-interference" and Fillmore's hiding behind a straddling version of popular sovereignty, he judged that only Frémont offered an unequivocal defense of the nation from proslavery aggression. Some months before the election that would see the Democrats carry New Jersey on a minority vote, with the opposition seriously divided, Hodge set out his views in a letter to his brother:

> I hear you are a Fillmore man. That is better than going for Buchanan. I am for Fremont. Not for the man, but for the platform. I would not vote for my father if he endorsed the Cincinnati resolutions; and Fillmore has committed himself to worse nullification than South Carolina ever dreamt of. He has drawn a broader line between the North and South than was ever drawn before, and exalted the 300,000 slave-holders into an equivalent of the 20,000,000 of the freemen, entitled to an equal share in the government of the country. I think the great danger to the country and to the cause of justice and good government is from the divisions and concessions of the North.[68]

Hodge's embrace of Republicanism may, as John W. Stewart has implied, have reflected a shift in his views on slavery itself, as he came to see more clearly the racial underpinnings of the peculiar institution.[69] More certainly we can conclude that his support of the new party was a measure of his belief in the existence of an ever more audacious Slave Power determined to divert the Union from the direction intended by its history and founders. A decade earlier he had considered the annexation of Texas a crime against conscience carried out to advance the interests of slaveholders; he had similarly opposed the Mexican War.[70] During the political crisis of 1849-50 he ridiculed and condemned the radical Southern caucus in Washington over their defense of an abominable slave-trade in the nation's capital and their "most unreasonable" antagonism towards the free states.[71] He took alarm over Southerners' subsequent covetous designs on

68. C. Hodge to H. L. Hodge, 8 July 1856 [misdated 1850 by Archibald Alexander Hodge], in Hodge, *Hodge*, pp. 393-94. Buchanan electors secured 47 percent of the New Jersey vote, Fillmore 29 percent, and Frémont 24 percent. The respective figures for the nation as a whole were 46 percent, 21 percent, and 33 percent. Gienapp, *Origins of the Republican Party*, pp. 405-6; Anbinder, *Nativism and Slavery*, p. 265n.
69. Stewart, *Mediating the Center*, pp. 74-85.
70. C. Hodge to H. L. Hodge, 26 Mar., 2 May, 30 Oct. 1844, 4 Nov. 1847, PCH.
71. "It is really dastardly that the north has so long submitted to that abomination. A member of congress [recounts] . . . that on one occasion he was standing with a large num-

Cuba. His essay on "Civil Government" in 1851, though designed as an emollient to sectional abrasions, deprecated "a certain class of southern politicians" driven to secure disproportionate political power for the South in national government.[72] Now these same men had perpetrated the scandalous Kansas policy, and whereas in the 1840s Hodge had been ready to acquiesce in political action that he judged wrong but constitutional, he was no longer ready to submit. The Slave Power's influence he saw reaching new heights in the Dred Scott decision, which formally overturned the constitutional construction that had held sway from Washington to the death of Clay, from the Northwest Ordinance of 1787 to the compromise measures of 1850 — namely, that Congress had the right to ban slavery from the federal territories. Hodge accused these "extreme men of the Calhoun school" of effecting a "revolution" that had replaced the municipal theory of slavery with one based on the slaveholder's right to the protection of his property under the federal flag.[73] His dismay was compounded by the complicity of his Old School colleagues, notably Thornwell and Benjamin Palmer, in this "reckless violation of historical truth," the culmination of the corresponding advance among the Southern clergy of "the new, unscriptural, and anti-Christian sentiment" that slavery was a positive good.[74]

Thus Hodge's votes for Frémont in 1856 and Abraham Lincoln four years later, though indicating a remarkable distance traveled since 1850, were in his own mind simply a conservative attachment to what he believed the traditional interpretation of slavery's constitutional status in the Union. His defense of the Constitution against revolutionary theorists was the political equivalent of the theological trenches he dug around the Westminster Confession. When he cast his ballots he figuratively rubbed shoulders with those of a radical Free Soil or even abolitionist temper, but it was despite this, and out of a common concern to stand by the Founding Fathers' perceived intentions, that he found himself in

---

ber of fellow members at the door of Brown's Hotel, when about 60 negroes chained in a row, were driven by. As soon as they got opposite the Hotel, they all set up, 'Hail Columbia happy land &c' & sung it with a loud voice. The Southerners present could not stand it." C. Hodge to H. L. Hodge, 25 Jan. 1849; see also C. Hodge to H. L. Hodge, 7 Dec. 1849, PCH.

72. C. Hodge to H. L. Hodge, 1 Sept. 1851, PCH; Hodge, "Civil Government," pp. 126-27.

73. C. Hodge to H. L. Hodge, n.d. [c1860-1], CHMC-PTS; C. Hodge to J. C. Backus, 28 Dec. 1860, in Hodge, *Hodge,* pp. 464-65.

74. Charles Hodge, "The Church and the Country," *BRPR* 33 (Apr. 1861): 348-75; C. Hodge to H. L. Hodge, 18 Feb. 1861, PCH; Charles Hodge, "Short Notices. *Thanksgiving Sermon* . . . By the Rev. B. M. Palmer, D.D.," *BRPR* 33 (Jan. 1861): 167-71.

the Republicans' embrace. This was exactly what Salmon P. Chase and other Republican leaders, including Lincoln himself in his Cooper Union speech in February 1860, had intended: to represent their party to a cross-section of political temperaments as the conservative heirs of the Republic's essentially antislavery founders.[75] It was sufficient to ensure that Hodge, joined in 1860 by thousands of other conservative ex-Whigs, was as immune to the appeal of John Bell's Constitutional Unionists as he had been to the Fillmorites four years earlier, despite their explicit ambition to reach men of his conservative outlook and political ancestry.[76]

Hodge gave no indication that he considered his political path from Federalist to Whig to Republican to be anything other than a consistent progress. Through these years he sought the election of political administrations that would respect social order and encourage the economic activity and meritocratic opportunities of responsible, self-disciplined, self-improving, and publicly educated citizens — all within a moral framework that fused the doctrines of Reformed Protestant Christianity with stable republicanism. Thus the stamp of the proto-Whig of 1830, politically inspired by Sabbatarianism, would continue to mark the budding Republican of the late 1850s, when Hodge, now striving for the enforcement of Sabbath laws in the teeth of freethinking immigrants and diffident Christians, still linked respect for the Protestant Sabbath with family integrity, the nation's economic well-being, and healthy republican government. The Whig admirer of Yankee enterprise effortlessly put on the clothing of a "free labor" Republican.[77] The continuities persisted after the Civil War, as his core conservatism went on shaping his view of public affairs, and most notably his reactions to the influential radical elements within the Republican party. But this final phase of Hodge's politics is best explored after first addressing the challenge that secession and Civil War presented to his political Unionism.

III

The remorseless unfolding of events in the months following Lincoln's election drew Hodge into what was to be, politically speaking, the most

75. Eric Foner, *Free Soil, Free Labor, Free Men: The Ideology of the Republican Party before the Civil War* (New York: Oxford University Press, 1970), pp. 73-102; Roy P. Basler, ed., *The Collected Works of Abraham Lincoln*, 9 vols. (New Brunswick, N.J.: Rutgers University Press, 1953-55), vol. 3, pp. 522-50.

76. Carwardine, *Evangelicals and Politics*, pp. 296-307.

77. Hodge, "Sunday Laws," pp. 733-36, 767; Foner, *Free Soil*, pp. 11-72.

intense and controversial phase of his life. The urgency and import of the issues, which transcended partisan politics, made it much easier for church leaders, even those previously disdainful of political "meddling," to speak out, and Hodge needed little encouragement to do so. For over three decades he had been alert to the dangers of sectional alienation in both church and state, shrewdly aware of the implications for the political Union of ecclesiastical schism, and realistic from an early date about the disruptive potential of secessionist doctrine. The polarizing implications of the Nat Turner rebellion of August 1831 had not escaped him, nor had the significance of the Nullification crisis of 1832-33. Jackson's proclamation, despite the "imbecility" of the president himself, commanded his admiration for its Federalist, Websterian rejection of the state-compact theory of the origins of the federal government, but he could see that if nullifiers should ever turn into seceders "they have the opinion and sympathy of a large portion of the South in their favor."[78] Hodge was able to take a more relaxed view of "Southern gasconade" and abolitionist "fuss" and "nonsense" in the congressional battles of the early 1840s, but he was sharply alert to the disunionist dangers lurking in the congressional warfare of 1849-50.[79]

The crisis that broke late in 1860 forced Americans to ask themselves what the Union was worth. Hodge himself considered it beyond price: the question was rather like having "to estimate in dollars and cents the value of . . . [a] father's blessing or . . . [a] mother's love." The theme of the superiority of the United States over other countries had been present in his private reflections and published writings for many years. Though stopping well short of crude chauvinism, he was convinced of America's greatness and power, and its role as exemplar to the wider world. He extolled his fellow citizens' material advantages and enterprise; their "comfort, independence, and cultivation"; their inheritance of fused political and religious liberties within a Protestant culture; and their escape from the feudal rigidities and the "socialistic anarchy" to which they reactively gave rise in the Old World. Those benefits flourished under the protection of a

78. Hodge reflected astringently, "I should feel still more rejoiced at the character of [the proclamation] . . . if I thought the old gentleman understood it, or knew what he said"; he was mistaken in believing that it was not in fact the work of Secretary of State Livingston. C. Hodge to H. L. Hodge, 1 Mar., 17 July 1830, 19, 29 Nov., 4 Dec. 1832, 9 Jan., 1 Mar. 1833, PCH; C. Hodge to H. L. Hodge, 1 Oct. 1831, 15 Dec. 1832, 23 Jan. 1833, in Hodge, *Hodge*, pp. 230-33; William H. Freehling, *Prelude to Civil War: The Nullification Controversy in South Carolina, 1816-1836* (New York: Harper & Row, 1966), p. 267.

79. C. Hodge to H. L. Hodge, 18 June 1841, in Hodge, *Hodge*, p. 344.

Union that Hodge considered perpetual. Americans were tied by bonds of kin, language, religion, physical geography, and history (quite apart from political covenants), which it would be "moral degradation to disregard," for their blood had been shed in a common cause, and "their ashes lay mingled in the same graves." The Union had an organic life that bespoke a real homogeneity: "It is not a mere association, such as binds together nations of different races, languages, and political institutions, as in the Austrian empire. . . . It cannot be permanently dissevered."[80]

When the election of the "Black Republican," Lincoln, prompted Southern disunionists single-mindedly to embark on their secessionist course, Hodge reacted with much the same exasperation he had expressed in respect of Southern radicals' threats of withdrawal in 1850 ("Men might as well prescribe decapitation for the head-ache, as the destruction of the confederacy as a cure for the present difficulties").[81] His celebrated article, "The State of the Country," was written in response to South Carolina's "lamentable" threat to leave the Union, though it would appear only after the Palmetto State had passed its secession ordinance.[82] It reflected Hodge's alarm at Southern separatism and his anxiety over what he termed "the poltroonery of Northern men who go down on their knees and call themselves the sole wrong-doers" — a dig at Presbyterian colleagues, notably Henry A. Boardman, who sought to prevent the publication of an article they feared would prove a firebrand. (It also shrewdly anticipated the bewildering annual message to Congress of his fellow Old School Presbyterian, James Buchanan, in which the president declared the federal government impotent in the face of a secession movement he deemed unconstitutional.)[83] Taking seriously the threat of an independent confederacy of all fifteen slave states, and determined to meet the most terrifying challenge to the law-abiding Whig temperament since the founding of the republic, Hodge set out two main lines of argument. He told Southerners that they entirely misread Northern opinion, which was not, as they claimed, fatally poisoned with abolitionism and atheism, nor hostile to Southern interests. (As he later summarized his position, in a

---

80. C. Hodge to A. Alexander, 2 Nov., 21 Dec. 1826; C. Hodge to S. Hodge, 10 Jan. 1827; C. Hodge to H. L. Hodge, 29 Dec. 1851, in Hodge, *Hodge,* pp. 106-12, 115, 203, 352-55, 359-60, 394; Charles Hodge, "Anniversary Address," *The Home Missionary* 2 (July 1829): 17-18; Hodge, "The State of the Country," pp. 2-3, 33.

81. Hodge, "Civil Government," p. 127.

82. Hodge, *Hodge,* p. 462; C. Hodge to H. L. Hodge, 22 Nov. 1860, PCH.

83. C. Hodge to H. L. Hodge, 13 Dec. 1860, PCH; James M. McPherson, *Battle Cry of Freedom: The Civil War Era* (New York: Oxford University Press, 1988), pp. 246-51.

letter to Thornwell, "If Southern men knew the North as we know it, they would no more think of secession than they would of suicide.") Equally, he insisted that secession was an absurdity, a crime, and an illegitimate, unconstitutional means of redressing the felt wrongs of Southerners.[84]

Hodge's article was widely reprinted in the religious press. Circulating in pamphlet form, it reached a far wider audience than did most of his political writings.[85] But though welcomed (and distributed) by Unionists, it provoked bitter condemnation within the South, including sections of his own church, and lost him close friends and erstwhile admirers.[86] Thornwell, Charles Colcock Jones, and other Old School Presbyterians lamented that even the once-moderate Hodge had been infected by the abolitionist virus, and had now become violent against his old colleagues. William Madison Cunningham of LaGrange, Georgia, regretted a diabolical symbiosis: through Hodge, "Black Republicanism has become an angel of light," but "in thus canonizing and sanctifying the Republican party" Hodge had "himself become assimilated to and imbued with the spirit of that foul and fiendish" force.[87] Severely taken aback by their response, Hodge wrote to the southern Presbyterian press, as well as to particular colleagues, to insist that his article had allocated blame evenhandedly. It was not he but the Southern radicals who had shifted their ground. "People rushing along on a railroad see the trees and fences flying in the opposite direction. So our brethren of the Gulf States who are hurrying from all their old positions, think that it is not they, but others

84. Hodge, "The State of the Country," pp. 3-4 and passim; C. Hodge to J. H. Thornwell, 3 Jan. 1861, in Hodge, *Hodge,* pp. 462-63.

85. Hodge, "The Princeton Review on the State of the Country," pp. 628-30. Neither of the two modern classics that address the secession winter in the North — Kenneth M. Stampp, *And the War Came: The North and the Secession Crisis, 1860-61* (Baton Rouge: Louisiana State University Press, 1950) and David M. Potter, *Lincoln and His Party in the Secession Crisis* (New Haven: Yale University Press, 1942), give any space to Hodge, and they virtually ignore the churches. Yet Hodge's pamphlet sparked serious public debate, North and South, in the early part of 1861.

86. For the breach with John Leighton Wilson, see Stewart, *Mediating the Center,* pp. 92-93. "Perhaps you saw the paragraph quoted from a Southern paper stating that it was a great mistake that the Southern Christian had not prayed for my death as I had lived a long life & was now doing more harm than good." C. Hodge to H. L. Hodge, 6 Sept. 1861, PCH.

87. Hodge, "The Church and the Country," pp. 328-32; Hodge, "The Princeton Review on the State of the Country," pp. 628-39; Robert Manson Myers, ed., *The Children of Pride: A True Story of Georgia and the Civil War* (New Haven: Yale University Press, 1972), pp. 645, 648-51. Other Old School Northerners previously well regarded by their Southern colleagues and now, like Hodge, losing their esteem included Samuel I. Prime and Nathan Rice. Carwardine, *Evangelicals and Politics in Antebellum America,* p. 289.

who are in motion."[88] Far from joining with the abolitionists, his article had explicitly condemned them. "Abolitionist" and "Republican" were not interchangeable labels. He recognized the justice of the South's concern over fugitive slaves: the federal authorities had the duty of ensuring full compensation to all who suffered otherwise irrecoverable loss. Unlike hard-line Free Soilers, he offered the restoration of the Missouri Compromise line as a solution to the territorial issue.[89]

Hodge certainly believed that in this contribution to the public debate he had burnished the bridge-building credentials he had earned in both ecclesiastical and civic spheres over the previous quarter century. The scriptural injunction to Christians to avoid "party spirit" found a ready match in Hodge's temperamental disposition to seek harmony in the face of schism and conflict, through dialogue and understanding. Thus in the mid-1830s he sought to prevent what he regarded as an unnecessary secession from the Presbyterian church by the Old School "ultras"; the harmony at the Old School annual assembly in 1860, a surprise after the agitation of previous years, gave him enormous pleasure. International disputes, as over Oregon, and sectional abrasions, as in the crisis of 1850, prompted similar calls for reconciliation. Hodge's natural emollience was reinforced by geographical location and personal milieu. Born and bred in the lower North, a teacher of students recruited mainly from the middle tier of states, slave and free, and a man of strong lifelong friendships with many from the upper South, Hodge was most at ease with those who had a similar vested interest in ensuring that the center did indeed hold.[90] These were the people that Hodge sought most to influence when he wrote "The State of the Country": moderates and conservatives in both sections. Believing he spoke for "the people of God in the North & West" and nine out of every ten readers of the *Princeton Review,* he judged the article would temper "the *uncompromising* spirit of [Republican] party leaders" and make them more amenable to John Crittenden's compromise proposals; equally, it would help reassure and strengthen the Unionist majority in the slave states and marginalize the disunionist hotheads.[91]

88. Hodge, "The Church and the Country," p. 329.

89. C. Hodge to J. H. Thornwell, 3 Jan. 1861, and C. Hodge to H. A. Boardman, 17 Jan. 1861, in Hodge, *Hodge,* pp. 462-63, 465-66.

90. Hodge, *Hodge,* pp. 34-35, 43-46, 52-53, 159-62, 253-54, 291-310, 445.

91. C. Hodge to J. Leighton Wilson, 3 Jan. 1861, CHMC-PTS; C. Hodge to H. A. Boardman, 17 Jan. 1861, in Hodge, *Hodge,* pp. 465-66. Hodge was cheered by the endorsements and supportive letters he received from across the country, from Douglas and Breckinridge Democrats, Constitutional Union men, and from Republicans: they provided

Hodge's approach was flawed, however. First, he seriously misread the temper of the South, overestimating the depth of Unionism within the cotton states and underestimating the extent to which, as fellow conservative Robert J. Breckinridge put it to him, "force, and terror, and delusion" were pushing the revolution forward.[92] There was no shame in Hodge's misapprehension: it was not the prerogative of an ivory-tower professor only. Lincoln and most Republican leaders made a similar mistake.[93] Secondly, by the time his essay appeared, and the rolling tide of secession was underway, urgent calls for the preservation of the Union — historically the agenda of the mediators and reconcilers — themselves took on a sectional and threatening aspect, at least in the deep South: in the face of *de facto* separation, Unionism equated with coercion. Thus Hodge the champion of a perpetual Union wrestled with Hodge the peacemaker. Fearful of war, the Unionist surrendered. Hodge followed Buchanan in proposing a convention of all the states to secure a peaceful separation "by the common consent of the parties," with the proviso that secession be repudiated and "the rights and essential interests of the North as well as the South" be secured.[94] He also began to distance himself from his unequivocal Republicanism of November, declaring that his vote had been for Lincoln "not as a Republican, but as the opposition candidate" (a statement which raises more questions than it answers, given that there were three such candidates from which to choose), and claiming not to have read or (less plausibly) known anything of the party's Chicago Platform.[95] This was a shift of position that took him closer to the "poltroonery" of more equivocal Northern conservatives, but it was as much a measure of the instability of the rapidly changing political terrain as of his own vacillation.

Hodge's pragmatic concession to the reality of the new Southern con-

---

ammunition against correspondents like John Miller, who judged that Hodge's article would "denationalize the seminary & confine it to the Northern States." J. Miller to C. Hodge, 7 Jan. 1861, CHMC-PTS; Hodge, "The Church and the Country," pp. 330-31.

92. R. J. Breckinridge to C. Hodge, 19 Jan. 1861, CHMC-PTS.

93. Potter, *Lincoln and His Party*, esp. pp. 219-48, 315-35.

94. C. Hodge to J. H. Thornwell, 3 Jan. 1861, in Hodge, *Hodge*, p. 463; Hodge, "The Church and the Country," p. 339; Hodge, "The Princeton Review on the State of the Country," pp. 634-35. Hodge was not alone in hinting at a constitutionally negotiated breakup of the Union; see Chester Forrester Dunham, *The Attitude of the Northern Clergy toward the South 1860-65* (Toledo, Ohio: The Gray Co., 1942), pp. 71-76; Peter J. Parish, "The Instruments of Providence: Slavery, Civil War and the American Churches," in *Studies in Church History*, vol. 20: *The Church and War*, ed. W. J. Sheils (Oxford: Blackwell, 1983), pp. 33-34.

95. Hodge, "The Church and the Country," p. 333.

federacy was short-lived. When South Carolinians turned their guns against Fort Sumter, he knew "the case was essentially altered." Contributing to the sharp metamorphosis in Northern evangelical feeling in April 1861, Hodge abandoned the scheme of peaceful separation and berated the South for its "unreasonable, ungrateful, and wicked" attempt on the life of the "glorious" Union.[96] Thereafter Hodge's Unionism never wavered, though his unsuccessful efforts during the spring and early summer to maintain his denomination's unity gave off different and confusing signals. Before the war broke out he had hoped that Presbyterians would "contribute to the restoration of our political union" by presenting "to the world the edifying spectacle of Christian brotherhood unbroken by political convulsions."[97] A few weeks into hostilities, his vote in the General Assembly against the Spring resolutions, which called on Presbyterians to declare their loyalty to the Federal Government, was prompted as much by that pre-war aspiration as by his principled objection to the blurring of the line between spiritual and civil authority. But the image of Hodge and a small handful of the Assembly resisting the patriotic indignation of the Philadelphia press and a shower of Unionist telegrams, and refusing to join with their fellow ministers in a chorus of "The Star-Spangled Banner" at the Lord's table, prompted some to conclude that the minority's sympathies lay with the rebels. William McMichael told Hodge that they were regarded as having endorsed *"the doctrine of secession as held by the South."* Noting that only "one class — and one class only — give our course in the Assembly an unqualified approval," the pro-Southern Breckinridge Democrats, he added, "I do not feel sure you will receive this announcement with unmingled pleasure."[98]

McMichael was right: in Hodge's cosmology these Democrats represented the forces of evil. They had played an essential part in "the long-continued machinations" to establish an independent confederacy that would operate in the interests of the South's 350,000 slaveholders. The Slave Power, in Hodge's quintessential Republican analysis, had acted like a spoiled child who, until Lincoln's election and the Union's refusal to

96. Charles Hodge, "The General Assembly," *BRPR* 33 (July 1861): 559; Hodge, "The Princeton Review on the State of the Country," pp. 634-35. The drawing together of Northern evangelicals in support of the Union flag is described in Moorhead, *American Apocalypse,* pp. 35-41, and Dunham, *The Attitude of the Northern Clergy,* pp. 76-80.

97. Hodge, "The Church and the Country," pp. 326, 376.

98. Hodge, *Hodge,* pp. 22-23, 491ff; Hodge, "The General Assembly," pp. 542-68; W. McMichael to C. Hodge, 26 June 1861, CHMC-PTS.

"love . . . legalize and extend" slavery, had always got her own way.[99] Unable to advance by constitutional means, these Southerners had turned to conspiracy and subterfuge, to keep the federal forts in the South vulnerable to attack from disunionists armed with weapons amassed by disloyal public servants.[100] Their evil dream, Hodge believed, was a slave empire, "in which capital will own labour; in which one race shall have all wealth and power, and the other shall be slaves — not for a time, or during a transition state, but permanently, as the best organization of society." Thus the blessed Union ("founded by God . . . to be the home of the free, the relief of the oppressed, the instrument in his hand for the dissemination of Christianity and civil liberty throughout the world") had been deliberately overthrown to extend "barbarism, ignorance, degradation, and misery of the majority of the people."[101]

Hodge, then, was in no doubt that the wickedness of the Confederacy's ends, the exaltation of an unscriptural form of slavery, was equaled only by the wickedness of its means: a revolutionary assault on the Union. A struggle for national existence, to subdue rebels who had sinned in disobeying the properly constituted authorities, could be nothing other than a just and godly war.[102] The apocalyptic strain and exotic millennialism that James H. Moorhead has exposed among many Civil War evangelicals was missing from Hodge's writings during the conflict, but there was no lack of certainty in the righteousness and universal significance of the cause for which his fellow-citizens were dying in their hundreds of thousands.[103] Surveying the battlefield failures in the summer of 1862, Hodge told his brother: "I still have full confidence that God is on our side, and that He will bring us safe, and I trust purified, out of all our troubles." Six months later, in the even bleaker aftermath of Fredricksburg, he called for Unionists to be "[c]onfident in the justice of the national cause, assured that God is on our side," though by now his expectations of the outcome

99. Hodge, "England and America," pp. 150, 165. The choice of possessive pronoun is Hodge's.

100. Hodge specifically indicted Secretary of War John B. Floyd. Hodge, "England and America," p. 173.

101. Hodge, "England and America," pp. 150-77; Hodge, "The Princeton Review and the State of the Country," pp. 631-33, 640.

102. Charles Hodge, "The General Assembly," *BRPR* 34 (July 1862): 519-21. The issue of the just war, and the justification of the present struggle, was widely and energetically addressed, with few evangelical voices raised in opposition to the chorus to which Hodge so vigorously contributed. See Parish, "The Instruments of Providence," pp. 298-307; and Dunham, *The Attitude of the Northern Clergy,* pp. 111-18.

103. Moorhead, *American Apocalypse,* pp. 56-65; Stewart, *Mediating the Center,* p. 109.

were less assured: "We do not say that success will certainly attend the right. The wrong in this world, which for a time is the kingdom of Satan, often triumphs. But we do say, that it is a thousand-fold better to be defeated with the right, than to be triumphant with the wrong."[104]

His published essays and private correspondence reveal Hodge as a lucid and trenchant commentator on the war's management and strategy, both military and political. Through newspaper reports and personal connections, most notably his brother-in-law, General David Hunter, he maintained a remarkable grip on the detail of events.[105] Unlike many, he did not underestimate the size of the challenge facing the Lincoln administration. In his judgment, the eleven rebel states, drawing on their own considerable resources in population and materiel, were logistically at a tenfold advantage over an enemy contending with hugely extended lines of supply and communication. Hodge saw his own role, as the Union confronted this "herculean task," to be that of expositor, moral guide, and shaper of opinion.[106]

His first extended examination of war issues, an essay for the *Princeton Review* in January 1862, was directed as much at the British public as the American. "England and America" was composed during the deep crisis over the American seizure of the British steamer, *The Trent,* with its undiplomatic cargo of Confederate envoys. The vituperative British reaction seemed to the Anglophile Hodge to confirm beyond all doubt the deeply disturbing impression that had steadily grown since the start of hostilities: that "[c]onstitutional, anti-slavery England throws the whole weight of her sympathy in favour of this unrighteous pro-slavery rebellion." British vessels had used the West Indies as a base from which to break the Union blockade of Southern ports; rebel ambassadors had been received in London; the British press, including evangelical religious journals that should have known better, had been contemptuous of Lincoln's professed reasons for going to war. A profoundly indignant Hodge thus wrote to show his British readers that they had "joined the wrong against the right" and had unwittingly given their moral support to "a pro-slavery rebellion," "an unrighteous effort to establish a government whose cornerstone is domestic slavery."[107] There is no way of precisely computing the

104. C. Hodge to H. L. Hodge, 15 July 1862, in Hodge, *Hodge*, p. 475; Charles Hodge, "The War," *BRPR* 35 (Jan. 1863): 168-69; C. Hodge to H. L. Hodge, 15 Apr. 1865, PCH.

105. See, for example, C. Hodge to H. L. Hodge, 24 July 1861, in Hodge, *Hodge,* pp. 472-74; C. Hodge to H. L. Hodge, 8 Apr. 1863, CHMC-PTS.

106. Hodge, "The War," p. 168; Hodge, *Hodge*, pp. 470-71.

107. Hodge, "England and America," pp. 147-77; Hodge, *Hodge*, pp. 468-69.

influence of the essay: we may simply note that Hodge's voice gave additional color to that chorus of American evangelical and humanitarian voices that very slowly and jerkily brought progressive opinion in Britain to recognize the moral imperatives behind the Union's war aims.[108]

Hodge similarly invoked conscience and moral purpose in his efforts to build the widest possible base of domestic support for the war. True to his essentially consensual understanding of the social process, he used the pages of the *Princeton Review* to remind "all good men" of their duty harmoniously to rally to government: the Union administration was the agent of national purposes carried out on national principles. Consciously avoiding appeals to party sentiment, he showed how in both its ends and its means the government was operating in the best national interest.[109]

Hodge's analysis of the administration's war aims provided a philosophical and practical defense of Lincoln's handling of the issues of Union and emancipation. In the same month that the president issued his Emancipation Proclamation, Hodge published his essay on "The War." He insisted that the preservation of the Union and Constitution was the one and only proper object of the conflict — as had been set out in the congressional (Crittenden-Johnson) resolutions in the early months of the war. To make abolition an objective in itself, as radical evangelicals had been urging ever more insistently, would be doubly mistaken and invite certain defeat. First, it would be morally wrong. True, slavery in the United States had become "a burden and curse," but that in itself did not justify the catastrophe of war. "Nothing can be a legitimate object of war but something which a nation has not only a right to attain, but which it is also bound to secure." What made the present conflict just was the Union's moral obligation to suppress a rebellion that threatened its very existence.[110] Secondly, a change in declared war aims would be inexpedient, for it would shatter the coalition of Republicans and Democrats, conservatives and radicals, on which victory depended; that, surely, had been the

108. Betty Fladeland, *Men and Brothers: Anglo-American Antislavery Cooperation* (Urbana: University of Illinois Press, 1972), pp. 382-410; Peter J. Parish, *The American Civil War* (New York: Holmes & Meier, 1975), pp. 381-89.

109. Hodge, "The War," pp. 141, 155, 168; Charles Hodge, "Retrospect of the History of the Princeton Review," in the *Index to the Princeton Review* (Philadelphia: Peter Walker, 1871), p. 35; Hodge, *Hodge*, pp. 460-61.

110. "The difference between [emancipation's] being a means and an end, is as great as the difference between blowing up a man's house as a means of arresting of a conflagration, and getting up a conflagration for blowing up his house." Hodge, "The War," p. 152.

implication of the fall 1862 elections, when Democrats were able to exploit the fears over emancipation and racial amalgamation to make significant congressional gains. The lesson, then, was clear: "We must keep right, and we must keep united, or we must be defeated."[111]

In Hodge's view, Lincoln's Emancipation Proclamation did nothing to change or compromise the Union's stated objectives. Declaring free those slaves in areas still under Confederate control Hodge considered a legitimate weapon of war for the commander-in-chief, especially when the rebels had persistently refused all opportunity to return to the Union on terms that protected their peculiar institution. Yet the reality of the Proclamation, as both Lincoln and Hodge understood, was to push events in such a way as to blur the distinction between previously stated means and ends. Preservation of the Union was still the ostensible objective, but it would hardly be a Union for slaveholders. Hodge acknowledged this when he wrote that remaining true to the original war aims would not only ensure victory, but would mean "that the abolition of slavery will follow in a natural and healthful manner." Though the Proclamation (morally grand as it was) did no more than instruct military officers "to regard and treat all slaves who come within their power as freemen," this was still enough to produce radical change over time. By the summer of 1864 Hodge, along with the whole northern Old School General Assembly, had come to the view that for the preservation of "our national life . . . slavery should be at once and for ever abolished" across the whole Union.[112] Hodge and his fellow conservatives now stood on the same ground that more radical antislavery evangelicals had reached from opposite premises.[113]

Hodge similarly endorsed Lincoln's policy regarding civil liberties. The issues of arbitrary arrest, press censorship, and conscription rivaled the questions of race and emancipation in divisiveness. Subjecting the administration's actions to the test of moral law, Hodge judged that Lincoln had

111. Hodge, "The War," pp. 150-55.

112. Hodge, "The War," pp. 166-67; Hodge, "The Princeton Review and the State of the Country," pp. 638-41; Charles Hodge, "The General Assembly," *BRPR* 36 (July 1864): 538-51; Hodge, "The Princeton Review on the State of the Country," pp. 640-41.

113. Parish, "The Instruments of Providence," p. 311. For radical voices, see Victor B. Howard, *Religion and the Radical Republican Movement 1860-1870* (Lexington: University of Kentucky, 1990), pp. 1-89; Moorhead, *American Apocalypse*, pp. 96-104; John R. McKivigan, *The War against Proslavery Religion: Abolitionism and the Northern Churches 1830-1865* (Ithaca: Cornell University Press, 1984), pp. 183-201; James M. McPherson, *The Struggle for Equality: The Abolitionists and the Negro in the Civil War and Reconstruction* (Princeton: Princeton University Press, 1964), pp. 52-307.

used these means in strict proportion to the threat facing the Union, and within the limits imposed by the Constitution. Loyal to its ideals of liberty and constitutional order, the government had ensured the humane treatment of Confederate prisoners, shown respect for rebels' private property, and refused to consider stirring up servile rebellion. Hodge reflected privately, during the summer disappointments of 1862, on "the great advantages of a military despotism in time of war over a republic"; later, in public, he declared that the real danger to American liberties lay in "the masses" and in "State pride," not the federal authorities, as evidenced in the outbreak of the rebellion itself. Hodge, the law-and-order Whig, fearful of Democratic populism, saw no threat of presidential despotism.[114]

The citizen's duty to this legitimate government was one of cheerful obedience. "[W]e are bound not to despond," Hodge wrote at one of the lowest points of a war that induced in him sleeplessness, tears, and depression. In all likelihood his public grappling with the meaning of Union calamities, the need for sacrifice, and the acceptance of burdens was at least in part a means of personal therapy. As John W. Stewart has remarked, it seems improbable that Hodge's explanations of the inscrutable relationship between God's judgment and human suffering would have occasioned much cheer amongst his readers. But his repeated message of obedience to the government, and avoidance of "factious opposition" even in the face of the folly and misjudgment of particular leaders, made its own contribution to the remarkable public loyalty to the Union cause over four bloody years.[115] Though a handful of militant abolitionists and a more numerous minority of peace Democrats bitterly demurred, most evangelicals echoed Hodge's insistence on public loyalty to an administration whose moral authority derived from God. James H. Moorhead has eloquently described how the repressive mentality that characterized most pro-Union ministers "contributed to the blurring of lines between dissent and disloyalty."[116]

114. Hodge, "The War," pp. 155-65; C. Hodge to H. L. Hodge, 15 July 1862, in Hodge, *Hodge*, p. 475; Hodge, "The Princeton Review on the State of the Country," p. 636.

115. Hodge, "The War," pp. 142-47; Hodge, "The Princeton Review on the State of the Country," pp. 634-36; Stewart, *Mediating the Center*, pp. 98, 100-101.

116. Moorhead, *American Apocalypse*, pp. 133-63 (quotation on p. 151). For a review of Old School Presbyterian voices, less insistently political than most but very generally supportive of the Union, and of the denomination's minority of provocatively mute pastors (notably William Plumer of Western Theological Seminary and S. B. McPheeters of St. Louis) see Lewis Vander Velde, *The Presbyterian Churches and the Federal Union* (Cambridge: Harvard University Press, 1932), pp. 280-333.

In line with his own precepts, Hodge kept private his sometimes-sharp criticism of the management of the Union war effort. Halleck, whose appointment to chief command he had initially welcomed as a means of ending the "confusion" caused by Stanton at the War Department, he soon judged an utter failure; the administration's efforts to explain as accidental the "inexcusable and criminal sacrifice of life" at Fredricksburg suggested that "God had given up our rulers to fatuity."[117] His criticisms included Lincoln, whom he believed to be sometimes too obstructed by radical Republicans to be entirely his own master. In public, however, he defended the President from attack: "We do not claim for Mr. Lincoln the graces which a dancing-master can bestow," he wrote quite early in the war. "But we do regard him as a man of mind, of unimpeachable integrity, of unbending firmness, of kind and gentle feelings, and of genuine simplicity of character," whose qualities would secure him a place in Americans' affections second only to Washington. Hodge's admiration grew to the point that his tribute to the assassinated president as "a great man" marked both the depth of his own profound grief and his belief that over time Lincoln had grown into the presidency, which he had graced with sagacity, personal integrity, simplicity, fixity of purpose, pragmatism, and a spirit of conciliation. Even so, Hodge's preference for Lincoln over George McClellan as presidential candidate in 1864 was by no means clear-cut. Ever since McClellan's impressive work in organizing the Army of the Potomac in 1861, Hodge had remained his unstinting admirer, and regarded the Democratic nominee as "a gentleman, a Christian, and a man of superior ability." Decisively, however, the candidate was tied to a party whose peace wing had fashioned a "mean, contemptible, and treacherous" platform. Hodge considered McClellan "a first-rate Captain in a very bad ship, and with a horribly bad crew. . . . I have no notion of going to sea with him. I wish and pray for his defeat, because I do not wish to see the Democratic party, which has brought all these troubles and horrors upon us, restored to power."[118] Behind Hodge's support for the broad-based

---

117. C. Hodge to H. L. Hodge, 15 July 1862, 7, 24 Dec. 1862, in Hodge, *Hodge,* pp. 475-80; C. Hodge to J. C. Backus, 31 Jan. 1863, PCH. Not surprisingly, Hodge voted the Republican ticket in November 1862, "though not satisfied with the powers that be." C. Hodge to H. L. Hodge, 4 Nov. 1862, PCH.

118. Hodge, "England and America," pp. 152-53; Hodge, *Hodge,* pp. 482-83; Hodge, "President Lincoln," pp. 445-46; C. Hodge to H. L. Hodge, 7 Sept. 1864, 15 Apr. 1865, PCH. Hodge and his brother were sharply divided in their estimate of McClellan, whom Hugh criticized for having endorsed the conservative peace Democrat, George Woodward, for governor of Pennsylvania in 1863, and for "disingenuously" maintaining that the Democratic platform

"Union" ticket in 1864 (which hauled in the evangelical vote even more powerfully than had the Republicans in 1860)[119] lay an inflexible and nearly lifelong partisan aversion to the values and philosophy of Jackson and his heirs.

Hodge's dallying with a presidential candidate who did not see emancipation as an essential condition of peace was an indication of his continuing conservatism even within the radicalizing context of war. After Appomattox, with the Union saved, that conservatism more thoroughly reasserted itself. Hodge accepted that God's principal purpose in inflicting the war had been the "sudden and final overthrow" of a system of slavery that had been immune to gradual reform. But besides this great radical alteration to the American social landscape, the conflict was also designed to confirm and clarify certain continuities in the country. It had determined limits of states' powers, but not obliterated those powers; brought to full consciousness a pre-existing but partially dormant sense of nationality; developed the nation's embryonic power and resources; and carried to new degrees of intensity the spirit of benevolence, humanitarianism, and religious devotion.[120] It was in this context of the reassertion and intensification of established habits that Hodge addressed the issues facing the political nation on the return of peace: the treatment of the Confederates, the organization of post-emancipation society, and the rights of the freedmen.

In Lincoln the conciliator, Hodge found a spiritual brother. In line with much Northern opinion, he unreservedly endorsed the principles on which the President built his reconstruction policy during the later stages of the war. Lincoln, he explained, had been right to distinguish between the wickedness of the sin (Southern slavery; rebellion) and those caught up in it, who might not necessarily be wicked people. Provided there were no threat to the nation's security, the guiding principles in the treatment of former rebels should be magnanimity, generosity, and the avoidance of judicial vengeance.[121] Hodge's instinctive preference for reconciliation was

in 1864 was compatible with loyal Unionism. C. Hodge to H. L. Hodge, 16 Sept. 1864, in Hodge, *Hodge*, pp. 480-81. See also Stephen W. Sears, ed., *The Civil War Papers of George B. McClellan: Selected Correspondence, 1860-1865* (New York: Ticknor & Fields, 1989), p. 524.

119. Howard, *Religion and the Radical Republican Movement*, pp. 68-89; Stephen L. Hansen, *The Making of the Third Party System: Voters and Parties in Illinois, 1850-1876* (Ann Arbor: UMI Research Press, 1980), pp. 141-43. See also Dale Baum, *The Civil War Party System: The Case of Massachusetts, 1846-1876* (Chapel Hill: University of North Carolina Press, 1984), pp. 91, 95-100.

120. Hodge, "President Lincoln," pp. 439-43.

121. Hodge, "President Lincoln," pp. 450-56.

undoubtedly reinforced by his concern to reestablish once-close friendships disrupted by war. The "long and affectionate embrace" that he and his lifelong friend John Johns enjoyed after several years of enforced separation was a metaphor for the broader national reconciliation that Hodge desired.[122] One element in that process, he was sure, was the healing of Presbyterian divisions. He deeply deplored the sour actions of the General Assembly of May 1865. Meeting under the dark shadow cast by Lincoln's death, the majority of ministers approved the punitive "Pittsburgh orders," which made repentance of the sin of secession the terms of Southerners' readmission. Apart from being beyond the legitimate sphere of the church, Hodge complained, the orders operated in defiance of Christ's appeal for his people "to be united in one organic body." The reunion of sectionalized churches was "almost indispensable" to the political reconciliation the government and "all good citizens" deeply desired. Hodge echoed the Republican *New York Times* in criticizing both Presbyterian and Congregational churches for missing an opportunity to follow the emollient example of the Episcopalians.[123]

Hodge similarly endorsed Lincoln's insistence that the rebel states abolish slavery before they could be fully reintegrated into the Union. Both men tenaciously held to the truth that "all men are by nature one." Hodge found in "the great scriptural truth of the unity of the human race as to origin and species" the iron argument against enslavement as a permanent condition. With Lincoln he maintained that, regardless of skin color and "unessential differences in the varieties of men, . . . every man fit to be free (and not otherwise) was entitled to be free; that every man able to manage property had the right to hold property; and that every man capable of discharging the duties of a father is entitled the custody of his children." Equally, "every man who has the intelligence and moral character necessary to the proper exercise of the elective franchise is entitled to enjoy it, if compatible with the public good." Hodge took a colorblind view of suffrage while retaining his lifelong concern to limit the privilege to those with the necessary moral and intellectual equipment to exercise it for the common good.[124]

122. They met in May 1866. Johns, Bishop of Virginia in the Protestant Episcopal Church, apparently said, "Charley, you have been a bad boy, but I'll forgive you." Hodge, *Hodge*, pp. 564-65. See also C. Hodge to F. McFarland, 15 July 1869, CHMC-PTS.

123. Hodge, *Hodge*, pp. 491-98; Hodge, "The Princeton Review and the State of the Country," pp. 651-55; Charles Hodge, "The General Assembly," *BRPR* 37 (July 1865): 496-514; J. C. Backus to C. Hodge, 28 June 1866, CHMC-PTS.

124. Charles Hodge, "Examination of some Reasonings against the Unity of Mankind,"

These twin ambitions of magnanimity towards the white South and rights for the freedmen proved the crux of Reconstruction politics. Andrew Johnson, though entering the White House with a reputation as the scourge of the Slave Power, would soon disappoint those congressional Republicans who sought a radical re-ordering of the Southern social and political order. Faced with a choice between the rehabilitation of the secessionist leaders and the destruction of a caste system, the Negro-hating Tennessean chose the former. His increasingly powerful Republican critics were driven by a variety of motives, of which the most potent were the desire to exercise political control over the postwar South and ensure the dead had not died in vain, the vengeful wish to punish the instigators of war, and real humanitarian concern for the vulnerable ex-slaves.[125] In the power struggle between the executive and legislative branches, Hodge's private sympathies lay at first with the president. When Johnson vetoed the Freedmen's Bureau Bill, designed to extend the life and expand the role of the wartime agency, he readily took Johnson's part against his moderate and radical critics. Hodge's view was much of a piece with the position he had taken over the Pittsburgh orders, and if made public would perhaps have reinforced the charges of "lukewarm loyalty and half-hearted devotion to the country" that had been leveled at him in the summer of 1865.[126] But as events developed during 1866, with the further alienation of moderate and conservative Republicans from the president, and with the Democrats reasonably hoping to make electoral capital out of Republican divisions, Hodge found his own course (yet again) shaped by his anti-Democratic animus. He had no enthusiasm for the Fourteenth Amendment, which opened the door to black suffrage, and which he feared would be used punitively in the South by the Radicals (who included "such outrageously wicked men as [Ben] Butler and [Thaddeus] Stevens") to give "the whole power to the negroes and a few hundred renegade white men in every State." Even so, he could not tol-

---

BRPR 34 (July 1862): 435-64; Hodge, "President Lincoln," pp. 456-57. For Lincoln's conversion to limited black suffrage in the reconstructed South, see LaWanda Cox, *Lincoln and Black Freedom: A Study in Presidential Leadership* (Urbana: University of Illinois Press, 1981), especially pp. 117-31; and Phillip Shaw Paludan, *The Presidency of Abraham Lincoln* (Lawrence: University of Kansas Press, 1994), pp. 263-66, 277-78, 308-10.

125. Eric L. McKitrick, *Andrew Johnson and Reconstruction* (Chicago: University of Chicago Press, 1960); Kenneth M. Stampp, *The Era of Reconstruction 1865-1877* (New York: Knopf, 1965), pp. 83-154; Eric Foner, *Reconstruction: America's Unfinished Revolution 1863-1877* (New York: Harper & Row, 1988), pp. 228-80.

126. C. Hodge to H. L. Hodge, 26 Feb. 1866, in Hodge, *Hodge,* p. 485; Hodge, "The Princeton Review on the State of the Country," pp. 636-37, 656-57.

erate voting for a party that had been "to a large extent disloyal" in the war. When Johnson Republicans and Democrats allied behind a Copperhead gubernatorial candidate in the fall elections in Pennsylvania, Hodge was utterly appalled.[127]

*   *   *

During the nervous days that marked the descent into war, Hodge maintained that he had "never taken any interest or part in politics as between one party and another, between bank and anti-bank, tariff and anti-tariff"; his chronic concern, he maintained, was "only between righteousness and unrighteousness." If in denying the influence on himself of party feeling Hodge was the victim of rhetorical self-deception (an understandable corollary of a last, desperate attempt at sectional bridge-building), he also provided an essential clue to his political journeying. "In this world," he would write, "life is a constant struggle against the causes of death. Liberty is maintained only by unsleeping vigilance against the aggressions of power; virtue is of necessity in constant antagonism to vice, and truth to error."[128] In early manhood and middle age Hodge located that unrighteousness and those aggressions of power within the "infidel" populism of Jackson's Democracy. In joining battle with the Jacksonians, Hodge the conservative sought to defend the social order and control democratic political change, but in his Reformed concern for embattled Sabbatarians and vulnerable Indians there were already signs of a moral exasperation that might modify Princeton's reputation as "the great conservative influence" in the nation. The Hodge who privately judged that Jackson's treatment of the Georgia missionaries was a sufficient offense against conscience to warrant rebellion expressed the same righteous indignation that would later lead him to identify with Free Soilers seeking to fashion an antislavery Kansas. That indignation drew him into a Republican party whose sectional orientation repelled many of his Old School colleagues in the free states. It prompted, in "The State of the Country," a moral indictment of Southern secessionists that his Presbyte-

127. C. Hodge to H. L. Hodge, 3 Oct. 1866, in Hodge, *Hodge*, p. 486; McKitrick, *Andrew Johnson and Reconstruction*, p. 409. It is more than likely that Hodge's particular animus against Thaddeus Stevens was influenced by the congressman's reputation as a libertine and trickster. McKitrick, *Andrew Johnson and Reconstruction*, pp. 262-63. When it came to the impeachment proceedings against Johnson, Hodge took the president's side. C. Hodge to H. L. Hodge, 12, 19 May 1868, PCH.
128. Hodge, "The Church and the Country," p. 333; Hodge, *Hodge*, pp. 255-56.

rian associates on both sides of the Mason-Dixon line regarded as provocative and dangerous. Hodge continued to regard himself as a conservative defender of ancient constitutional landmarks, but his political course between 1854 and 1861 made its own contribution to the sectional polarization he so deeply deplored.

Hodge's political influence cannot be precisely measured, though there is no doubt that his vigorous essays and the ministry of his thousands of students ensured that a Reformed understanding of public duty and citizenship continued to shape popular thinking about politics. It is clear too that the electoral triumphs of the young Republican party depended on its reaching well beyond the limits of the Free Soil combinations that preceded it, and that without the support of ex-Whigs and conservative evangelicals of Hodge's stamp, especially in the states of the lower North, Lincoln would surely have suffered defeat. The Republican coalition comprised in part an amalgam of radical, moderate, and conservative evangelicals, one whose significance grew even more important during the war itself, as the Lincoln administration strove to sustain a vigorous Union sentiment in the face of mounting war-weariness. Hodge's writings in celebration of the national cause and in defense of the energetic actions of the Union government contributed to the preservation of that evangelical coalition and, by extension, to Lincoln's remarkable re-election in 1864 and eventual Unionist victory.

Only with the Radical Republicans' takeover of Reconstruction policy did that broad-based evangelical coalition begin to fall apart, as Hodge's own hostility to the Radicals' schemes made clear.[129] The Union saved, he returned to the role of reconciler and intersectional bridge-builder that he had pursued for much of the pre-war period. Throwing off the despondency that so oppressed him during the war, he recovered his essential optimism: as he told Bishop Johns in 1874, "I really believe that the world, on the whole, is getting better, and that the cause of Christ is on the advance." Though he continued to harbor reservations about mass democracy and the threat to government from party hacks and placemen, he

---

129. For the psychological exhaustion of Northern evangelicals in confronting the problems of the postwar South, their shallow understanding of the operations of the free economic market, and their widespread acceptance of the return to white supremacy and racial segregation in the ex-Confederate states, see Moorhead, *American Apocalypse,* pp. 112-23, 178-217. Howard, *Religion and the Radical Republican Movement,* pp. 90-211, offers a meticulous examination of radical evangelical views on postwar policy towards the South and the ex-slaves, but asserts rather than proves their political influence, and gives little sense of the internal strains that Reconstruction policy set up within evangelical Protestantism.

could take pleasure in the resilience of American republicanism, the deepening sense of nationhood, the increased authority of government, and the country's striking economic advance. By the time of his death the insistent drum beat of sectionalism, the accompaniment of his prime, had yielded to the politics of compromise and consensus. But the reunion of 1877 was secured on terms that left the interests of the freedmen dangerously exposed. Hodge died soon thereafter. We are left with a question that may prompt an intuitive guess, but no sure answer: which would more profoundly have shaped his course towards the post-Reconstruction South, his emollient conservatism or his concern for righteousness?

Charles Hodge's Antislavery Moment

ALLEN C. GUELZO

$10 Reward

RUNAWAY from the Subscriber living in Monmouth county, near the Court-House, a black boy, of a lightish colour, named Elias; but since, it is said, has changed his name, and calls himself Bob. He is about 5 feet 9 inches high, rather slender built, a little round shouldered, about 19 years of age; on his under lip has a scar occasioned by the kick of a horse, and on the main joint of his little finger, on his right hand, has a scar, which he received by the cut of a scythe; one of his big toes has been split by the cut of an axe. He had on when he left home, a dark homespun drab cloth coatee, mixed satinet pantaloons, and black hair cap. He took another suit with him, which he was seen dressed in at Hightstown, on Sunday evening last, white hat, striped roundabout, and tow trowsers. Whoever will take up said boy and return him to the subscriber, shall receive the above reward, with all reasonable charges.

This broadside, advertising for the return of a runaway slave, is not an uncommon document from the antebellum American republic. What is sur-

I want to acknowledge the assistance of several individuals in locating documents and sources for this paper, most importantly Graham R. Hodges (Colgate University), Elizabeth Epstein (New Jersey State Archives), Mark Noll (Wheaton College), Raymond Cannata (Princeton Theological Seminary), and Peter Wallace (University of Notre Dame).

prising about it is that it was published, not in the slaveholding Southern states, but in New Jersey, and not in the eighteenth century, when slaveholding was still prevalent in most of the North, but in September of 1830, more than a quarter-century after New Jersey passed an emancipation statute that supposedly made it a "free" state.[1] Like many other places in the North, the 1804 New Jersey emancipation statute only created a gradual timetable for the elimination of slavery, and even though the process was hurried somewhat in 1846 when the legislature turned New Jersey's 700 remaining slaves into "apprentices" whose subsequent offspring would be automatically free, nevertheless those "apprenticeships" were for life.[2] Slavery in New Jersey was far from a clearly marked category.

The ambivalence of New Jersey's status as a "free" state provides an ironically appropriate backdrop to Charles Hodge, whose attempts as a theologian and intellectual to come to terms with slavery were fully as mottled as those of his adopted state. Nothing has more severely compromised Hodge's moral standing in the intellectual history of the American nineteenth century than his well-known and persistent refusal to condemn the exploitation of human beings as slaves, and his insistence from his first published writing on slavery in 1836 until the very eve of military emancipation during the Civil War that slavery was justifiable and abolition unjustifiable. This has not made for comfortable reading among the friends of his theology, and accordingly a number of them have attempted to qualify and sometimes condone Hodge's unapologetic support of slavery. William A. Barker, for instance, insisted that Hodge was actually more "ready to welcome and support emancipation when the tortuous course of Providence finally did produce it" than his writings might indicate; Peter Wallace and Mark Noll have gingerly suggested that Hodge occupied a "centrist" position that deplored both abolitionism and proslavery advocacy; and John Stewart believes that Hodge actually shifted positions over time from an unreflective endorsement of slavery to a more integrated

1. The original of William Van Dorn's broadside is in the collections of the Monmouth County Historical Association and is reproduced in Graham Russell Hodges, *Slavery and Freedom in the Rural North: African-Americans in Monmouth County, New Jersey, 1665-1865* (Madison: University of Wisconsin Press, 1997), p. 176.

2. William Freehling, *The Road to Disunion*, vol. 1: *Secessionists at Bay, 1776-1854* (New York: Oxford University Press, 1990), pp. 138-141; Paul Finkelman, *Slavery and the Founders: Race and Liberty in the Age of Jefferson* (Armonk, NY: M. E. Sharpe, 1996), pp. 57-79; Finkelman, "Slavery, the 'More Perfect Union,' and the Prairie State," *Journal of the Illinois State Historical Association* 80 (Winter 1987): 248-69; Daniel R. Ernst, "Legal Positivism, Abolitionist Litigation, and the New Jersey Slave Case of 1845," *Law and History Review* 4 (Fall 1986): 364-65.

concern for racial unity.[3] But other observers have been less patient with Hodge. Larry Tise's comprehensive survey of proslavery argumentation and ideology singles out Hodge's writings as "the most important and instructive contributions toward the formation of a national proslavery ideology of any nineteenth century American"; Leonard J. Trinterud's sesquicentennial essay on Hodge concluded sadly, "Until the last he sought to play down controversy and to conciliate the South in every possible way"; and even Hodge's Old School contemporary disgustedly remarked that Hodge "has done more to pervert the public mind on the subject of slavery than any hundred men in the Church."[4]

Hodge's understanding of slavery is a large mystery in a small place, and so it is easy to dismiss the confusing readings of Hodge's ideas as embarrassing, but fundamentally irrelevant, to a larger appreciation of Charles Hodge, or the outcome one might expect from the study of an intellectual venturing far from his real expertise. No one, I suspect, would object to such a dismissal more vehemently than Charles Hodge. What most commentators on Hodge have missed in evaluating Hodge's unlovely pronouncements on slavery is the personal context of slavery for Charles Hodge, for both Hodge and Princeton Theological Seminary were deeply entwined with slaveholding, both as a national ideological problem but also as an immediate, backyard practice in a state where slavery had far from faded by the time Hodge wrote his first and most sensational essay on slavery in 1836. Slavery was also thickly interwoven into the fabric of Hodge's notions of social and political economy, especially as a conservative Whig. But the very structure of that experience and that thought led Hodge, by the oddest of logic, to an antislavery moment that both unnerved him and unnerved the religious component of the entire proslavery argument. Charles Hodge on slavery is, by this measure, both less and more mysterious than he has seemed.

3. Barker, "The Social Views of Charles Hodge (1797-1878): A Study in 19th Century Calvinism and Conservatism," in *Presbyterian: Covenant Seminary Review* 1 (1975): 14; Peter Wallace, "The Defense of the Forgotten Center: Charles Hodge and the Enigma of Emancipation in Antebellum America," unpublished paper, 1996, pp. 41-42; Mark Noll, "The Civil War in the History of Theology," unpublished paper, 1994, pp. 12-14; John W. Stewart, *Mediating the Center: Charles Hodge on American Science, Language, Literature, and Politics* (Princeton: Princeton Theological Seminary, 1995), pp. 85-86.

4. Tise, *Proslavery: A History of the Defense of Slavery in America, 1701-1840* (Athens: University of Georgia Press, 1987), p. 278; Trinterud, "Charles Hodge," in *Sons of the Prophets: Leaders in Protestantism from Princeton Seminary* (Princeton: Princeton University Press, 1963), pp. 35, 37.

If New Jersey had been a "free" state after the pattern we usually associate with "free" states before the Civil War, there might be some excuse for Hodge's willingness to condone slavery, on the ground that Hodge lacked sufficient personal familiarity with the hideous abuses of the slave system to erase his indifference. But no such excuse actually exists in the case of Charles Hodge. Born in Philadelphia in 1797, he grew up in a district on Water Street, north of Market Street, where the first federal census indicated that at least nineteen slaves lived.[5] By the time Hodge moved to New Jersey, first as a student at the College of New Jersey and then at the new Princeton Theological Seminary, New Jersey had already enacted its gradual emancipation program, but the immediate environs of Hodge's Princeton in Mercer County were among those least eager to begin the long walk toward the ending of slavery. Agitation for emancipation had actually begun in New Jersey as early as 1780, but it had met with four successive legislative rebuffs between 1780 and 1794, and the gradual emancipation bill which finally passed the legislature in 1804 only restrained the continuance of slavery by providing that the children of slaves born after July 4, 1804, would be freed at age twenty-five in the case of a male child or twenty-one if female.[6] The result was that, for nearly a generation after the 1804 emancipation statute, slavery remained a relatively undisturbed feature of New Jersey life. In rural Hunterdon County, which bordered on Hodge's Princeton, the proportion of slaves in the population had actually been on the rise by the time of the 1804 emancipation statute, and slave sales of "a healthy young black woman . . . principally employed in cooking and housework" or of "the time of a Black Man Who has four Years to Serve" and who "has been accustomed to Farming" remained common. The last slave sale in Hunterdon County did not occur until 1836, and nine slaves were still held in bondage there as "apprentices" until at least 1850.[7]

The situation in Princeton itself was, if anything, even more unattractive. By the time of the 1830 federal census, Charles Hodge's Princeton still held twenty-one slaves in bondage in 1830; and the total "colored" population of Princeton gave the college town one of highest

5. *Heads of Families At the First Census of the United States Taken in the year 1790* (Washington, 1908), pp. 217-219.

6. Arthur Zilversmit, *The First Emancipation: The Abolition of Slavery in the North* (Chicago: University of Chicago Press, 1967), pp. 141, 152, 159, 175, 192-93; Hodges, *Slavery and Freedom*, pp. 148-49.

7. Hubert G. Schmidt, *Rural Hunterdon: An Agricultural History* (New Brunswick, N.J.: Rutgers University Press, 1946), pp. 247, 249, 250; Edgar J. McManus, *Black Bondage in the North* (Syracuse, N.Y.: Syracuse University Press, 1973), p. 184.

concentrations of black residents in the state. Although most of the black population was classified as "free," the term "free" had various levels of meaning in New Jersey that the census forms did not accommodate, and the unusually high number of "free colored" persons recorded in the immediate environs of Nassau Hall and in the boarding houses used by non-resident students raises an interesting question about how free many of Princeton's black population actually were.[8] This question is complicated by the unusually high percentages of Princeton students from slaveholding states. Since before the Revolution, New Jersey's relaxed attitude toward slavery and the unwillingness of the college's leadership to make slavery an issue made the college a highly popular alternative for the education of the sons of Southern gentry. Between 1800 and 1860, as much as one-third of the student population (which reached 341 undergraduates in 1861) was drawn from slaveholding states.[9] In 1848, out of a total enrollment of 257 students, there were 25 Virginians, 18 North Carolinians, and 45 others drawn from the deep South.[10] Whig Hall, which had included Charles Hodge as a member during his undergraduate days, had a long history of Southern predominance in its membership (Jefferson Davis was elected an honorary member in 1847), and debates on slavery in Whig Hall in 1802, 1817, 1819, 1839, and 1851 uniformly resulted in condemnations of emancipation, colonization, and William Lloyd Garrison.[11]

The climate of opinion at Princeton Theological Seminary was just as heavy with proslavery influence. In 1828, the seminary's sixteenth year of operation, students from slaveholding states comprised 21 percent of the student body (23 out of 108 students); ten years later, that proportion had increased to a quarter of the theological students (22 out of 92), and another decade on, Southerners still accounted for over 20 percent of the student population.[12] The core group of professors — Archibald

---

8. *Fifth Census of the United States* (Washington, 1948), Microfilm 19, Roll 83, pp. 304-6.

9. George R. Wallace, *Princeton Sketches: The Story of Nassau Hall* (New York: G. P. Putnam's Sons, 1893), p. 96.

10. H. L. Savage, *Nassau Hall, 1756-1956* (Princeton: Princeton University Press, 1956), p. 151.

11. Jacob N. Beam, *The American Whig Society* (Princeton: Princeton University Press, 1933), pp. 162-63.

12. *Catalog of the Officers and Students of the Theological Seminary, Princeton, New Jersey, January, 1828* (Princeton, 1829); *Catalog of the Officers and Students, Theological Seminary at Princeton, New Jersey* (Princeton: John Bogart, n.d.); *Catalog of the Theological Seminary of the Presbyterian Church, Princeton, New Jersey, November 1847* (Princeton: John T. Robinson, 1848).

Alexander, Samuel Miller, James Waddell Alexander, Joseph Addison Alexander, and Hodge — had numerous personal connections with slaveholding and the South. Archibald Alexander, a Virginian, deplored slavery as a system and kept no slaves during his career at Princeton, but he had concluded early on that "it is not my business to meddle" with slavery.[13] Samuel Miller was the son of a slaveholder, and though early in his career Miller had preached against "political and domestic slavery" as "inconsistent with *justice*," by 1830 in Princeton Miller owned a slave himself and was counseling emancipation in "a gradual manner."[14] And despite the fact that James Waddel Alexander was satisfied that "in a church of Jesus Christ, there is neither black nor white; and that we have no right to consider the accident of color in any degree," none of the Princeton Seminary faculty seem to have raised a protest over the decision of Princeton's First Presbyterian Church, after its rebuilding program in 1837, to segregate its black communicants, and in 1846 to force them into an entirely separate black congregation.[15] Emancipation in Princeton was, on the whole, a desirable goal but one that possessed no urgency, one that could be postponed so indefinitely that the right moment need never occur.

Least of all did Charles Hodge protest. For one thing, Hodge was a "cotton" Whig, which is to say that though he had scant political sympathy for the Democratic party and its increasingly Southern constituency from 1830 until 1860, his Whiggish commitment to the supremacy of national union disposed him toward co-operation rather than confrontation with Southerners, and especially Southern Whigs. Cotton Whigs like Amos Lawrence and Rufus Choate might personally abhor slavery, but they were unwilling to disrupt the national union, the national economy, and the Constitution in order to do anything about it.[16] Oddly enough, Hodge's Whiggism did not sit all that easily beside his Old School

13. Lefferts A. Loetscher, *Facing the Enlightenment and Pietism: Archibald Alexander and the Founding of Princeton Theological Seminary* (Westport, Conn.: Greenwood Press, 1983), pp. 56, 83-84, 181; William K. Selden, *Princeton Theological Seminary: A Narrative History, 1812-1992* (Princeton: Princeton University Press, 1992), p. 45.

14. Samuel Miller, Jr., *Life of Samuel Miller* (Philadelphia: Claxton, Remsen and Haffelfinger, 1869), vol. 1, pp. 91-94.

15. James Hall, ed., *Forty Years Familiar Letters of James W. Alexander* (New York: C. Scribner, 1860), vol. 1, p. 260, and vol. 2, p. 65; David Calhoun, *Princeton Seminary* (Edinburgh: Banner of Truth Trust, 1994), vol. 1, pp. 324-32.

16. Thomas H. O'Connor, *Lords of the Loom: The Cotton Whigs and the Coming of the Civil War* (New York: Scribner, 1968), pp. 58-59; Thomas Brown, *Politics and Statesmanship: Essays on the American Whig Party* (New York: Columbia University Press, 1985), p. 79.

Presbyterianism. Most Old School Presbyterians — and along with them most ultra-confessionalists among high-church and Anglo-Catholic Episcopalians, Lutherans, and Mercersburg German Calvinists — generally aligned themselves behind the Democratic party from the 1820s onwards.[17] The Whigs promoted themselves as the party of "improvement," whether that meant personal self-improvement and social or career mobility, or support for national programs of commercial "improvements," and they evoked faint response among Old Schoolers who mourned the damage "improvement" inflicted on organic agrarian cultures and the overweening optimism with which it overrode theological warnings about the inability or cupidity of human nature.[18]

Hodge's Whiggism, however, really lay only just across the boundary from the Old School Democrats he otherwise loathed, with the old Federalism rather than the new National Republicanism Henry Clay had carved from the Jeffersonian stock in the 1820s. "He was trained by his family in the opinions of the old Federalist party of Washington, Hamilton and Madison, and he held them tenaciously as principles to the end of his life," wrote Hodge's son, Archibald Alexander Hodge.[19] Hodge himself gloried in the consciousness that "every drop of blood in our veins is of the old federal stock. . . . We never had a blood relation in the world, so far as we know, who was not a federalist in the old sense of the word."[20] He regretted the mobility and commotion of a self-improved society, and although he admitted that "noise, nonsense, and at times violence are the price of liberty," he could not escape the conviction that the rule of the worst by the best was clearly for the best. "If we could have a Republic with the right of suffrage restricted to householders, who can read and write, and have been at least ten years in the country, we could get along grandly," Hodge advised his brother and lifelong confidante, Hugh Lenox

17. Richard Carwardine, *Evangelicals and Politics in Antebellum America* (New Haven: Yale University Press, 1993), p. 118; see also Carwardine's "Antinomians and Arminians: Methodists and the Market Revolution," in *The Market Revolution in America: Social, Political, and Religious Expressions, 1800-1880,* ed. M. Stokes and S. Conway (Charlottesville: University of Virginia Press, 1996), pp. 296-97.

18. Harry Watson, *Liberty and Power: The Politics of Jacksonian America* (New York: Hill and Wang, 1990), p. 186; Daniel Walker Howe, *The Political Culture of the American Whigs* (Chicago: University of Chicago Press, 1979), p. 21; Howe, *Making the American Self: Jonathan Edwards to Abraham Lincoln* (Cambridge: Harvard University Press, 1997), p. 139.

19. A. A. Hodge, *The Life of Charles Hodge, D.D.* (New York: C. Scribner's Sons, 1880), p. 230.

20. Hodge, "The Church and the Country," *Biblical Repertory and Princeton Review* 23 (April 1861): 333 (hereafter *BRPR*).

Hodge, in 1837, "But a democracy with universal suffrage will soon be worse than an aristocracy with Queen Victoria at the head."[21] The fundamental line that placed Hodge on the side of Whiggism was his reverence for the national union, and its supremacy over any form of local, sectional, or parochial loyalty:

> The union of these states is a real union. It is not a mere association, such as binds together nations of different races, languages, and political institutions, as in the Austrian empire. Our outward union is the expression of inward unity. . . . Besides the bonds of union above adverted to, this country is geographically one. . . . The country is thus physically one, and therefore its organic life is one.[22]

Division was Hodge's great dread: no matter whether the traumatic division of his family as a child by his father's premature death, the division of the Scriptures by German critics, or the division of the Presbyterian church by the rock-hard hostility of the Old Schoolers in the schism of 1837, Hodge found security instead in coherence and loyalty. "There are so many geographical and sectional causes of disunion," Hodge wrote to his brother in 1839, "that I am very much afraid that if once deprived of the bond of a common . . . name, and of common property, we shall be split into insignificant fragments."[23]

So, when Archibald Alexander Hodge wrote that his father "had a poor opinion of President Jackson, and of the Locofoco party," the younger Hodge was putting the case with unbecoming mildness.[24] Charles Hodge detested Andrew Jackson — "the President General" — and the Democrats with an unbridled loathing; they were, in his mind, the party of an unscrupulous alliance of Southern agrarians and "foreigners and Catholics, aliens and enemies really of the country" who hoped to conquer by playing one class off against another.[25] The Nullification Crisis cheered him only for the hope that it might "prognosticate a breaking up of the Jackson party. As nothing worse can well take its place, I'm for a change. . . ."[26]

---

21. Hodge to H. L. Hodge, August 1, 1837 (Box 10, File 3) and June 18, 1841 (Box 11, File 1), in Charles Hodge Papers (CO 261), Firestone Library, Princeton University (hereafter Hodge Papers); A. A. Hodge, *Life of Charles Hodge,* pp. 233, 344.

22. Hodge, "The State of the Country," *BRPR* 23 (January 1861): 2-3.

23. Hodge to H. L. Hodge, March 27, 1839, in Box 10, File 4, Hodge Papers.

24. A. A. Hodge, *Life of Charles Hodge,* p. 230.

25. Hodge to H. L. Hodge, December 16, 1844, in Box 11, File 2, Hodge Papers; A. A. Hodge, *Life of Charles Hodge,* p. 349.

26. Hodge to H. L. Hodge, March 9, 1831, in Box 9, File 3, Hodge Papers.

When it didn't, and the "splitting up of the anti-Jackson men into Calhoun, Clay & Wirt factions" seemed likely to "burden the country with the present Miserable incumbent for another term," Hodge concluded that "I think I could in such a case join a rebellion with a clear conscience, as I am sure I would with a full heart."[27]

But like the Cotton Whigs, Hodge pulled short of blaming such a rebellion on the influence of a "Slave Power." When Henry Clay lost his third and final bid for the presidency in 1844, Hodge was convinced that the election had been lost in New York, and that "the silly Abolitionists decided the State, and that again decided the country."[28] He found "the dreadful excitement on the negro question" after the Nat Turner uprising "deplorable," but his biggest anxiety was that sensational Northern newspaper accounts "will serve to exasperate the feelings of the South against the North, although it will be more than ever unreasonable."[29]

It did nothing to assuage his suspicion of the unreasonableness of anti-slavery Northerners that so many of them were New Schoolers with whom he already had deep intellectual disagreements about the nature and priorities of Calvinist theology. Like other Old School Presbyterians, Hodge looked askance at the revival-oriented, Edwardsean Calvinism of New England. "New England men have been . . . long accustomed to regard the six Eastern states as the whole world, and to consider the works of Edwards, West, Bellamy, and a few others, as the only theological writings extant," Hodge complained on the eve of the New School–Old School schism.[30] New Schoolers — and especially those who emerged from the nest of the Yale Theological Department — had defective conceptions of the atonement, a slipshod doctrine of the church (based on a fractious model of congregational independence and visible-saint membership), and, thanks to Jonathan Edwards and Nathaniel William Taylor, an incoherent notion of the operation of the human will that opened a window onto Pelagianism, or at least onto an overconfident notion of self-improvement. The defects in that theology, Hodge was convinced, had led ineluctably to abolitionism: Edwards's definition of true virtue as "love to Being in general" had passed in Samuel Hopkins's hands into the New Divinity doctrine of absolute "disinterested benevolence," and as such it induced New Schoolers like Charles Finney and Albert Barnes to fasten onto abolition and demand the excom-

27. Hodge to H. L. Hodge, October 1, 1831, Box 9, File 3, Hodge Papers.

28. Hodge to H. L. Hodge, June 18, 1841 (Box 11, File 1) and December 16, 1844 (Box 11, File 2), in Hodge Papers; A. A. Hodge, *Life of Charles Hodge,* pp. 344, 349.

29. Hodge to H. L. Hodge, October 1, 1831, Box 9, File 3, in Hodge Papers.

30. Hodge, "The General Assembly of 1836," *BRPR* 8 (July 1836): 463.

munication of slaveholders as the most obvious application of the New School's rigorist ethics. "The spirit of censoriousness, of denunciation, of coarse authoritative dealing, and the whole array of new measures," declared Hodge in 1844, "were the natural fruit of the New Divinity, and especially of their opinion that a change of heart was a change of purpose, which a man could effect as easily as change his route on a journey."[31]

But much as Hodge's politics and theology conspired quite sufficiently to deaden any sense of outrage over slavery and position him among the most conservative of the Cotton Whigs, the most personal reason for Hodge's indifference was that he had evidently dabbled in slaveholding himself. In 1828, frustrated "with changing servants so often," Sarah Bache Hodge persuaded her husband "to purchase the time of some girl whom she could venture to control," and in December, Hodge "found one sixteen year old who has five years to serve" (in other words, a black female born after the 1804 emancipation statute and bound to serve until achieving age twenty-one) and bought her "for seventy-five dollars."[32] This slave shows up in the 1830 census as "free colored," either because the census-taker simply miscategorized her or because she was not actually bound for life like other slaves in Princeton, such as Samuel Miller's slave; but the same census also shows a similar entry for a "free colored" man in the Hodge household, who may have been the rented slave, Cato, for whom Hodge paid "$100 a year" in 1829, or a free black named John whom Hodge paid "50 cts." a week "& his clothes wh. is the same as giving him a dollar." Either way, Hodge was seeking to employ a worker "whose wages will not probably amount to as much as we should otherwise have to pay" — in other words, to avoid the costs of free or wage labor — to help manage his household or to cultivate the "six acres of ground, immediately adjoining the Seminary property to the westward" that he purchased in 1830, and that his crippled, arthritic leg prevented him from farming with his own hands.[33]

Charles Hodge could not condemn slavery without condemning his whole intellectual milieu, and without acknowledging his own personal complicity in slaveholding, neither of which he ever did in his lifetime; and he could not accommodate attacks upon slavery as immoral and grounds for excommunication without allowing himself to become immoral and an excommunicate, which would have spelled more clearly

---

31. Hodge, "Abolitionism," *BRPR* 16 (October 1844): 547.

32. Hodge to H. L. Hodge, December 12, 1828, in Box 9, File 3, Hodge Papers.

33. *Fifth Census of the United States,* Microfilm 19, Roll 83, p. 304; Hodge to H. L. Hodge, March 18, 1829, in Box 9, File 3, Hodge Papers; A. A. Hodge, *Life of Charles Hodge,* p. 228.

than anything else the personal threat of division and alienation. Rather than remaining complacent, Hodge took "as much interest in this whole matter as any other individual in our church," wrote an appreciative Charles Colcock Jones, the proslavery Presbyterian apostle of Georgia slave missions, "& we have no one whose views are more extended & intelligent & just."[34] All of which means that when Hodge came to write his first major essay on slavery in 1836, the hand and mind that composed it were already deeply committed — much more than Hodge's apologists have recognized — to the rationalization of slavery as an institution, and to the dismissal of abolition as an unnecessarily divisive force in American and Presbyterian life.

Hodge's essay on slavery was also the most comprehensive statement he ever made of his ideas on the subject. The immediate cause for the essay was the publication of the aged Unitarian stalwart William Ellery Channing's *Slavery* in 1835, a short book that was less important for its arguments than for the highly conservative Channing's decision to come down off the fence and endorse abolition. For all of his abrasive anti-Calvinist reputation, Channing's affection for Scottish common sense philosophy, his political loyalties to Henry Clay, and his hostility to the Transcendentalists established significant areas of common ground with Hodge, so his decision finally to condemn slavery as an evil institution offered a muted challenge to men of similar mind like Hodge.[35] But behind Channing's book were more stormy developments: in 1819 the debate over the admission of Missouri as a slave state had awakened a controversy over the future of slavery in the republic, and it was followed through the 1820s by schemes for emancipation and colonization on the one hand and stand-pat defenses of the legitimacy of slavery on the other. In 1831 William Lloyd Garrison published the first issue of his sensational abolitionist newspaper *The Liberator*, followed (in what seemed to Southerners to be unseemly proximity) by Nat Turner's short-lived but bloody slave revolt in Virginia, the abolition of slavery in the British West Indies, the organization in December 1833 of the American Anti-Slavery Society by the New School laymen Arthur and Lewis Tappan, and a campaign by the Society in 1835 to mass-mail abolitionist periodicals — the newspaper *Human*

34. Jones to Hodge, August 4, 1847, in Box 16, File 71, Hodge Papers.

35. Channing's *Slavery* is included in *Works of William E. Channing, D.D.* (Boston: American Unitarian Association, 1886), vol. 2, pp. 5-153; see also Daniel Walker Howe, *The Unitarian Conscience: Harvard Moral Philosophy, 1805-1861* (Cambridge: Harvard University Press, 1970), pp. 289-94, and Andrew Delbanco, *William Ellery Channing: An Essay on the Liberal Spirit in America* (Cambridge: Harvard University Press, 1981), pp. 164-65.

Rights, the magazine *Antislavery Record,* the Tappans' journal, *Emancipator,* and a children's publication, *The Slave's Friend* — to unsmiling Southern post offices.[36] And the agitation dropped onto Hodge's doorstep when abolitionist New Schoolers in the General Assembly of 1835 offered a se-ries of antislavery resolutions attacking slavery as "a heinous sin" and call-ing for the excommunication of slaveholders. Not coincidentally, the New Schoolers set Hodge's teeth further on edge by establishing a rival theo-logical seminary in New York City.[37]

Consequently, Channing's slim book was hardly more than Hodge's pretext for a position paper aimed at abolitionism in general and the threat of New School theological predominance in the Presbyterian church. "Every one must be sensible that a very great change has, within a few years, been produced in the feelings, if not the opinions of the public in relation to slavery," Hodge acknowledged at the beginning. "The sub-ject of slavery is no longer one on which men are allowed to be of no mind at all," and especially in "almost every ecclesiastical society." But the cause of this change, Hodge warned, was not some rising swell of moral con-science, but rather "the conduct of the abolitionists" with their provoca-tive "denunciations of slaveholding, as man-stealing, robbery, piracy, and worse than murder. . . ." It pained Hodge to see so venerable a figure of conservative Unitarianism as Channing swept up by this, and not surpris-ingly Hodge believed that this had led Channing into a fundamental mis-construction of what made slavery such a problem. Channing, partly in an effort to accommodate his fellow Cotton Whigs but also partly in a practical recognition that it was unjust to demonize all slaveholders, had portrayed slavery itself as the evil, brutalizing master and slave alike.[38] What Hodge asserted was the exact opposite: slavery itself was not an evil, and was probably as much a good as any other social system. "The as-sumption that slaveholding is itself a crime, is not only an error, but is an error fraught with evil consequences." If slavery was a crime, then "we might expect to hear the interpreters of the divine will, saying that a sys-tem which leads to such results is the concentrated essence of all crimes,

---

36. Freehling, *Road to Disunion,* pp. 291-292; Bertram Wyatt-Brown, *Lewis Tappan and the Evangelical War Against Slavery* (Cleveland: Press of Case Western Reserve University, 1969), pp. 143-45.

37. C. C. Goen, *Broken Churches, Broken Nation: Denominational Schism and the Coming of the Civil War* (Macon, Ga.: Mercer University Press, 1985), pp. 68-78; H. Shelton Smith, *In His Im-age, but . . . : Racism in Southern Religion, 1780-1910* (Durham, N.C.: Duke University Press, 1972), pp. 77-94.

38. Channing, *Slavery,* in *Works,* vol. 2, p. 75.

and must be instantly abandoned on pain of eternal condemnation." But the unarguable fact was that the apostles said nothing of the sort, "and we cannot now force them to say it."

> It is on all hands acknowledged that, at the time of the advent of Jesus Christ, slavery in its worst forms prevailed over the whole world. The Savior found it around him in Judea; the apostles met with it in Asia, Greece, and Italy. How did they treat it? Not by denunciation of slaveholding as necessarily and universally sinful. Not by declaring that all slaveholders were men-stealers and robbers, and consequently to be excluded from the church and the kingdom of heaven. . . . If we are right in insisting that slaveholding is one of the greatest of all sins; that it should be immediately and universally abandoned as a condition of church communion or admission into heaven, how comes it that Christ and his apostles did not pursue the same course?[39]

Hodge was unmoved by counter-arguments from politics or economics. "It is . . . argued" by Channing "that slavery must be sinful because it interferes with the inalienable rights of men." But Hodge, the birthright Federalist, knew of no such inalienable Jeffersonian rights. "Slavery, in itself considered, is a state of bondage, and nothing more," and involves simply an obligation "to labour for another, who has the right to transfer this claim of service, at pleasure." If that involved "the loss of man of the rights which are commonly and properly called natural," it was no more than what happened when societies necessarily "deprive any set of men of a portion of their natural rights." Only in a Lockean state of nature can anyone claim to perfectly possess all of their natural rights; the need to enter into society means the surrendering of some portion of those rights, and the right to liberty is no more inalienable than any other right of which society deprives people from time to time. Nor was it the task of Christianity to try to decide what rights might be inalienable and what not. "Christianity," wrote Hodge in one of his most profoundly conservative assertions, "was never designed to tear up the institutions of society by the roots," much less to do it "after a pattern cut by the rule of abstract rights." The Roman Empire, after all, had been a "cruel despotism" that lacked much sense of any rights, and when "the licentiousness, the injustice, the rapine and murders of those wicked men" rolled in full force onto the public stage, the Christians "condemned" them "with the full force of

39. Hodge, "Slavery," *BRPR* 8 (April 1836): 268, 270, 273, 275, 277, 280, 284, 298.

divine authority." But they never condemned the Roman *system:* "the mere extent of their power, though liable to abuse, they left unnoticed."[40] Similarly, slavery as a *system* was no more objectionable to Christianity than the Roman Empire. Both might be unpleasant, and even abusive, but Christianity treated them alike as simply fallible human social expedients to be endured by souls whose citizenship was in heaven, not as moral offenses to be expunged.

This satisfied Hodge's deep-seated Calvinistic propensity to locate sin within the concrete ethical situation of individual people, rather than removing it to the morally safer distance of a social institution. And it certainly satisfied both Old Schoolers who distrusted the New School enthusiasm for disinterested benevolence and slaveholding Presbyterians who (Hodge knew well) could easily respond to New School agitation by taking their congregations and their support someplace other than the General Assembly and, of course, Princeton Seminary. But it was precisely on the cusp of this endorsement of slavery as a permissible, and even tolerable, social system that Hodge's antislavery moment occurred, and occurred almost as the concomitant of every argument he had thus far mustered in slavery's defense.

Channing had insisted that the slave system was evil, but that slaveholders, individually considered, were not. By inverting Channing's argument, Hodge was compelled to grasp and reverse the other part of the proposition, that individual slaveholding did not make masters evil, and claim that it was individual masters who were precisely the problem. A slave is *property,* Hodge wrote; but *property,* in this sense, is strictly an economic relation, and the possession of property "must of necessity vary according to the nature of the object to which it attaches." Consequently, when "it is said that one man is the property of another, it can only mean that the one has a right to use the other *as a man,* but not as a brute or thing." *Property* gives "no sanction to the employment of any and every means which cruelty, suspicion, or jealousy may choose to deem necessary. . . ." Slavery, therefore, cannot be termed *evil* if it is considered as a *system* of holding property, but slaveholders can become evil themselves by abusing their slave property. This meant, in particular terms, that

> if any man has servants or others whom he separates after marriage, he breaks as clearly a revealed law as any written on the pages of inspiration, or on the human heart. If he interferes unnecessarily with

40. Hodge, "Slavery," pp. 280, 289, 292.

the authority of parents over their children, he again brings himself into collision with his Maker. . . . If he deliberately opposes their intellectual, moral, or religious improvement, he makes himself a transgressor.[41]

This kind of exception-making had a fairly long intellectual history, going back to William Paley's distinction between ownership of property in a slave's *labor* rather than in a slave's *person,* and it was even a familiar part of proslavery arguments from William A. Smith to James Henley Thornwell.[42] It has also been dismissed, as William Freehling remarks, "because of the misconception that [it] was boring and simplistic"; what Freehling and John Ashworth have both noticed is that, at the same time as it rebuffed the abolitionist claim for slavery's evil, it also made impossible the countervailing claim that slaveholders increasingly wanted to make, that slavery was a positive *good.*[43] It could not be a good, according to Hodge, if it involved such offenses against Christianity as the breaking up of families or the denial of opportunities for "intellectual, moral, or religious improvement," and the possibility hung in the air that if it could be demonstrated that such offences were part of a particular arrangement of slavery, that particular arrangement (although not slavery itself) could be condemned as sinful. This involves some measure of what appears at first glance to be very fine grinding, but it was in fact lethal to Southern slavery, since the legal power to break up families and punish "improvement" was precisely what Southern slave laws embodied and what Southern slaveholders considered their rightful dominion. And had Hodge been as simple-minded in his rationalization of slavery as Tise and Trinterud suggest, Hodge's logical next step would have been no next step at all, but instead a withdrawal into the safe confines of what slavery ought to be rather than a criticism of what it was.

But this was what Hodge did not do, and for an unpredicted moment, Hodge suddenly began prophesying the end of slavery. "If it be asked what

41. Hodge, "Slavery," pp. 293, 296, 303.

42. See Smith's *Lectures on the Philosophy and Practice of Slavery* (Nashville: Stevenson and Evans, 1856), pp. 276-328, and Thornwell's "Relation of the Church to Slavery" and "The Christian Doctrine of Slavery," in *Collected Writings of James Henley Thornwell* (Columbia, S.C., 1873), vol. 4, pp. 386, 396-97, 403, 413-15, 419-34.

43. Freehling, "James Henley Thornwell's Mysterious Antislavery Moment," in *Journal of Southern History* 57 (August 1991): 391-92; John Ashworth, *Slavery, Capitalism, and Politics in the Antebellum Republic,* vol. 1: *Commerce and Compromise, 1820-1850* (New York: Cambridge University Press, 1995), pp. 213-14.

would be the consequence of thus acting on the principles of the gospel, of following the example and obeying the precepts of Christ" — or in other words, what should slavery look like if it really limited itself to an economic relationship and permitted the "improvement" of the slaves? — Hodge answered, "the gradual elevation of the slaves in intelligence, virtue and wealth." But a slave possessing "intelligence, virtue and wealth" was an oxymoron; slaves possessing those qualities would quickly find ways to stop being slaves, or else masters would quickly find it "no longer desirable or possible to keep them in bondage," and slavery would disappear. Hodge unblinkingly agreed: follow his prescription and the result would inevitably be "the peaceable and speedy extinction of slavery." And what then would become of these self-improved slaves? "It may be objected that if the slaves are allowed so to improve as to become freemen, the next step in their progress is that they should become citizens. We admit that it is so." And he did not balk at the fundamental serpent of race in this equation. "The fact that the master and slave belong to different races" was irrelevant to the question: "Still they are men; their colour does not place them beyond the operation of the principles of the gospel, or from under the protection of God." If civil integration proved impossible, then Hodge was willing to consider "dividing the land" and creating "distinct communities," or else colonization. But one race does not have "a right to oppress the other."[44]

That Hodge could move almost at once from marshalling together Christ and the apostles to defend slavery, to a moment of apparently sober entertainment of black emancipation and civil rights presents a double somersault of dizzying proportions. But Hodge saw no hidden contradictions: "We have little apprehension that any one can so far mistake our object, or the purport of our remarks, as to suppose either that we regard slavery as a desirable institution, or that we approve of the slave laws of the South." And he saw no contradiction for one basic reason: this was a formula for avoiding division — division in the Presbyterian church, division in the national Union, and above all division within his own seminary and its supporters. Southerners could be placated by his approval of slavery, New Schoolers could be placated by his bow toward ultimate emancipation, and a "long-continued conflict" and even "the disunion of the states" and "a desolating servile insurrection" could be avoided. And if this form of gradualism seemed to impatient abolitionists to be instead a formula for doing nothing until some long-delayed "improvement" magi-

44. Hodge, "Slavery," pp. 300, 304-5.

cally allowed "their chains thus gradually to relax, until they fall off entirely," Hodge had his own Princeton — perhaps even his own six acres — to point to as a laboratory for how slavery could yield gradually to freedom without exactly doing anything to abolish it. In that sense, Charles Hodge was not proposing a mere policy formula for dealing with slavery; he was describing what he hoped was his own management of the dilemma.[45]

Despite Charles Hodge's historical reputation as the doyen of Old School Presbyterian orthodoxy, Hodge and the Princetonians were treated in the 1830s by Old School bitter-enders as soft and unreliable toward the New Schoolers. John Williamson Nevin would later testify that Hodge, Alexander, and Miller had sold too much of their souls to "the unchurchly scheme," and none of them were able to prevent Northern Old Schoolers from striking an alliance with slaveholding Southern Presbyterians at the 1837 General Assembly to exscind the four New School synods and nearly 100,000 New School communicants from the Presbyterian church.[46] This did not get rid of a persistent minority of abolitionists in the General Assembly, nor did it stop suspicious Old School presbyteries from threatening to withhold support from the seminary if it failed to espouse Old Schoolism with sufficient vigor, and it placed a tremendous amount of pressure on Hodge as the editor of the *Princeton Review* to prove Princeton's worthiness and, incidentally, pacify the even more critical Southern voice in the General Assembly.[47] He returned to slavery as a subject briefly in 1838 in a review of several New School authors on the subject (the principal being Oberlin College faculty member James A. Thome), but only to reiterate that abolitionism was in "direct collision with the scriptures." He still believed that "it would . . . be a great point gained, if it could be made to appear incontestably that the interests of the slaveowner are promoted by every improvement in the condition of the slave, and even by his full emancipation," but he had no explicit recommendations for bringing that about. To the contrary, he preferred to blame the abolitionists and their "fanatical denunciation of slave-holding, as at all times and under all circumstances a most heinous sin" for making Southerners more truc-

45. Hodge, "Slavery," pp. 300, 301, 302, 304.

46. Theodore Appel, *The Life and Work of John Williamson Nevin, D.D., LL.D.* (Philadelphia: Reformed Church Publication House, 1889), p. 48; George Marsden, *The Evangelical Mind and the New School Presbyterian Experience: A Case Study of Thought and Theology in Nineteenth-Century America* (New Haven: Yale University Press, 1970), pp. 65-66.

47. E. Brooks Holifield, *The Gentlemen Theologians: American Theology in Southern Culture, 1795-1860* (Durham, N.C.: Duke University Press, 1978), pp. 177-78.

ulent and more willing to embrace the idea that slavery is a "good and desirable institution."[48]

An 1844 review of Old Schooler George Junkin's proslavery tirade, *The
Integrity of our National Union vs. Abolitionism,* gave Hodge another opportunity to prove his *bona fides* to unpersuaded Old Schoolers, and he once
again defined slavery as "simply the right of possession and use" like any
other property, and therefore "not in itself a crime" or "evil in its own nature." The hole he had opened in the proslavery argument concerning
the jeopardy the specific wrongdoings of masters or legislatures brought
onto the whole slave system was now filled up by the denial that Southern slavery "makes a man a thing in distinction from a person. . . . Under
no system of slave laws that ever existed, is a slave regarded otherwise
than as a person, that is, an intelligent, moral agent." If anything, Hodge
now suggested, Southern slavery might actually be morally superior to
industrial wage labor. "We believe it to be true, that the slaves of the
south, as a general rule, are better compensated, than the great body of
operatives in Europe. We believe also that taking them as a class, their intellectual, moral and religious condition is better." But even if the slave
laws had their defective provisions, Hodge now added that there was
nothing the Presbyterian church could do about it. "It is plain that the
church has no responsibility and no right to interfere with respect to the
slave laws of the South."[49] When the abolitionist minority in the General
Assembly of 1845 pressed for a redefinition of the Assembly's stance on
slavery, the motion was crushed by a resounding condemnation of "modern abolitionism."[50] Charles Hodge's antislavery moment appeared to be
over.

The fading of that moment tracked the flagging of the abolitionist
movement. In 1840 the American Anti-Slavery Society split over the issue
of women in leadership, while Garrison split American abolitionism even
further by his attacks on former colleagues as "morally defunct," on "political abolitionists" and on organized religion.[51] It was not in the end the
abolitionists who rescued abolition, but rather the slaveholders, first by
staging a vain and costly effort to gag discussion of antislavery in the

48. Hodge, "West India Emancipation," *BRPR* 10 (October 1838): 607, 613.

49. Hodge, "Abolitionism," *BRPR* 16 (October 1844): 554, 555, 556, 576, 580.

50. John R. McKivigan, *The War Against Proslavery Religion: Abolitionism and the Northern
Churches, 1830-1865* (Ithaca, N.Y.: Cornell University Press, 1984), p. 83.

51. Louis Filler, *The Crusade Against Slavery, 1830-1860* (New York: Harper, 1960), p. 156;
Russell B. Nye, *William Lloyd Garrison and the Humanitarian Reformers* (Boston: Little, Brown,
1955), pp. 126-48.

House of Representatives between 1841 and 1844, and then by pushing the United States (with Andrew Jackson's lieutenant, James Knox Polk, in the White House) into the annexation of Texas and a war with Mexico in order to expand the territorial horizons of slavery. The same Old Schoolers who had deplored abolitionist agitation as just one more species of New Divinity aggression now cranked around to behold an equally unwelcome challenge to Old School orthodoxy in the form of James Henley Thornwell's "strict-construction" Presbyterianism, and Charles Hodge cranked around with them.[52] In his commentary on the General Assembly of 1846, Hodge suddenly declared that he did not "see how any Christian can say that" slavery "is a desirable condition, or that the ignorance and degradation without which slavery cannot exist, should be perpetuated." This was a startling re-awakening of his antislavery moment, if only because of the suggestion that the idea of slavery, which Hodge had previously uncoupled from the abuses of specific slave systems, might not be able to be separated from "ignorance and degradation" after all. He continued to insist that "slaveholding is not in itself sinful," but he now closed the gap between slaveholding *itself* and the "many things which slaveholders often do, and too often justify, which are sinful, such as keeping their slaves in ignorance, preventing their hearing the gospel, disregarding their conjugal and parental rights, denying to them the right of property, and the like." Only four years after suggesting moral parity between wage labor and slavery, Hodge denied that he had ever said anything of the sort: "This is a doctrine which had few, if any, advocates even among men of the world, in this country, until within a few years; and we know of no presbyterian minister who has ever avowed it."[53]

Hodge had been able to keep his antislavery moment reasonably at bay by distinguishing between slavery *itself* and the South's actual slave laws, insisting that evils in the latter did not compromise the moral neutrality of the former. This, as events were demonstrating, allowed Hodge a remarkable degree of flexibility, since he could accordion the distance between the two depending on how closely he wanted to judge the approximation of the one to the other or by fixing the proper definition of slavery so high that no slaveholders could hope to accommodate it and still have slavery. Just how high he was willing to fix it was illustrated by his second great essay on the question, a highly favorable review in the Oc-

---

52. James O. Farmer, *The Metaphysical Confederacy: James Henley Thornwell and the Synthesis of Southern Values* (Macon, Ga.: Mercer University Press, 1986), pp. 184-85.

53. Hodge, "General Assembly," *BRPR* 18 (July 1846): 425, 426.

tober 1849 *Biblical Repertory* of border state Old Schooler Robert J. Breckinridge's plea for emancipation in Kentucky, *The Question of Negro Slavery and the New Constitution of Kentucky*. The stately Breckinridge was anything but a wild-eyed abolitionist, and his vain attempt to persuade Kentucky to abandon slavery as a doomed system set the perfect contrast for Hodge to the gathering demands of the lower South for the extension of slavery into the Mexican Cession. "We have ever maintained that slaveholding is not in itself sinful," Hodge reiterated for the sake of continuity, "but the right to hold slaves does not imply the right to treat them as brutes, or as mere chattels." The shift of voice here is critical, since the 1836 essay on slavery had established an equilibrium between slavery and bad slaveholding as though the two could be chosen between; the Breckinridge review now as much as admitted that this had been a sleight of hand. "Slavery implies perpetual ignorance and perpetual degradation," Hodge wrote; and *because* of that, rather than *in spite* of that, "in almost all slave states there are enactments, the design of which is to prevent the intellectual and social improvement of the blacks." The accordion closed: slavery in the abstract might not be evil, but to practice slavery "in almost all" cases leads the slaveholder to practice evil. On that logic, Hodge concluded, "Emancipation is not only a duty, but it is unavoidable."[54]

Precisely because Hodge's ideal notion of slavery allowed for "gradual improvement," and because "gradual improvement must lead to gradual emancipation," it was now clear to Hodge that the obstacle in the path of slavery's proper development toward oblivion had to be a "mass of slaveholders" who opposed improvement, which in Hodge's mind meant the mass of Southern Democrats. What had killed Breckinridge's noble program for Kentucky emancipation was "the whole tendency of our system . . . to throw the actual power into the hands of the masses," where a slaveholding Democratic elite could easily whip up poor whites into a racial frenzy against black emancipation. "This is the reason why a few thousand slaveholders wield the authority of a whole state, and make the majority of the people think they are contending for their own rights and interests, while in fact they are contending for the exclusive advantage of a small minority." The Whig program, however, offered a better solution: gradually emancipate the slaves and satisfy the demands of improvement, and then colonize the freedpeople to satisfy the racism of the whites. "While . . . we joyfully admit the negro race to be bone of our bone and

54. Hodge, "Emancipation," *BRPR* 19 (October 1849): 601, 603, 604.

flesh of our flesh, to be brethren of the same great family to which we ourselves belong," nevertheless "The whites, and especially the less cultivated portion of them, revolt at the idea that the distinction between themselves and those whom they have always looked upon as their inferiors, should be done away." Hence, "the greatest of all temporal blessings" would be the great Whig solution, colonization "to the rising republic of Liberia."[55] The evils of slavery were the fault of the slaveholders, not slavery itself; the evils of racism were the fault of the Democrats, not white supremacy.

If this was not quite a perfect antislavery moment, it was enough to wake up Hodge's readers. Philadelphia Old Schooler Henry A. Boardman surprised Hodge by assuming "that I had changed my ground on the slavery question," and Lewis Tappan curiously wrote to Hodge a month after the Breckinridge review was published to "inquire whether your views on the subject of American slavery have undergone any change since the publication of your views in the Biblical Repertory of April 1836, and whether you do not now believe that voluntary slaveholding shall deprive a man of fellowship as a Christian."[56] Hodge did not, and the settlement of the Mexican cession through the Compromise of 1850 once more cooled Hodge's emancipation rhetoric. Even though the Compromise badly split the Whigs and laid the foundation for the disintegration of the Whig party over the following six years, Hodge rejoiced in the dissipation of "secession or separation of the Union," and not only endorsed the Fugitive Slave Law but settled back into his more customary criticism of "the violent denunciations of slaveholders, in which a certain class of northern writers habitually indulge."[57] He did not settle for long, though. As with many other Northern Whigs, the introduction of the Kansas-Nebraska bill in 1854 (by Democrat Stephen Douglas), the Dred Scott decision in March 1857 (written by Andrew Jackson's old lieutenant, Roger Taney), and the determination of a Democratic administration under James Buchanan to back up a proslavery regime in the Kansas Territory were revelations that the 1850 Compromise had been a cruel hoax, fobbed off on a gullible public by the "Slave Power." Hodge was astounded by the Dred Scott decision, not so much because it denied Scott any standing as an American citizen, but because it opened up a limitless vista for the expansion and perpetuation of

---

55. Hodge, "Emancipation," pp. 587-588, 590, 596-597.

56. Tappan to Hodge, November 25, 1849, in Box 19, File 1, and Hodge to H. A. Boardman, December 28, 1860, Box 14, File 23, Hodge Papers.

57. Hodge, "Civil Government," *BRPR* 23 (January 1851): 125-126, 129-130.

slavery, and made nonsense of Hodge's expectation that "improvement" could occur gradually within the slave system. "All the history of the country is against it," Hodge protested to his brother, "In 1800, 1806, 1809, 1820, then in 1836, and 1848 acts were passed all founded on the principle that Slavery might be prohibited in the Territories."[58]

But the threat of disunion was now so palpable that Hodge could hardly afford publicly to indulge his antislavery moment. He turned Republican and voted for Frémont in the 1856 election, not so much because he loved Frémont (who was a Roman Catholic) but because he hated the Democrats and believed that Millard Fillmore, the last feeble Whig presidential candidate, had "committed himself to worse nullification than South Carolina ever dreamt of."[59] And he contented himself, in his annual commentaries on the General Assembly in the *Review*, with criticizing Thornwell and the Old School abolitionists alike.[60] It was not until after the election of Lincoln in November 1860, when South Carolina finally declared for outright disunion, that Hodge's antislavery moment appeared for the third and last time, and when it did, it clarified beyond question what the driving forces behind that moment had all along been.

The months between South Carolina's secession and the outbreak of the Civil War were a torment for Hodge, who had been taught as a good Whig to prize the unity as much as the liberty of the republic as its principal political virtues. He pleaded with Southern Old Schoolers like Robert Lewis Dabney to believe "that the great majority of the North condemn . . . the language, spirit, & conduct of the abolitionists" and assured Dabney of what he himself did not personally believe, that "As to the Territories, the people of the North admit that they are common property & that the people of the South have exactly the same rights in them as the people of the North."[61] In two articles for the January and April 1861 issues of the *Repertory*, Hodge endorsed the Crittenden Compromise, urged that "the Missouri Compromise be restored . . . abrogation of which is the immediate source of all our present troubles," and denied that the election of a Republican president was any worthwhile excuse for secession. "That party is not an anti-slavery, much less an abolition party," Hodge insisted; on the

58. Undated fragment of a letter of Hodge to H. L. Hodge, Princeton Theological Seminary Archives.

59. Hodge to H. L. Hodge, July 8, 1856, in Box 12, File 2, Hodge Papers; see also A. A. Hodge, *Life of Charles Hodge,* pp. 393-94.

60. Hodge, "The General Assembly," BRPR 31 (July 1859): 592, 616.

61. Hodge to R. L. Dabney, December 15, 1860, in Robert Lewis Dabney Papers, Historical Foundation of the Presbyterian and Reformed Churches, Montreat, North Carolina.

contrary, it was little more than the old Whigs revived "who desired to enter their protest against the repeal of the Missouri Compromise, and the attempts to force slavery upon Kansas, joined by thousands who wish for a protective tariff, and thousands more, who, from dislike of one candidate, and distrust of another, preferred to vote for Mr. Lincoln." That Lincoln himself was a "Henry Clay Whig" who denied any intention to interfere with slavery in the slave states only made Hodge's task lighter, and made secession more easy to condemn as a selfish sectional plot to "promote the prosperity of the cotton states" and "be relieved from the great national burden and from commercial restrictions."[62]

Hodge did not, significantly, believe that his articles had any chance "of producing the slightest impression on disunionists." He wrote them, as he explained to Henry A. Boardman, because there "are many conservative men at the South who wish to have their hands strengthened, to whom it will be a matter of importance to have it proved that the whole North is not abolitionized."[63] But behind even that motivation for avoiding national disunion was an even more anxious motivation for preserving the union of the nation and the church for Princeton, since a divided nation, like a divided church, could do nothing but damage to the seminary. "If I am to believe a tenth of what I hear," he confided to Boardman, "I never wrote any thing for the Review likely to do the Seminary and all concerned greater service." Pacifying and unifying gestures over slavery and disunion, not to mention definitions of slavery flexible enough to expand and contract with the appearance of Hodge's antislavery moment, were fundamentally guided by what conduced to the survival of Princeton Seminary and by what a life lived in Princeton had taught him about the nature of slavery. "Brethren at the west write," Hodge told Boardman, "that it [the January 1861 article on "The State of the Country"] has done more than they can well express" — not, ultimately, to save the Union or demonstrate the true nature of slavery and abolition, but "to sustain the old School cause & strengthen confidence in Princeton."[64] Disunion threatened Princeton and threatened Hodge; hence, what threatened disunion was what determined the emergence of Charles Hodge's antislavery moment.

Of course, once the Confederates made secession a fact, all restraint on the final emergence of that antislavery moment gradually dissolved.

---

62. Hodge, "The State of the Country," pp. 5, 12, 36.

63. Hodge to H. A. Boardman, December 16, 1860, in Box 14, File 23, Hodge Papers.

64. Hodge to H. A. Boardman, January 17, 1861, in Box 14, File 23, Hodge Papers.

Hodge hoped against hope that Southern Old Schoolers could be kept part of the General Assembly despite secession, but "Presbyterians were in arms against Presbyterians," and Northern Old Schoolers (appropriately stimulated by Gardiner Spring, a New School sheep in Old School wolves' clothing) voted overwhelmingly "in favour of an open declaration of loyalty to the Constitution and the Federal Government." Hodge agreed that "the course of the South, in its attempt to break up our glorious Union, is unreasonable, ungrateful, and wicked," but he begged the restless majority of the Assembly to split a hair in the name of unity: the South might be wrong in thinking secession legal, but that was a political thought, and the Assembly had no business designating which political thoughts were legal and which were not. It was an argument wasted on an assembly packed with angered Northerners and giddy Southerners, eager to proclaim (as Thornwell's associate, Benjamin Palmer, declared) slavery "a Divine Trust," and so the Old School General Assembly itself was divided, with the Southern Presbyterians lost for more than a century and (as Hodge carefully noted) "three hundred subscribers" to the *Repertory* gone "at one blow."[65] He stubbornly hoped that an adjusted settlement to the war could bring them all back, and he opposed emancipation on the grounds that it would make a negotiated peace in the Civil War impossible. "We are not advocates of the immediate and universal emancipation of the slaves," Hodge wrote in the late spring of 1862, just as Abraham Lincoln was privately concluding that negotiated peace was an illusion and emancipation unavoidable. "We believe such emancipation would be a dreadful calamity to the blacks, as well as to the whites."[66] And he kept on opposing emancipation as a point of no return right up to the final issue of the Emancipation Proclamation. "We do not say that the emancipation of the slaves may not be a legitimate means for the prosecution of the war," but it was a solution too close to "blowing up a man's house as a means of arresting a conflagration" for Hodge's edgy fears of disintegration and disunity. "If the abolition of slavery be made, either really or avowedly, the object of the war, we believe we shall utterly fail." Improvement, he continued to argue, and not emancipation was the "natural and healthful manner" for "the abolition of slavery."[67]

---

65. Hodge, "The General Assembly," *BRPR* 33 (July 1861): 542-43, 559; Thomas Cary Johnson, *The Life and Letters of Benjamin Morgan Palmer* (Richmond, Va.: Presbyterian Committee of Publication, 1906), p. 206; Hodge, "The Princeton Review on the State of the Country and of the Church," *BRPR* 37 (October 1865): 657.

66. Hodge, "The General Assembly," *BRPR* 34 (July 1862): 521.

67. Hodge, "The War," *BRPR* 35 (January 1863): 151, 152.

But once it became clear to Hodge that the Confederacy would fight for disunion to the last slave, Hodge surrendered not only to the inevitability of abolition, but also to the collapse of virtually all of his precious distinction between slavery *itself* and slaveholding. With little in the way of a slaveholding constituency left in the General Assembly (even the border state gradualist, Robert J. Breckinridge, supported Lincoln and acted as temporary chair of the Baltimore convention that re-nominated Lincoln for the presidency), Hodge now closed the accordion between slavery *itself* and evil slaveholding, and he approved a General Assembly resolution in 1864 branding slavery as "an evil and guilt" on the grounds that "that concrete system with which the people of this country are familiar . . . is designed and adapted to keep a certain class of our fellow-men in a state of degradation. . . ." Hodge now was willing to agree, as though it had never been at all clear before, that slavery "is the system which declares, with the force of law, that a slave cannot marry; which forbids his being taught to read and write; which allows of the forcible separation of husbands and wives. . . ." He did not permit it to close quite so much, though, that he could be accused of inconsistency. "One of the saddest proofs of the injustice of Southern laws is, that after more than a century, the vast body of the slaves of the extreme Southern states are in a condition of the greatest degradation," Hodge announced, but he wanted it "distinctly understood, that we have not changed our ground on the subject of slavery. We hold now precisely what we held in 1836, when the subject was first argued in these pages."[68] There was, in the end, no disunity Hodge dreaded more than the discovery of disunion within himself.

In practical terms, though, this permitted Hodge to reduce his idea of slavery to the thinnest and most useless of abstractions, and to indulge Union partisanship to the hilt. "The South has always been treated as a spoilt child, to which the other members of the family gave up for sake of peace," Hodge disgustedly remarked in 1862, and he was delighted with "the great victories in which it has pleased God to crown our arms at Mobile and Atlanta." He thought "highly" of George McClellan, but he voted for Lincoln in 1864 "because I do not wish to see the Democratic Party, which has brought all these troubles and horrors upon us, restored to power."[69] He feared that Sherman's march to the sea would be "a mistake.

68. Hodge, "The General Assembly," *BRPR* 36 (July 1864): 545, 548.

69. Hodge, "England and America," in *BRPR* 34 (January 1862), p. 165; Hodge to H. L. Hodge, September 7, 1864, and September 16, 1864, Box 12, File 3, Hodge Papers; A. A. Hodge, *Life of Charles Hodge*, p. 481.

But it has turned out right," and he rejoiced in December 1864 "that the end cannot be far off."[70] He genuinely mourned the assassination of Lincoln as "the saddest day in the whole history of our nation," and he was "exasperated . . . almost to madness" when "some of the Democrats here in this town openly rejoiced when the news of Mr. Lincoln's murder arrived."[71] But there is nothing in Hodge's utterances during the war that showed much enthusiasm for the centrality of emancipation to the war effort. His mid-course *Repertory* commentary on "The War" in 1863 still discouraged vigorous moves toward emancipation, and the article made him anxious only to find out from his brother whether his war-diminished readership did "not think my War Article in the last number of the Princeton Review is not pretty orthodox."[72] Once the war was over, Hodge urged re-admission of the Southerners (though not the New Schoolers) to the General Assembly, praised Andrew Johnson's presidential reconstruction policies as "consummate wisdom," and regretted that "Stevens, Wade, Sumner [and] Wilson" seemed to want nothing less than "universal suffrage & the disenfranchisement of the white population in the South, giving the whole power to the negroes & a few hundred renegade white men in every state."[73] He did not live long enough to offer a distinction between segregation *itself* and the evils of Jim Crow.

And yet, if Hodge's record on slavery and slaveholding is poor enough to invite sarcasm, it is also worth remembering that he did actually have an antislavery moment, and it was such moments, and not the squalling of the Garrisonians, that prevented most Northerners from settling idly down beside slavery, and that, once disunion and blood-letting had set the table, allowed abolition to become a national goal. The critical aspect of Hodge for us to understand is not that he condoned slavery in the abstract, but that his abstract definition of slavery made it forever impossible for him wholeheartedly to support Southern slavery, and made it possible for him to swing like a gate toward antislavery whenever the Southern hand in the General Assembly weakened. He was, in that sense, more antislavery than any slaveholder could possibly have liked, and when on the eve of the Civil War E. N. Elliott re-published (without permission) Hodge's 1836 "Slavery" essay in his sensational collection *Cotton Is King and Pro-Slavery Arguments,* Elliott prudently trimmed out all of Hodge's

70. Hodge to H. L. Hodge, December 21, 1864, in Box 12, File 3, Hodge Papers.
71. Hodge to H. L. Hodge, April 15, 1865, in Box 12, File 3, Hodge Papers.
72. Hodge to H. L. Hodge, January 27, 1863, in Box 12, File 3, Hodge Papers.
73. Hodge, "The General Assembly," BRPR 37 (July 1865): 511-13; Hodge to H. L. Hodge, October 5, 1866 and December 25, 1868, in Box 12, File 3, Hodge Papers.

antislavery moment on the inevitability of slavery *itself* tending toward improvement and emancipation. That single excision testified more loudly than all of Hodge's admirers' protests to the poisonous capabilities of Hodge's moment. And yet, at the end of the day, Hodge remains a disappointment, and perhaps a crueler disappointment than even his critics have claimed, because Hodge did actually see what truth and justice were tending toward, and refused to hasten it even after Appomattox. That refusal, however, was a measure not so much of Hodge's intellectual frailty as it was of his oversize anxieties for the national union, for the union of the Presbyterian church, and for the survival of his own beloved Princeton. Princeton, and New Jersey, had taught him that no hurry was needed or desired on the subject of slavery, that "peaceful and natural modes of death" for slavery were the best remedy, and so the antislavery moment might stretch out to infinity. The real measure of Hodge's failing was that not even war could teach him more than that.

AFTERWORD

Where Does One Find the Legacy of Charles Hodge?

JAMES H. MOORHEAD

The legacy of Charles Hodge has been inescapably tied to subsequent Presbyterian controversies. In the decades after his death, liberal theology, the historical-critical study of the Bible, and scientific theories such as evolution made further inroads in Presbyterian pulpits and seminaries. Beginning in 1892, the General Assembly sought to shore up orthodoxy by pushing for a restrictive interpretation of the Westminster Confession of Faith, the denomination's official creed. On a number of occasions, the Assembly enumerated allegedly essential tenets of the Westminster Confession — for example, the inerrancy of Scripture — and thus in theory made assent to these doctrines mandatory for every Presbyterian minister. During the early 1920s, archconservatives sought to enforce a restrictive view of Presbyterian identity by purging theological liberals from the church. Faced with the prospect of protracted conflict and possibly schism, the Assembly retreated to a more moderate position. In 1926 and 1927, it adopted a report denying that any General Assembly possessed the power to define categorically the essential articles of the Westminster Confession. In effect, this action declared unconstitutional previous Assembly attempts to dictate the essentials and thus safeguarded a degree of theological pluralism within the denomination.[1]

1. The most detailed account of this theological struggle remains Lefferts A. Loetscher, *The Broadening Church: A Study of Theological Issues in the Presbyterian Church since 1869* (Philadelphia: University of Pennsylvania Press, 1954). See also Bradley J. Longfield, *The Presbyterian Controversy: Fundamentalists, Modernists, and Moderates* (New York: Oxford University Press, 1991), and George M. Marsden, *Fundamentalism and American Culture: The Shaping of Twentieth-Century Evangelicalism, 1870-1925* (New York: Oxford University Press, 1980), pp. 109-18.

Princeton Seminary was deeply involved in the controversies. Archibald A. Hodge (1823-86), the eldest son of Charles Hodge and successor to his father in the chair of didactic and polemical theology, co-authored with Benjamin B. Warfield (1851-1921) the article "Inspiration," published in the *Presbyterian Review* in April 1881. That article refined the argument for the inerrancy of Scripture and became a rallying cry for many conservatives. As A. A. Hodge's successor at Princeton, Warfield in turn stressed the necessity of the objective truth of the Bible and of the doctrines drawn from it. Unless Christians firmly avowed that truth, faith might dissolve into vague or subjective intuitions. In the 1920s, J. Gresham Machen (1881-1937), who had taught at Princeton since 1906, became the intellectual leader of Presbyterians seeking to purify the church of modernism. In his landmark *Christianity and Liberalism* (1923), Machen insisted that Christianity and liberalism were entirely different faiths and that liberals had no legitimate place in the ministry of the Presbyterian church. This aggressive policy divided the faculty of Princeton Seminary. Although all of the professors were doctrinally conservative, a minority deeply regretted what one of their number called the "theological panic" they believed Machen represented. Discerning no widespread Presbyterian defection from the historic Christian faith, they presented their conservatism in a more irenic fashion than Machen and were prepared to work with moderate liberals in order to further the unity and mission of the denomination. The General Assembly of 1926 appointed a special committee to investigate the divisions within the seminary. After conducting on-campus interviews with faculty and students, the committee recommended in 1928 and the General Assembly approved the following year a reorganization of the seminary. The restructuring augured a more theologically inclusive stance for the institution; and after 1936, when John Alexander Mackay (1889-1983) became president of the seminary, faculty appointments began to signal a broader theological perspective. Machen did not wait to see his worst fears realized. Along with several other Princeton professors, he resigned in 1929 to found Westminster Theological Seminary in Philadelphia. By 1936, Machen's deepening disputes with the Presbyterian Church in the U.S.A. led to his defrocking and to his participation in the founding of a new denomination, soon called the Orthodox Presbyterian Church.[2]

---

2. See Loetscher, *Broadening Church,* pp. 136-47; D. G. Hart, *Defending the Faith: J. Gresham Machen and the Crisis of Conservative Protestantism in Modern America* (Baltimore: Johns Hopkins University Press, 1994). The significant role of John A. Mackay in redefining

For those who lived through them, these events were traumatic and shaped the way they and later generations perceived what had gone before. Henceforth the legacy of Charles Hodge would be viewed through the lens of the 1920s and 1930s. For example, at the close of a recent two-volume history of Princeton Theological Seminary written out of deep sympathy with Hodge, David B. Calhoun observes, "Old Princeton ceased to exist in 1929." For the author this was a sad moment when the Presbyterian church "chose institutional unity and undermined not only its own history but its own integrity." Although Calhoun acknowledges that some influence of the old tradition lingered at Princeton and within the Presbyterian Church (U.S.A.), he leaves no doubt that by and large the glory departed from Israel in 1929. Yet according to Calhoun, the glory lives on elsewhere. "It is strong," he writes, "within the Orthodox Presbyterian Church, the Presbyterian Church in America, other Presbyterian denominations, and at theological seminaries, such as Westminster, Covenant, and Reformed." Calhoun's study serves as a reminder that for many conservative Protestants, Hodge and old Princeton represent a live theological option, not merely a historical curiosity; and they proudly claim as theirs what they believe Princeton Seminary and most Presbyterians abandoned in 1929.[3]

And what of Princeton itself? What of subsequent generations of theological professors who have taught at Hodge's institution? How have they understood his legacy and their relationship to it? In an essay prepared for the sesquicentennial of the seminary in 1962, theologian Hugh Thompson Kerr observed, "It is no secret that many contemporary professors at the Seminary feel completely out of touch theologically with their predecessors of a generation or more ago. . . ." Kerr was not apologetic about this fact. If anything, he rejoiced in the movement away from a theology he considered inadequate. Old Princeton was tempted, Kerr asserted, "in the direction of a cloistered scholasticism patterned after post-Reformation orthodoxy." Although "a highly cerebral theological tradition, . . . it often resulted in an intellectualism unrelated to vital religion, the currents of secular and scientific thought, and the practical life of the Church." Thus the changes that had come to the seminary represented a positive devel-

---

Princeton Seminary has not yet received the historical research or attention needed. For an overview of Mackay's life and work, see "Memorial Minute: John Alexander Mackay, 1889-1983," *Theology Today* 40 (Jan. 1984): 453-56. The "theological panic" reference is found in Loetscher, *Broadening Church*, p. 143.

3. David B. Calhoun, *Princeton Seminary*, vol. 2: *The Majestic Testimony, 1869-1929* (Edinburgh: Banner of Truth Trust, 1996), pp. 398, 428.

AFTERWORD

opment and were actually in accord with the deeper wellsprings of the Reformed tradition. The shift from the old Princeton to the new was a re-
invigoration of the tradition, not a defection from it. It was an instance of
fulfilling "the categorical imperative that the church, reformed, must ever
be reformed."[4]

The differences between these interpretations are obvious. In the one
view, old Princeton embodied the verities of the Christian faith. Its demise
was a tragedy mitigated only by the fact that when the light died in Princeton it was relit elsewhere. From the other perspective, old Princeton was
badly flawed, and its transformation saved the school from theological
sclerosis. Yet one assumption shared by Calhoun and Kerr is perhaps as
significant as their vast differences. Both take for granted that the 1920s
plowed a glacial moraine through the history of the seminary and thus utterly separated the old Princeton from the new. This perception has endured because, in the main, it is true. But it is not the whole truth. It over-
simplifies the story of a complex theological development and thus makes
it harder to assess the legacy of Charles Hodge in a nuanced fashion.

One oversimplification resulting from emphasis upon the 1920s is to
suggest that everything in the Princeton Theology before that decade was
of a single piece or at least tending in the same direction. In this view,
Archibald Alexander and Samuel Miller, the seminary's first professors,
founded the tradition that Charles Hodge codified, A. A. Hodge and B. B.
Warfield then defended, and for which J. Gresham Machen ultimately left
Princeton. Sydney E. Ahlstrom's *A Religious History of the American People*
(1972), still one of the most widely used texts in courses dealing with the
religious history of the United States, illustrates this interpretation.
Ahlstrom treats Hodge and the Princeton Theology in the context of what
he calls "dissent and reaction in Protestantism" — that is, as one of the
sources of the fundamentalist-modernist controversy. Ahlstrom writes:

> The Princeton Theology, expounded for a half-century by Charles
> Hodge and published in systematic form both by him and by his son,
> won acceptance far and wide as the strength and stay of embattled
> conservatism. And during the 1880s this dogmatic tradition gained
> further support from Benjamin B. Warfield (1851-1921), who brought
> great theological and historical prowess to the defense of the Re-
> formed tradition, and new rigidity into the doctrine of scriptural in-

4. Hugh T. Kerr, ed., *Sons of the Prophets: Leaders in Protestantism from Princeton Seminary*
(Princeton: Princeton University Press, 1963), pp. xii, xiii.

330

spiration. Each of Warfield's great interests, Reformed doctrine and biblical inerrancy, provided a major theme in the "Fundamentalist Controversy" that raged within Northern Presbyterianism.[5]

Ahlstrom is, of course, correct in discerning a trajectory from the Hodges to Warfield to the fundamentalist controversy. Many of the essays in this volume have echoed and confirmed this assessment. Thus James Turner writes of the "air of melancholy [that] hangs about Hodge's career." For "in the end neither his learning nor his ascendance could protect his worldview from being swept under the tide of historicism. At Princeton itself a remnant of loyalists did continue Hodge's work, but in the twentieth century even they were forced to abandon ship and ended marooned on the margin of American culture."

Yet there is another question that needs to be asked: What else, if anything, was in the life and thought of Hodge that cannot be plotted along the arc to Warfield and Machen? The contributors of this volume have demonstrated that there was more. Mark Noll gives us an important clue to finding another part of Hodge when he encourages readers to look beyond the latter's *Systematic Theology*. Often those who understand Hodge as a so-called scholastic theologian preparing the way for fundamentalism focus primarily upon that three-volume work. With its air of delivering eternal verities unrelated to time and place, the *Systematic Theology* can indeed bear that interpretive construction. But Noll insists that this work is not the only key to Hodge. Rather than being the *summa* or the "capstone" of his career, that work should be understood according to another metaphor. It is "a caboose — stately, impressive, and hard to miss though it may be — at the end of a very long train." More characteristic of the majority of "cars" on Hodge's "train" were the hundreds of pages he wrote in the *Princeton Review* or in monographs. These works, far from seeming timeless intellectual exercises, passionately engaged then-contemporary issues. E. Brooks Holifield's essay emphasizes a similar point. While Hodge's successors may have tried to push him "into the tight boundaries of the Darwinian and infallibility debates," he was in his own context an exemplification of "the nascent ideal of the professional theologian as an incisive broad-ranging thinker able to comment on any question of theology that might arise."

One might press Holifield's point even further, for Hodge had a breadth of concern and commitment beyond systematic theology nar-

---

5. Sydney E. Ahlstrom, *A Religious History of the American People* (New Haven: Yale University Press, 1972), pp. 813-14.

AFTERWORD

rowly conceived. Hodge's serious reservations about Darwin's theory notwithstanding, Ronald Numbers's essay makes clear that the Princeton professor maintained a lifelong engagement with the sciences. Whether attending lectures on physiology and medicine, inviting scientists to gatherings in his home, or publishing articles on the latest scientific developments in the *Princeton Review,* he exhibited an abiding zeal for science. His interest in politics and economics was equally broad. Usually well informed and often opinionated in regard to public issues, his passion for politics moved him successively through Federalism, anti-Jacksonism and the Whig Party, and ultimately to Lincoln and the Republicans. Behind this engagement was his Reformed conviction that Christians had an obligation to shape the civic order, and thus it "was entirely in character," Richard Carwardine writes, "that under his editorial direction the *Biblical Repertory and Princeton Review* should admit essays and reviews, some from his own pen, that at times turned it into something of a polemical political journal." The essays in this book also hint (though the issue needs to be explored further) at the extent to which Hodge the systematic theologian was a churchman — often a mediating and pragmatic one at that. As the split between Old and New School Presbyterians loomed in the 1830s, Hodge had strong sympathies with the Old School's theology; but, fearing that the most hard-line Old Schoolers would divide the church, he urged moderation. Only when the split became unavoidable did he adopt the partisan Old School stance for which he is often remembered. The same desire for conciliation prompted his desperate attempt to hold the Southern and Northern wings of the Old School together even as the nation was dividing in 1861.

Of course one must not, in overreaction to one stereotype of Hodge, create another. If he was not a twentieth-century fundamentalist born out of season, neither was he a centrist or moderate by later standards. The essays in this volume attest that he was indeed conservative on most issues. For example, Brian Gerrish and E. Brooks Holifield demonstrate that Hodge remained largely oblivious to the virtues of liberal theologies such as those of Schleiermacher or Bushnell. (Hodge's appreciation for Bushnell's *Christian Nurture* and its critique of revivalistic individualism was perhaps the chief exception.) David Kelsey notes that Hodge, while open in principle to the historical-critical study of the Bible, in fact often approached Scripture in a pre-critical fashion. Moreover, Hodge's vision of what Louise Stevenson calls "manly ministers" scarcely allowed women to appear on the radar of consciousness. Likewise, his "antislavery moment," as Allen Guelzo styles it, was hedged by evasions and compromises.

In short, the essays in this volume do not require that one jettison the image of Hodge as a theological and social conservative, but they do point to complexities that commentators, whether friendly or hostile to the Princeton professor, often miss. They serve as reminders that Hodge's life and thought, understood in their own context, were more than foreshadowings of subsequent events. Once this fact is grasped, then one may discover more nuanced answers than are often given to the question: "Where does one find the legacy of Charles Hodge?"

The usual response, as already noted, traces the legacy along a path from Hodge to Warfield and thence to Machen and those like him who seceded from the Presbyterian Church in the U.S.A. and from mainstream Protestantism. That perception is only partly correct, for old Princeton before the reorganization of 1929 was not a monolith. Despite significant theological continuities, there were also very important differences. In Warfield's writings were the hints of a growing doctrinal intransigence, testifying that at least in tone a subtle shift from Hodge had already occurred. The transformation was even more pronounced by the time Machen arrived on the scene. In his willingness (and, at times, even his eagerness) to divide the Presbyterian church over doctrine, one sees an ecclesiology at variance with that of Hodge's more temperate approach to the Old School–New School rupture and to the subsequent split of Northern and Southern Old Schoolers. Moreover, Machen and Hodge offered different approaches to the issue of Christianity's public role. As one recent sympathetic biographer has noted, Machen was a libertarian distrusting efforts to legislate morality. In him one discerns a stance more akin to the Southern Presbyterian concept of the "spirituality of the church" than to the typically Reformed notion of Hodge that faith had to shape the public order. This difference, of course, is not surprising in view of the fact that Machen grew up in a Baltimore family where Southern Presbyterian traditions were revered. To make these observations, one must again hasten to add, is *not* to deny the important continuities linking Hodge to Machen. It is to assert, however, that the conservative Protestants who claimed to have inherited Hodge's mantle did not receive it whole or unaltered.

And is it possible that one may also find the legacy of Hodge where it supposedly ceased in 1929 — in the institution where Hodge taught, in the Presbyterian denomination to which he belonged, and in the wider mainstream Protestantism of which that denomination has been a conspicuous representative? The mere suggestion will strike many as an impertinence. Those who self-consciously claim Hodge's legacy will not be eager to share it with those whom they regard as its betrayers. By contrast, most mainstream Protestants seldom think of Hodge; but those who do, wishing themselves rid of him, will probably greet the notion of his persisting legacy with an enthusiasm akin to Ebenezer Scrooge's when he encountered the ghost of Jacob Marley. Yet the idea of a legacy of Hodge outside conservative sectors of Protestantism is not fanciful. Hodge's eagerness (at least at certain points in his career) to mediate theological disputes and his engagement with the social, political, and cultural trends of his day are more characteristic of mainstream religion than of the fundamentalism with which Hodge is usually associated.

Perhaps, then, one may tentatively answer the question of Hodge's legacy by saying that it bifurcated in the 1920s. His doctrinal commitments, narrowed and made more rigid, were claimed by some conservative Protestants, while his broader concerns with modern thought and culture were maintained by the school where he had taught and by mainstream Protestantism, albeit without the specific theological underpinnings Hodge had given those concerns. Further research would, of course, be needed to sustain or to nuance this judgment. In any event, the time has come for serious historical investigation of a figure who has too often been either a bogey or an icon to later generations.

Bibliography of the Works
by and about Charles Hodge

COMPILED BY JOHN W. STEWART

EDITOR'S NOTE: I am especially grateful for the untiring assistance of
Joe L. Coker, a Ph.D. candidate at Princeton Theological Seminary, and
the invaluable advice of William A. Harris, Librarian for Archives and Special Collections at the same seminary. This bibliography remains incomplete and is still a "work in progress." That incompleteness, as others have
remarked, is an indication of the depth, breadth, and continuing interest
in the work and influence of Charles Hodge.

An outline of the Bibliography is as follows:

I. The Published Works by Hodge
   A. Books
   B. Pamphlets
   C. Articles published in the *Biblical Repertory and Princeton Review*
   D. Articles in Other Journals
   E. Sermons
   F. Incidental Writings
II. Unpublished Works and Manuscripts by Hodge
III. Published Works about Hodge
   A. Nineteenth-Century Works
   B. Twentieth-Century Works
IV. Unpublished Works about Hodge
V. Bibliographies for Hodge's Works by Other Scholars

JOHN W. STEWART

I. THE PUBLISHED WORKS BY HODGE

A. Books (listed chronologically)

A Dissertation on the Importance of Biblical Literature. Trenton: George Sherman, 1822.

The Place of the Bible in a System of Education: A Sermon Preached in Philadelphia. Philadelphia: American Sunday School Union, 1832.

Commentary on Romans: Designed for Students of the English Bible. Philadelphia: Gregg & Eliot, 1835. [In print, Grand Rapids: Eerdmans, 1990; Edinburgh: Banner of Truth, 1997; and Wheaton: Crossway Books, 1994.] This work went through several editions, the last in 1884. It was also translated into French in 1841 and published in England and Scotland. For a history of this publication see the editor's comments in the 1884 edition.

Questions on the Epistle to the Romans: Designed for Bible Classes and Sunday Schools. Philadelphia: Gregg & Elliot, 1835.

The Constitutional History of the Presbyterian Church in the United States of America. 2 vols. Philadelphia: William S. Martien, 1839-40.

The Way of Life. Philadelphia: American Sunday-School Union, 1841. [In print, Edinburgh: Banner of Truth Trust, 1978. Reprinted in *Charles Hodge: The Way of Life.* Ed. Mark A. Noll. New York: Paulist Press, 1987.]

A Commentary on Romans: Abridged by the Author for Use of Sunday Schools and Bible Classes. Philadelphia: Henry Perkins, 1843.

Theological Essays: Reprinted from "The Princeton Review." New York: Wiley and Putnam, 1846. [By Hodge et al.]

What Is Presbyterianism? An address delivered before the Presbyterian Historical Society at their anniversary meeting in Philadelphia on Tuesday evening, May 1, 1855. Philadelphia: Presbyterian Board of Publication, 1855.

A Commentary on the Epistle to the Ephesians. New York: Carter & Bros., 1856. [In print, Wheaton: Crossway Books, 1991.]

An Exposition of the First Epistle to the Corinthians. New York: Carter & Bros., 1856. [In print, Edinburgh: Banner of Truth, 1978; and Wheaton: Crossway Books, 1995.]

Essays and Reviews: Selections from "The Princeton Review." New York: Robert Carter & Brothers, 1857.

An Exposition of the Second Epistle to the Corinthians. New York: Carter & Bros., 1857. [In print, Edinburgh: Banner of Truth, 1978, and Wheaton: Crossway Books, 1995.]

Systematic Theology. 3 vols. New York: Charles Scribner and Co., 1871 [vols. 1 and

2]; New York: Scribner, Armstrong, and Co., 1872 [vol. 3]. Reprint, Peabody, MA: Hendrickson, 1999.

Systematic Theology. Abridged edition with study notes and index. Edited by Edward N. Gross. Grand Rapids: Baker Book House, 1992.

What Is Darwinism? New York: Scribner, Armstrong, and Company, 1874. [Reprinted in *What Is Darwinism? and Other Writings on Science and Religion.* Ed. Mark A. Noll & David N. Livingston. Grand Rapids: Baker Book House, 1994.]

Index to Systematic Theology. New York: Scribner, Armstrong, and Company, 1877.

Discussions in Church Polity: From the Contributions to "The Princeton Review." Ed. William Durant. New York: Charles Scribner's Sons, 1878. This large work extracted and reprinted Hodge's thoughts about ecclesiology originally presented in the *Biblical Repertory and Princeton Review.*

Conference Papers: Or Analyses of Discourses, Doctrinal and Practical; Delivered on Sabbath Afternoon to the Students of the Seminary. New York: Charles Scribner's Sons, 1879. [Reprint, *Princeton Sermons: Outlines of Discourses, Doctrinal and Practical, at Princeton Theological Seminary.* London: Banner of Truth, 1958.]

B. Pamphlets

Introductory Lecture Delivered in the Theological Seminary, Princeton, N.J. Nov. 7, 1828. N.p.: Connolly & Madden, n.d.

A Brief Account of the Last Hours of Albert B. Dod. Princeton: John T. Robinson, 1845.

Reunion of the Old and New School Presbyterian Churches. New York: Charles Scribner and Company, 1867.

Address of Rev. Charles Hodge, D.D., at the Conference of Commencement Week, Saturday, April 26, 1873. N.p., n.d.

A Solemn Question! Can the Protestants Conscientiously Build up the Churches of the Pope? Halifax: Nova Scotia Printing Co., 1873.

Proper Method of Dealing with Inquirers. New York: American Tract Society, 1876.

The Teaching Office of the Church. New York: Board of Foreign Missions, 1882.

The Rights of General Assembly Not to be Annulled by Any Assumed Authority of the Presbyteries; Their Relations to Each Other Defined by Dr. Hodge in "The Princeton Review." New York: E. B. Treat, 1896. [Also published by Anson D. F. Randolph & Co., 1896. Contains extensive excerpts from articles by Hodge.]

Adequate Support of the Ministry: Sustentation Fund. Princeton: Blanchard, n.d.
How is the Sabbath to be Sanctified? Bellefonte, Pa.: Bellefonte Press Co., n.d.
Sunday Laws: Or Shall the Sabbath be Protected? Philadelphia: Presbyterian Board
   of Publication, n.d.

C. Articles published in the
Biblical Repertory and Princeton Review

EDITORS' NOTE: First, this journal had several title changes for this journal, beginning with *Biblical Repertory,* then *Biblical Repertory and Theological
Review, Biblical Repertory and Princeton Review* and later, *Princeton Review.* In
the nineteenth century others usually referred to it as simply *The Princeton
Review.* Second, these volumes have anonymous "Short Notices" and "Literary Intelligences." As editor of the journal, Hodge undoubtedly wrote
many of these brief commentaries, but their authorship cannot be positively identified. Third, Hodge's account of the history of the journal, an
index, and short biographies of the journal's many authors may be found
in *The Biblical Repertory and Princeton Review: The Index Volume, 1825-1868*
(Philadelphia: Peter Walker, 1871). Finally and most importantly, Hodge's
entire journal has now been placed online by the University of Michigan's
in its "Making of America" series and can be accessed through http://
moa.umdl.umich.edu

The Biblical Repertory and Theological Review (1825-28)

   Vol. 1 (1825)

"Introduction." Pp. iii-vi.
"Proposal for the Periodical Publication of a Collection of Dissertations,
   Principally in Biblical Literature." Pp. 1-3.

The Biblical Repertory and Princeton Review (The New Series 1829-68)

   Vol. 1 (1829)

   JANUARY   "Introductory Lecture Delivered in the Theological Seminary,
                Princeton, NJ November 7, 1828 . . ." Pp. 75-98.
      JULY   "Public Education . . ." Pp. 370-410.
                "On the Sonship of Christ." Pp. 429-56. [Hodge's authorship of
                this two-part article is ambiguous.]

OCTOBER   "On the Sonship of Christ." Pp. 457-80.
"Remarks of the Editors on the Foregoing Strictures." Pp. 602-38.

Vol. 2 (1830)

JANUARY   "Professor Stuart's Postscript to His Letter to the Editors of the *Biblical Repertory.*" Pp. 122-45.
APRIL   "Regeneration and the Manner of its Occurrence, a Sermon . . . by Samuel H. Cox." Pp. 250-97.
JULY   "Review of an Article in the June number of the *Christian Spectator*, entitled, 'Inquiries Respecting the Doctrine of Imputation.'" Pp. 425-72.

Vol. 3 (1831)

JANUARY   "The *American Quarterly Review* on Sunday Mails." Pp. 86-134.
JULY   "Review of Sprague's *Lectures to Young People.*" Pp. 295-306.
"The *Christian Spectator* on the Doctrine of Imputation." Pp. 407-43.
OCTOBER   "Remarks on Dr. Cox's Communication." Pp. 514-43.

Vol. 4 (1832)

JANUARY   "Hengstenberg's Vindication of the Book of Daniel." Pp. 48-71.
APRIL   "The New Divinity Tried . . ." Pp. 278-304.

Vol. 5 (1833)

JANUARY   "Suggestions to Theological Students . . ." Pp. 100-113.
JULY   "*A Commentary on the Epistle to the Romans* . . . by Moses Stuart." Pp. 381-416.

Vol. 6 (1834)

APRIL   "Lachmann's New Testament." Pp. 269-81.
OCTOBER   "The Act and Testimony." Pp. 505-22.

Vol. 7 (1835)

JANUARY   "Act and Testimony, No. II." Pp. 110-34.
APRIL   "*Notes, Explanatory and Practical, on the Epistle to the Romans* . . . by Albert Barnes." Pp. 285-340.
JULY   "The General Assembly of 1835." Pp. 440-82.
OCTOBER   "*Narrative of the Visit to the American Churches* . . . by Andrew Reed and James Matheson . . ." Pp. 598-626.

Vol. 8 (1836)

JANUARY "*Commentar über den Brief Pauli an die Römer.* Von L. J. Rückert . . ." or "Rückert's Commentary on the Romans." Pp. 39-51.

APRIL "*Slavery.* By William E. Channing . . ." Pp. 268-305.

JULY "The General Assembly of 1836." Pp. 415-76.

Vol. 9 (1837)

JANUARY "*A Plea for Voluntary Societies and a Defense of the Decisions of the General Assembly of 1836 against the Strictures of the Princeton Reviewers and others.* By a member of the Assembly . . ." or "Voluntary Societies and Ecclesiastical Organizations." Pp. 101-52.

APRIL "1. The Greek Testament, with English notes . . . by . . . S. T. Bloomfield . . . 2. The New Testament arranged in Historical and Chronological order . . . by Rev. George Townsend . . ." Pp. 266-98.

JULY "The General Assembly of 1837." Pp. 407-85.

Vol. 10 (1838)

JANUARY "*Tracts for the Times.* By members of the University of Oxford . . ." or "Oxford Tracts." Pp. 84-119.

APRIL "1. *Facts and Observations* . . . by James Wood . . ." or "State of the Presbyterian Church." Pp. 243-70.

JULY "The General Assembly of 1838." Pp. 457-503.

OCTOBER "1. *An Account of the present state of the Island of Puerto Rico.* By Colonel Flinter . . . 2. W. India Emancipation. By John A. Thorne . . ." Pp. 602-44.

Vol. 11 (1839)

JULY "*A Brief History and Vindication of the Doctrines received and established in the Churches of New England* . . . by Thomas Clapp . . ." Pp. 369-404.

"General Assembly of 1839." Pp. 416-448.

OCTOBER "*Decretum Synodi Nationalis Ecclesiarum Reformatarum Galliae initio Anno 1645* . . . ab Andrea Riveto . . ." or "Testimonies on the Doctrine of Imputation." Pp. 553-79.

"Letters to the Rev. Professor Stuart by Daniel Dana . . ." or "Dr. Dana's Letters." Pp. 584-96.

Vol. 12 (1840)

JANUARY "*A Discourse on the Latest Form of Infidelity* . . . by Andrews Norton . . ." or "The Latest Form of Infidelity." Pp. 31-71.

APRIL "Davies's *State of Religion among the Dissenters in Virginia*" or "Presbyterianism in Virginia." Pp. 169-205.

"*A Treatise on Justification.* By George Junkin" or "Junkin on Justification." Pp. 268-82.

JULY "*A History of the Rise, Progress, Genius and Character of American Presbyterianism* . . . by William Hill . . ." Pp. 322-50.

"Catalogue Collegii Neo-Caesariensis . . ." or "New Jersey College and President Davies." Pp. 371-93.

"The General Assembly of 1840." Pp. 411-31.

OCTOBER "*Sectarianism is Heresy* . . . by A. Wylie." Pp. 465-81.

"*The Substance of a Discourse* . . . by J. C. Coit . . ." or "Discourse on Religion by Mr. Coit." Pp. 582-99.

Vol. 13 (1841)

JULY "*A Brief Examination* . . . by George W. Doane . . ." or "Bishop Doane and the Oxford Tracts." Pp. 450-62. [Co-authored with J. A. Alexander.]

Vol. 14 (1842)

JANUARY "*Sermons on Important Subjects.* By . . . Samuel Davies . . . With an Essay on the Life and Times of the Author. By Albert Barnes . . ." Pp. 142-69.

APRIL "*The History of Christianity* . . . By . . . H. H. Milman . . ." Pp. 236-66.

JULY "The General Assembly of 1842." Pp. 472-523.

OCTOBER "*The Divine Rule of Faith and Practice.* By William Goode . . ." or "Rule of Faith." Pp. 598-630.

Vol. 15 (1843)

JANUARY "*The Marriage Question* . . . by Parsons Cooke." Pp. 182-90.

APRIL "Rights of Ruling Elders." Pp. 432-43.

JULY "The General Assembly of 1843." Pp. 407-69.

Vol. 16 (1844)

JANUARY "Proceedings of the General Assembly of the Free Church of

Scotland, May 1843." Pp. 86-119. [Co-authored with J. A. Alexander.]

APRIL   "Neander's *History of the Planting of the Church*." Pp. 155-83.

"The Claims of the Free Church of Scotland. By Thomas Smith." Pp.
229-61.

"Presbyterian Government not a Hierarchy, but a Commonwealth . . .
by Robert J. Breckinridge." Pp. 276-306.

JULY   "The General Assembly of 1844." Pp. 418-53.

OCTOBER   *"The Integrity of our National Union vs. Abolitionism* . . . by Rev.
George Junkin" or "Abolitionism." Pp. 545-81.

Vol. 17 (1845)

JANUARY   *"Sacerdotal Absolution: A Sermon* . . . by M. A. Curtis." Pp. 43-61.
[Co-authored with J. A. Alexander.]

*"Christ, The Only Sacrifice: or the Atonement in its Relations to God
and Man. By Nathan S. S. Beman*." Pp. 84-138.

APRIL   *"The Arguments of Romanists from the Infallibility of the Church and
Testimony of the Fathers on behalf of the Apocrypha, discussed and
refuted,* by James H. Thornwell." Pp. 268-82.

JULY   "The General Assembly." Pp. 428-71.

OCTOBER   *"Principles of Protestantism* . . . by Philip Schaff" or "Schaff's Protestantism." Pp. 626-36.

Vol. 18 (1846)

JANUARY   *"A Treatise on the Scriptural Doctrine of Original Sin* . . . by H. A.
Boardman" or "The Original State of Man." Pp. 67-81.

"The Unity of the Church. By Henry Edward Manning" or "Theories of the Church." Pp. 137-58.

APRIL   "Essays in the *Presbyterian* by Theophilus on the question: Is
Baptism in the Church of Rome Valid?" or "Is the Church
of Rome a Part of the Visible Church?" Pp. 320-44.

JULY   "The General Assembly." Pp. 418-56.

"Lectures on Biblical History . . . by William Neill." Pp. 456-61.

OCTOBER   *"Evangelische Kirchen-Zeitung.* Herausgegeben von C. W. Hengstenberg" or "Religious State of Germany." Pp. 514-46.

"The Catholic News Letter, St. Louis . . ." or "The Late Dr. John
Breckinridge." Pp. 585-89.

*"Lectures on Mental Philosophy and Theology. By James Rich-
ards* . . ." or "Life and Writings of Dr. Richards." Pp. 589-
600.

Vol. 19 (1847)

APRIL   *"Lectures on Systematic Theology . . .* by Rev. Charles Finney." Pp. 237-77.

JULY   *"An Earnest Appeal to the Free Church of Scotland, on the subject of Economics.* By Thomas Chalmers" or "Support of the Clergy." Pp. 360-78.
        "The General Assembly." Pp. 396-444.

OCTOBER   *"Discourses on Christian Nurture.* By Horace Bushnell." Pp. 502-39.

Vol. 20 (1848)

APRIL   *"The Mystical Presence. A Vindication of the Reformed or Calvinistic Doctrine of the Holy Eucharist.* By John W. Nevin" or "Doctrine of the Reformed Church on the Lord's Supper." Pp. 259-97.
        "Das Leben Johann Calvin's. Ein Zeugniss für die Wahrheit, von Paul Henry" or "Henry's Abridged Life of Calvin." Pp. 278-305. [Hodge's authorship of this article is disputed.]

JULY   "The General Assembly of 1848." Pp. 403-51.
        "The Power of the Pulpit. By Gardiner Spring." Pp. 463-89. [Co-authored with J. A. Alexander.]

Vol. 21 (1849)

JANUARY   "American Board of Commissioners for Foreign Missions. Special Report of the Prudential Committee . . ." or "American Church Boards . . ." Pp. 1-42.

APRIL   *"God in Christ; Three Discourses . . .* by Horace Bushnell." Pp. 259-97.

JULY   "The General Assembly." Pp. 422-57.

OCTOBER   *"The Question of Negro Slavery and the New Constitution of Kentucky.* By Robert J. Breckinridge" or "Emancipation." Pp. 582-607.

Vol. 22 (1850)

APRIL   *"Memoirs of Rev. Walter M. Lowrie . . .* by his Father." Pp. 280-312.

JULY   "The General Assembly." Pp. 441-83.

OCTOBER   *"The Theology of the Intellect and that of the Feelings.* By Edwards A. Park" or "Professor Park's Sermon." Pp. 642-74.

Vol. 23 (1851)

JANUARY   "*Conscience and the Constitution.* By Moses Stuart" or "Civil Government." Pp. 125-58.

APRIL   "Remarks on the *Princeton Review,* Vol. XXII. No. IV. Art. VII. By Edwards A. Park . . ." or "Professor Park's Remarks." Pp. 306-47.

JULY   "The General Assembly." Pp. 521-53.

OCTOBER   "*Unity and Diversities of Belief even on Imputed and Involuntary Sin* . . . by Edwards A. Park . . ." or "Professor Park and *The Princeton Review.*" Pp. 674-95.

Vol. 24 (1852)

JULY   "The General Assembly." Pp. 462-501.

Vol. 25 (1853)

APRIL   "The Idea of the Church." Pp. 249-90.

JULY   "The Idea of the Church." Pp. 339-89.

"Theology in Germany." Pp. 430-50. [Hodge's authorship of this article is disputed.]

"The General Assembly." Pp. 450-528.

OCTOBER   "Visibility of the Church." Pp. 670-85.

Vol. 26 (1854)

JANUARY   "*The Conflict of Ages* . . . by Edward Beecher" or "Beecher's Great Conflict." Pp. 96-138.

"*History of the Apostolic Church* . . . by Philip Schaff." Pp. 148-93.

APRIL   "*A Vindication of the Doctrine of the Church of England on the Validity of the Orders of the Scotch and Foreign Non-Episcopal Churches.* By W. Goode" or "The Church of England and Presbyterian Orders." Pp. 377-404.

JULY   "*Denominational Education.* By R. J. Breckinridge" or "The Education Question." Pp. 504-44.

"The General Assembly." Pp. 545-80.

Vol. 27 (1855)

JANUARY   "*The Life of Archibald Alexander.* By James W. Alexander" or "Memoir of Dr. Alexander." Pp. 133-59.

APRIL   "*The Truth and Life* . . . by Charles P. McIlvaine" or "Bishop McIlvaine on the Church." Pp. 350-59.

JULY   "Eutaxia; or, the Presbyterian Liturgies" or "The Presbyterian Liturgies." Pp. 445-67.

"The General Assembly." Pp. 467-542.

Vol. 28 (1856)

JANUARY   *"The Church Review and Register* for October 1855. Art. VI. 'Professor Hodge on the Permanency of the Apostolic Office.'" Pp. 1-38.

APRIL   *"The Elements of Psychology* . . . by Victor Cousin. Translated by Caleb S. Henry . . ." or *"The Princeton Review* and Cousin's Philosophy." Pp. 331-87.

JULY   "The General Assembly of 1856." Pp. 552-90.

OCTOBER   "The Church — Its Perpetuity." Pp. 689-715.

Vol. 29 (1857)

JANUARY   "Free Agency." Pp. 101-35.

JULY   "The General Assembly of 1857." Pp. 440-97.

"On the Action of Our Church Courts in Judicial Cases, and Suggestions in Reference to Them." Pp. 497-506.

"Report on the History and Recent Collation of the English Version of the Bible . . . of the American Bible Society . . ." or "The American Bible Society and its New Standard Edition of the English Version." Pp. 507-42.

OCTOBER   *"The Inspiration of Holy Scripture* . . . by William Lee" or "Inspiration." Pp. 660-98.

Vol. 30 (1858)

APRIL   *"The Tecnobaptist.* By R. B. Mayes" or "The Church Membership of Infants." Pp. 347-89.

JULY   "The General Assembly." Pp. 533-70.

OCTOBER   "Adoption of the Confession of Faith." Pp. 669-92.

"The Revised Book of Discipline." Pp. 692-721.

Vol. 31 (1859)

JANUARY   *"The Testimony of Modern Science to the Unity of Mankind* . . . by J. L. Cabell" or "The Unity of Mankind." Pp. 103-49.

APRIL   "Demission of the Ministry." Pp. 360-70.

JULY   "The General Assembly." Pp. 538-618.

OCTOBER   *"History of the Institution of the Sabbath Day, its Uses and Abuses.* By William Logan Fisher" or "Sunday Laws." Pp. 733-67.

Vol. 32 (1860)

JANUARY   *"Christian Life and Doctrine.* By the Rev. W. Cunningham" or "What Is Christianity?" Pp. 118-61.

APRIL   *"The First and Second Adam. The Elohim Revealed* . . . by Samuel J. Baird." Pp. 335-76.

JULY   "Reid's Collected Writings. Preface, Notes, and Supplementary Dissertations by Sir William Hamilton . . ." or "Sir William Hamilton's Philosophy of the Conditioned." Pp. 472-510. [Possibly co-authored with Francis A. March.]
"The General Assembly." Pp. 511-46.
"Presbyterianism." Pp. 546-67.

Vol. 33 (1861)

JANUARY   "The State of the Country." Pp. 1-36.

APRIL   "The Church and the Country." Pp. 322-76.

JULY   "The General Assembly." Pp. 511-68.

Vol. 34 (1862)

JANUARY   "Are There Too Many Ministers?" Pp. 133-46.
"England and America." Pp. 147-77.

JULY   "Examination of some Reasonings against the Unity of Mankind" or "Diversity of Species in the Human Race." Pp. 435-64.
"The General Assembly." Pp. 464-524.

Vol. 35 (1863)

JANUARY   "The War." Pp. 140-69.

JULY   "The General Assembly." Pp. 439-99.

OCTOBER   "Relation of the Church and State." Pp. 679-93.

Vol. 36 (1864)

JANUARY   "Can God Be Known?" Pp. 122-52.

JULY   "The General Assembly." Pp. 506-74.

Vol. 37 (1865)

JANUARY   "Nature of Man." Pp. 111-35.

APRIL   "The Principles of Church Union, and the Reunion of the Old and New-School Presbyterians." Pp. 271-313.

JULY   "President Lincoln." Pp. 435-58.
"The General Assembly." Pp. 458-514.

OCTOBER   "The *Princeton Review* on the State of the Country and of the Church." Pp. 627-58.

Vol. 38 (1866)

JANUARY   "Sustentation Fund." Pp. 1-24.
APRIL   "*The Vicarious Sacrifice* . . . by Horace Bushnell." Pp. 161-94.
JULY   "The General Assembly." Pp. 425-500.

Vol. 39 (1867)

JULY   "The General Assembly." Pp. 440-522.

Vol. 40 (1868)

JANUARY   "Presbyterian Reunion. By the Rev. Henry B. Smith D.D. Reprinted from the *American Presbyterian and the Theological Review*, October 1867." Pp. 53-83.
APRIL   "*Representative Responsibility* . . . by Henry Wallace." Pp. 219-45.
JULY   "Professor Fisher on the *Princeton Review* and Dr. Taylor's Theology." Pp. 368-98.
"The Protest and Answer." Pp. 456-77.

Vol. 41 (1869)

JULY   "The New Basis of Union." Pp. 462-66.
OCTOBER   "Morell on Revelation and Inspiration." Pp. 489-511.

The Princeton Review

Vol. 42 (1870)

JULY   "The Trial Period in History." Pp. 411-25.

Vol. 43 (1871)

JANUARY   "Preaching the Gospel to the Poor." Pp. 83-95.
APRIL   "The Relation of Adam's First Sin to the Fall of the Race." Pp. 239-62.

Presbyterian Quarterly and Princeton Review

New Series, Vol. 5 (1876)

APRIL   "Christianity Without Christ." Pp. 352-62.

D. Articles in Other Journals

"The State of Religion in France." *Christian Advocate* 2 (October 1827): 449-53; (November 1827): 499-502.

"Anniversary Address to the American Home Missionary Society." *The Home Missionary* 2 (June 1, 1829): 3-20.

"Mr. Editor." *Presbyterian* 2 (May 9, 1832): 51.

"Princeton Theological Seminary." *Presbyterian* 6 (January 7, 1836): 2. [Co-authored with Archibald Alexander and Samuel Miller; also in *The New-York Observer*, December 26, 1835.]

"To the Christian Public." *Presbyterian* 6 (April 30, 1836): 70.

"A Correction of Dr. Elliot's Statement." *Presbyterian* 12 (August 20, 1842): 134.

"Narrative of the State of Religion." *Presbyterian* 16 (June 13, 1846): 94.

"The Teaching Office of the Church." *Missionary Chronicle* (June 1848): 9-11.

"The Late Dr. J. W. Alexander." *Presbyterian* 29 (August 13, 1859): 130.

"Dr. Hodge's Remarks at the Seminary." *Presbyterian* 30 (February 11, 1860): 22.

"A Communication from Rev. Charles Hodge, D.D." *The Central Presbyterian* (January 19, 1861).

"Protest of Dr. Hodge and Others." *Presbyterian* 31 (June 8, 1861): 90.

"The Bible in Science." *The New York Observer* (March 26, 1863): 98-99.

"Dr. Hodge's Address at the National Sabbath Convention." *Presbyterian* 33 (December 5, 1863): 193.

"Another Letter from Dr. Hodge to the Rev. David Wills." *Presbyterian* 36 (August 18, 1866): 2. [Reprinted from the *Macon* (Ga.) *Daily Telegraph*.]

"The First Princeton Professors." *Presbyterian* 45 (May 15, 1875): 7.

"Testimonial to A. H. Ritchie's picture, 'Mercy Knocking at the Wicket Gate,' from Bunyan's *Pilgrim's Progress*." *Presbyterian* 45 (December 25, 1875): 10.

"A Last Word." *New York Independent*, May 9, 1878. [Reprinted in *The Presbyterian*, September 27, 1879.]

"An Unpublished Letter of Dr. Hodge to Dr. S. S. Schmucker, On Christian Union." *The Lutheran Church Review* 18 (April 1899): 207-13.

"Unity of the Church." *Christianity Today* 2 (May 26, 1958): 23-27.

E. Sermons

The Place of the Bible in a System of Education: A Sermon, Preached in Philadelphia, at the Request of the American Sunday-School Union, May 21, 1832. Philadelphia: American Sunday School Union, 1833. [Also published in *Sermons Delivered at the Anniversaries of the American Sunday-School Union.* Philadelphia: American Sunday-School Union, 1834.]

A Sermon, Preached in Philadelphia, at the Request of the American Sunday-School Union, May 21, 1832. Philadelphia: American Sunday-School Union, 1833.

A Discourse Delivered at the Funeral of Mrs. Martha Rice, March 7, 1844. Princeton: n.p., 1844.

"Faith in Christ, The Source of Life," in *The Princeton Pulpit.* Ed. by John T. Duffield. New York: Charles Scribner, 1852. Pp. 74-94.

"Sermon by Charles Hodge," in *Sermons Preached Before the Congregation of the Presbyterian Church, Corner of Fifth Avenue and Nineteenth Street, at the "Memorial Services," October 9, 1859, Appointed in Reference to the Death of Their Late Pastor, James Waddell Alexander.* New York: Anson D. F. Randolph, 1859. Pp. 3-22.

"Funeral Address Delivered in the First Presbyterian Church, Burlington, New Jersey, on the 30th of July, 1860," in *Memorial of Cortlandt Van Rensselaer.* Philadelphia: C. Sherman & Son, 1860. Pp. 8-17. [Also published in *The Presbyterian Magazine* 10 (September 1860): 388-95.]

"Funeral Sermon, by the Rev. Charles Hodge, D.D.," in Thomas L. Janeway, *Memoir of the Rev. Jacob J. Janeway, D.D.* Philadelphia: Presbyterian Board of Publication, 1861. Pp. 277-96.

A Discourse Delivered at the Re-Opening of the Chapel, September 27, 1874. Princeton: Chas. S. Robinson, 1874.

Conference Papers, or Analyses of Discourses, Doctrinal and Practical, Delivered on Sabbath Afternoons to the Students of the Theological Seminary, Princeton, New Jersey. New York: Charles Scribner's Sons, 1879. [Also published as *Princeton Sermons: Outlines of Discourses, Doctrinal and Practical.* . . . London: T. Nelson, 1879.]

F. Incidental Writings

"On the Necessity of a Knowledge of the Original Languages of the Scriptures," in *The Annual of the Board of Education of the General Assembly of the Presbyterian Church in the United States.* Vol. 1. Ed. John Breckinridge. Philadelphia: Russell & Martien, 1832. Pp. 195-214.

"Nature of the Atonement," in *The Spruce Street Lectures: Delivered by Several Clergymen, During the Autumn and Winter of 1831-32.* Philadelphia: Russell & Martien, 1833. Pp. 143-69.

"Introduction," in *The Faithful Mother's Reward.* Philadelphia: Presbyterian Board of Publication, 1853.

"The Bible Argument on Slavery," in *Cotton is King, and Pro-Slavery Arguments: Comprising the Writings of Hammond, Harper, Christy, Stringfellow, Hodge, Bledsoe, and Cartwright, on This Important Subject.* Ed. E. N. Elliott. Augusta, Ga.: Pritchard, Abbott & Loomis, 1860. Pp. 841-877.

"The Fugitive Slave Law," in *Cotton is King, and Pro-Slavery Arguments: Comprising the Writings of Hammond, Harper, Christy, Stringfellow, Hodge, Bledsoe, and Cartwright, on This Important Subject.* Ed. E. N. Elliott. Augusta, Ga.: Pritchard, Abbott & Loomis, 1860. Pp. 809-40.

"Address of Dr. Hodge," in *A Discourse Delivered at the Funeral of Rev. John McDowell, D.D.* Philadelphia: William S. & Alfred Martien, 1863. Pp. 22-24.

On Praying and Giving Thanks for Victories: a correspondence between Rev. J. M. MacDonald and Rev. Dr. Hodge. Princeton: n.p., 1864.

"Address," in *Memorial of Rev. Peter O. Studdiford, D.D., Late Pastor of the Presbyterian Church of Lambertville, New Jersey, Who Departed this Life June 5th, 1866.* Philadelphia: Published by the Session, 1866. Pp. 33-35.

"Address of Welcome on Behalf of the Board of Trustees," in *Inauguration of James McCosh, D.D., LL.D., as President of the College of New Jersey, Princeton, October 27, 1868.* New York: Robert Carter and Brothers, 1869. Pp. 10-12.

"Letter to Pius the Ninth, Bishop of Rome," reprinted in French in *Acta Et Decreta: Sacrorum Conciliorum Recentiorum. Collectio Lacensis.* Vol. 8. Ed. S. J. E. Domo et al. (Friburgi, Brisgoviae: Herder, 1870-90), 1135-37. The original manuscript of this important letter is in the Firestone Library, Princeton University. Hodge wrote the letter on behalf of a committee from two American Presbyterian denominations explaining why these two denominations refused to attend the Vatican Council (1869).

"Retrospect of the History of the *Princeton Review*," in *The Biblical Repertory and Princeton Review Index Volume, from 1825-1868.* Philadelphia: Peter Walker, 1871. Pp. 1-39.

"Address," in *Proceedings Connected with the Semi-Centennial Commemoration of the Professorship of Rev. Charles Hodge, D.D., LL.D., in the Theological Seminary at Princeton, N.J., April 24, 1872.* New York: Anson D. F. Randolph & Co., n.d. Pp. 49-54.

"Introduction," in James B. Ramsey, *The Spiritual Kingdom: An Exposition of the First Eleven Chapters of the Book of Revelation.* Richmond: Presbyterian Committee of Publication, 1873. Pp. i-xxxv. [In print, Carlisle, Pa.: Banner of Truth Trust, 1977.]

"The Unity of the Church Based on Personal Union with Christ," in *History, Essays, Orations, and Other Documents of the Sixth General Conference of the Evangelical Alliance.* Ed. Philip Schaff and S. Irenaeus Prime. New York: Harper & Bros., 1874. Pp. 139-44.

"Prayer by Rev. Charles Hodge, D.D.," in *A Memorial Of Joseph Henry.* Washington: Government Printing Office, 1880. Pp. 13-14.

"Autobiography," in A. A. Hodge, *The Life of Charles Hodge, D.D., LL.D.* London: T. Nelson & Sons, 1881. Pp. 1-38.

II. UNPUBLISHED WORKS AND MANUSCRIPTS BY HODGE

Princeton Theological Seminary, Princeton, New Jersey

The Department of Archives and Special Collections at the Speer and Luce Libraries houses the single largest collection of Hodge's manuscripts. In addition to manuscripts of numerous lectures and hundreds of sermons and talks, the collection contains manuscripts of several of Hodge's major works, including his *Systematic Theology* and *Constitutional History of the Presbyterian Church.* The collection also includes a significant amount of correspondence between Hodge and various persons as well as personal memorabilia and lecture notes taken by Hodge's students.

Princeton University, Princeton, New Jersey

The Hodge Papers held by Firestone Library's Special Collections department contains lecture notes by Hodge as well as several manuscripts, including those of sermons, articles for the *BRPR*, and books such as *What Is Darwinism?* and the *Commentary on Romans.* The bulk of the collection, however, is made up of correspondence to and from Hodge. This extensive collection of letters includes correspondence with family members and over 430 other correspondents.

Rutgers University, New Brunswick, New Jersey

The Special Collections department at Alexander Library holds two files of papers by Hodge. One contains manuscripts for "Are There Too Many Ministers?" and "England and America," while the other contains correspondence between Hodge and several persons, including Francis March, William S. Martien, Phineas D. Gurley, and C. Cuyler.

Montreat, North Carolina

Hodge documents are included in the McFarland Papers and in the John Wilson papers at the Presbyterian archives.

New Jersey Historical Society, Newark, New Jersey

Letters from Hodge are contained in the "Princeton, NJ, manuscripts, 1842-1918" collection and in the Hornblower Papers.

Presbyterian Historical Society, Philadelphia, Pennsylvania

The University of Vermont, Burlington, Vermont

The Bailey/Howe Library Special Collections houses the James Marsh collection, which contains several letters from Hodge.

Library of Congress, Washington, D.C.

The Manuscript Division holds three volumes of lectures by Hodge dating from 1854-1855.

III. PUBLISHED WORKS ABOUT HODGE

A. Nineteenth-Century Works

"The Act and Testimony, Once More." *The Christian Intelligencer and Evangelical Guardian* 5 (December 1834): 351-53.

Adger, John B. "Calvin Defended Against Drs. Cunningham and Hodge." *The Southern Presbyterian Review* 27 (January 1876): 133-66.

———. "Calvin's Doctrine of the Lord's Supper." *The Southern Presbyterian Review* 36 (October 1885): 785-800.

———. "*The Life of Charles Hodge . . .* by his son, A. A. Hodge." *The Southern Presbyterian Review* 32 (January 1881): 134-43.

———. "Northern and Southern Views of the Province of the Church." *The Southern Presbyterian Review* 16 (March 1866): 384-411.

Aiken, Charles A. "A Tribute Introductory to the Opening Lecture of the Session of 1878-9, Princeton Theological Seminary, September 6, 1878," in *Dis-*

courses Commemorative of the Life and Work of Charles Hodge, D.D., LL.D. Philadelphia: Henry B. Ashmead, 1879. Pp. 21-23.

Alexander, James W. *The Life of Archibald Alexander, D.D.* New York: Charles Scribner, 1854.

"American Presbyterian History." *The New Englander* 8 (February 1850): 89-106.

Atwater, Lyman H. *A Discourse Commemorative of the Late Dr. Charles Hodge delivered in the Chapel of the College of New Jersey by request of the President, October 13th, and repeated in the First Presbyterian Church, Princeton, at the request of its session, Oct. 20, 1878.* Princeton: C. S. Robinson, 1878.

————. "Dr. Forbes on Romans, vs. Dr. Hodge." *The Presbyterian Quarterly and Princeton Review* 2 (January 1873): 164-73.

————. *The First Adam and the Second: The Elohim Revealed in the Creation and Redemption of Man.* Philadelphia: Parry & McMillan, 1860. [See pp. 435-51.]

————. "*The New Englander,* April 1868, Article IV, Entitled, 'The *Princeton Review* on the Theology of Dr. N. W. Taylor'" or "Professor Fisher on the *Princeton Review* and Dr. Taylor's Theology." *Biblical Repertory and Princeton Review* 40 (July 1868): 368-98.

————. *A Rejoinder to the "Princeton Review," Upon the Elohim Revealed, Touching the Doctrine of Imputation and Kindred Topics.* Philadelphia: Joseph M. Wilson, 1860.

"The *Biblical Repertory* on the Doctrine of Imputation." *The Quarterly Christian Spectator* 3 (September 1831): 497-512.

Boardman, Henry A. "Memorial Discourse Delivered in the First Presbyterian Church, Princeton, N.J., April 27, 1879," in *Discourses Commemorative of the Life and Work of Charles Hodge, D.D., LL.D.* Philadelphia: Henry B. Ashmead, 1879. Pp. 27-70.

Briggs, Charles Augustus. *American Presbyterianism, Its Origin and Early History.* New York: Charles Scribner's Sons, 1885.

————. *Whither? A Theological Question for the Times.* New York: Charles Scribner's Sons, 1889.

Buttz, Henry A. "Rev. Charles Hodge, D.D., LL.D." *The National Repository* 5 (January 1879): 60-66.

"Case of the Rev. Mr. Barnes." *The Quarterly Christian Spectator* 3 (June 1831): 292-336.

Chadwick, J. W. "Two Presbyterian Professors." *The Nation* 31 (1880): 381-82.

"Charles Hodge." *The Biblical Repertory and Princeton Review: Index Volume from 1825-1868.* Philadelphia: Peter Walker, 1871. Pp. 200-211.

"*A Commentary on the Epistle to the Ephesians* by Charles Hodge." *The Evangelical Review* 8 (October 1856): 289-90.

"*A Commentary on the Epistle to the Ephesians* by Charles Hodge." *The Journal of Sacred Literature and Biblical Record* 4 (October 1856): 215.

"*A Commentary on the Epistle to the Ephesians* by Charles Hodge." *The Theological and Literary Journal* 9 (July 1856): 170.

"*Commentary on the Epistle to the Romans* by Charles Hodge." *The British and Foreign Evangelical Review* 14 (July 1865): 656-58.

"*Conference Papers.*" *Bibliotheca Sacra* 36 (July 1879): 587-88.

"*Conference Papers* . . . by Charles Hodge." *The New Englander* 38 (September 1879): 727.

"*Conference Papers* . . . by Charles Hodge." *The Presbyterian Review* 1 (1880): 195-97.

"Cousin and the Princeton Reviewer." *The Church Review and Ecclesiastical Register* 9 (October 1856): 358-74.

Cox, Samuel H. "Reply of Dr. Cox." *Biblical Repertory and Princeton Review* 3 (October 1831): 482-514.

Cunningham, William. "Dr. Hodge and the *Edinburgh Witness.*" *Presbyterian* 30 (March 31, 1860): 50.

————. "Dr. Hodge's *Essays and Reviews.*" *The British and Foreign Evangelical Review* 6 (July 1857): 687-715.

Dabney, Robert Lewis. "*Conference Papers* . . . by Charles Hodge." *The Southern Presbyterian Review* 30 (July 1879): 606-8.

————. "Doctrine of Original Sin." *The Southern Presbyterian Review* 35 (October 1884): 583-610.

————. "Hodge's *Systematic Theology.*" *The Southern Presbyterian Review* 24 (April 1873): 167-225.

————. *Syllabus and Notes of the Course of Systematic and Polemic Theology Taught in Union Theological Seminary, Virginia.* 3d ed. Asbury Park, N.J.: Presbyterian Publishing Co., 1885.

"Danville Versus Princeton." *Methodist Quarterly Review* 24 (November 1886): 145-59.

"Death of Dr. Charles Hodge." *The Evangelical Repository and United Presbyterian Worker* 55 (August 1878): 123-24.

"The Death of Dr. Hodge." *Princeton Press* (June 22, 1878): 2.

Discourses Commemorative of the Life and Work of Charles Hodge. Philadelphia: Henry B. Ashmead, 1879. Essays by William Paxton, Charles A. Aiken, Henry A. Boardman, and a Minute adopted by the Board of Trustees of Princeton Theological Seminary.

"Discussions in Church Polity." *Bibliotheca Sacra* 36 (July 1879): 584-87.

"Dr. Dabney on Immediate Imputation." *The Southern Presbyterian Review* 24 (January 1873): 30-65.

"Dr. Hodge on 'The Lutheran Doctrine' of the Person of Christ." *The Quarterly Review of the Evangelical Lutheran Church* 2 (April 1872): 256-80.

"Dr. Hodge on the Resurrection." *The Theological and Literary Journal* 10 (October 1857): 247-83.

"Dr. Hodge's Commentary on Romans in French." *Presbyterian* 11 (March 27, 1841): 50.

Dwight, Timothy. "*The Life of Dr. Charles Hodge.*" *The New Englander* 40 (March 1881): 222-46.

————. "Princeton Exegesis: A Review of Dr. Hodge's Commentary on Romans V.12-19." *The New Englander* 27 (July 1868): 551-603.

————. "Princeton Exegesis, No. II: Its Dealings with the Testimony of the Scriptures Against the Doctrine of a Limited Atonement." *The New Englander* 28 (April 1869): 361-405.

————. "A Review of the Biography of Charles Hodge." *The New Englander* 40 (1881): 222-46.

Elliot, E. N., ed. *Cotton Is King, and Pro-Slavery Arguments.* Augusta, Ga.: Pritchard, Abbott & Loomis, 1860. Two articles from the *BRPR* were reprinted here: "The Bible Argument on Slavery" (1836) and "The Fugitive Slave Law" (1857). In the light of the deletions made by this Southern editor, it is instructive to compare Hodge's original articles with the edited versions in *Cotton is King.* It remains undetermined whether Hodge approved the incorporation of his articles in this volume.

Ellis, G. E. "The New Theology." *The Christian Examiner and Religious Miscellany* 62 (May 1857): 321-69.

Etter, John Wesley. "The Atonement." *United Brethren Review* 3 (July 1892): 206-18; and 4 (October 1892): 364-71.

"*An Exposition of the First Epistle to the Corinthians* by Charles Hodge." *The New Englander* 16 (February 1858): 194-95.

"*An Exposition of the First Epistle to the Corinthians* by Charles Hodge." *The Theological and Literary Journal* 10 (July 1857): 169.

"*The First Adam and the Second* . . . by Samuel J. Baird." *The Presbyterian Quarterly Review* 8 (April 1860): 683-85.

Fisher, George P. "The Augustinian and the Federal Theories of Original Sin Compared." *The New Englander* 27 (July 1868): 468-516.

————. "Dr. N. W. Taylor's Theology: A Rejoinder to the *Princeton Review.*" *The New Englander* 27 (October 1868): 740-63.

————. "Original Sin: The State of the Question." *The New Englander* 18 (August 1860): 694-710.

————. "The *Princeton Review* of January." *The New Englander* 28 (April 1869): 406-8.

————. "The *Princeton Review* on the Theology of Dr. N. W. Taylor." *The New Englander* 27 (April 1868): 248-84.

Forbes, John. *Analytical Commentary on the Epistle to the Romans, Tracing the Train of Thought by the Aid of Parallelism.* Edinburgh: T & T Clark, 1868.

Girardeau, John L. "Theology as a Science, Involving an Infinite Element." *The Southern Presbyterian Review* 27 (July 1876): 462-85.

Grayson, William John. *Reply to Professor Hodge on the "State of the Country."* Charleston: Evans & Cogswell, 1861.

Hageman, John F. *The History of Princeton and Its Institutions.* 2d ed. Philadelphia: J. B. Lippincott & Co., 1879. [See pp. 354-58.]

Hawley, James Marvin. "The Image of God." *Methodist Quarterly Review* 23 (January 1886): 17-40.

Hill, William. *A History of the Rise, Progress, Genius, and Character of American Presbyterianism: Together with a Review of "The Constitutional History of the Presbyterian Church in the United States of America, by Chas. Hodge, D.D. Professor in the Theological Seminary, at Princeton, N.J."* Washington City: J. Gideon, Jr., 1839.

Hodge, Archibald Alexander. *The Life of Charles Hodge D.D., LL.D.: Professor in the Theological Seminary Princeton, N.J.* New York: Charles Scribner's Sons, 1880.

————. *Questions on the Text of the Systematic Theology of Dr. Charles Hodge.* New York: Charles Scribner's Sons, 1885.

"Hodge on Ephesians." *The Presbyterian Magazine* 6 (June 1856): 275-77.

"Hodge on First Corinthians." *The Presbyterian Magazine* 7 (November 1857): 511-14.

"Hodge on Presbyterianism." *The New Englander* 14 (February 1856): 1-32.

"Hodge on the Romans (Earl of Chichester's comments)." *Presbyterian* 15 (October 4, 1845): 158.

"Hodge's *Discussions on Church Polity.*" *The New Englander* 38 (January 1879): 148-49.

"Hodge's *Systematic Theology* (vol. II)." *The New Englander* 31 (April 1872): 371-72.

"Hodge's Theology." *The American Presbyterian Review* 3 (October 1871): 651.

"*Index to Systematic Theology* by Charles Hodge." *Bibliotheca Sacra* 31 (April 1874): 195-97.

"*Index to Systematic Theology* by Charles Hodge." *The Quarterly Review of the Evangelical Lutheran Church* 3 (October 1873): 618.

"Infant Salvation." *The American Church Review* 26 (October 1874): 519-25.

"*Introductory Lecture . . . by Charles Hodge.*" *The Quarterly Register and Journal of the American Education Society* 1 (April 1829): 216-19.

Irvin, W. *"The Life of Charles Hodge . . . by his son, A. A. Hodge."* The Presbyterian *Review* 2 (January 1881): 199-201.

Knox, John. "The Presbytery of Oxford and Dr. Hodge." *Presbyterian* 36 (May 5, 1866): 3.

Krauth, Charles P. *Infant Baptism and Infant Salvation in the Calvinistic System: A Review of Dr. Hodge's Systematic Theology.* Philadelphia: Lutheran Book Store, 1874.

————. "A Review of Dr. Hodge's *Systematic Theology* with Special Reference to the Question of Infant Baptism and Infant Salvation, in the Calvinistic System." *The Mercersburg Review* 21 (January 1874): 99-159.

Landis, Robert W. *The Doctrine of Original Sin as Received and Taught by the Churches of the Reformation Stated and Defended: And the Error of Dr. Hodge in Claiming that this Doctrine Recognizes the Gratuitous Imputation of Sin, Pointed Out and Refuted.* Richmond: Whittet and Shepperson, 1884.

————. "The Gratuitous Imputation of Sin." *The Southern Presbyterian Review* 27 (April 1876): 318-53.

————. "Imputation, Part I." *The Danville Quarterly Review* 1 (September 1861): 390-427.

————. "Imputation, Part II, Antecedent Imputation and Supralapsarianism." *The Danville Quarterly Review* 1 (December 1861): 553-613.

————. "Imputation, Part III, Imputation and Original Sin." *The Danville Quarterly Review* 2 (1862): 58-111, 248-82, 514-78.

————. "'Unthinkable' Propositions and Original Sin." *The Southern Presbyterian Review* 26 (April 1875): 298-315.

"The Late Mrs. Hodge." *Presbyterian* 20 (January 12, 1850): 6.

"The Life of Charles Hodge . . . by his Son, A. A. Hodge." The Baptist Review 3 (1881): 130.

"The Life of Charles Hodge . . . by his son, A. A. Hodge." Bibliotheca Sacra 38 (July 1881): 591-92.

"The Life of Charles Hodge, D.D." *London Quarterly Review* 59 (October 1882): 56-73.

Linday, Thomas M. "The Doctrine of Scripture: The Reformers and the Princeton School." *The Expositor* 1, Fifth Series (1895): 278-93.

"Literary Review" [of *Systematic Theology*, vol. 1]. *The Congregational Quarterly* 13 (October 1871): 604-5.

"Literary Review" [of *Systematic Theology*, vol. 2]. *The Congregational Quarterly* 14 (April 1872): 333-35.

MacDonald, James Madison. *On Praying and Giving Thanks for Victories: a correspondence between Rev. J. M. MacDonald and Rev. Dr. Hodge.* Princeton: n.p., 1864.

MacGregor, James. "Dr. Charles Hodge and the Princeton School." *The British and Foreign Evangelical Review* 23 (July 1874): 456-69.

———. "Review of *Systematic Theology,* by Charles Hodge." *The British and Foreign Evangelical Review* 21 (1872): 384-85.

McMaster, Gilbert. "Review of Hodge on the Epistle to the Romans." *The Literary and Theological Review* 3 (September 1836): 398-422.

Miller, John. *Fetich in Theology: Or, Doctrinalism Twin to Ritualism.* New York: Dodd and Mead, 1874. [Same as *The Congregational Quarterly* 16 (1874): 619-21.]

Mills, Henry. "Exegesis of Romans, 9:2,3." *The Literary and Theological Review* 3 (1836): 331-45.

"Minute Adopted by the Board of Directors of the Princeton Theological Seminary at their Annual Meeting, Held April 29, 1879," in *Discourses Commemorative of the Life and Work of Charles Hodge, D.D., LL.D.* Philadelphia: Henry B. Ashmead, 1879. Pp. 73-75.

"The Modern Doctrine of the Unknowable." *The Southern Presbyterian Review* 27 (October 1876): 662-96.

Nevin, John W. "Doctrine of the Reformed Church on the Lord's Supper." *The Mercersburg Review* 2 (September 1850): 421-548.

———. "Dr. Hodge on the 'Mystical Presence.'" *The Weekly Messenger of the German Reformed Church* 13 (May 24-August 9, 1848).

———. "Hodge on the Ephesians." *The Mercersburg Review* 9 (January 1857): 46-83.

———. "Hodge on the Ephesians, Second Article." *The Mercersburg Review* 9 (April 1857): 192-245.

Park, Edwards A. "Dr. Hodge's *Systematic Theology.*" *Bibliotheca Sacra* 29 (July 1872): 553-60.

———. "New England Theology; with Comments on a Third Article in the *Biblical Repertory and Princeton Review,* Relating to a Convention Sermon." *Bibliotheca Sacra* 9 (January 1852): 170-220.

———. "Remarks on the *Biblical Repertory and Princeton Review,* Vol. XXII. No. IV. Art. VII." *Bibliotheca Sacra* 8 (January 1851): 135-80.

———. "Unity Amid Diversities of Belief, Even on Imputed and Involuntary Sin; with Comments on a Second Article in the *Princeton Review* Relating to a Convention Sermon." *Bibliotheca Sacra* 8 (July 1851): 594-647.

Patton, Francis Landey. "Charles Hodge." *The Presbyterian Review* 2 (January 1881): 349-77.

Paxton, William M. "Address by William M. Paxton, D.D., of New York, at the Obsequies of the Rev. Dr. Hodge, in the First Presbyterian Church of Princeton, N.J., June 22, 1878," in *Discourses Commemorative of the Life and*

Work of Charles Hodge, D.D., LL.D. Philadelphia: Henry B. Ashmead, 1879. Pp. 5-18.

Peck, T. E. "*Discussions in Church Polity* . . . by Charles Hodge." *The Southern Presbyterian Review* 30 (January 1879): 187-91.

Pond, Enoch. "The Atonement, in Its Relations to God and Man." *Bibliotheca Sacra* 19 (October 1862): 685-706.

———. "Dr. Hodge and New England Theology." *Bibliotheca Sacra* 30 (1873): 371-81.

"The *Princeton Review* and the Office of Ruling Elder." *Spirit of the XIX Century* 2 (May 1843): 315-16.

Proceedings Connected with the Semi-Centennial Commemorative of the Professorship of Rev. Charles Hodge, D.D, L.L.D, April 24, 1872. New York: Anson D. F. Randolph, 1872. [See also *The Southern Presbyterian Review* 24 (July 1873): 461-63.]

"Professor Hodge on the Permanency of the Apostolic Office." *The Church Review and Ecclesiastical Register* 8 (October 1855): 406-25.

"Professor Hodge's Exposition of II Corinthians." *The New Englander* 18 (February 1860): 217-18.

"Recent English Commentaries on Paul's Epistle to the Ephesians." *The British and Foreign Evangelical Review* 6 (October 1857): 933-60.

"Remarks on Protestant and the *Biblical Repertory*, Respecting the Doctrine of Imputation." *The Quarterly Christian Spectator* 3 (March 1831): 162-68.

The Reviewer Reviewed: Or, An Answer to Strictures Contained in the Princeton Biblical Repertory, for July, 1840, on Dr. Hill's History of the Rise, Progress, Genius, and Character of American Presbyterianism. New York: Printed for the Author, 1842.

"Review of *A Commentary on the Epistle to the Ephesians*, by Charles Hodge." *Methodist Quarterly Review* 10 (July 1856): 452.

"Review of *Commentary on the Epistle to the Romans*, by Charles Hodge." *Methodist Review* 69 (January 1887): 148-49.

"Review of *Conference Papers*, by Charles Hodge." *Methodist Review* 61 (July 1879): 590-91.

"Review of *Conference Papers*, by Charles Hodge." *Southern Presbyterian Review* 30 (July, 1879): 606-9.

"Review of *Conference Talks*, by Charles Hodge." *New York Times*, May 6, 1879, p. 3.

"Review of *Discussions in Church Polity*, by Charles Hodge." *Methodist Review* 61 (January 1879): 166-67.

"Review of Dr. Hodge's System of Theology." *New Englander* 30 (1871): 744-45.

"Review of *Essays and Reviews,* by Charles Hodge." *Methodist Quarterly Review* 11 (January 1857): 146-47.

"Review of *Essays and Reviews,* by Charles Hodge." *Methodist Review* 39 (April 1857): 311-13.

"Review of *An Exposition of the First Epistle to the Corinthians,* by Charles Hodge." *Methodist Review* 39 (July 1857): 483.

"Review of *Proceedings Connected with the Hodge Semi-Centennial.*" *Southern Presbyterian Review* 24 (July 1873): 461-63.

"Review of *Systematic Theology,* by Charles Hodge." *Methodist Review* 55 (July 1873): 500-503.

"Review of *Systematic Theology,* by Charles Hodge." *New York Times,* October 23, 1871, p. 2.

"Review of *Systematic Theology,* vol. 2, by Charles Hodge." *The Nation* 446 (January 15, 1874): 44-46.

"Review of *Systematic Theology,* vols. 1 and 2, by Charles Hodge." *Methodist Review* 54 (April 1872): 337-38.

"Review of *Unabridged Commentary on Romans,* new ed., by Charles Hodge." *Presbyterian* 36 (May 26, 1866): 1.

"Review of *The Way of Life.*" *Presbyterian* 12 (May 21, 1842): 83.

"Review of *What Is Darwinism?,* by Charles Hodge." *Methodist Review* 56 (July 1874): 514-16.

"Review of *What Is Darwinism?,* by Charles Hodge." *Methodist Review* 64 (July 1882): 586-92.

"Review of *What Is Darwinism?,* by Charles Hodge." *The Nation* 465 (May 28, 1874): 348-51.

"Review of *What Is Darwinism?,* by Charles Hodge." *New York Times,* July 2, 1874, p. 2.

Rice, John H. "The *Princeton Review* on the State of the Country." *Southern Presbyterian Review* 14 (April 1861): 1-44.

Salmond, Charles Adamson. "Dr. Charles Hodge." *The Catholic Presbyterian* 5 (January-June 1881): 56-66.

———. *Princetoniana: Charles and A. A. Hodge: With Class and Table Talk of Hodge the Younger.* New York: Scribner & Welford, 1888.

Schaff, Philip. *Theological Propaedeutic.* 8th ed. New York: Charles Scribner Sons, 1909. [First published 1892. See pp. 390ff.]

Shedd, William G. T. "Questions on the Text of the *Systematic Theology* of Charles Hodge . . . by A. A. Hodge." *The Presbyterian Review* 6 (April 1885): 371-72.

Smith, Henry Boynton. *The Reunion of the Presbyterian Churches, Called New School and Old School: A Reply to the "Princeton Review."* New York: William

Sherwood, 1867. [Reprinted from *American and Presbyterian Theological Review* 5 (October 1867): 624-65.]

———. "*Systematic Theology* . . . by Charles Hodge." *The Presbyterian Quarterly and Princeton Review* 2 (April 1872): 395-400.

Stebbins, R. P. "The Andover and Princeton Theologies." *The Christian Examiner and Religious Miscellany* 52 (May 1852): 309-35.

Stowe, Calvin E. "Hodge's Commentary on Romans (last edition)." *Bibliotheca Sacra* 22 (January 1865): 159-62.

Stuart, Moses. "Postscript," in *An Examination of the Strictures Upon the American Education Society, in a Late Number of the Biblical Repertory, originally published in that work*. Boston: Flagg & Gould, 1829. Pp. 33-48.

———. "Remarks of Protestant on the *Biblical Repertory*." *The Quarterly Christian Spectator* 3 (March 1831): 156-62.

"*Systematic Theology* . . . by Charles Hodge." *The American Church Review* 25 (April 1873): 293-96.

"*Systematic Theology* by Charles Hodge." *The Baptist Quarterly* 6 (January 1872): 115-16.

"*Systematic Theology* by Charles Hodge." *The Baptist Quarterly* 6 (April 1872): 248-49.

"*Systematic Theology* by Charles Hodge." *The Baptist Quarterly* 7 (January 1873): 124-25.

"*Systematic Theology* by Charles Hodge." *The British Quarterly Review* 55 (January 1872): 164.

"*Systematic Theology* by Charles Hodge." *The British Quarterly Review* 55 (April 1872): 309-10.

"*Systematic Theology* by Charles Hodge." *The British Quarterly Review* 59 (January 1874): 157.

"*Systematic Theology* by Charles Hodge." *The Mercersburg Review* 19 (April 1872): 318-21.

"*Systematic Theology* by Charles Hodge." *The Mercersburg Review* 20 (January 1873): 177-79.

"*Systematic Theology* . . . by Charles Hodge." *The Presbyterian Quarterly and Princeton Review* 2 (January 1873): 174.

"*Systematic Theology* by Charles Hodge." *The Quarterly Review of the Evangelical Lutheran Church* 3 (January 1873): 156-57.

"Theological Science in America." *The Mercersburg Review* 20 (April 1873): 317-24.

Thornwell, James H. "The *Princeton Review* and Presbyterianism." *Southern Presbyterian Review* 13 (January 1861): 757-810.

"Unitarian View of the Park and Hodge Controversy." *Presbyterian* 22 (July 3, 1852): 106.

"A Voice from Princeton, N.J., and the American Sunday School Union." *The Millennial Harbinger*, 3d series, 1 (January 1844): 33-35.

Wallace, Benjamin J. "The 'Presbyterian Magazine' and the 'Spirit of American Presbyterianism.'" *The Presbyterian Quarterly Review* 2 (September 1853): 206-46.

————. "The Spirit of American Presbyterianism." *The Presbyterian Quarterly Review* 1 (December 1852): 473-523.

Watts, Robert. "The Late Dr. Hodge." *The British and Foreign Evangelical Review* 27 (October 1878): 699-724.

"*The Way of Life* . . . by Charles Hodge." *The American Quarterly Register* 14 (May 1842): 419.

"*What Is Darwinism?*" *The New Englander* 33 (July 1874): 594.

"*What Is Darwinism?* by Charles Hodge." *The American Church Review* 26 (April 1874): 316-19.

Wright, George F. "Dr. Hodge's Misrepresentations of President Finney's System of Theology." *Bibliotheca Sacra* 33 (April 1876): 381-92.

Woodberry, George Edward. "Johnson's Garrison, and Other Biographies." *The Atlantic Monthly* 47 (April 1881): 558-67.

B. Twentieth-Century Works

Ahlstrom, Sydney E. "The Scottish Philosophy and American Theology." *Church History* 24 (September 1955): 257-72.

————. *The Shaping of American Religion*. Princeton: Princeton University Press, 1961.

Ambrose, Vernon. "Charles Hodge," in *The Cambridge History of American Literature*. Ed. Carl Van Doren. New York: Macmillan, 1921, Vol. 3, pp. 201-5.

Anderson, Robert A. *A Bicentennial Remembrance: Charles Hodge, 1797-1877: A Look at the Life and Witness of the Great Princeton Theologian*. Charlotte, N.C.: Fundamental Presbyterian Publications, 1997.

Albritton, James McLean. "Slavery, Secession, and the Old School Presbyterians: James Henley Thornwell and Charles Hodge on the Relationship Between Church and State." *Southern Historian: A Journal of Southern History* 21 (Spring 2000): 25-39.

Alexander, George. "The Glory of Ministry," *The Princeton Seminary Bulletin* 21 (November 1927): 2-5.

Aucker, W. Brian. "Hodge and Warfield on Evolution." *Presbyterion: Covenant Seminary Review* 20 (Fall 1994): 131-42.

Baker, David W. "Dr. Charles Hodge: Down-to-Earth Theologian." *Eternity* 9 (June 1958): 20.

Balmer, Randall. "The Princetonians and Scripture: A Reconsideration." *Westminster Theological Journal* 44 (1982): 352-65.

————. "The Princetonians, Scripture, and Recent Scholarship." *Journal of Presbyterian History* 60 (Fall 1982): 267-70.

Barker, William S. "The Social Views of Charles Hodge (1797-1878): A Study in Nineteenth-Century Calvinism and Conservatism." *Presbyterion: Covenant Seminary Review* 1 (Spring 1975): 1-22.

Beam, Jacob N. "Charles Hodge's Student Years in Germany." *Princeton University Library Chronicle* 8 (April 1847): 103-39.

Bie, Linden J. de. "The Spoils of War in Nineteenth-Century American Eucharistic Controversy." *Pro Ecclesia* 4 (Fall 1995): 431-41.

Bodo, John R. *The Protestant Clergy and Public Issues, 1812-1848.* Princeton: Princeton University Press, 1954.

Bozeman, Theodore Dwight. *Protestants in the Age of Science: The Baconian Ideal and American Antebellum Religious Thought.* Chapel Hill: University of North Carolina Press, 1977.

Brown, Jerry Wayne. *The Rise of Biblical Criticism in America, 1800-1870: The New England Scholars.* Middletown, Conn.: Wesleyan University Press, 1974.

Butler, Diana Hochstedt. "Review of *The Way of Life,* by Charles Hodge." *Fides et Historia* 21 (June 1989): 87-88.

Bruce, Frederick F. "Review of *A Commentary on the Epistle to the Ephesians,* by Charles Hodge." *Evangelical Quarterly* 26 (July 1954): 184-85.

————. "Review of *Commentary on the Epistle to the Romans,* by Charles Hodge." *Evangelical Quarterly* 26 (July 1954): 184-85.

————. "Review of *An Exposition of the First Epistle to the Corinthians,* by Charles Hodge." *Evangelical Quarterly* 26 (July 1954): 184-85.

Calhoun, David B. *Princeton Seminary.* 2 vols. Edinburgh: Banner of Truth, 1994, 1996.

Carey, Jonathan Sinclair. "For God or Against Him: Princeton, Orthodoxy and Transcendentalists." *American Presbyterians* 64 (Winter 1986): 243-58.

Carwardine, Richard J. *Evangelicals and Politics in Antebellum America.* New Haven: Yale University Press, 1993.

Cashdollar, Charles D. "The Pursuit of Piety: Charles Hodge's Diary, 1819-1820." *Journal of Presbyterian History* 55 (1977): 267-74.

————. *The Transformation of Theology, 1830-1890.* Princeton: Princeton University Press, 1989.

The Centennial Celebration of the Theological Seminary of the Presbyterian Church in the United States of America at Princeton, New Jersey. Princeton: Princeton Theological Seminary, 1912. There are many references to Hodge by his students and contemporaries in this large and congratulatory volume.

Coker, Joe L. "Exploring the Roots of the Dispensationalist/Princetonian 'Alliance': Charles Hodge and John Nelson Darby on Eschatology and Interpretation of Scripture." *Fides et Historia* 30 (Winter/Spring 1998): 41-56.

Conkin, Paul K. *The Uneasy Center: Reformed Christianity in Antebellum America.* Chapel Hill: University of North Carolina Press, 1995.

Coleman, Michael C. *Presbyterian Missionary Attitudes Toward American Indians, 1837-1893.* Columbia: University of Missouri Press, 1985. See comments about the influence of Hodge.

Conser, Walter H. *Church and Confessions: Conservative Theologians in Germany, England and America, 1815-1866.* Macon, Ga.: Mercer University Press, 1984.

———. *God and the Natural World: Religion and Science in Antebellum America.* Columbia: University of South Carolina Press, 1993.

Danhof, Ralph J. *Charles Hodge as Dogmatician.* Goes, The Netherlands: Osterbaan and le Cointre, 1929.

Daughters, Kenneth A. "Review of *The Way of Life,* by Charles Hodge." *Journal of the Evangelical Theological Society* 31 (December 1988): 497-98.

Davis, D. Clair. "Princeton and Inerrancy: The Nineteenth-Century Philosophical Background of Contemporary Concerns," in *Inerrancy and the Church.* Ed. John D. Hannah. Chicago: Moody Press, 1984. Pp. 359-78.

Dawson, David G. "A Recurring Issue of Mission Administration." *Missiology* 25 (October 1997): 457-65.

Dillenberger, John. *Protestant Thought and Natural Science: A Historical Study.* Nashville: Abingdon Press, 1960.

Duncan, J. Ligon III. "Divine Passibility and Impassibility in Nineteenth-Century American Confessional Presbyterian Theologians." *Scottish Bulletin of Evangelical Theology* 8 (Spring 1990): 1-15.

Farina, John. "General Introduction," in *Charles Hodge: The Way of Life.* Ed. Mark A. Noll. New York: Paulist Press, 1987. Pp. ix-x.

Farmer, James O. *The Metaphysical Confederacy: James Henley Thornwell and the Synthesis of Southern Values.* Macon, Ga.: Mercer University Press, 1986.

Flower, Elizabeth, and Murray G. Murphey. *A History of Philosophy in America.* Vol 1. New York: Capricorn Press, 1977.

Fuller, Donald, and Richard Gardiner. "Reformed Theology at Princeton and Amsterdam in the Late Nineteenth Century: A Reappraisal." *Presbyterion: Covenant Seminary Review* 21 (Spring 1995): 89-117.

George, Alexander. "The Glory of the Ministry." *Princeton Seminary Bulletin* 21 (November 1927): 2-5.

Gerrish, Brian A. *Tradition and the Modern World: Reformed Theology in the Nineteenth Century.* Chicago: University of Chicago Press, 1978.

Gerstner, John H. "The Contributions of Charles Hodge, B. B. Warfield, and J. Gresham Machen to the Doctrine of Inspiration," in *Challenges to Inerrancy: A Theological Response.* Ed. Gordon Lewis and Bruce Demarest. Chicago: Moody Press, 1984. Pp. 347-81.

Gillette, William. *New Jersey Blue: Civil War Politics in New Jersey, 1854-1865.* New Brunswick: Rutgers University Press.

Goen, C. C. *Broken Churches, Broken Nation.* Macon, Ga.: Mercer University Press, 1985.

Grau, Jose. Review of *Teologia Sistematica,* by Charles Hodge. *Reforma* 8 (1995): 11-14.

Gregory, Frederick. "The Impact of Darwinian Evolution on Protestant Theology in the Nineteenth Century," in *God and Nature: Historical Essays on the Encounter Between Christianity and Science.* Ed. David C. Lindberg and Ronald L. Numbers. Berkeley: University of California Press, 1986. Pp. 369-90.

Gundlach, Bradley J. "McCosh and Hodge on Evolution: A Combined Legacy." *Journal of Presbyterian History* 75 (Summer 1997): 85-102.

Harrill, J. Albert. "The Use of the New Testament in the American Slavery Controversy: A History of the Hermeneutical Tension Between Biblical Criticism and the Christian Moral Debate." *Religion and American Culture* 10 (Summer 2000): 149-86.

Hart, Darryl G. "Divided Between Heart and Mind: The Critical Period for Protestant Thought in America." *Journal of Ecclesiastical History* 38 (April 1987): 254-70.

———. "Poems, Propositions, and Dogma: The Controversy Over Religious Language and the Demise of Theology in American Learning." *Church History* 57 (September 1988): 310-21.

———. "Review of *The Way of Life,* by Charles Hodge." *Fides et Historia* 22 (Winter-Spring 1990): 65-66.

Hatch, Nathan O., and Mark A. Noll. *The Bible In America: Essays in Cultural History.* New York: Oxford University Press, 1982.

Helseth, Paul K. "Right Reason and the Princeton Mind: The Moral Context." *Journal of Presbyterian History* 77 (1999): 13-28.

Hewitt, Glenn A. *Regeneration and Morality: A Study of Charles Finney, Charles Hodge, John W. Nevin, and Horace Bushnell.* Brooklyn: Carlson Publishing, 1991.

―――――. "Review of *The Way of Life*, by Charles Hodge." *Journal of Religion* 69 (April 1989): 305.

Hicks, Peter. *The Philosophy of Charles Hodge: A 19th Century Evangelical Approach to Reason, Knowledge and Truth.* Lewiston: Edwin Mellen, 1997.

Hoekema, Anthony A. "Review of *Systematic Theology*, by Charles Hodge." *Calvin Theological Journal* 24 (April 1989): 207.

Hoeveler, J. David. *James McCosh and the Scottish Intellectual Tradition.* Durham: Duke University Press, 1981.

Hoffecker, W. Andrew. "Beauty and the Princeton Piety," in *Soli Deo Gloria: Essays in Reformed Theology.* Ed. R. C. Sproul. Nutley, N.J.: Presbyterian and Reformed Pub., 1976. Pp. 118-33.

―――――. "Charles Hodge," in *Dictionary of Christianity in America.* Ed. Daniel G. Reid et al. Downers Grove, Ill.: InterVarsity Press, 1990. Pp. 537-38.

―――――. "The Devotional Life of Archibald Alexander, Charles Hodge and Benjamin Warfield." *Westminster Theological Journal* 42 (Fall 1979): 111-29.

―――――. *Piety and the Princeton Theologians: Archibald Alexander, Charles Hodge, and Benjamin Warfield.* Philipsburg, N.J.: Presbyterian and Reformed Publishing Co., 1981. [Also published by Baker Book House, 1981.]

Hogeland, Ronald W. "Charles Hodge, The Association of Gentlemen and Ornamental Womanhood: A Study of Male Conventional Wisdom, 1825-1855." *Journal of Presbyterian History* 53 (1975): 239-55.

Holifield, E. Brooks. *The Gentlemen Theologians: American Theology in Southern Culture, 1795-1860.* Durham: Duke University Press, 1978.

―――――. "Mercersburg, Princeton and the South: The Sacramental Controversy in the Nineteenth Century." *Journal of Presbyterian History* 54 (1976): 238-57.

Hollinger, David, and Charles Capper. *The American Intellectual Tradition.* Vol. 2, 2d ed. New York: Oxford University Press, 1989.

Hood, Fred J. *Reformed America: The Middle and Southern States, 1783-1837.* University, Ala.: The University of Alabama Press, 1980.

Hovenkamp, Herbert. *Science and Religion in America, 1800-1860.* Philadelphia: University of Pennsylvania Press, 1978.

Howe, Daniel W. *The Political Culture of the American Whigs.* Cambridge: Harvard University Press, 1979.

Illick, Joseph E. "The Reception of Darwinism at the Theological Seminary and the College at Princeton, New Jersey." *Journal of the Presbyterian Historical Society* 38 (1960): 152-65, 234-43.

Jamison, Wallace N. *Religion in New Jersey: A Brief History.* Princeton: D. Van Nostrand Press, 1964.

Jodock, Darrell. "The Impact of Cultural Change: Princeton Theology and Scriptural Authority." *Dialog* 22 (1983): 21-29.

————. "Review of *The Way of Life*, by Charles Hodge." *Critical Review of Books in Religion* 1 (1989): 328-31.

Kelsey, David H. *The Uses of Scripture in Recent Theology.* Philadelphia: Fortress Press, 1975.

Kemeny, Paul C. *The Nation's Service: Religious Ideals and Educational Practice, 1868-1928.* New York: Oxford University Press, 1998.

Kennedy, Earl William. "From Pessimism to Optimism: Francis Turretin and Charles Hodge," in *Servant Gladly: Essays in Honor of John W. Beardslee III.* Ed. J. Klunder and R. Gasero. Grand Rapids: Eerdmans, 1989. Pp. 104-16.

————. "Review of *Systematic Theology*, by Charles Hodge." *Reformed Review* 46 (Autumn 1992): 84-85.

Knight, George W. "Subscription to the Westminster Confession of Faith and Catechisms." *Presbyterion: Covenant Seminary Review* 10 (Spring-Fall 1984): 20-55.

Kuklick, Bruce. *Churchmen and Philosophers: From Jonathan Edwards to John Dewey.* New Haven: Yale University Press, 1985.

Kull, Irving S. "Presbyterian Attitudes Towards Slavery." *Church History* (June 1838): 101-14.

Livingstone, David N. "Darwinism and Calvinism: The Belfast-Princeton Connection." *Isis* 83 (1992): 408-28.

————. *Darwin's Forgotten Defenders: The Encounter Between Evangelical Theology and Evolutionary Thought.* Grand Rapids: Eerdmans, 1987.

————. "The Idea of Design: The Vicissitudes of a Key Concept in the Princeton Response to Darwin." *Scottish Journal of Theology* 37 (1984): 329-57.

————, D. G. Hart, and Mark A. Noll, eds. *Evangelicals and Science in Historical Perspective.* New York: Oxford University Press, 2002.

Loetscher, Lefferts A. *The Broadening Church: A Study of the Theological Issues in the Presbyterian Church Since 1869.* Philadelphia: University of Pennsylvania Press, 1954.

————. *Facing the Enlightenment: Archibald Alexander and the Founding of Princeton Theological Seminary.* Westport, Conn.: Greenwood Press, 1983.

March, Wallace Eugene. "Charles Hodge on Schism and Civil Strife." *Journal of the Presbyterian Historical Society* 39 (June 1961): 88-97.

Marsden, George M. "The Collapse of American Evangelical Academia," in *Faith and Rationality: Reason and Belief in God.* Ed. Alvin Plantinga and Nicolas Wolterstorff. Notre Dame: University of Notre Dame Press, 1983. Pp. 219-64.

————. *The Evangelical Mind and the New School Presbyterian Experience*. New Haven: Yale University Press, 1970.

————. *Fundamentalism and American Culture: The Shaping of Twentieth-Century American Evangelicalism*. New York: Oxford University Press, 1980.

May, Henry F. *The Enlightenment in America*. New York: Oxford University Press, 1976.

Moore, James R. *The Post-Darwinian Controversies: A Study of the Protestant Struggle to Come to Terms with Darwin in Great Britain and America, 1870-1900*. Cambridge: Cambridge University Press, 1979.

Muller, Richard A. "Giving Direction to Theology: The Scholastic Dimension." *Journal of the Evangelical Theological Society* 28 (June 1985): 183-93.

Mullin, Robert B. "Biblical Critics and the Battle Over Slavery." *Journal of Presbyterian History* 61 (Summer 1983): 210-26.

Murchie, David N. "Charles Hodge and Jacksonian Economics." *Journal of Presbyterian History* 61 (Summer 1983): 248-56.

————. "From Slaveholder to American Abolitionist: Charles Hodge and the Slavery Issue," in *Christian Freedom: Essays in Honor of Vernon C. Grounds*. Ed. Kenneth Wozniak and Stanley Grenz. Lanham, Md.: University Press of America, 1986. Pp. 127-52.

Nelson, John Oliver. "Charles Hodge (1797-1878): Nestor of Orthodoxy," in *The Lives of Eighteen From Princeton*. Ed. Willard Thorpe. Princeton: Princeton University Press, 1946.

Nichols, James H., ed. *Romanticism in American Theology: Nevin and Schaff at Mercersburg*. Chicago: University of Chicago Press, 1961. [See ch. 4, "The Reformed Doctrine of the Lord's Supper Recovered."]

————, ed. *The Mercersburg Theology*. New York: Oxford University Press, 1966.

Nichols, Robert H. "Charles Hodge," in *Dictionary of American Biography*. Vol. 9. Ed. Dumas Malone (New York: Charles Scribner's Sons, 1932). Pp. 98-100.

Noll, Mark A. "Charles Hodge," in *American National Biography*. Ed. John A. Garrity and Mark C. Carnes. New York: Oxford University Press, 1999.

————. "Charles Hodge," in *Historical Handbook of Major Biblical Interpreters*. Ed. Donald K. McKim. Downers Grove, Ill.: InterVarsity Press, 1998.

————. "Common Sense Traditions and American Evangelical Thought." *American Quarterly* 37 (1985): 216-38.

————. "Introduction," in *Charles Hodge: The Way of Life*. Ed. Mark A. Noll. New York: Paulist Pres, 1987. Pp. 1-44.

————. "The Princeton Review." *Westminster Theological Journal* 50 (Fall 1988): 283-304.

————. "The Princeton Theology," in *The Princeton Theology*. Ed. David F. Wells. Grand Rapids: Baker Book House, 1989. Pp. 13-36.

————. *The Princeton Theology, 1812-1921: Scripture, Science, and Theological Method. From Archibald Alexander to Benjamin Breckinridge Warfield*. Grand Rapids: Baker Book House, 2001.

Olbricht, Thomas H. "Charles Hodge as an American New Testament Interpreter." *Journal of Presbyterian History* 57 (Summer 1979): 117-33.

Phipps, William E. "Asa Gray's Theology of Nature." *American Presbyterians* 66 (Fall 1988): 167-75.

Pierard, Richard V. "Review of *The Way of Life*, by Charles Hodge." *Christian Scholar's Review* 19 (1990): 309-10.

Pope, Earl A. *New England Calvinism and the Disruption of the Presbyterian Church*. New York: Garland Press, 1987.

Roberts, Jon H. *Darwinism and the Divine in America: Protestant Intellectuals and Organic Evolution, 1859-1900*. Madison: University of Wisconsin Press, 1988.

Rogers, Jack B. *Scripture in the Westminster Confession: A Problem of Historical Interpretation for American Presbyterians*. Grand Rapids: Eerdmans, 1967.

————, and Donald K. McKim. *The Authority and Interpretation of the Bible: An Historical Approach*. San Francisco: Harper & Row, 1979.

Russ, Pulliam. "Review of *Systematic Theology*, by Charles Hodge." *Eternity* 39 (December 1988): 40-41.

Sandeen, Ernest R. "The Princeton Theology: One Source of Biblical Literalism in American Protestantism." *Church History* 31 (September 1962): 307-21.

————. *The Roots of Fundamentalism: British and American Millenarianism, 1830-1930*. Chicago: University of Chicago Press, 1970.

Scott, Hugh Lennox. *Some Memories of a Soldier*. New York: The Century Company, 1928. H. L. Scott was a grandson of Charles Hodge and mentions his grandfather.

Scott, William B. *Some Memories of a Paleontologist*. Princeton, N.J.: Princeton University Press, 1939. W. B. Scott was a grandson of Charles Hodge and mentions his grandfather.

Shriver, George H. "Passages in Friendship: John W. Nevin to Charles Hodge, 1872." *Journal of Presbyterian History* 58 (Summer 1980): 116-22.

Silva, Moisés. "Old Princeton, Westminster, and Inerrancy," in *Inerrancy and Hermeneutic: A Tradition, A Challenge, A Debate*. Ed. Harvie Conn. Grand Rapids: Baker Book House, 1988. Pp. 67-80.

Smart, Ninian, ed. *Nineteenth-Century Religious Thought in the West*. 3 vols. New York: Cambridge University Press, 1985.

Smith, Elwyn A. *The Presbyterian Ministry in American Culture: A Study of Changing Concepts, 1700-1900.* Philadelphia: The Westminster Press, 1962.

Smith, H. Shelton, Robert T. Handy, and Lefferts A. Loetscher. "Church Boards Versus Voluntary Societies," in *American Christianity,* vol. 2, *1820-1960: An Historical Interpretation with Representative Documents.* Ed. H. Shelton Smith, Robert T. Handy, and Lefferts A. Loetscher. New York: Charles Scribner's Sons, 1963. Pp. 88-92.

Smith, James H., and A. L. Jamison, eds. *The Shaping of American Religion.* Princeton: Princeton University Press, 1961.

Smith, Timothy L. *Revivalism and Social Reform in Mid-Nineteenth-Century America.* Nashville: Abingdon Press, 1957.

Smylie, James H. "Charles Hodge (1797-1878)," in *Makers of Christian Theology in America.* Ed. Mark G. Toulouse and James O. Duke. Nashville: Abingdon Press, 1997. Pp. 153-60.

————. "Review of *The Way of Life,* by Charles Hodge." *Church History* 58 (March 1989): 116-17.

————. "Writings That Have Shaped Our Past." *American Presbyterians* 66 (Winter 1988): 213-332.

Soon, Gil Huh. *Presbyter in Volle Rechten: Het Debat Tussen Charles Hodge en James H. Thornwell over Het Ambt Van Ouderling.* Groningen, Netherlands: De Vuurbaak, 1972.

Speer, Robert E. "Charge to the President." *The Princeton Seminary Bulletin* 31 (April 1937): 2-6. This article contains several references to Hodge.

Stein, Stephen J. "Stuart and Hodge on Romans 5:12-21: An Exegetical Controversy About Original Sin." *Journal of Presbyterian History* 47 (December 1969): 340-58.

Stevens, George Barker. *The Christian Doctrine of Salvation.* New York: Charles Scribner's Sons, 1905. [See pp. 181-86.]

Stewart, John W. "Charles Hodge," in *Encyclopedia of The Reformed Faith.* Ed. Donald K. McKim. Louisville: Westminster/John Knox Press, 1992. Pp. 174-76.

————. "Hodge, Charles (1797-1878)," in *Dictionary of the Presbyterian and Reformed Tradition in America.* Ed. D. G. Hart. Downers Grove, Ill.: InterVarsity Press, 1999. Pp. 122-23.

————. *Mediating the Center: Charles Hodge on American Science, Language, Literature, and Politics.* Princeton: Princeton Theological Seminary, 1995.

Stoneburner, John. "Review of *The Way of Life,* by Charles Hodge." *Religion and Intellectual Life* 6 (Fall 1988): 132-35.

Taylor, Marion Ann. *The Old Testament in the Old Princeton School (1812-1929).* Lewiston, N.Y.: Mellen Research Press, 1992.

Tise, Larry. *Proslavery: A History of the Defense of Slavery, 1701-1840.* Athens: University of Georgia Press, 1987.

Trinterud, Leonard. "Charles Hodge (1797-1878): Theology — Didactic and Polemical," in *Sons of the Prophets.* Ed. Hugh T. Kerr. Princeton: Princeton University Press, 1963. Pp. 22-38.

Troxel, A. Craig. "Charles Hodge on Church Boards: A Case Study in Ecclesiology." *Westminster Theological Journal* 58 (Fall 1996): 183-207.

Turner, James. *Without God, Without Creed: The Origins of Unbelief in America.* Baltimore: Johns Hopkins University Press, 1985.

VanderVelde, Lewis G. *The Presbyterian Churches and the Federal Union, 1861-1869.* Cambridge: Harvard University Press, 1932.

Van Huyssteen, J. Wentzel. *Duet or Duel? Theology and Science in a Postmodern World.* Harrisburg, Pa.: Trinity Press, 1998. See ch. 3.

Wallace, Peter J. "The Defense of the Forgotten Center: Charles Hodge and the Enigma of Emancipationism in Antebellum America." *Journal of Presbyterian History* 75 (Fall 1997): 165-77.

———. "Foundations of Reformed Biblical Theology: The Development of Old Testament Theology at Old Princeton." *Westminster Theological Journal* 59 (Spring 1997): 41-69.

———, and Mark A. Noll. "The Students of Princeton Seminary, 1812-1929: A Research Note." *American Presbyterians* 72 (1994): 203-15.

Welch, Claude. *Protestant Thought in the Nineteenth Century.* 2 vols. New Haven: Yale University Press, 1985.

Wells, David F. "Charles Hodge," in *Reformed Theology in America: A History of Its Modern Development.* Ed. David F. Wells. Grand Rapids: Baker Book House, 1997. Pp. 39-64.

———. "Charles Hodge," in *The Princeton Theology.* Ed. David F. Wells. Grand Rapids: Baker Book House, 1989. Pp. 37-62.

———. "The Debate Over the Atonement in 19th-Century America: Aftermath and Hindsight of the Atonement Debate." *Bibliotheca Sacra* 145 (January-March 1988): 3-14.

———, ed. *Southern Reformed Theology.* Grand Rapids: Baker Book House, 1989.

Wells, Jonathan. "Charles Hodge on the Bible and Science." *American Presbyterians* 66 (Fall 1988): 157-65.

———. *Charles Hodge's Critique of Darwinism: An Historical-Critical Analysis of the Nineteenth-Century Debate.* Lewiston, N.Y.: Edwin Mellen Press, 1988.

———. "The Stout and Persistent *Theology* of Charles Hodge." *Christianity Today* 18 (1974): 1278.

———, ed. *The Princeton Theology.* Grand Rapids: Baker Book House, 1989.

Wilcox, David L. "Three Models of Making: Prime Mover, Craftsman, and King — Alternate Theistic Frameworks For Teaching Origins." *Perspectives on Science and Christian Faith* 39 (December 1987): 212-20.

Willis, E. David. "The Material Assumptions of Integrative Theology: The Conditions of Experiential Church Dogmatics." *Princeton Seminary Bulletin* 2 (1979): 232-50.

Willis-Watkins, E. David. "Charles Hodge's Systematic Theology." *American Presbyterians: Journal of Presbyterian History* 66 (Winter 1988): 269-72.

Wilson, R. Jackson, ed. *Darwinism and the American Intellectual.* 2d ed. Chicago: University of Chicago Press, 1989.

Woodbridge, John D., and Randall H. Balmer. "The Princetonians and Biblical Authority: An Assessment of the Ernest Sandeen Proposal," in *Scripture and Truth.* Ed. D. A. Carson and John D. Woodbridge. Grand Rapids: Zondervan, 1983.

IV. UNPUBLISHED WORKS ABOUT HODGE

Balmer, Randall H. "The Old Princeton Doctrine of Inspiration in the Context of Nineteenth Century Theology: A Reappraisal." Th.M. thesis, Trinity Evangelical School, 1981.

Balzer, Joel. "A Comparison of Charles G. Finney's View of Sin With That of Charles Hodge." M.A. thesis, Simpson College, 1988.

Berg, Kenneth. "Charles Hodge, Controversialist." Ph.D. dissertation, University of Iowa, 1952.

Carl, Harold F. "Found in Human Form: The Maintenance and Defense of Orthodox Christology by Nineteenth Century American Reformed Theologians." Ph.D. dissertation, Westminster Theological Seminary, 1992.

Clyde, Walter R. "The Development of American Presbyterian Theology, 1705-1823." Ph.D. dissertation, Hartford Theological Seminary Foundation, 1939.

Dahl, James David. "Charles Hodge: Defender of Piety. A Study of the Relationship of Piety and Theology as Seen Through his Various Writings and his Critique of Schleiermacher." Ph.D. dissertation, Trinity Evangelical Divinity School, 1996.

Davis, Dennis Royal. "Presbyterian Attitudes Toward Science and the Coming of Darwinism in America, 1859-1929." Ph.D. dissertation, University of Illinois, 1980.

Deifell, John J. "The Ecclesiology of Charles Hodge." Ph.D. dissertation, University of Edinburgh, 1969.

Gardner, Richard. "Princeton and Paris: An Early Nineteenth Century Bond of Mission." Unpublished paper, Princeton Theological Seminary Archives, 1994.

Goodwin, Russell Dixon. "Viable Ecumenicity as Presented in the Nineteenth Century Evangelical Perspective of Dr. Charles Hodge." M.A. thesis, Hartford Seminary, 1970.

Gundlach, Bradley J. "The Evolution Question at Princeton, 1845-1929." Ph.D. dissertation, University of Rochester, 1986.

Hofecker, Andrew W., Jr. "The Relation Between the Objective and Subjective Aspects in Christian Religious Experience: A Study in the Systematic and Devotional Writings of Archibald Alexander, Charles Hodge, and Benjamin B. Warfield." Ph.D. dissertation, Brown University, 1970.

Jang, Sung Shik. "Contextualization in Princeton Theology, 1822-1878: Scottish Common Sense Realism and the Doctrine of Providence in the Theology of Charles Hodge." Th.M. thesis, Westminster Theological Seminary, 1993.

Johnson, Deryl Freeman. "The Attitudes of the Princeton Theologians Toward Darwinism and Evolution from 1859-1929." Ph.D. dissertation, University of Iowa, 1969.

Jones, Charles A. "Charles Hodge, the Keeper of Orthodoxy: The Method, Purpose and Meaning of His Apologetic." Ph.D. dissertation, Drew University, 1989.

Kennedy, Earl William. "An Historical Analysis of Charles Hodge's Doctrine of Sin and Particular Grace." Ph.D. dissertation, Princeton Theological Seminary, 1968.

Kim, Ki-Hong. "Presbyterian Conflict in the Early Twentieth Century: Ecclesiology in the Princeton Tradition and the Emergence of Presbyterian Fundamentalism." Ph.D. dissertation, Drew University, 1983.

Knaak, Patric J. "An Exposition and Analysis of Charles Hodge's Conception of Limited Atonement." M.A. thesis, Wheaton College, 1995.

Lazenby, Henry F. "Revelation History in the Theologies of Karl Barth and Charles Hodge." Ph.D. dissertation, University of Aberdeen, 1984.

McAllister, James L., Jr. "The Nature of Religious Knowledge in the Theology of Charles Hodge." Ph.D. dissertation, Duke University, 1957.

Murchie, David N. "Morality and Social Ethics in the Thought of Charles Hodge." Ph.D. dissertation, Drew University, 1980.

Nelson, John Oliver. "The Rise of the Princeton Theology: A Genetic History of American Presbyterianism until 1850." Ph.D. dissertation, Yale University, 1935.

Plaster, David R. "The Theological Method of the Early Princetonians." Th.D. Dissertation, Dallas Theological Seminary, 1989.

Richards, Walter Wiley. "A Study of the Influence of Princeton Theology upon the Theology of James Petigru Boyce and His Followers with Special Reference to the Work of Charles Hodge." Th.D. dissertation, New Orleans Baptist Theological Seminary, 1964.

Scovel, Raleigh D. "Orthodoxy in Princeton: A Social and Intellectual History of Princeton Theological Seminary, 1812-1860." Ph.D. dissertation, University of California, 1970.

St. Amant, Penrose. "The Rise and Early Development of the Princeton School of Theology." Ph.D. dissertation, University of Edinburgh, 1952.

Stewart, John W. "The Tethered Theology: Biblical Criticism, Common Sense Philosophy, and the Princeton Theologians, 1812-1860." Ph.D. dissertation, University of Michigan, 1990.

Torbett, David. "Theology and Slavery: Charles Hodge and Horace Bushnell on the Problem of African American Slavery in the United States." Ph.D. dissertation, Union Theological Seminary and the Presbyterian School of Christian Education, 2002.

Wells, John C. "Charles Hodge's Critique of Darwinism: The Argument to Design." Ph.D. dissertation, Yale University, 1986.

Wilhelm, Paul A. "A Victim of Sectional Theologies: Parochial Schools in the Presbyterian Church in the Crossfire Between Charles Hodge and James Henley Thornwell." M.A. thesis, Vanderbilt University, 1999.

V. BIBLIOGRAPHIES FOR HODGE'S WORKS BY OTHER SCHOLARS

Armstrong, William P. "Index of the *Presbyterian and Reformed Review* IX (1900)–XIII (1902) and *The Princeton Theological Review* (1903)-XXVII (1929)." *Princeton Theological Review* 27 (July 1929): 487-587.

Biblical Repertory and Princeton Review. Index Volume from 1825 to 1868. Philadelphia: Peter Walker, 1870-1871.

Burr, Nelson R. "The Princeton Theology," in *A Critical Bibliography of Religion in America.* Vol. 4. Ed. James Ward Smith and A. Leland Jamison. Princeton: Princeton University Press, 1961. Pp. 999-1003.

Dulles, Joseph H. "Index to Volumes I-X, 1890-1899." *Presbyterian and Reformed Review* 10 (October 1899): 727-98.

Gapp, Kenneth S. "The *Princeton Review* Series and the Contribution of Princeton Theological Seminary to Presbyterian Quarterly Magazines."

Unpublished ms., 1960. Special Collections, Luce and Speer Libraries, Princeton Theological Seminary, Princeton.

"Index of References to Rev. Charles Hodge, D.D., Found in the Files of the *Presbyterian* from 1831-1877." Unpublished MS, n.d. Special Collections, Luce and Speer Libraries, Princeton Theological Seminary, Princeton. [In the Charles Hodge Collection, box 31, file 13.]

Kennedy, Earl William. "Authors of Articles in the *Biblical Repertory and Princeton Review*." Typescript, Speer Library, Princeton Theological Seminary, 1963.

————. "Writings about Charles Hodge and His Works. Principally as Found in Periodicals Contained in the Speer Library of Princeton Theological Seminary for the Years 1830-1880." Unpublished ms., 1963. Special Collections, Luce and Speer Libraries, Princeton Theological Seminary, Princeton.

Noll, Mark A. "Select Bibliography," in *Charles Hodge: The Way of Life*. Ed. Mark A. Noll. New York: Paulist Press, 1987. Pp. 280-82.

————. *The Princeton Theology, 1812-1921: Scripture, Science and Theological Method from Archibald Alexander to Benjamin Warfield*. Grand Rapids: Baker Book House, 2001. This work contains an extensive bibliography about Hodge. The author of this bibliography is deeply indebted to Professor Noll, especially for his accounting of unpublished manuscripts about Hodge.